The Making of the Modern Canon

VISION, DIVISION AND REVISION:
THE ATHLONE SERIES ON CANONS

This series moves the canon debate of the 1980s forward into a new multidisciplinary and cross-cultural phase by investigating problems of canon formation across the whole humanistic field. Some volumes will explore the linguistic, political or anthropological dimensions of canonicity. Others will examine the historical canons of individual disciplines.

Series Editor: Professor Jan Gorak, University of Denver

VISION, DIVISION AND REVISION:
THE ATHLONE SERIES ON CANONS

The Making of the Modern Canon

Genesis and Crisis of a Literary Idea

Jan Gorak

ATHLONE
London & Atlantic Highlands, NJ

First published 1991 by The Athlone Press Ltd
1 Park Drive, London NW11 7SG and
171 First Avenue, Atlantic Highlands, NJ 07716

© Jan Gorak 1991

British Library Cataloguing in Publication Data
Gorak, Jan *1952-*
   The making of the modern canon: genesis and
   crisis of a literary idea
   1. Literature. Critics
   I. Title
   801.95

   ISBN 0-485-11388-0

Library of Congress Cataloging in Publication Data
Gorak, Jan, *1952-*
   The making of the modern canon: genesis and crisis of a literary idea/
Jan Gorak.
     p.   cm.   (Vision, division, and revision)
   Includes bibliographical references and index.
   ISBN 0-485-11388-0
   1. Criticism. 2. Canon (Literature). 3. Frye, Northrop.
   4. Gombrich, E. H. (Ernst Hans), 1909-. 5. Kermode, Frank, 1919-.
   6. Said, Edward W. I. Title. II. Series
PN81.G64 1991
801'.95-dc20

Typeset by Blackpool Typesetting Services Ltd, Blackpool, UK
Printed in Great Britain by Billings, Worcester

Contents

Series Editor's Preface

The last years of a century characteristically present the opportunity to review the assumptions and anxieties of the era which is passing and to anticipate the key conceptualizations and paradigms of the era yet to come. Twentieth-century artists and intellectuals, who have produced an unprecedented harvest of methodological innovation, terminological self-scrutiny, and wide-ranging theoretical inquiry, seem unlikely to neglect this opportunity. As we reflect on the past and anticipate the future, many of our contemporary academic and intellectual debates manifest our increasing concern with the formation, transmission, and validation of valued works. In this context, the canon debate, which has been in progress since the early 1980s, has both reinforced and modified our intellectual habits. The debate has reinforced the sustained meta-critical investigation into our artistic, cultural, and political institutions and agencies which has been mounted with increasing sophistication and commitment throughout the twentieth-century. Yet the intense scrutiny currently being given to 'the Canon' and canons also signals an unprecedented need to relate our artistic achievements and aspirations to the structures of perception, culture, education, class, gender, and ethnicity posited in a wide range of newly constituted and reconstituted fields of contemporary inquiry – feminism, cultural studies, semiology, and many others of note.

Its intimate involvement in the development of these fields is one of the reasons the editors of this series think the canon debate is now entering a new, extended, multidisciplinary, and cross-cultural phase. Because they make no pretence of knowing the shape of the cultures and disciplines which will emerge from this ferment, the editors will not attempt to prescribe the intellectual affiliations and procedural choices of contributors to the series. Instead, they hope to include in the series works which will enlarge our understanding of modern academic canons and encourage the scrutiny of historically important canons in fields such as literature, theatre, cinema, art, history, politics, philosophy, education, anthropology, archaeology, religion, and the history of science. Some volumes in the series will deal with general and theoretical problems: the creation and the transmission of cultural values; the sociology and psychology of cultural or intellectual elites; the benefits and conflicts associated with the application of canons to particular fields; the emergence of opposing canons and assumptions in those fields; and the counter-values articulated by marginalized or numerically dominant but culturally underrepresented groups. Other volumes will focus on specific constituencies, important periods, or decisive crises in the history of western or other cultural canons. These more specialised volumes may analyse the canon-making role of a dominant or marginalized group, or the important works and characteristic modes of interpretation of a particular community or intellectual circle. The editors envisage a series which will foreground important theoretical contributions on key canonical concepts and issues without slighting challenging empirical investigations of significant canons and canon-makers.

The editors are particularly interested in extending the canon debate beyond the ideological frame of reference it currently inhabits. While the demythologizing approach to the so-called 'Great Tradition' or canon of 'Great Books' has produced some of the most important and influential studies of the last decade, other areas of investigation now command increasingly urgent attention. For this reason, the editors especially welcome studies which scrutinize the linguistic, epistemological, anthropological, sociological, and historical dimensions of the canon. However, the only agenda for the series lies in its editors' belief that twentieth-century conditions have turned 'the Canon' and canons into plurisignificant and multifunctional phenomena. For this reason, contributors should not feel constrained to conform to any currently dominating ideology or ethos or method of conducting critical inquiry. Their sole obligation will be to discuss one or more facets of past or present canon-formation, to illuminate an episode from the history of the canon, or to scrutinize a key concept for understanding present and future academic or artistic canons. In this way, it is hoped that the series will enrich, enliven, and enhance our understanding of an important item in our cultural lexicon. The editors do not nail their colours to the mast of the old or even, as is more usual, to the new. They hope instead to provide a forum for a variety of writers to add their voices to a debate which will shape the way we transmit and transform the humanities in the twenty-first century.

Foreword

Until surprisingly recently, readers of very different political persuasions agreed on the liberating potential of certain works of art and aesthetic ideas. A conviction that 'throughout the long history of art, and spite of changes in taste, there is a standard which remains constant' enabled Herbert Marcuse to undertake in *The Aesthetic Dimension* a radical critique of Marxist theories of art. The *Scrutiny* group, who conducted a long battle against Marxism, launched their famous journal by announcing that they would be 'actively concerned for standards'. And the standard for the standards in these very different instances became a short-list of recurring authors and topics – the contradictions of capitalist society, the value of subjectivity or inwardness, the high status of Baudelaire and Shakespeare – a list which attracted ever-increasing volumes of critical, scholarly, historical, biographical, and textual exegesis in virtually all the human sciences.

Today, however, an increasing proportion of our critical discourse exhibits little willingness to congregate around these venerable figures and themes. The 'standard' invoked by Marcuse and Leavis alike has become 'the Canon' of contemporary criticism, the subject of exactly the same kind of radical critique for which 'the standard' used to supply the source. Instead of measuring modern decline by the illumination shed by *Middlemarch*, contemporary critics prefer to consider how far *Middlemarch* itself tacitly colludes in the repressive hierarchies that characterize modern society. How did such a drastic change occur in reading habits and interpretative conventions? Does the emergence of an avowedly anti-canonical wing inside the academy portend the beginning of a new, secular, democratic order? Or does it merely transfer the transgressive rhetoric literary critics have always liked to brandish to the objects they formerly held aloft as trophies?

Whatever its ultimate motives, the new willingness to relate 'the academic canon' or 'the literary canon' to the activities of some dominant political order or ideology extends across unexpected frontiers. A situation in which both William Bennett and Jonathan Culler agree that 'the Canon' does indeed preserve the orthodoxies of a particular world view indicates how far we have travelled from Leavis and Marcuse. Yet, on the question of canons, both radicals and conservatives converge in another, and much more misleading way. They both invoke an abstract, hypostatized 'Canon' rather than explore the circulation and function of actual historical canons in specific communities, institutions, and individual critical careers. This book maps the operations of some of these canons. My discussion is intended to pave the way for a more realistic appraisal of both the imaginative possibilities and the cultural limitations presented by canons present and past.

The historical evidence amassed in *The Making of the Modern Canon* indicates that no homogenizing entity called 'the Canon' ever existed. The various meanings ascribed to the term *canon* – a standard, a sublime truth, a rule, a master-work, an artistic model, and, latterly, a book-list for educational use – stretch across some very different cultural lexicons and have elicited correspondingly diverse methods of transmission. Even inside the various Christian communities – communities often seen as responsible for the restrictive ur-Canon of modern literary study – there have always been commentators who reminded their readers, with Brevard Childs, that 'the canon did not descend from heaven'.

If this is true of sacred canons, one can only wonder what deities presided at the birth of the modern secular canon. For a long time secular critics preferred to demonize the market and apotheosize the author, whom they frequently transposed to an imaginary milieu – an organic society, a vanished agrarian idyll invented by a community of nostalgic idealists. More recently, Francis Haskell and Pierre Bourdieu have shown the inadequacy of a cultural history that pits a freedom-loving avant-garde or intelligentsia against a reactionary bourgeoisie. The market conditions in which nineteenth-century French artists were forced to operate actually extended the roles available to them in certain crucial respects. They could draw their subject matter from wider sources and call on more diverse canons of taste because they were situated in a society which exhibited an unprecedented heterogeneity. Sound historical evidence supports the idea that modern culture bequeaths artists and critics a multiplicity of reference points against which to define their activities.

When our heresies start to look as homogeneous as our orthodoxies, then it is time to start rewriting our philosophies of culture. Even today, among canonical radical critics these philosophies involve a larger element of nostalgia than one might expect. Clearly, Leavis's 'wheelwright's shop' conforms to *Scrutiny's* programme of impassioned conservatism. But what of Raymond Williams's 'knowable community' or Walter Benjamin's 'storyteller'? Without these backward-looking complexes of value, the work of both these critics would look more programmatic and less deeply felt. Canons, which enjoy a strikingly close association with small artistic groups and movements, may well belong with these instances of nostalgia for a hand-made world of primary loyalties. One of the pivotal arguments of this book is that we should create an enlarged category of 'canonical discourses' before we subsume 'the Canon' under the repressive properties currently ascribed to 'Discourse'.

Before we abandon the canonical monuments and *topoi* altogether, it may be useful to reflect on some perplexing issues as yet unraised in our contemporary canon wars. What does it mean when the responsibility for cultural choice becomes delegated to a single professional group, however broadly that group aims to recruit? A long established usage links the term *canon* with the patterns and formulae which aid the production of works of art. Should we really be happy to see this association dwindle into their exegesis?

Etymologically, the term *canon* refers to a rod or reed. An appropriate figure for the contemporary understanding of the word might be Prospero's staff – an instrument of coercion more than magic, and on the very brink of being abandoned. Do we want to retrieve the staff for another generation or is it best to jettison it without more ado? It is hoped that *The Making of the Modern Canon* will furnish the evidence which can help us formulate some answers to these questions.

Although I suspect that any one of them would attack such questions very differently from me, I must thank the following people. Brian Southam of Athlone first encouraged me to write on canons, while Gillian Beaumont supplied editorial assistance and some unexpected encouragement. Irene Gorak assisted this project from its inception to its execution. George Hunter and Claude Rawson have helped me immeasurably over the years, and I should like to thank them too.

Introduction:
The Canon Debate

ARGUMENTS AGAINST THE CANON

Coleridge remarks in *Aids to Reflection* that 'There are cases, in which more knowledge of more value may be conveyed by the history of a *word*, than by the history of a campaign'.[1] By the same token, the history of a word will sometimes thrust it into the turmoil of a campaign, as a history of the words 'liberty' or 'empire' would certainly bear out. In recent years, a history of the word 'canon', understood by Richard Ohmann as 'a shared understanding of what literature is worth preserving' and by Alastair Fowler as the 'limited field' we 'criticize and theorize about',[2] would describe its recruitment in a campaign to reform the teaching of the humanities which itself dates back to the 1960s. As Robert von Hallberg observes, 'a canon is commonly seen as what other people, once powerful, have made and what should now be opened up, demystified, or eliminated altogether'.[3]

Criticism mounted against 'the canon' in the last ten years runs to thousands of pages penned by some of the most authoritative voices in contemporary criticism. In the mountain of hostile testimony, two main charges recur. First, many writers assume that the canon operates as an instrument of principled, systematic exclusion, although little evidence of this charge is actually adduced. The canon, they tell us, reinforces ethnic and sexual assumptions; it reflects passively the ethos or ideology of a particular society or group. 'It is probably quite accurate', Lillian Robinson observes, 'to think of the canon as an entirely gentlemanly artifact.' The gentlemanly consensus which restricts discussion to certain authors also conceals unjust preferences for particular kinds of writing – for tragedy over memoir, epic over confession, and so on. Social and sexual injustice begets intellectual confusion, as the tour from one masterpiece to another leaves a student with a passive, consumer's impression of the broader literary culture. Because it confines discussion to 'the informal agglomeration of course syllabi, anthologies, and widely commented-upon

1

"standard authors" that constitutes the canon as it is generally understood',[4] the idea of 'literature' current in academic circles has narrowed to an unacceptable degree. Robinson wants to redress this narrowness by including confessions, diaries, exhortatory and occasional pieces – the full spectrum of written communication – in her definition of literature. In her view, those responsible for the modern academic canon have set up an exclusive list of works worth reading, without defending the criteria for their evaluations or admitting the claims of any society outside the circle of male humanist intellectuals.

The second charge against the canon is an institutional one. Many critics of the canon see it as a vehicle or medium for the transmission of a fixed set of orthodox values and responses. In this way, the canon subserves some larger theory about literary criticism as a vehicle tied to the mechanisms which keep cultural power in the hands of a conservative minority. Jonathan Culler, who wants the modern university to function as a 'producer of knowledge', objects to what he sees as a state-sponsored dictum that 'gives criticism the role of interpreting the canon, elucidating the "core" of knowledge to be conveyed'. To fetter literary studies with conveyor-belt learning inevitably reduces its status, since, Culler argues, 'few would seriously suggest that physicists or historians should restrict their work to what can be communicated to 19-year-olds'.[5] The spectacle of generations of adolescents all sitting down again to read *King Lear* every October provides a potent reminder of the intellectual inertia of the canonical disposition.

It is but one of the ironies of the current debate that a series of academic attacks on the canon has centred on the canon-making role of the academy itself. With the waning of Arnold Bennett's man of letters and Virginia Woolf's common reader, the classroom becomes the universally acknowledged site for the perpetuation of canonical texts. For this reason, students of the composition, formation, and transmission of the modern literary canon pay much – not always friendly – attention to its sponsorship by educational institutions. The demystification of canon formation undertaken by such critics as Richard Brodhead and Jane Tompkins has uncovered a complex system of promotion, publicity, and politics behind an author as unquestionably canonical as Nathaniel Hawthorne. For Tompkins especially, entry to the canon becomes understood as conformity with the interests of a dominant political or intellectual group. Continued canonical esteem asks that the same cliques produce regular testimonies of worth. Instead of emphasizing the intrinsic merits of the canonical text or reinforcing its traditional cultural status,

Tompkins associates it with a network of promotions resting on a conspiracy between inertia and propaganda, or what Richard Ohmann calls 'a contest for cultural hegemony . . . carried on behind the scenes or in the seemingly neutral marketplace'.[6] From *Paradise Lost* to *Moby-Dick*, canonical works ally themselves with a spectrum of vested interests that include male dominance, Anglo–Catholic orthodoxy, national self-definition, and professional aggrandizement.

The conviction that the canon survives only by virtue of institutional control and sponsorship has made it difficult to argue for the intrinsic merit and genuine worth of the works included in it. It is traditional to suggest that some works are more linguistically or aesthetically rewarding or more humanly moving than others, and that this explains their status as objects of study. This appeal to emotional or evaluative criteria has fallen dramatically out of favour. For example, Jane Tompkins's *Sensational Designs* (1985) examines the political factors behind Hawthorne's place in the canon of American literature, showing that his original audience lumped him squarely among 'the sentimental novelists' a modern academic readership statutorily deplores. Tompkins argues that Hawthorne's rise to professorial esteem reflects his privileged place among the New England intellectual aristocracy. Behind Hawthorne's status as a masterpiece, she detects the corporate workings of 'the machinery of publishing and reviewing'.[7]

Tompkins's work gains further weight from the arguments of Richard Brodhead in *The School of Hawthorne* (1986). Brodhead traces the present 'curricular' version of Hawthorne to an early-twentieth-century 'modernization of the American literary past' which accompanied 'the rise of a new formation of the professoriate'.[8] In sharp contrast, Hawthorne's initial place in the canon of American letters depended on an alliance between Democratic politics and a New England literary clique. Instead of becoming a canonical author because he faced up to 'the problem of evil' in a way his Transcendentalist contemporaries could not (as F. O. Matthiessen proposed), Hawthorne's early rise to canonical fortunes coincides with his involvement in the Democratic Party machine (he wrote a campaign biography of Franklin Pierce and served as US consul in Liverpool). Viewed by Matthiessen as the epitome of the solitary, alienated genius, Hawthorne is resituated in Brodhead's book at the heart of a complex system of cultural, academic, aesthetic and political alliances. In the work of Brodhead and Tompkins, the substitution of a system of textual politics for essentialist validation demystifies the process of canonization.

The School of Hawthorne pushes back to the nineteenth century a process of institutionalized canon formation which many contemporary critics see as a peculiarly modern phenomenon. Yet arguably, Brodhead's book hardly goes back far enough. It would be more accurate to note an association of *canon* with teaching, aesthetic creation, and cultural self-definition that reaches back to the ancient world. As the next chapter will show, the lost *Canon* of Polycletus (445 BC) contained a set of precise mathematical calculations for the proportions of the human body that was used by generations of art students. By the Renaissance these calculations were lost, but, in a typical development in the history of the canon, Polycletus's own statuary had become identified with the proportions of nature.

Even so, the story of canon formation does not always tell of an evolving and stabilizing consensus. At a very early stage in its history, the range of meanings ascribed to *canon* widens and becomes highly controversial. Indeed, as soon as it reaches beyond measurement, *canon* becomes embroiled in controversy. Plato and Aristotle use the word in the course of their attempts to teach deeply conflicting moral and ethical systems. Early Christian bishops and scholars use it to characterize the inspired books that underpin a series of controversial models for the growth of ecclesiastical institutions. As we shall see, the selection of books accepted as 'canonical' by early Christian communities emerged only at the end of a series of bitter internal disputes. These communities did not recognize the same books as divinely inspired; not all members of the same community agreed on the exact number of the canonical books; the arguments used to legitimate the canonical works were more context-specific than the timeless narratives they were designed to underprop; and the works themselves proved as hospitable to interpretation as any modern-day text: for all these reasons the possibility for argument proved enormously wide.

CANON AND CANONS

The subsequent chapters will show that *canon* can become a focus for debate in any period in which artists, critics, philosophers or theologians try to match an inherited body of texts, practices, or ideas to their perceived present and future cultural needs. The association between canons, pedagogy, artistic creation and cultural valuation dates back to the ancient world; the complex balance and interplay of interests around a canonical work present a problem almost from the start of the history of the idea. Fascinating in their own right, past discussions among ancient craftsmen and philosophers also throw considerable light on the canon debate inside contemporary communities of interpreters. In *Canons*, a revealing collection of essays by prominent members of the American academy, Robert von Hallberg links the current debate about the nature and function of the canon to a growing concern with the public dimension of critical activity. 'We are most curious now', he says, 'about those points where art seems less private than social.' He suggests that 'interest in canons is surely part of a larger inquiry into the institutions of literary study and artistic production'.[9] Such interests lead naturally to the intriguing examinations of the institutions of literary criticism, of the history of academic disciplines, and of the mechanisms of cultural control undertaken by Gerald Graff, Richard Bridgman, and Jonathan Arac.[10]

Even so, what these examinations so far lack is a sense of the historical dimension of the present debate. All too casually, critics refer to the 'eighteenth-century canon' or the 'Victorian canon' as primitive equivalents of the disputed modern curriculum. Attacked on one side as a privileged receptacle of traditional readings, praised (if increasingly infrequently) as the preserver of cultural value, the entity commonly called 'the canon' appears, one way or another, to be a permanent part of our intellectual landscape. Yet as late as 1981, M. H. Abrams failed to include *canon* in the fourth edition of his standard reference source *A Glossary of Literary Terms*. Since most anti-canonists agree that the canon exerts its greatest impact in the classroom, Abrams's omission seems a puzzling one. The graduate-school counterpart to his glossary, the *Princeton Encyclopedia of Poetry and Poetics*, swelled from 300 to 992 pages between its publication in 1965 and its first major revision in 1974. Yet in neither of these incarnations did it make room for 'canon', despite finding space for accounts of 'tradition', 'tragic flaw', and even 'poet laureate'.

When basic sources break the silence about the canon, they voice the same reservations we pride ourselves on articulating today. For instance, René Wellek and Austin Warren's *Theory of Literature* (1956) includes a chapter on 'Evaluation' which repeatedly emphasizes that 'no literary critic can . . . attach himself to so barren and pedagogic an absolutism as that of the "fixed rank"'. The authors specifically distance themselves from 'authoritarianism and its canonical list', emphasizing that 'the desire to affirm in some form the objectivity of literary values does not require commitment to some static canon, to which no new names are added and within which no shifts of rank may occur'.[11] When contemporary critics cite the postwar years as the era when the limited modern canon became entrenched in the curriculum, they occlude the work of earlier writers who opposed the currency of the 'fixed rank' almost as categorically as themselves.

If basic modern sources yield no specific information on the history of the canon, then the makers of modern criticism furnish little further help. Samuel Johnson asks himself what qualities make a work endure, but he does not characterize these qualities, nor the works possessing them, as 'canonical'. The later volumes of Coleridge's *Collected Works* refer to 'canon law' and canons of logic, but not 'the literary canon' or even 'the canons of criticism'. Matthew Arnold conducts a tireless campaign for 'criticism' and 'culture', but he never marches under the banner of the 'canon'. A phalanx of institutional vested interests, all employing 'the canon' as a way of controlling the cultural market, fixing literary standards and selecting literary texts, becomes harder to find in direct proportion to one's distance from contemporary testimony.

It is asserted that the modern canon exists only in order to conserve existing institutional practices and definitions; that it requires teachers of the humanities to transmit time-honoured platitudes; that it favours a privileged set of writings that alone constitute 'literature', while conspiring to conceal the way those writings become the basis for the curriculum; and that it compounds these sins of omission and commission by employing methods of reading that remove favoured authors and texts from the processes of struggle and conflict which have deeply shaped our common culture. As I shall argue in the chapters which follow, our contemporary concern with the shared assumptions, beliefs and rules governing the selection of valued art-works has much in common with earlier debates on the nature and focus of canonical activity. What has been lost in the flurry of contemporary argument is a sense of the historical dimensions of that debate.

The present book attempts to restore to the canon some episodes from its lost history, and this is why it offers a different method and a varying set of governing assumptions from some of the 'canon-busters', as Gerald Graff has called them, whose arguments have stimulated the current debate. First, it examines the actual process of canon formation, a process often neglected in arguments which highlight the canon's role as a vehicle for institutional vested interests. *The Making of the Modern Canon* investigates this process in two main ways: historically, in Chapters 1 and 2, which trace the history of *canon* from classical and early Christian usage to the early modern period; and genetically, in Chapters 3 to 6, each of which examines the development of an exemplary modern maker or unmaker of canons. The critics to be discussed in Chapters 3 and 4 alert us to the existence of a wider postwar movement to incorporate into the canon an unprecedented range of artistic processes and works. Those to be discussed in Chapters 5 and 6 allow us to scrutinize two influential contemporary attempts to rearrange the canon, to nudge literary works into a more plural and socially responsive order. In this way, *The Making of the Modern Canon* sets two hugely influential modern canon-makers, E. H. Gombrich and Northrop Frye, against two critics whose work reflects a mixture of fascination and suspicion about canons, Frank Kermode and Edward Said. As I shall show, all four critics share a fascination with the canon as an entrée to a self-determining and potentially liberating imaginative world. If Gombrich and Frye perhaps press *canon* too hard in their attempt to defend it, Kermode and Said show the impossibility of expelling it completely from any ambitious and responsive critical system.

This focus on the evolution and working of particular critical canons clearly sets the whole idea of the canon in a more sympathetic light than appears from the institutional approaches represented in von Hallberg's collection. For if the historical approach lessens the authority of the canon, it also underlines the sheer variety of the ideas and forms different periods and critics have attached to it. In effect, *The Making of the Modern Canon* examines the term 'canon' from the classical period until the present day, laying particular emphasis on three points: first, the sheer range of the propositions linked to the idea (as we shall see, the word *canon* has been attached to almost every form of discourse and genre from fairy tale to divine pronouncement to artist's sketchbook); second, the irony by which the most significant critics of the canon also function as its defenders; and third, the tendency throughout their history for canons to survive not by the fiat of authoritarian dogma but by a combination of narrative suggestiveness and ineradicable cultural need.

This wide canvas shows that critics of the modern academic canon often stake their case on an ultra-conservative idea that only a very small number of writers have actually called into play. The contemporary view of the canon as an instrument of exclusion reinforces the confusion made by F. R. Leavis and the *Scrutiny* group between a canonical text and a classical text. In this way, existence inside the canon becomes tied to a limited number of texts of unassailable importance and an equally restrictive set of authoritative critical interpretations, while existence once the canon has been demolished becomes equated with the study of a shifting body of texts which are felt to be more responsive to evolving ethnic and sexual needs.

Unfortunately, this simple opposition distorts the complex and still evolving history of the Anglo-American canon. As we shall discover, especially in the chapters on Kermode and Said, the battle for the canon has been repeatedly fought but never unequivocally won. On the contrary, the long and complex history of *canon* follows a far more tentative, even confused, line of development than most contemporary commentators have taken into account. Throughout that history, a succession of artists and critics has repeatedly tried to wrest the canon from the hands of rivals they conceive of as limiting its reference and censoring its force. It is worth noting at the outset that T. S. Eliot, a figure often blamed for our current canonical malaise, on several occasions attacks *canons* on the same grounds for which he now finds himself attacked: the grounds of exclusion and repression. Eliot left it to others to formulate the Ur-text of the restrictive modern canon; he spent much of his own career energetically conducting his highly idiosyncratic version of the current debate.

Too often, the contemporary canon debate identifies the 'restrictive', 'unresponsive' Anglo-American canon with the work and influence of Eliot and his followers. Yet as we shall see, the actual 'canons' invoked by such arch-canonizing figures as F. R. Leavis, R. P. Blackmur and John Crowe Ransom do not always fulfil our need to see an earlier generation of critics as imprisoned in the world of utter repression and restriction from which we ourselves have heroically broken free. However great their prestige among their own contemporaries and students, these critics offer no more than an influential minority view of the literary canon. Another equally significant (and very long) line of critics has always taken a more inclusive approach, seeking to understand the canon not as an authoritarian tool but as an imaginative possibility associated with a reasonable, culturally reponsive set of critical values. In a discussion of the careers of these less often cited canon-makers, a permanent set of canonical problems gradually begins to reveal itself. Far from being a new debate, the debate about the canon has constantly returned to the same problems: the need for some version of a canon in order to transmit to the next generation works of cultural value and to show the interrelationships between valued works; the tendency of the canon, once explicitly formulated as a canon, to freeze responses to the texts inside it and to exclude other, currently less recognized texts. Let us now trace these problems to their beginnings by pursuing the earliest appeal to *canons* in the life and culture of Ancient Greece.

1

More Than Just a Rule:
The Early History of the Canon

FROM MEASUREMENT TO VALUE:
THE FIRST GREEK CANONS

Herbert Oppel considered that 'the word *kanōn* illuminates the whole course of Greek civilization'.[1] A map of the word's early application would certainly stretch across a bewildering variety of activities, while its users would figure in any anthology of the most important classical authors. They include Plato, Aristotle, Euripides, Demosthenes, Epicurus, Polycletus, Plutarch, Epictetus and Lucian. In the classical period, canons underpin the first chapters of 'how to' textbooks and explain the achievement of sculptural masterpieces. Canons govern practical activities such as building a temple, and artistic pursuits such as decorating it; contemplative pursuits such as moral philosophy, and early scientific accounts of the laws of nature. Canons play an important part in the composition of music and speeches, the construction of buildings and sculpture, the selection of authorities for writing history, philosophy and rhetoric, the organisation of time into significant units of measurement, and the framing of patterns to regulate the behaviour of human beings and heavenly bodies. In short, the testimony of classical authors rehearses many of the issues thrown out in the contemporary canonical debate, while exhibiting a similar lack of unanimity. No review of the classical evidence will support any nostalgia for a time when everyone agreed about the unquestioned authority behind the word *canon*. If such a time ever existed, it did not exist in the world of antiquity.

Three important meanings of *canon* currently in use present it as a teaching guide, a norm or rule, and a list of basic authorities. Each of these meanings resides embryonically in the classical Greek word *kanōn*, whose earliest meaning is glossed in Liddell and Scott's *Greek-English Lexicon* as 'any straight rod or bar'. The many uses of the word collected by the editors (several of them from Homer) refer to the rods that run across a shield, the rods used in weaving, the beams used in scales, the keys and stops of flutes, and the level or

9

plumb line used by a carpenter or mason. K. von Fritz has argued that the common denominator linking these usages lies in the property of *straightness*, a quality which made it easy for *kanōn* to be subsequently understood as a rule or standard.[2] When modern critics describe a work as a 'yardstick' for future achievement or as a 'milestone' for a particular genre, they may unconsciously act in the spirit of the earliest Greek speakers, who gradually pushed *canon* from mensuration to evaluation.

With the rise of *canon* as evaluation comes evidence that the earlier use as *measure* fell into disfavour. Oppel points out that Aristophanes and Plato both attack the Sophists for measuring their sentences less by the matter or the sense than by the length or *kanones*. Some early musicologists, also regarded unfavourably by later authors, composed by rigid mathematical laws also known as *kanones*. In other words, almost from the very start of its history writers on the canon have regarded it as an inherited set of rules and practices to be broadened, sophisticated, and generally loosened up. All these motives explain the background to Plato's interest in the canon and perhaps even the original motive behind his championship of the Socratic dialectic. In *Philebus* the mathematical activities measured by a canon, such as the construction of circles or straight lines, lead Socrates to envisage a similarly undeviating standard for moral philosophy. Pointing to the uniform, predictable standards of measurement available to the mason or carpenter, Socrates contrasts the uncertain materials and deteriorating equipment of the moral philosopher with the precise instruments available in the science of building. Among the instruments on which he looks so longingly are the mason or carpenter's 'rule [*kanoni*] . . . lathe, compasses, chalk-line, and vice'.[3] Failing to achieve such exactitude, Socrates develops instead what becomes in essence his rival canon, the dialectic, a battery of ever more profound questions he employs to disseminate uncertainties to an audience only too ready for trivial certainty.

Dialectic or mason's rule, both these classical ideas of canon share a concern with teaching and a belief in the close connection between teaching and creation. It is not surprising, therefore, that two of the most influential ancient canons appeared as teaching manuals. Polycletus and Epicurus both wrote substantial treatises (now lost) which they called *Canon*. When the *Canon* of Polycletus appeared around 454 BC, it set new standards for the representation of the human body. Erwin Panofsky has described how Polycletus devised his canon in accordance with the features of actual human subjects, in sharp contrast with his Egyptian successors, who evolved more abstract canons of representation from the stone, wood and marble of their artistic medium. Panofsky emphasizes the monumental consequences for Western art of the fact that Polycletus, unlike the Egyptians, defined and legitimized a canon which 'possessed a purely anthropometric character'.[4]

Polycletus's *Canon* also won prestige and authority from its association with his own creative work, especially his famous *Doryphorus*, a sculptural triumph, explains the nineteenth-century German critic C. O. Müller, which, 'whether this was the intention of the artist, or . . . the judgement of posterity, became a canon of the proportions of the human frame.'[5] Pliny the Elder's *Natural History* appeared three centuries after the death of Polycletus. Yet even at this late date, its author still sees Polycletus's statue as an exemplary achievement, suggesting that 'he alone of mankind is deemed by means of one work of art to have created the art itself'. Whatever complications and fissures appear even at this early stage in the history of the canon, it is worth remembering that for at least three centuries the closest connection persisted between canonical formulae and artistic creation. In fact, Pliny goes even further, suggesting that Polycletus 'made what artists call a canon, or model statue, from which they draw their artistic proportions, as from a sort of standard'.[6] Such a description has two effects. First, it lays the foundations for the idea of *canon* as a set of unsurpassable masterpieces to be studied and copied by all later practitioners in the field. Second, it suggests the transition of *canon* from a practical working blueprint to something like the Platonist's Idea. As understood by Pliny, Polycletus's canon no longer functions as a strictly practical framework to be deployed in the execution of certain specifically defined ends. As Pliny interprets it, the canon becomes a seed rather than a scheme, a seed that potentially contains a whole universe of measurements and future creation.

So successful was Polycletus's *Canon* that knowledge of it survived through generations of students in an increasingly wide orbit of disciplines. Its citation nearly three centuries later in Galen's *The Doctrines of Hippocrates and Plato* offers another telling instance of its survival. Even at considerable distance of both time and field, Galen's reference to Polycletus is worth examining closely as an instance of a recurrent phenomenon in the history of the canon, applied canonicity. Galen, a physiologist and anatomist writing in the first century, cites and views of Chrysippus, a Stoic philosopher of the third century BC. Three centuries before Galen, Chrysippus had already applied Polycletus's ideas to his own very different sphere of work. Chrysippus, Galen explains, holds that beauty does not consist in the elements but in the harmonious proportion of the parts, the proportion of one finger to the other, of all the fingers to the rest of the hand, of the rest of the hand to the wrist, of these to the forearm, of the forearm to the whole arm, in fine, of all parts to all others, as is written in the canon of Polycletus.[7]

To the modern reader, Galen's 'as is written in the canon of Polycletus' sounds almost scriptural; in fact, Galen's whole manner reminds us how early in its development the canon began to exceed the demands of the merely functional or instrumental, to cross the boundaries of disciplines and activities and to become an almost charismatic vehicle perceived as relevant to every sphere of human life. The *Canon* of Polycletus, like the sacred books of the Old Testament and the 'tradition' of T. S. Eliot, found itself accommodated to purposes its author could never have anticipated.

Polycletus's *Canon* certainly fulfilled one indispensable requirement of canonicity, the ability to be applied in contexts foreign to the circumstances that originally produced it. As Panofsky points out, Polycletus's *Canon* revolutionized contemporary practices by trying to capture the whole beauty of the human form. Instead of considering each part of the body separately according to established formulae, Polycletus related each part to its neighbour and tested its accuracy against the experienced reality of a human subject. Although he is less well known today than some of those he influenced, Polycletus represents one of the most important strands of classical thought, a strand stretching from Plato to Aristotle himself. All these authors emphasize the flexibility of the canon and the important of its adjustment to the human subjects it was designed to serve.

THE SEARCH FOR A HUMAN CANON: ETHICS AND THE STANDARD OF TRUTH

Once we pass from the artist's workshop to the world of moral philosophy, the other sphere with a major impact on our modern ideas of canon, the limitations in the notion of *canon* as a fixed rule or formula become much more apparent, since it is hard to define a set of exemplary standards which will measure a good man as surely as a fine statue. Certainly, there is no ethical equivalent to Polycletus's canon that will guarantee the successful achievement of goodness just as certainly as the satisfactory representation of a human figure. The strength of Polycletus's *Canon* lay in its subordinatation of formula to human perception and design. In the shift from sculpture to ethics the canon becomes, even more markedly than with Polycletus, a tacit framework by which to guide human behaviour rather than an explicit set of rules.

As Plato clearly intends to demonstrate, didactic works intended for the classroom need not gloss over the inherent uncertainty of the ethical field. A lost work by a major rival of Plato, Epicurus's *Of the Standard: A Work Entitled Canon*, introduced an opposed but equally strenuous ethical system to the writer's immediate circle of pupils. Like Polycletus and Plato, Epicurus outlasted his occasion, being quoted as an authority centuries later in Cicero's *On the Nature of the Gods* (45 BC) and Diogenes Laertius's *Lives of the Philosophers* (third century AD). Leaving no doubt as to Epicurus's stature, Cicero characterizes his *Canon* as 'that work of genius'.[8] Exhibiting similar commitment, Diogenes describes Epicurus's achievement in terms of a work 'which deals with the standard and the first principle, or the elementary part of philosophy', a work which has the status of a pioneering study as well as a teaching manual. According to Diogenes, Epicurus's *Canon* taught 'that our sensations and preconceptions and our feelings are the standards [*kritēria*] of truth; they regard our perceptions of mental processes as standards also.' Diogenes shares with Polycletus, Cicero and, apparently, Epicurus himself the conviction that elementary axioms and complex psychological treatises can share the same intellectual ground. In a sense, these early philosophers and aestheticians laid the seeds of the current debate about the canon by situating it in a peculiar border country where instructional norms and permanent monuments lie side by side.

Even so, not all classical moralists saw such undisputed lines of continuity between ancient, modern and future canons. Another very early development in classical literature is the use of the word *canon* and its cognates in exhortatory works intended to modify or attack contemporary practices. In these works we see the first signs of a set of books, not overtly presented as canonical, which become retrospectively canonized. Thucydides's *History* and the poetry of Homer are two notable instances of retrospective canon formation, a process that involves a work's adjustment to ends very different from those its author may have intended.

Around AD 162, for example, Lucian, writing in the middle of the Parthian war, ponders in a letter to his friend Philo the best motives for writing history. He contrasts the work of Thucydides, who constructed his *History of the Peloponnesian War* with an eye on posterity (as 'a possession for evermore', is how he formulates it) with the opportunistic scribbles of their contemporaries. Lucian sees an abyss between the historians who write according to Thucydides's yardstick and those who frame their chronicles according to contemporary opportunity or occasion. Contemporary historians 'may write better by applying this yardstick [*kanona*] if they think it accurate', Lucian observes. 'If they do not,' he adds, 'they must use the same rule to do their measuring [*metrounton to pragma*] as now'.[10]

Lucian's sharp contrast between the yardstick or standard for posterity [*kanon*] and the measure [*metron*] acceptable to circumstances [*pragma*] reflects a common distinction between a work worthy of posterity and a work written to attract contemporary attention. It is worth noting, however, that nowhere does Thucydides lay down laws for historical writing beyond those deducible from his own practices. Even so, his seriousness of concern and gravity of expression made him retrospectively canonical for an author writing five centuries later and, later still, for Byzantine teachers in the new world of the Christian academies.

Similarly, in his dialogue *Hermotimus* Lucian impresses on his Stoic interlocutor how contemporary ethical philosophers fall short of their professed ideals. After sketching out a vaulting paradigm of passionless perfection ('a type that feels no pain, one who is not dragged down by pleasure, who is never angry, but rises above envy, despises wealth, and is perfectly happy'), Lucian observes ironically that 'our canon and measure of the virtuous life must be like that'.[11] He secures his rhetorical success by wringing from Hermotimus the admission that no modern-day Stoic behaves in so exemplary a fashion. Demosthenes's *On the Crown* (330 BC) constitutes, like *Hermotimus*, a work of polemical intent. Demosthenes insists on the iniquity of 'this catalogue of traitors' contemporary Athens chooses to shelter. He contrasts these 'traitors' with Athenian heroes of the past, who offered 'the very standard and canon [*kanones*] of prosperity'. Like Lucian, Demosthenes makes a play of contrast between 'canon' and 'metron', suggesting that where the ancestors of present-day Athenians employed a noble spiritual standard or 'canon' in their moral behaviour, his contemporaries 'measure [*metrountes*] their happiness by their belly and their baser parts'.[12]

Today, 'the canon' is associated with an undisputed (often unidentified) ground of high culture which persisted from Dryden until the critical self-scrutiny of the 1980s. Sustained examination of the evidence shows, on the contrary, that a whole range of canons–canons technical and philosophical, deliberate and retrospective–already appear at an early stage in classical literature. Today, the erosion of genres in modern literature and art has simplified our idea of *canon* and laid an insupportable weight on the single institutional canon commonly invoked. In marked contrast, classical artists often worked by virtue of the inspired example supplied by a series of models. None of these canons had the status of all-purpose excellence; they were used instead to guide and measure an artist's efforts in a particular mode. The plurality of canonical models was matched by a similar diversity of function. As Müller pointed out, ancient canons functioned first as muses, then as mentors, sometimes as competitors, and finally as bridges towards an idealized perfection. For his contemporaries, Müller observes, Polycletus still ranked 'far behind Phidion in the fashioning of gods'.[13] Only for posterity did he achieve the status of an unsurpassable model of absolute perfection.

If classical authorities universally equate 'canon' with 'standard' or 'rule' they exhibit little unanimity about the workings of that rule. Euripides, for instance, invokes a 'canon' common to all human beings but by no means uniform or predictable in its operation. In *Hecuba* (*c*. 425 BC) the heroine contrasts the uncertain state of nature, where good stock can produce bad crops, with the more predictable course of human nature, where 'canon' represents some basic human substance encoded with an intuitive, unwritten sense of moral good. Hecuba insists that 'by honour's touchstone' [*kanoni tou kalou*] a human being can learn to recognize baseness'.[14] The wrongs piled on the conquered Trojan Queen during the course of the play stretch this maxim to its limits by subjecting her to a series of horrifying assaults and retaliations. In the bleak world of Euripidean drama, canons govern human behaviour without restraining it; moral laws explain individual motivation while undermining our sense of any larger order. Like Hecuba, the peasant at the beginning of *Electra* (*c*. 413 BC) opposes the judgement of the world to his own inward judgement. By defending his actions against the rules of a merely conventional propriety, the peasant plunges us into a world of mounting ethical uncertainties. 'If any call me a fool because I take a young maid to my home and do not touch her,' he challenges the audience, 'let him know that he measures chastity by his own soul's base measure [*ponērois kanosin*], as base as he is.'[15] For Euripides, the moral canon does not seem learned so much as innate, a sure and infallible guide to the way, for good or for ill, a given man or woman will judge any experience. Each human being has a measure, to be sure; yet that measure will be only as straight as the soul it occupies. And because the measure remains hidden from the public scrutiny or understanding, human conduct may appear unfathomable, veering from the ridiculous to the barbarous without apparent explanation.

The fatalism attached in antiquity to the notion of *canon* becomes apparent in Plutarch's first-century *Letter to Apollonius*. In this work Plutarch invokes *canon* for the purposes of moral consolation when the author advises his grieving correspondent, who has just lost a son, that 'the laws [*kanones*] of wisdom and of the other virtues must be followed for better fortune or for worse'.[16] Plutarch presents *canon* as a set of non-negotiable norms with unquestionable legitimacy in the sphere of moral conduct. By linking these canons of behaviour with the laws governing the fertility patterns of animals and the seasonal vicissitudes of the earth itself, he implies that canons exert their unalterable power independently of human will or choice.

In fact, one danger of invoking canons in the sphere of ethics rests in the tendency to raise the past above the present and the divine or mythical pattern above human free choice and deliberate action. By idealizing a human reason and culture which have disappeared, such mythical canons can introduce a falsifying sense of discontinuity between present and past. Yet as a historian, as opposed to a moral philosopher, Plutarch himself is keenly aware of this problem, for in his *Life of Solon* he rejects the binding authority of the 'so-called chronological canons [*kanosin*]' on two related grounds. First, many authorities unanimously agree on the importance of his own comparative type of historical narrative, which does not conform to traditional canons. Second, none of the sources responsible for those canons can 'bring their contradictions into any general agreement'.[17]

In fact, the further he travels from the ethical sphere, the more likely is Plutarch to attack the canonizing disposition itself. In his treatise 'How to Study Poetry', for instance, he conceives of poetry as a preparation for a sober philosophy purged of illusory idealism. Because it gives 'an imitation of character and lives, and of men who are not perfect or spotless', poetry seems preferable to the kind of philosophy which represents men as 'wise and honest, consummate kings, and standards [*kanones*] of all virtue and uprightness'.[18]

In this passage, Plutarch anticipates some of the ambivalence or contradictions of later canonists. The author of the *Lives* hardly seems the enemy of the exemplary; yet in 'How To Study Poetry' the exemplary comes under considerable fire. T. S. Eliot elevated 'tradition' into a canon as an alternative to the rigidity of early-twentieth-century criticism and the emotional luxuries of late-Victorian versifying. In the same way, Plutarch may have framed his treatise on poetry to attack contemporary orators, whom he associates with ritual invocation of outmoded formulae on the one side and with impossible standards of moral behaviour on the other.

ARISTOTLE'S LEADEN RULE

Aristotle's *Nicomachean Ethics* displays a similar moderation in its approach to canons. Aristotle wants to propagate a notion of *canon* which will serve human experience in a more flexible, less punitive way than absolute *law* [*nomos*]. He sees good human beings as able to adjust their field of vision, so that they can see 'the truth in each kind' while also acting in a sense as human canons, 'the standard and measure of the noble'.[19] In a different way from Polycletus, Aristotle gives 'measurement' a central role in his philosophy. He emphasizes that measurement governs many human affairs, extending far beyond mechanical and technical tasks. If Polycletus suggests that we measure horses and forms, Aristotle reminds us that we measure actions as well. Instead of a picture of human beings as measuring according to a *canon* conceived of as an unchanging ideal blueprint, Aristotle turns *canon* into an instrument which is itself shaped by the materials on which it works. In this way, his *canon* can support process and action as well as serving as a norm. It is the working flexibility of *canon* that Aristotle admires, a flexibility which he moves to a new centrality in human ethics.

Unlike Euripides, whose characters remain trapped in a bleak and divisive essentialism, Aristotle emphasizes the hopefulness of present and future human *action*. He reminds us that 'we measure even our actions, some of us more, some of us less'. Aristotle thinks that measuring and ruling are central human activities, so he by no means expects us to do without canons or to limit their sphere of influence. He particularly likes the way that a tacitly operating unwritten canon might extend to circumstances where the short letter of the law would seem unjust. This is why so much of his work encourages the emergence of basic, widely agreed canons of social behaviour which could serve as the subject of open discussion and be modified as circumstances change. It is, he notes, impossible to legislate for all occasions, but canons can account for contingencies in ways that laws cannot. 'There are some cases', he says, 'for which it is impossible to lay down a law'.[20] Against the rigidity of *nomos* he emphasizes the flexible, unwritten, and adaptable properties of *canon*.

When Aristotle characterizes 'the good man' as 'the standard and measure [*kanōn kai metron*] of the noble and pleasant', his conciliatory purposes become even more apparent in his careful choice of words. Some of his contemporaries opposed '*metron*' to '*kanōn*', presenting the former as a mere transitory measuring rod and the latter as the basis for lasting standards. In this context, it is significant that Aristotle simply yokes the two words together. In the same spirit of conciliation, he emphasizes the flexibility and repeated adjustments needed to support any lasting canon. His good or equitable man perceives 'the truth in each kind', applying rules which he adjusts according to circumstance. Later in his treatise, Aristotle contrasts the flexibility of a canon with the absolute quality of a law. He draws an analogy between *canon* and the deceptively light 'leaden rule' [*molibdinos kanōn*] used by the builders of Lesbos, a rule these clever builders adapted to their immediate purposes and materials. 'What itself is definite can be measured only by an indefinite standard', Aristotle observes. The rule, he continues, 'is not so rigid that it cannot be bent to the shape of the stone'.[21] In framing his own rule, the 'equitable man' will practise a similar flexibility. In encouraging the adoption of a negotiable canon constantly readjusted to the demands of the people who use it, Aristotle stands at the head of a line of critics who want to mitigate the effect of the 'hegemonic' canon invoked – not for the first time – in the contemporary canon debate. From Aristotle to Gombrich, these critics constantly return to two simple points: the practical usefulness of canons in so many spheres; and the need to shape those canons to the needs of the people who employ them.

Aristotle stands as the first in a line of humanists, from Erasmus to Frank Kermode, who prefer the compromises of *canon* to the full rigour of *law*. Yet Aristotle's triumph of conciliation also reminds us that ancient authorities disagreed no less intensely than their modern successors about the measuring rods to be applied as a canon. Some classical sources saw the canon as an almost inspired innate guideline or as a fluctuating set of human feelings; others understood it as a set of written instructions to inform students or as a storehouse of indisputable perfection; still others saw it, like Aristotle himself, as a basis for negotiation. Even at this early stage of its history, the word *canon* adds layers of complications, as it becomes the locus for a variety of activities from mathematics to ethics. While all these spheres indicate that the basic function of the canon is to regulate, it still remains unclear whether the canon regulates by virtue of a core of acquirable skills, by an internalized norm never formally learned, by an artistic masterpiece physically present before a pupil, or by a set of ideal forms a canonical work shadows forth.

'NEW CREATION':
THE EMERGENCE OF SACRED CANONS

In contemporary common usage, the phrase 'the canon' chiefly refers to the set of sacred texts a particular religious group accepts as permanently recording truths revealed to it by God. In the West Christianity becomes the central instance of such a canon, but similar 'canons' are assumed to exist for other religious groups.[22] This assumption is slightly misleading. For instance, although scholars refer to an 'Old Testament or Judaic canon', to speak of the Jewish 'canon' is, in fact, to conform to Christian usage. It is more accurate to say that Jewish religious practice revolves around 'the sacred writings', which are said to 'defile the hands' because of their holiness.[23] It is possible that these verbal distinctions may conceal even greater differences in the relationship of the two canons to the communities they represent. The Jewish sacred books show many links with significant events and crises in the history of the Jewish people, links which have not been traced for the Christian canon.

Even so, these differences should not obscure the similarities in the way the two faiths evolved and codified their respective canons. Some contemporary scholars view the definition of the Jewish sacred texts in terms of an ongoing battle among rival groups which lacks any high point of negotiated agreement. A more traditional account suggests that around AD 90, after nearly four centuries, the Council of Jamnia decided that a heterogeneous series of books known separately as the *Law*, the *Prophets*, and the *Writings* would constitute the limited set of sacred books henceforth accepted as binding on the Jewish people. By AD 400 a similar Christian canon lay in place, and Amphilochius, Bishop of Iconius, could end his catalogue of the Old and New Testament books by calling them 'perhaps the most reliable canon of the divinely inspired Scriptures'.[24] Beyond the shoals of editorial commentary, philological enquiry, theological controversy and palaeographic curiosity, Jew and Christian alike find inspiration and regulation in the limited totality of sacred books commonly referred to as their 'canon'.

The evolution of these closely related religious canons adds some important layers to the classical understanding of *canon*. First, the ultimate authority for the canon becomes divine rather than human, natural or instrumental. Second, *canon* becomes far more than a rule or formula: it becomes a total narrative contained in a sacred book. Third, that book becomes a closed narrative containing a retrospectively binding providential plot. And fourth, this plot governs every aspect of work, thought, public and private life in the religious community; it becomes, in effect, the basis for the canonization of everyday life. As we shall see, the early years of Church history mark a sustained attempt to incorporate *canon* into an institutional structure, so that it becomes the basis for a contract between the individual, the Christian community or state, and God.

Although the classical use of *canon* reflects the needs of the *polis*, it is Christian and Jewish authorities who align *canon* with the inherited traditions, present life, and future destiny of a particular community of beliefs. When contemporary critics present the 'cultural canon' as an all-powerful force, controlling our most intimate categories and ideas, they revert to early Christian and Jewish usage, which views the canon or accepted set of holy books as the inexhaustible, encyclopaedic narrative of a whole people, a narrative that comprehends everything from their required readings and codes of behaviour to their shared assumptions and manifest beliefs.

In this way, the Jewish and Christian understanding of *canon* extends the civic frame of reference the word possessed for the men and women of antiquity. For although classical authors refer, sometimes in grief as well as in deference, to the 'canonical' status of figures from the past, they never regard those figures as sealing a permanent contract between the individual and society. On the contrary, several classical writers object strongly to the exemplary instances which appear in the inherited writings of the *polis*. In the early Church, in sharp contrast, *canon* comes to signal the difference between human contingency and a divinely sanctioned order permanently inscribed in the accepted canonical books. That order is assumed by the Church Fathers to stretch across centuries and nations, serving as a permanent and universal framework binding humanity to God.

The strong sense of a communal narrative and destiny that emerges in the early Christian Church has its basis in a pattern already established in Jewish religious practice. The first seeds of the Jewish canon date as far back as 600 BC, when the destruction of the temple drove Israel into exile. At this point, Jews began to gather a disparate group of writings–chronicle, law, lament, epic, encyclopaedia–into a continuous story they called their Holy Book. During the same period, the manuscripts of the Pentateuch became commonly known as 'Torah' or 'Law'. In AD 90–95 the *Against Apion* of Josephus confirmed the importance of twenty-two volumes, a number corresponding to the letters of the Hebrew alphabet. 'Although such long ages have now passed,' Josephus writes, 'no one has ventured either to add, or to remove, or to alter a syllable; and it is an instinct with every Jew, from the day of his birth, to regard them as the decrees of God, to abide by them, and, if need be, cheerfully to die for them.'[25] In this disparate collection of writings, Josephus suggests that Jews witness at the same time a set of laws, a unified story, and an inspired revelation. And underpinning each of these is the long tradition of commentary of which he himself forms part, commentary by learned exegetes versed in Jewish tradition who apply the law to historical events and demonstrate its afterlife in contemporary purposes and conduct.

The tradition of learned commentary emphasizes the adaptability of the canon, its openness to adjustment by different members of a homogeneous community. We can balance this picture by emphasizing a recurrent feature of sacred and secular canons alike: their usefulness in forming and preserving the identity of a particular community at the expense of other communities. In *Against Apion*, Josephus emphasizes the limited number of books recognized by the Jewish community, a situation he contrasts with the easy-going eclecticism of the Greeks. In *Against Heretics*, Irenaeus defends Christian canons against their Gnostic and Manichaean mutations, while in *The City of God* Augustine directs his portrait of the ideal Christian community 'against the pagans'. Many generations later, Edward Said will argue that the canon of Western Orientalist scholars conspires against the cultures of the East. Canons are often defined as 'accepted standards'. But acceptance can also imply rejection, an underside of the canonizing disposition I have no wish to underplay.

Ratification of the Jewish canon took at least 700 years. Acceptance of the considerably less varied Christian canon still took 400 years, partly because the earliest Christians preferred eyewitness testimony and apostolic authority concerning the life of Jesus to literary or philosophical renditions of the principles of their faith. Such preferences die hard. As recently as 1983, the theologian James Barr argued that a written canon 'was not an essential part of the foundation plan of Christianity'.[26] As an historical scholar, Barr accepts the obligation of understanding the original audience for the Gospels, of reconstructing the framework of their expectations, and of mapping their philological and ideological horizons. As a practising Christian, he wants to penetrate the spiritual world of the pioneers in his faith. What is essential, suggests Barr, are the events, personalities and experiences behind the Gospel texts, not the texts themselves as verbal artifacts. For different reasons, the Catholic Church has long returned a similar verdict, presenting Scripture as less important than ecclesiastical authority, an authority sanctioned by its own binding 'canons' or rules. These sharply different emphases show that the Christian canon, like its Jewish antecedent, points in two different directions. On the one hand, it points to the Word of God as recorded in Scripture, a set of narratives inherited from the distant past; on the other hand, it describes the rites and rituals of an organised, institutionalized present-day ecclesia. To see Christianity as uniquely a religion of the book is to misrepresent its varied lines of descent and its institutional history. If it means anything at all in Christian history, *canon* must refer to the shifting balance between law, established usage, accredited authority, and accepted Scripture.

To complicate matters still further, one of the earliest authorities refers to none of these meanings of *canon*, but rather to a sense that words and rites alike wither in the light of striking experiences, the experiences of those who constitute true witnesses of Christ's divinity. The Letters of Paul identify 'canon' with the rules binding on Christians and exemplified in Christ's own life. In Galatians 6:15–16, Paul declares that for Christians 'circumcision is nothing; uncircumcision is nothing; the only thing that counts is new creation! All who take this principle [*kanoni*] for their guide, peace and mercy be upon them, the Israel of God!'[27] For Paul, a 'canon' erases rather than transmits established standards. Where Judaic law traps its followers in a matrix of ritual observances, Paul invokes the liberating law of Christ, which can alone forge the 'new creation' of the Christian promise.

In another letter Paul repeats the same uncompromising message. Rejecting 'the outward appearance' of religion, its imposing structure of priests, temples and scribes, he aligns himself at 2 Corinthians 10: 1–16 with 'the gentleness and magnanimity of Christ'. Characteristically, Paul's discourse oscillates between consolidation and expansion, claiming in one verse not to travel 'beyond the proper limits', but promising his hearers soon afterwards to 'carry the gospel to lands that lie beyond you'. At one point, Paul contrasts pagan thinkers, who 'measure themselves [*eautous metrountes*] on their own' and in this way 'find in themelves their standard [*sugkrinontes*] of comparison', with Christians, whose 'sphere is determined by the limit [*metron tou kanonos*] God laid down for us'. Commentators have disputed whether 'the limit' to which Paul lays claim refers to a geographical entity or to his charismatic construction of his own apostolic mission. In either case, he lends conviction to many later voices of anti-institutional defiance. For Paul, as Martin Luther emphasized, turns conventional valuations inside out, kicking away the machinery that intervenes between the believer and God. 'The rule of which Paul speaks', notes Luther, 'is alone to be blessed . . . in which we live in Christian faith and become a new creature.'[28] For classical thinkers, a person possessed a canon; for Paul, the canon possesses the person. In effect, Paul reimagines the canon, transforming it from a classical pedagogic instrument or ritualized Jewish covenant into a dynamic, unpredictable, transcendent mission ultimately identified with Christ himself.

Yet almost despite Paul's efforts, the canon he bequeathed to posterity proved surprisingly open to the needs of the Church's diverse leaders and followers and, in the process, to Hellenistic and Judaic modification. In a sense, the complexity of the Christian canon reflects the extensive cultural borrowing of the early Church. When early Christians invoke canons in instructional manuals they assimilate Greek practices, while the actual organization of their Church owes much to the example of its Roman rulers. Christian ecclesiastical canons parallel the hierarchical centralized structures that enabled Rome to stretch itself from a province to a worldwide empire. Similarly, in presenting the canon as a set of sacred books associated with a fixed set of rituals and observances, holy days and fast days, Christians incorporate important aspects of the Jewish *Law*.

They also borrow from Jewish sources the crucial principle of personal canonization. If Philo of Alexandria (Philo Judaeus) characterizes Abraham as 'himself a law and an unwritten statute', then Christians of a Pauline disposition apply this 'law' to Jesus himself. If Philo suggests that each of the prophets becomes an 'exemplar of the wisdom [*sophias kanōn*] they have gained, Abraham by teaching, Isaac by nature, Jacob by practice',[29] then the early Church apportions similar virtues among the various apostles. And in another borrowing with crucial consequences for the modern *canon*, Christians perpetuate and rival the Jewish tradition of exegetical commentary. In fact, authorities such as Augustine and Aquinas carry these commentaries even further by developing a massive set of concordances between the New Testament and the Old, a process which absorbs centuries of world history into a pattern foreshadowed by a single sacred canonical work.

RULES FOR THE CONFIRMATION OF FAITH: THE CANONIZATION OF EARLY CHRISTIAN LIFE

Absorbing all these currents, Christian canons oscillate through the centuries between rule books, instructional digests, institutional ground-plans, the workings of Providence as demonstrated through the instrument of history, and clerically sanctioned sacred texts. The old association of *canon* with teaching manuals resurfaces in St Basil the Great's fourth-century *Detailed Rules*, a set of prerscriptions governing almost every aspect of the daily life of monks. Athanasius's *On Virginity*, a work described by Johannes Quasten as a 'manual for the Christian virgin',[30] encourages the canonization of everyday Christian existence by outlining step by step the process which brings the Christian virgin nearer to the vision of God. His work, which combines Hellenistic didacticism with a Jewish love of rite and observance, shows the willingness of early Christian authorities to employ the canon as a sort of providential syllabus. Similarly, when the Reformation Cardinal Cajetan characterizes the Old Testament books as 'rules for the confirmation of faith . . . for the edification of the faithful' ['*canonici . . . regulares ad firmandum . . . ad aedificationiem fidelium*'[31]], he combines the pedagogic function of the classical canon and the ritual observances of the Jewish canon with the missionary construction imparted by St Paul. As late as 1588, the Elizabethan cleric William Whitaker superimposes a Christian superstructure on a classical and Jewish base when he characterizes the canonical Scriptures as prescribing to us 'what we must believe, and how we ought to live: so that we should refer to this test our whole faith and life, as the mason or architect squares his work by the line and plummet'.[32] In Christian eyes, the canonical writings become foundation stones believer use to construct a new life, enabling them to see a new world by virtue of the truths revealed in a sacred book.

One would think that a Church centred on the Pauline dispensation would regard 'the canon' as a divine innovation, a charismatic departure from all existing traditions. A look at the foundations of the Christian canon shows, on the contrary, that the early Church established its preferred texts and codes of practice as much by borrowing as by origination and more by disputation than by miracle. Look, for instance, at Irenaeus of Lyons's second-century disquisition *Against Heresies* (AD 181–2), one of a series of works which argue the need and clear the field for a closed list of clerically authorized, divinely unified canonical texts. Irenaeus sets himself against the challenge to continuous teaching mounted by the Valentinians and other Gnostic groups. At this point no officially sanctioned list of Christian Scriptures yet existed. Even so, Irenaeus still refers to 'the writings (*graphas*)' accepted by ecclesiastical and apostolic tradition as binding on Christians. Irenaeus contrasts the unity and integrity of these writings with the distorted, contextless citations of the Gnostics. He describes the code of textual harassment that allows these heretics to chip away at the Scriptures, turning them into a *cento* of occult narratives which conform to previously held beliefs about creation, judgement, and other key religious matters. Irenaeus compares the Gnostics' mangled mutant of Scripture with the ingenious versions of Homer produced by generations of commentators. He argues that the Gnostic interpreters, like the editors of Homer, operate by redistributing lines, collage-fashion, from their proper places to sections of the text where they can participate in an occult narrative, a narrative that matches carnal desires more closely than spiritual needs. Irenaeus figures the clash of world views as a clash of narratives. In this way, he reminds us of the heterogeneous properties – code of law, community history, nascent body of dogma – surrounding a canon not yet established in its clerical role at the time of writing, but struggling for dominance, like Eliot's 'tradition', by the scribe's own executive will.

Confronted with this early and intriguing example of poststructuralist free play of interpretation, Irenaeus affirms the integrity of a harmonious set of Christian practices that begin with baptism, centre on the orderly presentation of the holy Scriptures, and end in the believer's reunion with God. For Irenaeus, each separate Christian observance contributes to a canon [*kanona*] or 'rule of truth'[33] that maps out the course of Christian existence from birth to death. As he presents it, the sum of Church law and clerically authorized Scriptures is a structure in which text, tradition and proper authority create a temporal human existence with the shapeliness and sequence of a story. Securely lodged in the believer's spirit, this 'canon of truth' expels the ghost and annihilates the authority of rival beliefs. As renaeus expands and consolidates it, the Christian 'canon' sets the conditions for an existence always ready, already blessed, conforming in the minutest actions of daily life to the words spoken by Jesus and the norms maintained by his Church. Already, the canonical flexibility welcomed by Aristotle is becoming less important than a capacity to conform, to fulfil the expectations set by a transcendent authority.

Irenaeus testifies to a Church challenged by alternative religious teachings from an early date. But is this a Church hardened by internal divisions or a Church revitalized by its encounters with alien traditions? Certainly, it is possible to argue that the canons of the early Church evolved dialogically, or at least controversially, in the context of debate with opposing factions and philosophies. For instance, Clement of Alexandria's lost *Ecclesiastical Canon* (only a fragment survives) bore the subtitle *Against the Judaizers*. Some may think that this phrase promises the worst kind of authoritarian excess sheltering behind the word *canon* throughout its history. Others might argue that these early ecclelsiastical canons survived so long precisely because they were forced to take account of diverse cultures. In fact, most of Clement's career, especially his largest work, the third-century *Stromata (Miscellanies)*, shapes up as an intercultural dialogue, and this dialogue modifies the shape of the *canons* Clement invokes. This lengthy work (unfinished at his death in AD 215) offers a loosely woven series of meditations on the relationship between Christian faith and pagan philosophy, the 'law' as understood by Christian, Jewish and classical cultures, and the relationship between true and false *gnosis*. Many biblical scholars credit the *Stromata* with lifting the Christian community above the turmoil of sectarian debate. Johannes Quasten, for instance, thinks that Clement 'proved that the faith and philosophy, Gospel and secular learning, are not enemies but belong together'. Quasten argues that Clement, through his work as a Christian bishop of a multicultural Jerusalem, came to believe that 'all secular learning serves theology'.[34] As Clement relays them, the canons of the Church become crucial instruments in the Christian's independence from the corruptions of secular govern- ment and the argumentative conventions of pagan philosophy. In his view, 'the discord of the sects' need not discourage philosophical and political debate. No Christian need feel distracted by the plurality of opinion or oppressed by the laws of the marketplace and the polity. Instead, by observing 'the canon [*canona*] of the Church' and 'the rule [*kanona*] of faith',[35] Christians can feel confident of freeing them- selves from spiritual error, whatever discord they encounter in the secular field.

The 'rule of faith' and 'the canon of the Church' bear on the conduct of believers. In part, this conduct will conform to rules or 'canons' decided by ecclesiastical authorities. But the original source for these rules remains the Word of God expressed in the canonical Scriptures. How does Clement conceive of this Word? Although he accepts the injunction to proclaim the Gospel 'from the housetops', Clement does not confuse volume with simplicity. Instead, he characterizes the scriptures as difficult and mysterious but absolutely binding. He thinks that 'the canon [*kanona*] of truth explaining the Scriptures' will always appear dark to anyone outside the Church. Only those who 'receive and observe it according to the ecclesiastical rule [*kanona*]' will understand it.[36] A public Church complements a complex figurative text; entry into the first becomes a prerequisite for comprehension of the second.

Like Irenaeus, Clement opposes the concordant unity of God's narrative as revealed in Scripture to the opportunistic revisions of the heretics. Like Irenaeus too, he sees the scriptural canon as giving birth to a secondary canon of binding institutional practices, practices incumbent on all 'those who receive and observe, according to the ecclesiastical rule, the exposition of the Scriptures as explained by him', the appointed preacher. For those ignorant on the point, Clement explains that 'the ecclesiastical rule is the concord and harmony of the law and the prophets in the covenant delivered at the coming of the Lord'.[37] In Clement's hands the ecclesiastical canon, clearly understood now as a mutually reinforcing code of practices and set of texts, imprints the authority of Christian revelation over all rival systems of belief, explaining history's larger providential pattern as well as the actions of the individual believer.

Clement and Irenaeus both see Scripture as the basis for the Church's charismatic mission. Such an enormous responsibility made it all the more important to know the exact boundaries of Scripture and to regulate its interpretations through appropriate channels. How else could the ingenious exegetical endeavours of a Montanus or a Valentinus be fought off, or the rigoristic exclusions of a Marcion be defeated? In the early years of the Church, when gospels multiplied and their authority dwindled, it became especially pressing and difficult to agree on a list of accepted canonical works. In this atmosphere, it is hardly surprising that around AD 140 Marcion, the son of a bishop, furnished a list that excluded all sources except a severely edited Gospel of St Luke, ten Pauline epistles, and his own *Antitheses*. Four years later Marcion was expelled from the Church. Even so, Marcion's list spurred others to follow his example, and for some time his exclusionary principle exerted considerable influence on Church authorities. For instance, Eusebius describes Origen's early treatise 'On the Gospel According to Matthew' as a work 'defending the canon of the Church' in which Origen 'testifies that he knows only four Gospels'. Eusebius then quotes Origen's explanation of what he has 'learnt by tradition concerning the four Gospels, which alone are unquestionable in the Church of God under heaven'.[38]

In the *Decrees of the Synod of Nicea* (*c.* 350) Athanasius acknowledges that a book called *The Shepherd* enjoys a certain esteem among Christians. Even so, the book does not, he judges, 'belong to the canon [*kanonos*]'.[39] Seventeen years later, in a festal letter, Athanasius lists for the first time the twenty-seven canonical books of the new Testament, and insists that the words preserved by Jesus's witnesses and those first entrusted with their transmission must not be mixed with less authoritative testimony. Conceding that other works may instruct beginners, he emphasizes that only a select list of authorized books have canonical status [*biblia kanonizomena*]. 'Our whole scripture is divinely inspired,' he asserts, 'and contains books not infinite in number but finite and comprehended in a single canon.'[40] By 380, Amphilochius of Iconius had compiled a list of canonical works which he characterizes as directly inspired by God. In 400, Isidore of Pelusium fused the 'canon of truth' invoked by Irenaeus and Clement of Alexandria with canonical lists compiled by Athanasius and Amphilochius. 'Let us examine the canon of truth', Isidore remarks. 'I mean the divine scriptures.' He then furnishes his list of canonical books. In the same year, Macarius Magnes speaks for the first time of 'the canon of the New Testament'.[41]

Unlike the classical canons, the Christian canon represents a shared clerical initiative and its maintenance becomes a public responsibility. Athanasius's 'Festal Letter', in which he lists the canonical works, has many of the qualities associated with Christian canonicity. In fact, the very idea of a festal letter alerts us to the ecclesiastical checks that regulated the life of the early Christian community. Shortly after the feast of the Epiphany, Alexandrian bishops would publicly announce the date of Easter and the beginning of Lent. The letter announcing these dates contained a mixture of discussion, proselytization, and affirmation. This is the context of Athanasius's letter, which reaffirms the strength of ecclesiastical authority and the saving properties of the Scriptures against the facile ingenuity of the unauthorized books. By 'canon', Athanasius understands an authorized selection of works that regulate the lives of the faithful. 'These', he says 'are the fountains of salvation, that they who thirst may be satisfied with the living words they contain.' Even so, the inspiring power of the sacred writings must subdue itself to what he calls 'the teaching of piety'.[42] Athanasius will not allow the words of Scripture to escape the nets of doctrine and custom woven by the church.

From an early date, the idea of an 'ecclesiastical canon' suggests not just a set of texts and a codified set of rules but a complex unity of practices, rituals and writings which the leaders of the Christian community want to transmit to the next generation of believers and to circulate among an expanding circle of present-day members. This complex and interpenetrating set of ideas means that however much our subsequent reading of secular canonical works may owe to methods pioneered in biblical exegesis, an enormous gulf still separates the Christian canon from its literary counterpart. For the

Christian, the canonical text remains essentially vehicular: it transports divine revelation, facilitates missionary exhortation, and underwrites ecclesiastical authority. Secular critics, who may voluntarily adhere to a cognate set of affiliations, still invoke the canons of Aristotle more readily than the canon of Athanasius, even though they may see the secular works they discuss as exerting a profound 'sacred' charge. In fact, one of the complications attached to the modern secular use of 'canon' remains the numinous resonance it borrows from its sacred counterpart.

In an early Christian context, 'canon' refers both to a set of ecclesiastical practices and to a list of inspired texts. Taken together, the two canons fuse into the storylike unity that prefigures the destiny of every believer. However, 'canon' in the early Church fulfils still a third role, in supplying the common past and shared norms which will bind together the Christian community. Always intensely aware of the dangers of persecution, the early Christian hierarchs impressed on their followers the need for unity and unanimity by appealing to 'the canon'. Eusebius's *Ecclesiastical History* describes many occasions when, disturbed by reports of internal dissent, the bishops recalled the Church's supposedly more unified past. At one time, as the late-second-century Hegissipus fervently puts it, the Church resembled 'a pure and uncorrupted virgin'. In those days, only a few Christians threatened 'to corrupt the healthful rule [*kanona*] of the Saviour's preaching'.[43]

Yet as Hegissipus must surely have known, Christian congregations already enjoyed a long history of resistance to legislated ecclesiastical *canons*. As early as the last decade of the first century, during a heated argument between an authoritative institutional centre and a dissenting province, Clement of Rome tries to calm the restless church at Corinth. Clement reminds the Corinthians that they share with the rest of the Church a common past in Christ, a mission for the present, and a hope for the future. Confronted by the persecuting forces of Nero, Clement uses the same form of argument as Hegissipus. Although the Church is still in its infancy, he speaks with the authority of centuries, urging the Corinthians to adhere 'to the glorious and venerable rule [*kanona*] of our tradition'. Like so many defenders of the canon after him, Clement acts as a spokesman for the cause of order, cautioning the Corinthians 'to remain in the rule of subordination' and 'to manage their households with seemliness, in all circumspection'. Canons aid the cause of peaceful self-government, unbroken tradition, and central, legitimate authority. Clement begs the dissidents to observe 'the appointed rule of his own ministration with all dignity'.[44]

In all these cases, Christ's role as preacher and leader gives authority to the later theory and practice of ecclesiastical leadership. Polycrates of Asia describes 'the rule of faith' that regulates his conduct at the Passover, sanctions the authority of his episcopacy, and ensures the wide dispersal of God's word. The ultimate canon, Polycrates assures his followers, lies not in any worldly structure but only in Christ and in God. This explains why 'it is better to obey God rather than men'.[45] In the same uncompromising spirit, Clement of Alexandria describes an ideal order visible beyond the repeated outbursts of sectarian conflict. That order, as housed in the ancient Church, becomes the cradle of 'the ecclesiastical canon'. That canon encourages not fanciful readings of disputed texts but rather 'the exactest knowledge and the truly best set of principles'.[46] Such canons elicit obedience from those who wish to call themselves the children of God. They possess the sanction of tradition and stamp their authority on history. To act in conformity with them is to ensure the fulfilment of the good news promised in Scripture. The early Christians expected to see a fulfilment of this promise during their own lifetimes. As such expectations faded, canons remained and provided a matrix of texts and observances, a strong foundation in the shifting winds of historical change.

Once established in its own right, divorced from Jewish, Gnostic, and heathen observances, divorced even from Scripture itself, this 'ecclesiastical canon' produced a series of secondary canons designed to regulate the conduct of believers in ways that ranged from the legislative, as in canon law, to the practical, as in the so-called canonical epistles, which ruled on dietary and disciplinary matters. (In 300 Church councils ruled that these should be known henceforth simply as *Canons*.) Once decreed acceptable to Church tradition, these legislative canons proliferated. Basil the Great's fourth-century *Detailed Rules*, mentioned earlier, illustrates how such rules were applied by Christian communities increasingly remote from direct apostolic witness. Basil's experience as an official visitor to monasteries had acquainted him with the disciplinary problems of an institution outside the chains of command enforced in the central episcopal order. How could the teachings authorized by the precedent of Christ and the apostles be adjusted to suit monastic conditions? Since the monastery Superior continued the mission of Christ, he also shared Christ's responsibilities as a preacher. But what rules governed behaviour inside the monastery during the Superior's absence's? The prospect of many monks all talking at once and in random order did not seem like God's scheme applied to earthly conditions. Basil accordingly emphasizes the binding power 'of the rule [*kanonos*] and of tradition'.[47] Observance of these monastic canons entailed a strict division of the day and the periodic separatioin of monks to meditate on the Order's 'rules and traditions' in the security of their individual cells.

In Basil's cells many modern readers will see the forerunner of the Victorian panopticon. However, Gregory of Nazianzus, Basil's long-time friend, offers the different perspective of a participant. As he rides away from his friend's monastery, Gregory re-creates in his mind a kind of canonical pastoral, the vision of a society in which practical duties (wood-chopping, housework) link with devotional observances in a chain of continuous spiritual enrichment. What some might view as a canonical obstacle course, Gregory recalls as a structured set of operations aimed at 'the contest and incitement of virtue . . . secured by written rules and canons'.[48] By viewing each separate rule as an episode in a larger narrative designed to promote the cause of holiness, Gregory incorporates rote observance into an imaginatively satisfying quasi-aesthetic structure.

AUGUSTINE'S CLOSED CANON

Even so, the ultimate authority for such observances always remains in doubt in a religious institution whose ultimate canon rests in Christ himself. Does *canon* refer to a codified set of rules or to the charismatic possibility offered by the example of Jesus? A recurring problem in the Christian community is the authority for the institutional rules and the institutional role of the charismatic leader. In the shift from St Paul to St Gregory, the word *canon* appears to change into its opposite, as the apostle's intense spiritual vision yields to the institutional structures described by his successors. Even so, such a shift seems almost easy to grasp in comparison with some of the usages that follow. The immensely complicating middle term so far omitted is, of course, the holy text which joins at their source the inspired narratives of the apostles and the rudiments of later ecclesiastical doctrine.

In the course of transforming itself from a ministry to an institution, the early Church understood that the charisma of the canonical texts needed to be harnessed to a more reasonable, persuasive framework than Paul appeared to offer. This is why the subsequent history of canon formation involves the ecclesiastical authorities in a complex interplay of regulation, persuasion, education and administration. In the process, the scriptural canon becomes a kind of liminal institution situated at the very threshold of cerebration and calibration, a guarantee not just of Christian unity but of Christian selfhood and Christian culture. In Augustine's *The City of God* (413–26) the idea of the canon as an authoritative list of sacred books, to be consulted before and beyond all others, is presented as part of an indispensable social need to regulate, limit and co-ordinate what a given community understands by 'the Word of God'.

Writing with an inescapable sense of distance from the original Christian mission, Augustine demonstrates the precarious balance of institutional, theological, charismatic and epistemological pressures held in place by the newly established scriptural canon. He makes much of the unanimity of canonical testimony, constrasting it with the disarray and cacophony of philosophy denied the benefit of revelation. Before such a canon existed, he observes, no possibility for certainty lay open to mankind. Augustine draws on the theme iterated by Irenaeus and Clement when he says that the Hellenistic system of education, with its bias towards the recondite and exclusive, produced nothing more satisfying than 'a few babblers engaged in quarrelsome debates in schools and gymnasia'. (Tolerance in matters of *canon* surfaces only intermittently after Aristotle.) Developed on such a shaky foundation, no canon could remain truly fixed. Broadening this point into a kind of argument from success, Augustine then remarks that 'whole peoples, townspeople and rustics alike, learned and unlearned together, peoples so many in number, so great in size, have believed that "when the apostles wrote their books God was speaking to them or through them" '. History supports this widespread popular belief. After examining the dates of the Hebrew prophets and the 'inspired' classical authors, Augustine concludes that 'not even these preceded in time our genuine theologian, Moses, who gave a truthful account of the one true God, and whose writings now stand first in the authorized canon'. He then adds, somewhat disingenuously, that the number of the canonical books is, miraculously, just right: 'There were bound to be few of them, so that what ought to be precious in the eyes of religion should not be cheapened by abundance; and yet not so few that their agreement should not be wonderful'.[49] Augustine shortens the gap between the the world of history (a veil of tears and disorder) and the world of canonical revelation by insisting that *history* conforms to *canon* in the same way that the Old Testament conforms to the New. In his writings, the canonical Scriptures gain a new shape and relevance as the foundation plan for the future city of God.

The new demands of pattern and coherence that Augustine makes of the Scriptures would seem to encourage the provision of ever higher standards of textual and lexical accuracy. Since the Old Testament was written in classical Hebrew and Aramaic and the New Testament was written in a Greek dialect, a predominantly Latin-speaking audience faced a momentous task in penetrating the original meaning of the authentic texts. Augustine sidesteps this whole problem by quoting from whatever text serves his doctrinal purposes. His implicit assumption is that the canonical Scriptures remain important in themselves, almost despite their words and irrespective of their audience's capacity to understand them. Augustine simultaneously believes that the Scriptures are all-important and that they are unfathomable and dark. This paradox encourages him to disregard sound editorial principles and to cite whatever text suits the doctrinal point he needs to make.

Of course, this attitude is far from unknown in literary criticism. Throughout his career, G. Wilson Knight used a one-volume obsolescent edition of Shakespeare, so as not to disturb by editorial apparatus the words of a writer he regarded as canonically obscure. In the same way, Augustine considered the editorial labours of Jerome and Origen less useful than the faith needed to penetrate the scriptural mysteries. After listing the 'canon of the Scriptures' in *On Christian Doctrine* (396–427) Augustine emphasizes that these books must be read 'even if they are not understood', because 'those things which are manifest' serve 'to illuminate those things which are obscure'. He cannot conceive of a textual and lexical authority sufficient to purge the Scriptures of all mystery. He even hints that such clarity would ferment an anti-canonical spirit, since obscurity 'was provided by God to conquer pride by work'.[50]

Augustine recognizes that the best guarantee of the difficulty, mystery and harmony he cherishes will come from a closed canon – the wider the range of witnesses, the more unlikely the submission of a unanimous verdict. Even so, he wants that unanimity to exceed the bounds of rationality. He remains unsatisfied by the 'philosophy' of the Greeks; he wants the Christian canon to be 'wonderful' as well as concordant. In *The City of God* the values of originality, authenticity and unanimity all underpin the regulative authority of the Christian canon. Taken together, observes Augustine, the Scriptures reveal a mysterious concord latent in the universe as a whole. Outside the canon he sees only dissent and misery; inside it, he finds the sole hope for certainty and salvation. Because he sees the stakes as so immeasurably high, he impresses on his audience again and again the need for consensus. After examining a series of rival quests for universal paradigms – Jewish, Greek, Egyptian – he takes pride in the fact that in Christianity 'our canon of sacred books is fixed and bounded' and is, moreover, 'far from disagreeing in any respect'.[51] Taken as a whole, *The City of God* represents one of the strongest arguments yet made for a closed canon based on a restricted number of uniquely privileged texts.

Such a view involves the term *canon* in a 180-degree turn from the position endorsed by Aristotle. Aristotle understands *canon* as a flexible measuring rod for human activities, whereas Augustine sees it as the only intermittently comprehensible source of a divine plan. Future generations of sacred and secular critics will often seek to combine elements of both positions, despite the contradictions in which this involves them. Later critics want their canonical authors to appear mysterious and endlessly fascinating but also to serve as the source, as Scripture was for Augustine, of the binding traditions that regulate a community. But the same critics also want their own activities to conform to rational principles. They want a *Tempest* that conforms to the theatrical conventions of the Jacobean stage while simultaneously supporting the mysteries of loss and renewal described by Colin Still or the myths of immortality celebrated by G. Wilson Knight.

One cannot stress too strongly, however, that if the early Church Fathers read the Scriptures with great subtlety, they did so as authorities in a hierarchical, legislating Church. When Augustine distinguishes between 'things to be enjoyed' and things 'to be used', the contemporary reader inevitably recalls Roland Barthes's description of the *jouissance* promised by the literary text.[52] Yet to call Christianity the religion of the book is to overlook the way the interpretative excess of an Augustine bolsters doctrinal authority. In practice, Augustine's interpretative, scholarly and historical skills all drive the scriptural text towards conformity with established ecclesiastical practice. His interpretative play always serves homiletic and dogmatic purposes. His canon plays off incompatible ends that are ultimately resolvable only in the eyes of faith. Just as the difficult text underwrites the public authority of the Church, so the limited number of canonical books germinates the limitless vistas of interpretative significance. Ecclesiastical authorities establish procedures of great refinement in order to measure the status and heighten the significance of the books included in their own authorized Scriptures.

THE BURDEN OF UNDERSTANDING:
THE CANON IN THE CHRISTIAN COMMUNITY

As the simplicity of the original Christian mission recedes from view, Church leaders find themselves involved in increasingly complex arguments about the definition and boundaries of the scriptural canon. Rufinus, a fifth-century priest and editor, distinguishes in his *Commentarius in symbolum Apostolorum* (*Commentary on the Apostles' Creed, c.* 404) between the canon of inspired books and books acceptable to the faith but not divinely inspired. Rufinus notes that 'catechumens receiving their first lessons in the Church' must turn to the works of the sacred canon in order to reach 'the well-springs from which their draughts of the Word of God must be taken'. Like the *Canon* of Polycletus, the sacred canon fuses elementary instruction and ultimate inspiration. Even so, other works have other, less exalted and less practical uses. 'We should appreciate', Rufinus remarks, 'that there are certain other books which our predecessors designated "ecclesiastical" rather than "canonical".' He then cites as examples such apocryphal works as the Wisdom of Solomon, Ecclesiasticus, Tobit, Judith, and Maccabees. 'Canonical' books enjoy privileged forms of transmission and interpretation; the 'ecclesiastical' books 'handed down to us by the Fathers' become exhortatory and useful, but are not binding in matters of dogma. These are the books the authorities wish 'to be read in the churches', even as they direct 'that appeal should not be made to them on points of faith'.[53]

Yet despite Rufinus's formula for selective ecclesiastical readings from non-canonical books, the Old and New Testaments soon overtook all other sources for official Christian teaching. Beryl Smalley describes the Bible as 'a teaching book' for medieval churchmen, and as 'the only set book to be universally recognized' in medieval Europe.[54] The words of the Bible settled the beginning of every sermon, formed the basis for all existing dogma, tested the training of recruits to the clerical professions and the willingness to believe of ordinary Church members. In this context, it is hardly surprising to find Thomas Aquinas reiterating that the formidable apparatus of the medieval Church 'rests on the revelation made to the Prophets and Apostles who wrote the canonical books, not on a revelation, if such there be, made by any other teacher'. Earlier in the *Summa*, Aquinas introduces this distinction by applying Aristotle's idea that 'the virtuous man . . . sets the measure and standard for human acts' to Paul's formulation that 'the spiritual man judges all things'. Aquinas thinks that Paul's 'judgement' confirms Aristotle's 'measure', but not vice versa. The words of Scripture need no confirmation because they represent divine wisdom. By the same token, Christians must shape their souls by the new law established by Scripture rather than match Scripture to some previous system of beliefs. To enforce this point, Aquinas quotes Augustine:

> Only to those books or writings which are called canonical have I learnt to pay such honour that I firmly believe that none of their authors have erred in composing them. Other authors . . . I read to such effect that, no matter what holiness and learning they display, I do not hold what they say to be true because those were their sentiments.[55]

Devotional writers, like pagan philosophers, must be judged by their conformity to canonical Scripture, not by their pious or eloquent words.

Whether they offer a blueprint for the construction of a Christian self or the construction of a Christian city, limit the scope of Christian devotions or set those devotions in the wider context of ecclesiastical history, these increasingly complex clerical distinctions prove that the adoption of a fixed and closed Christian canon necessitated drastic changes in reading and in ideas of history and prophecy, all these undoubtedly accompanied by momentous revisions of social and personal experience. Very early in Christian history, the idea of the canon as a guarantee of minimum standards disappears entirely. Instead, the canon becomes a vehicle not just to reach posterity's favourable verdict but to achieve salvation itself. Canons provide a framework for the construction of a Christian soul, just as previously they had supplied the blueprint for the construction of a human image. They supply a pattern for experiencing reality according to the pattern of the Gospels; in a sense, like a work of art, their purpose becomes to make the Christian *see*.

Yet as the status of the canonical writings rises, they must withstand the pressure of ever-expanding frames of reference. And despite a sophisticated tradition of assertions to the contrary, acceptance of the scriptural canon as an exemplary narrative does not entail acceptance of a canon of binding ecclesiastical and social practices. Nor does acceptance of a closed canon of biblical texts guarantee consensus about their interpretation. Taken together, these two points explain why the hostility contemporary critics display towards the academic canon has long received powerful expression by reformers inside the Christian Church. The recurring tension in

Christian history between a canon that preserves the charismatic residue of divine revelation by means of an inspired collection of writings and a canon that reinforces centralized authority and codifies observances acceptable to such an authority has many points of contact with current academic controversies about the canon. The complex history of the canons bequeathed to later Christians by the early Church lies far beyond the scope of this brief discussion. I shall confine myself here to sketching out a few points relevant to our modern ideas about the literary canon, laying special emphasis on the variety of interpretations the officially 'closed' Christian canon continues to attract.

Perhaps predictably, the closure of the Christian canon expands its interpretative force, generating secondary, related canons which set forth rules governing every aspect of worldly Christian life, daily rules for participation in the community of belief, rules which constitute a kind of spiritual *Highway Code*. Unfortunately, not everyone follows this code, nor even agrees with the limits it sets up. Soon after Aquinas lays the question to its hermeneutic rest, firm pressure emerges to interpret the canon in an almost classical way, to understand it once again as a set of basic rules or code of practice, while at the same time attaching to its every, much-glossed, word a life-and-death force that is the very reverse of classical.

While defence of the canon by early and medieval churchmen reaches new heights of subtlety in the hands of those commissioned to perform it, the achievement of Luther and the Protestant Reformation lays the burden of interpretation in the hands of every believer. At the height of the Reformation, the epithet 'canonical' inspires as much mistrust as conviction. Martin Luther notoriously staked his life on the authority of the canonical Scriptures, while seeing no authority at all in the imposing ecclesiastical structures entrusted with their transmission. In the same spirit, Henry Crosse, a Puritan activist writing in the last days of Elizabeth I, uses the word as a litmus test for the reversion of the Christian Commonwealth to false ceremony and show. For Crosse, episcopal authority in all its pomp and glory merely travesties the Word of God. 'Wisdome in a ragged coat is seldom canonnicall',[56] he sardonically observes, a remark with which Luther would almost certainly agree.

While Luther acknowledges that 'the canonical books . . . lay the foundation of faith', he rejects much of the ecclesiastical and scholarly apparatus those books have amassed. In the preface to his translation of the New Testament, he observes that 'it would only be right and proper if this volume were published without any preface, or without any name on the title page, but simply with its own name to speak for itself'. By implication, he opposes the Church as an institution to the Word of God contained in Scripture. When Luther met the rival theologian Zwingli at the Colloquy of Marburg in 1529, his mistrust for exegetical ingenuity and established authority took little time to appear. Luther understood the history of the church as directing that 'When the Fathers speak, they are to be accepted in accordance with the canon of Scripture'. His rider, 'Whatever they appear to write contrary to Scripture must either be interpreted or be rejected',[57] effectively sets up a hierarchy that inverts accepted Catholic practice. For the established structure – Church, Scripture, interpreter – Luther substitutes a three-tier structure of his own – Scripture, interpreter, Church. From the Reformation onwards, an institutionally accredited class entrusted with the preservation and circulation of the canonical writings coexists with a new, urgent conviction that all members of the Christian community must understand – and behave as if they understand – the canonical words without any institutionalized intermediary.

The current of scepticism which the Reformation directed towards ecclesiastical institutions spreads in later periods towards the texts themselves. Throughout the later history of the Church, rational interpretation not just of ecclesiastical institutions but of the canonical Scriptures becomes in some quarters a Christian imperative. The result, as archaeological and palaeographic skills grow and the authority of science heightens, is that the unanimity of canonical testimony, which Augustine took for granted, can hardly withstand a battery of philological, textual and historical enquiries pointing to the heterogeneous materials collected in the Christian Bible. Unable to ignore the flood of scholarly material, some churchmen subject the canon to continuous interpretation, while others seek to understand it as a set of basic rules. Throughout the later history of the Church, some members want to pare the canonical writings down to a few simple, universal messages. For instance, E. M. Goulburn, Dean of Norwich and the writer of many nineteenth-century devotional works, thinks that 'an over-subtle scrutiny of the words of a sentence sometimes impairs our perception of its force'. Such a fate has befallen Scripture. In his bid to clear through the thickets of interpretative excess, Goulburn emphasizes the importance of practical codes of conduct, and behaviour which conforms to the basic rules of faith. In this context, he presents the Lord's Prayer as *the* essential text for Christians to know, 'a canon . . . for testing and correcting our spiritual state'.[58]

Against Goulburn's canonical minimalism Max Müller offers a different answer, suggesting that a community of believers should extend the same vigilance of understanding to its canonical writings as it applies to any written source. If by *religion*, observes Müller, 'we mean a body of doctrines handed down by tradition, or in canonical books', then we should agree to submit those books and traditions to the scientific scrutiny which has proved so profitable in the modern world as a whole:

> No one would venture, now-a-days, to quote from any book, whether sacred or profane, without having asked these simple and yet momentous questions: When was it written? Where? And by whom? Was the author an eye witness, or does he only relate what he has heard from others?

For Müller, canonical testimony maintains its authority by virtue of its conformity with the rules of ordinary discourse. Any higher authority it enjoys lies in what Müller proposes as the basis for a new religion based on a new canon, a canon situated beyond the frontiers of conflicting and assailable inherited texts. This canon or rule he describes as 'a faculty of faith in man, independent of all historical religions'.[59]

How have later Christians responded to these challenges? Goulburn's canonical minimalism and Müller's sceptical historicism present two sides of one coin, since they both ask revelation to conform to practical requirements. The link forged by the early Church between *canon* as ecclesiastical rule and *canon* as authorized texts begins to break apart when even a devout Christian such as Goulburn focuses attention on the texts that allay anxiety – concentrates, in other words, on immediate spiritual effect. Against this minimalist current lies a still-continuing tradition of learned exegesis, with its endless attempt to penetrate the 'otherness' of the scriptural writings or to redefine the grounds for their transcendent authority. Unlike some of their Victorian predecessors, a number of twentieth-century commentators have made a sustained attempt to bolster the authority of the canonical Scriptures. Even so, in recent years the question of canonical authority has proved a tricky one for theologians to answer – so much so, in fact, that the complexities of recent discussions would occupy the rest of this book. Instead of trying to follow the ramifications of current theological argument,

I shall conclude this discussion of the classical and Christian canons by focusing on a few developments of particular relevance to the current literary debate.

In answer to the 'scientific' demystifications of a Müller, some theologians have tried to reconstruct the experience and renegotiate the meaning of *canon* in both religious and historical terms. Brevard Childs, for instance, has used the idea to re-examine the Old Testament writings:

> The concept of canon implies that these writings have a function which is not exhausted by their original role in history, but they continue to function in the life of the church in each successive generation through the work of the Holy Spirit. By its . . . shaping of the tradition, the canon provides the hermeneutical key for the later generation of Christians to appropriate the ancient testimony for itself.[60]

Childs reattaches to the idea of *canon* the narrative dimension described by Irenaeus and Augustine, the orderly canon of texts and religious practices which has aesthetic qualities we normally find in art. Similarly, for James A. Sanders, the Old Testament canon endures not as a collection of prohibitions 'but because of its essential diversity, its own inherent refusal to absolutize any single stance as the only place where one might live under the sovereignty of God'. When he emphasizes the experience of exile at the heart of the Jewish canon, Sanders conforms to the pattern of modern experience reported by a Kafka or a Raymond Williams. When he aligns *canon* with 'the community's historic memory which is the locus of its identity',[61] he suggests its consonance with the deep hope for continuity in the midst of change that secular authorities from Matthew Arnold to Frank Kermode have associated with *culture*. When Sanders interprets *canon* as transmitting the eschatological fears and hopes of a particular community, he speaks of Scripture in terms that Northrop Frye and Walter Benjamin use to discuss the apocalyptic potential of art and mythology. Sanders's emphasis on its diversity not only validates the biblical canon for a plural society but renders it a potentially useful instrument for literary and cultural critics as well.

Some of these critics may be surprised to hear the Bible described as 'a veritable textbook in contemporization of tradition'.[62] Even so, the capacity to imagine the separate ordinances and commandments of the Church as an interrelated quasi-aesthetic structure has deep roots in the history of the Christian canon. As a practitioner of what he calls 'canonical criticism', Sanders discovers in the Bible the kinds of patterns earlier commentators found in Church customs and laws. Sanders's canon conforms to the assumptions of a plural society, while the canons of Irenaeus, Gregory and Augustine conform to their assumptions of a hierarchical universe. In both cases, however, the power of the canon lies in its ability to suggest the ultimate shape and destiny of Christian existence. All these writers agree that the Christian canon impresses on believers a set of values which scriptural narrative perpetually reconfirms.

The same power, of course, makes some notion of *canon* a potentially valuable, as well as dangerous, instrument for students of the humanities, who also possess their privileged works, monuments which the most ambitious students – T. S. Eliot or Northrop Frye, for example – have tried to collect into a similar imaginative unity. Like biblical scholars, students of the humanities hope their privileged works will survive the waning of the beliefs that originally produced them. Even if they disagree with Sir Walter Raleigh that *Paradise Lost* sets up a monument to dead ideas, many modern readers will agree with Raleigh that Milton's poem continues to beguile the mind and ear. Moreover, even as the ideas themselves wane, their efficacy in developing a community's sense of identity may still be acknowledged, in theology and the humanities alike. We shall see in later chapters that Frye views literary canons as storehouses of the basic myths and narratives of society as a whole, while Edward Said, who presents 'the canon' as the primal scene of social division, might none the less agree with Paul Ricoeur's hypothesis that through its canons a 'community recognizes what is consistent with its own existence, what founds it'.[63]

Ricoeur's formulation alerts us to the existence of an important group of theologians, themselves influenced by philosophers and literary critics, who seek to distance the idea of a *canon* from texts and ecclesiastical statutes alike, identifying it rather with the interpretative community as a whole. Ricoeur admits that only at the level of 'the confession of the community can I answer the question of canon'. For Ricoeur, a biblical text makes sense only when a Christian community uses it to direct its own spiritual experiences. Combining Aristotle's sense of canonical adaptability with Augustine's emphasis on the fixed, separate dispensation of the Christian community, Ricoeur presents the Christian canon as a kind of *contrat théologique*, by virtue of which interpretation becomes a continuous, organic process embracing both the earliest prophets and the latest hermeneutic critics. If the Christian canon is closed, it is because the Christian community as a whole chooses to close it. Closing the canon, observes emphatically Ricoeur is 'like an arbitrary act which became a kind of faith for the whole community, which hencforth is constituted by this closing of the canon'. Out of this closure comes a perpetual commitment to a faith defined in terms of a continuing process of interpretation, or what Ricoeur calls 'a wager: I risk my life on this whole and belong to it by this commitment, and I may win or lose'.[64]

In the field of secular literature, one would think that the risks would seem less momentous. Even so, borrowing from the pattern of canon formation presented by their Christian counterparts, the makers of the literary canon have set up a short-list of works which they expect to enjoy long-lasting public esteem. They have also tried to use these works to regulate subsequent production. The epic and tragic poets of antiquity, the seventeenth-century metaphysical poets, Mr Eliot and his disciples – these represent just a few of the canonical models held up by generations of critics for future creative achievement. Literary and cultural history also offers examples of rigoristic spirits eager to fuse their chosen works into a design for living, an inclination that manifests a desire to literalize the analogical relationship between sacred and secular canons. For some contemporary critics, this excessive zeal inextricably tethers canons to the repressive cause of an illegitimate authority.

One way to lessen the recurrent association of *canon* with such authority is to emphasize aesthetic shape and internal coherence as one of the ways by which a canon achieves legitimacy. Admittedly, this idea seems unlikely to mitigate the full force of the current blast of hostility to canons, and this is why the present chapter has also pointed to several other ways of legitimating the notion of *canon*: as an educational tool, as a framework for argument, a pretext for cross-cultural dialogue, an exemplary achievement, and so on. Few of these traditional senses of *canon* are currently recognized or even remembered. On the contrary, we shall see as the book proceeds that only a few twentieth-century critics exhibit any awareness of the plurisignificance underlying that most monolithic of words, 'canon'.

The pages have offered no more than a sketch of the early history of the canon – a history of the modification, arguably even the breakdown, of the most ambitious attempt to anchor a fixed canon encompassing a list of books and a set of rules to a closed providential narrative regulating every aspect of individual and communal existence. Even so, the examples of Goulburn, Müller and Ricoeur show that, right up to its breakdown, this grand totalizing canon generates new canons, new norms for the spiritual life. The larger pattern we can trace through both the classical and the Christian canons suggests a kind of cycle through which all canons must probably pass. The transformation of the Christian canon shows that if any idea of 'the canon' as monolithic and all-powerful ultimately proves a chimera, still 'canons' in mutation inevitably tend to reappear. Yet the practical success of these canons often depends not merely on their providing 'a measure' but on their providing 'the right measure'. And the right measure soon comes to be applied far beyond the range of the practical area for which it was originally developed. In its extended sense, *canon* no longer functions in a rational framework deployed by men and women whose purposes have been clearly and narrowly defined. Instead, it becomes the vehicle of posterity or of some unspecified *idea*. That idea is enlarged, modified, adds magical and institutional elements, and is challenged by its inheritors. To canonize is somehow to expand the dimensions of the given, to invest it with charismatic properties bestowed from a different region of experience. Those properties become manifest and codified, and soon find themselves under fire. The cycle begins anew.

2

A Whole World of Reading:
The Modern History of the Canon

It is not always easy to untangle the previous senses of *canon* which permeate modern, secular use or to pinpoint precisely when new senses appear. Certainly, after Christianity takes hold of it, the idea of the canonical book assumes a prominence unknown in the period of Aristotle or Polycletus. But what happens when *canon* finds itself applied to non-sacred books, to works that make no explicit claims to regulate or regenerate, works for which these claims must be made by readers themselves? It is not unknown for those entrusted with the transmission of secular works to students and the general public to discuss their chosen authors in almost evangelical terms, sometimes making explicit claims about their restorative and legislative force. Even his contemporaries credited Wordsworth with 'healing power'. During the same period, Shakespeare became a sacred genius for critics from Coleridge to G. Wilson Knight. These two notorious cases obscure the fact that in the last 200 years almost any author, from Gray to Barthelme, may attract equal or even higher praise.

What does this praise mean? The reader of St Paul will scarcely need reminding of the author's aims to counsel and exhort. Yet the reader of Shakespeare and Wordsworth, writers of continued esteem for the enormous readership which has existed for printed matter since the nineteenth century, undergoes a very different experience from the reader of St Paul. During the period of the printed book it is often difficult to determine whether 'canonical' refers to a way of reading or to a distinctive quality of certain texts. An added complication is a meaning carried over from both the classical and the Christian uses of the term, the association of *canon* not just with written teaching but with some internally accepted code shared by all members of a community of belief.

Because of the immense complexity of *canon* after the Renaissance, it may be as well to summarize some main strands bequeathed by the classical and Christian eras to modern secular authors. We have seen that behind the label *canon* lie four distinct kinds of canonical disposition. First, there is the Euripidean or Pauline sense of *canon* as a

44

troubling internal rule that sets the stage for some sublime intimation of a truth beyond the reach of publicly measurable experience. Second, there is the Aristotelian canon, a disposition to frame rules according to circumstance, mistrusting the absolutes of law and revelation alike. Third, there is the Gregorian disposition, eager to spin out some previously existing grand *canon* into an ever more minute set of practical injunctions. And finally there is the Augustinian canon, a closed set of sacred texts open to inexhaustible figurative application and interpretation, the occasion for evangelical activity among the laity, exegetical activity among the learned, and a distinct way of viewing and interpreting history with a correspondingly momentous effect on political, social and intellectual life.

THE CONTROVERSIAL CANONS OF CRITICISM

These very different referents behind the word *canon* make Thomas Wilson's apparently straightforward assertion in *The Arte of Rhetorique* (1553, 1560), 'such as all the world hath confirmed and agreed upon, that . . . is autentique and canonicall', a matter of hope rather than of observable reality. And in fact, as soon as Wilson refines his usage, the tensions behind 'canonicall' massively erupt. Wilson applies the apostle Paul's words on law, punishment and authority to Cicero, whose *Verrine Orations* against Gaius Verres sent at least one corrupt official into retirement. Even so, 'canonicall', explains Wilson, refers not to 'fables uttered among men', however powerful in a court of law, but only to 'an assured trueth left unto us by writing'. Not, however, all writing. Wilson specifically excludes the truths expressed in 'common' writing, reserving 'canonicall' for 'the wordes of a Doctor in the Church of God'. Nor will the words of any such 'Doctor' suffice; Wilson proposes as 'canonicall' only the words of an authentic apostle. And even then, not the 'worst' apostle, but only the apostle Paul, whose words, Wilson goes on, are not his own 'but rather the words of the Holy Ghost, speaking by the mouth of Paule'.[1]

By the end of Wilson's disquisition, 'canonicall' has shifted from a universally agreed principle to a scripturally authorized Christian message. So exclusive an authority would appear all too vulnerable at a time of heady doctrinal ferment, and soon the word *canon* becomes associated with savage controversy. Its close connection with bitterly disputed episcopal authority means that during the Reformation *canon* inspires as much mistrust as conviction, and when secular writing begins to engender its own rival 'canons', that mistrust quickly spreads. As we shall see, the belated emergence of *canon* in non-dogmatic, secular use in the eighteenth century occurs in contexts where its authority is by no means indisputable, where every prescription has its opposing rule.

Outside the field of sacred literature, *canon* in the eighteenth century generally refers to 'established usage' or 'customary practice'. Yet neither of these translates into 'reflex action' or 'unblinking orthodoxy'. A good example of the complex exhortatory or normative use of 'canon' appears in Christopher Smart's 'The Horatian Canons of Friendship' (1750), a poem ironically dedicated to William Warburton, a figure of much controversy in the history of the canon. Smart shows public civility as boosted by a set of standards for private conduct which he attributes to Horace rather than to any contemporary models for social behaviour. He sees the canons which would restore the Commonwealth to harmony as emerging from an alliance between civic responsibility and Christian conscience. Only vigorous private self-examination will resore the public life of what he ironically calls 'this golden and truly Augustan age'. He exhorts his readers to careful self-scrutiny, bidding them:

> Sift then yourself, I say, and sift again,
> Glean the pernicious tares from out the grain,
> And ask thy heart, if Custom, Nature's heir,
> Hath sown no undiscover'd fern-seed there,
> This be our standard then, on this we rest,
> Nor search the Casuists for another test.[2]

Smart's 'Canons of Friendship' combine a Pauline introspection with an Aristotelian willingness to apply rational values to public conduct. His faith in the power of reason over social phenomena is a well-known characteristic of eighteenth-century thought, but it has little in common with the short-lists of valued works we now associate with 'the canon'.

Although recent critical works have described an entity called 'the Augustan canon' or 'the eighteenth-century canon', such formulations reconstruct an earlier period in the light of contemporary paradigms. Eighteenth-century usage does not support any unqualified extension of *canon* to a context outside Scripture or antiquity. Neither Samuel Johnson's *Dictionary of the English Language* (1755) nor the dictionary of the French Academy furnishes an entry under 'canon' that refers to a list of valued secular texts, a set of lasting literary qualities, or a scale of permanent literary merit. Johnson's dictionary understands 'canonical' simply as 'according to the established rule; a law', and 'the Books of Holy Scriptures'. Diderot's *Encyclopaedia* (1751–80) defines 'canon' simply as a 'list of books recognized as divine',[3] in a particular community of belief. The writers then compare the less explicit canon of Jewish sacred books with the arbitrary and peremptory Christian notion of *canon* before quietly passing on to their second definition, *canon* as the barrel of a gun.

Even so, eighteenth-century authors begin to push the idea of *canon* in its modern direction when they develop a new self-consciousness about the value of national authors, whose works they think deserve a new 'scientific criticism' in possession of its own independent canons. For instance, Theobald's preface to his 1733 edition of Shakespeare describes his subject as 'a corrupt Classic', a genius whose permanent merit has become obscured by contemporary theatrical adaptations and editions (Pope's edition is especially singled out). To remedy this situation, Theobald promises editorial corrections of a kind already 'effected on ancient Writers', which aim at 'restoring to the Publick their greatest Poet in his original Purity'. He describes this endeavour as 'the first Assay of the kind on any modern Author whatsoever'.[4]

Theobald's aspirations outran his capacities. Accordingly, Warburton, whom Theobald had consulted as he prepared his edition, renewed the quest for a scientific criticism. In his 1747 edition of Shakespeare, Warburton accepts both the editorial responsibility for 'restoring the Poet's genuine text' and the importance of this task for the health of English letters. Warburton, like Theobald, considers Shakespeare an occasionally obscure author, and acknowledges his duty 'to illustrate the obscure Allusions . . . to explain the Beauties and Defects of Sentiment or Composition'. He emphasizes, however, that in carrying out these tasks he has proceeded systematically, and has 'religiously observed the severe Canons of literal Criticism'. Looking beyond his immediate author, Warburton wonders whether to furnish his readers with '*a body of Canons*, for literal Criticism. . . . To give the *unlearned reader* a just Idea, and consequently a better Opinion of the Art of Criticism, now sunk very low in the popular Esteem.'[5] Although he never supplied this theoretical adjunct to his activities, Warburton's Preface left no doubt of the high importance he ascribed to the editorial principles he employed.

In his famous statement of intention, Warburton invokes 'canons' as a set of rational principles consistently applied and subject to public scrutiny. He exhibits no direct concern with disturbing the status of the author he edits. His 'canons' aim rather to raise the stock of criticism itself by codifying a set of rules for establishing and annotating a standard text. On trial he imagines his own activities as an editor being judged by the established criteria of accuracy, consistency and learning. Conceived of in this way, 'canons' sanction the activity of the critic rather than establish the value of a work of art. They introduce the idea of a codified set of rules for commentary on a secular text. At this stage of literary history they function as a prologue to judgement rather than as an explicit set of judgements.

Warburton's Preface shows that the emergence of rules governing the interpretation and editing of secular texts precedes the emergence of binding canons which guarantee the value of these texts or arrange them with other texts in a ranked hierarchy. Yet despite the authority with which he presents them, Warburton's 'canons' gained no universal currency. Thomas Edwards found something inherently ridiculous in the very phrase 'canons', and in 1748 he published a malicious parody of Warburton's scientific pretensions in a pamphlet called *A Supplement to Mr. Warburton's Edition of Shakespear, Collected from the Notes in that Celebrated Work and Proper To Be Bound Up with It. The Canons of Criticism, and Glossary*. In a typical development in the history of the canon, Edwards's squib became popularly known as *The Canons of Criticism* and was subsequently reissued in an expanded edition with that title, running to seven editions by 1765. *The Canons of Criticism and Glossary* (1750) intensifies the assault on the integrity of Warburton's text in a section on 'The Canons or Rules for Criticism' which juxtaposes Edwards's parodic 'canons' with 'canons' extracted from Warburton's editorial notes.

In 'The Canons or Rules for Criticism' Edwards lays down twenty-five 'canons' which mimic Warburton's original headings and leave little doubt about his contempt for Warburton's high-sounding ineptitude. Edwards's revised rules for editors include such memorable advice as 'He may Interpret his Author so; as to make him mean directly contrary to what He says', and 'He may explane a difficult passage, by words absolutely unintelligible'. Edwards attacks Warburton for elevating his personal editorial habits into a set of absolute criteria for critical activity. He dislikes the excessive liberty of Warburton's emendations and the showiness of his annotations, which he characterizes as intended 'not so much to explane the Author's meaning, as to display the Critic's knowledge'. He even mimics the solemn impersonality of Warburton's commentary, noting that for such an editor 'it may be proper, to shew his universal learning, that He minutely point out, from whence every metaphor and allusion is taken'.[6] Other strictures imply that Warburton has wrested the final responsibility for meaning from the author, replacing it with his own self-importance.

Implicit in Edwards's sense of *canon* is the notion that a satisfactory edition or critical work will follow the author's intentions, establish these intentions rationally, and report on them intelligibly. Edwards does not anticipate a secular criticism that will borrow the exegetical ingenuity of its sacred and classical counterparts, however minutely it might examine the texts in its care. He sees interpretation as proceeding from obscurity to clarification, with 'canons' providing the minimum standards necessary to turn scholarship into a rational, consistent and properly auxiliary activity, an activity that will extend to Shakespeare the same respect given to the Scriptures and the classics.

Edwards's strictures on Warburton conceal a deep-seated mistrust of criticism that proves too ingenious, overreaching itself and usurping its occasion. In a sense, *The Canons of Criticism* stands at the beginning of a repeated episode in the history of the canon, an episode the equally witty A. J. A. Waldock repeats in his *Sophocles the Dramatist* (1951) when he turns to attack the inflated 'critical canons' of his day.[7] Waldock's targets include a historical scholarship that refuses to discriminate between the permanent and the contingent, a documentary fallacy that treats imaginative works as occasions for biographical speculation, and a pattern-making preference that ignores dramatic and verbal texture. Edwards and Waldock both illustrate the recurring tendency for critical laws to collapse when placed against concrete instances. The history of criticism invariably shows how watertight regulations become debating points or controversial targets. Critical canons rarely carry the force of laws. As the history of criticism amply evidences, they will provide at best the subject of rational debate or witty controversy.

Canons, as Warburton conceives them, work best on dead authors, who cannot take the liberty of arguing back. Later writers want to incorporate into the notion of *canon* an important agent excluded from Warburton's account, the creative artist whose works serve as the quarry for the critic's legislative energies. As we shall see, the rise of Romanticism sounded the death knell for Warburton's idea of a universally agreed set of secular critical canons, rules as indisputable and enforceable as the laws governing scriptural interpretation itself. Perhaps the surest sign of the decline of such regulations comes in 1801, in the Preface to the second edition of *Lyrical Ballads*. Wordsworth expresses the conviction that canons of criticism belong to an earlier and more artificial age, complaining bitterly about the rigidity of contemporary critics in their pursuit of critical rules:

> If in a Poem there should be found a series of lines, or even a single
> line, in which the language, though naturally arranged, and
> according to the strict laws of metre, does not differ from that of
> prose, there is a numerous class of critics who, when they stumble
> upon these prosaisms as they call them, imagine that they have
> made a notable discovery, and exult over the Poet as over a man
> ignorant of his own profession. Now these men would establish
> a canon of criticism which the Reader will conclude he must
> utterly reject if he wishes to be pleased with these volumes.[8]

Wordsworth agrees that poets should subscribe to 'the strict laws of
metre', as well as to other unspecified 'natural' conventions. Even so,
he disagrees with the idea that 'canons of criticism' constitute rules
guaranteeing a rational, scientific criticism. Instead, he views such
canons as instruments which impede a unique self-governing literary
creation.

The long descent of canons into the creative obloquy described by
T. S. Eliot in *The Sacred Wood* begins when Wordsworth firmly distinguishes 'canons of criticism' from the laws naturally followed by
poets themselves. He thinks that canons draw up boundaries the
authentic imagination will transgress. Canons block the passage of
experience from writer to reader which is permanently renewed in
any worthwhile work of art. Although they make an unlikely pairing,
Edwards and Wordsworth show the vulnerability of any permanent
'canons of criticism'. Such canons challenge the Pauline imperative of
every post-classical poet and also, by expanding the apparatus necessary to communicate with a work of art, they interfere between
reader and creator. Damned by poet and critic alike, the earliest appli-
cations of 'canon' to secular criticism do not support a rousing vote
of confidence in the universality or even the utility of critical canons.
The notion of permanent 'canons of criticism' was challenged prac-
tically at its birth, a casualty not just of the quest for poetic freedom
but of the historical sense of critics sceptical about raising the status
of a discipline traditionally regarded as ancillary to creation itself. As
ultimate criteria for valuable creative achievement or scientific scholarly endeavour, these 'canons' soon met intense opposition.

CANON IN THE CLASSROOM: RUHNKEN'S CLASSICAL LISTS

Warburton's attempt to define permanent, universal 'canons of
criticism' suffered another setback when knowledge of the art of
editing as carried out in other cultures became more widely diffused.

It is at this point, when critics begin to unearth the history of their discipline, that the modern idea of the canon as a 'list of required secular readings' first emerges. Warburton's application of 'canon' to the duties of an editor may have aroused hostility because of his hints of affiliation with scriptural precedent. During the next stage in the history of the word a more neutral usage becomes more popular. In 1768, the German classical scholar David Ruhnken set in motion an important shift in the modern history of *canon* by applying the word to the editorial and pedagogic activities of Aristophanes of Byzantium and Aristarchus. In effect, Ruhnken showed that even the heroic founders of second-century Byzantine scholarship selected and organized their material to meet the cultural needs of contemporary readers. In his 'Critical History of the Greek Orators', a frequently reprinted introduction to his edition of Rutilius Lupus, Ruhnken describes how these great Alexandrian teachers of oratory transmitted their knowledge to their students. 'From the great abundance of orators . . . they drew up into a canon at least ten they thought most important'.[9] As relayed by Ruhnken, Aristophanes's lists have the status of a syllabus: they are teaching lists that codify classroom practice. Ruhnken shows that once these ten authors became 'canonical' for students of rhetoric, other lists followed of epic, lyric and elegiac poetry, and so on.

Although the 'canons' of Warburton, Edwards and Ruhnken all refer to the activities of gentlemanly equals, *canon* in Ruhnken's sense also functions as a set of cultural choices. This explains why, after the publication of Ruhnken's book, it became common, if sometimes controversial, to extend the application of *canon* to any list of valuable inherited works. Rudolf Pfeiffer austerely characterizes the application of *canon* to a secular list of authors as 'a modern catachresis', while Nietzsche's adversary von Wilamowitz remained unconvinced about the authority of such a secondary use. Even so, classical scholars soon extended Ruhnken's usage from oratory to classical letters as a whole. A selection of Latin titles circulating after the appearance of Ruhnken's work shows the importance of his pioneering application: *On the So-Called Canon of Aristophanes and Aristarchus* (1876), *On the Canon of the Ten Attic Orators* (1883), *On the Canon of the Ten Orators* (1891), *Did Canons of Poets, Writers and Artists Exist during Antiquity?* (1897).[10]

To this day, the idea of *canon* as a list of standard texts relating to a particular culture or area remains a vital one, so that critics speak of 'the canon of Dutch seventeenth-century painting' or 'the canon of Attic authors'. But important as such a canon is, recent scholarship also emphasizes the even more basic function of the Byzantine canon as an institution preserving the life of an alien culture by means of classroom models. N. G. Wilson has expanded Ruhnken's account by describing the practical considerations governing the Alexandrian canon-makers, who accommodated pagan texts to a militant Christian culture by drawing up lists which met the specific requirements of different classroom subjects – rhetoric, history, and so on.[11] The tactic of allegorization, devised to reconcile pagan words with Christian revelation, was actually applied quite sparingly. Instead, the picture which emerges is one of busy classroom teachers trying to inculcate a flexible corpus of skills. Undoubtedly, the classroom selections of Byzantium guaranteed the survival of many texts. Even so, 'canon formation' in this context meant selection by teachers and circulation among generations of students in a vastly different cultural context from that assumed by the authors themselves. *Canon* in this sense suggests a list of works which preserve the life of a deceased foreign culture in markedly different contemporary conditions.

An important modern equivalent to the Alexandrian endeavour lies in the Victorian classical revival. In an enormous outpouring of pedagogic energy, generations of Victorian schoolmasters drilled their pupils in the fundamentals of a foreign tradition, and from the Victorian lists of classical authors prescribed in schools another *canon* soon emerged. Frank M. Turner has shown that for Victorian educators Homer became a second Scripture, the 'secular Bible' of a revitalized national culture built on the shoulders of an old one.[12] In creating this culture, a succession of nineteenth-century scholars, administrators and teachers transferred the roles and responsibilities of the Byzantine canonists to an industrial culture and created, in essence, the proliferating functions of the modern canon. The classical texts of nineteenth-century liberal education indirectly raise the standards of critical and philological investigation. Their permanent worth as guides to life provides a subject for reams of exhortatory prose. Classical works become the means of building basic skills in a classical language. And finally, the formidable apparatus of popularization – simplified excerpts, schoolbook abridgements and glossaries, discussion groups and periodical articles – relays the works to a broader readership.

WELTLITERATUR: THE CANONS OF ROMANTICISM

In this way, the masterpieces of antiquity become the subject of an enormous nineteenth-century effort to assimilate a long-extinct culture, with the labours of the Alexandrian rhetoricians serving as an implied or overt point of reference. The wide diffusion of Ruhnken's pioneering application of *canon* becomes apparent in the course of Taine's observations on Italian art in his *Travels in Italy* (1866). Taine praises Italian painters because 'they established principles and set up a canon for painters like the one the Alexandrians had previously established for orators and poets'.[13] Taine employs the word tentatively, as if he is aware that such a specialized instance will not permit universal application. Yet with his social scientist's caution he lags behind artistic enthusiasms, which had extended the usage of *canon* since the end of the eighteenth century. The conditions of modern literacy encourage readers and critics to see classical and modern culture as episodes in a common, still developing European inheritance, and in the process *canon* gathers its modern range of meanings: a general law; a special rule; an authoritative or religious text; a pedagogically useful text; an inspired or restrictive precursor. From now on in the history of the word, the contradictions in its usage loom larger, while the core of agreement becomes ever more closely questioned.

For instance, if a canon constitutes a list of texts, how are those texts selected? In his fragmentary essay 'Thoughts for an Oral Lecture on the New Universal History' (1754) Winckelmann suggests a simple rule for the formation of cultural canons: 'only the inventor, not the copyists; only the originals, not the compilers'. He then proceeds to catalogue a stellar canon whose quality is guaranteed by the extent of its exclusions: 'Galileo, Huygens, and Newton, not Viviani and L'Hospital; Corneille and Racine, not Boursault and Crébillon; Raphael, Spagnoli, and Rubens, not Penni, Piazzetta, and Jordaens; Buonarroti and Palladio, not Vanbrugh or Vischer'. On the grandest historical scale, the same principle governs Winckelmann's championship of ancient culture, which he proposes as the ultimate source of all worthwhile future production. Not surprisingly, his essay 'On the Imitation of the Painting and Sculpture of the Greeks' (1755) raises the canon of ancient art to virtually iconic force, informing readers in no uncertain terms that 'There is but one way for the moderns to become great . . . by imitating the ancients'. In several of his essays, Winckelmann interposes as permanent cultural models not just individual ancient works but ancient aesthetic principles, so that the Laocoön becomes a perfect statue while 'the rule of Polycletus' becomes 'a perfect rule of art'. It would seem difficult to provide a more absolute statement of the virtues of a restricted canon, bound by time and place but everlastingly important. Yet no account of Winckelmann's influence on the canons of later critics can ignore his urgent suggestion for a new, broad approach to cultural history, crossing established boundaries, presenting 'the famous discoveries in nature and art' as 'great events in the nation'.[14]

It becomes clear even in Winckelmann's massively exclusory criticism that in the changing circumstances of modern culture *canon* cannot be restricted to a short-list of approved ancient works. This thought was certainly in Novalis's mind when he announced to August Wilhelm Schlegel in 1797 that 'Shakespeare is a more excellent model [*Canon*] for the scholarly onlooker'.[15] Novalis must have felt unsure what kind of literature would emerge when the classical canon shed some of its authority, for to his private journal he confided his belief that 'the fairy tale is entirely the canon of poetry – everything poetical must be like a fairy tale'.[16] Such sentiments point to a revolution in literary history whose shape becomes evident only a century later when Viktor Shklovsky describes literary history as a process of perpetually canonizing the marginal. 'New forms in art', he asserts, 'are created by the canonization of peripheral forms. Pushkin stems from the peripheral genre of the album, the novel from horror stories, Nekrasov from the vaudeville, Blok from the gypsy ballad.'[17]

A few months after Novalis's letter to Schlegel, Schiller wrote to Wilhelm von Humboldt that Goethe and Homer formed 'the canon for all epic poets'.[18] This new current of canonical idealism transformed German literature. Schlegel's translations of Shakespeare followed in 1825–33. The Brothers Grimm produced their collection of fairy tales in 1812–13. If late-eighteenth-century German classical scholarship rediscovers the Alexandrian idea of the canon as a list of classroom models, German Romantic literature of the period assists at the rebirth of a canon that bursts out of its classical moulds. Revaluating Voltaire's barbarous Shakespeare, reimagining his plays as the raw materials of a visionary unity, an inspired source rather than a degraded exemplum, the German Romantic authors unleash *canon* as the source of a creative unity that cuts across individual works and nations. The *Weltliteratur* celebrated from Goethe onwards becomes a spiritual region sanctified by the imagination that tears down generic, national and historical boundaries.

Goethe's influence on this period of heroic eclecticism can hardly be overestimated. Eckermann records how a visit in January 1827 found the sage characteristically full of ideas, this time as a result of reading a Chinese novel. Goethe's encounter with the Orient provoked him into some more general reflections on literature and world culture. 'National literature', he observes, 'is now rather an unmeaning term; the epoch of World-Literature is at hand, and everyone must strive to hasten its approach.' Goethe next emphasizes that this global enterprise must not become waylaid by standardized or restricted canons. 'While we thus value what is foreign, we must not bind ourselves to some particular thing, and regard it as a model.' Nor should a new cultural relativism herald the death of the classical past. 'If we really want a pattern,' he adds, 'we must always return to the Ancient Greeks, in whose works the beauty of mankind is constantly represented. All the rest we must look at only historically; appropriating to ourselves what is good, so far as it goes.'[19] In effect, Goethe envisages a world literature organized around a two-tiered canon. The first tier will include the provisional, historical canons that furnish examples of specific artistic possibilities. The second 'supercanon' will store the permanent and universal records of artistic achievement. Goethe's 'new historicism' has no desire to destroy museums altogether. Instead, his is an art which will scan history and contemporary society in search of patterns. The era of *Weltliteratur* will call for pioneer-poets, ready to roam the world of culture with the energy of Keats's Cortez.

During the nineteenth century, *canon* bursts from the framework of antiquity to meet the demands of modernity. Instead of functioning as a set of inherited rhetorical or poetic practices it becomes a model for the whole imaginative life, an inspired pattern for future production across the borders of period or personal belief. In Schiller's new canon, Goethe can stand next to Homer, just as for A. W. Schlegel Shakespeare stands next to Aeschylus. What we might call the 'Romanticization' of the canon invests modern secular works with charismatic and inspirational values, replenishing literary history by supplying it with a dimension beyond the one supplied by chronology or received wisdom. Of course, there is a price to pay for admission to the 'charismatic' canon of creative artists. Schiller's translation of *Macbeth* moves at some distance from the original text, and a similar freedom characterizes the majority of early-nineteenth-century German translations. Even so, these virtual retellings of Shakespeare's stories derive strong justification from the writings of the German Romantic critics. For, as Friedrich Schlegel puts it, in a formulation that canonizes the breaking of canonical rules, 'every stage must be subject to peculiar laws and forms suitable to the period of time and character of the nation'.[20] In a historicizing age, canons do not wither away, but instead take on an even larger range of functions.

Some of these functions become apparent during the debate unleashed by the uncanonical writings of the British Romantic poets.

In 1808, Francis Jeffrey of the *Edinburgh Review* criticized Wordsworth's 'Lucy' poems for violating 'that eternal and universal standard of truth and nature, which every one is knowing enough to
recognize, and no one great enough to depart from with impunity'.[21]
In 1814, Jeffrey's campaign against Wordsworth came to a head in
a critique of *The Excursion* which anticipated a long-running Victorian controversy about the role of idiosyncrasy in poetry, the poet's
duties as communicator, and the importance of classical learning and
breadth of contact with modern literature. Jeffrey noted certain deficiencies of culture and expression. He went on:

> An habitual and general knowledge of the few settled and perma-
> nent maxims, which form the canon of general taste in all large and
> polished societies – a certain tact, which informs us at once that
> many things, which we still love and are moved by in secret, must
> necessarily be despised as childish, or derided as absurd, in all such
> societies, – though it will not stand in the place of genius, seems
> necessary to the success of its exertions.[22]

Today, it is all too easy to view Jeffrey's 'canon of general taste' in the
same spirit Wordsworth viewed the eighteenth-century 'canons of
criticism' – as disguising a few well-endowed prejudices with the
appearance of universal wisdom. The whole force of Wordsworth's
poetry, which is steeped in regional reference and marginalized
psychology, seems to speak against the validity of Jeffrey's canon. Yet
interest in such widely mastered and applicable 'maxims' was
perhaps not so utterly extinguished as Wordsworth hoped. In his
early writings, Coleridge himself speaks positively of 'the canons of
criticism'.[23] In a letter of 1802, he even promises Robert Southey that
he will act as 'arbitrator' between Wordsworth and the 'Old School'
by laying down 'some plain, & perspicuous, tho' not superficial,
Canons of Criticism respecting Poetry'.[24] It is a sign of Coleridge's
thoroughly modern difficulties with canons that this modest project
never appeared. Instead, he devotes many pages of *Biographia Literaria*
to a defence of the 'truths' contained in Wordsworth's poetry, even
though, echoing St Paul, he concedes that the poet has carried those
truths 'beyond their proper limits'. He still prefers Wordsworth's
truths to Jeffrey's maxims, which emerge, like Athena from the head
of Zeus, 'without a single leading principle established or even
announced'. Periodically in *Biographia Literaria* Coleridge turns aside
from the main course of his argument to attack contemporary
reviewers for failing to 'support their decisions by reference to fixed

canons of criticism, previously established and deduced from the nature of man'.[25] Needless to say, he himself provides no such canons. For the author of *Biographia Literaria*, struggling with a veritable arsenal of psychological, aesthetic, cultural and religious anxieties, a short-list of 'canons of criticism' seems no longer a practical proposition.

Later critics become increasingly convinced that fixed 'canons of criticism' will only endanger the growth of their newly hatched institutions. Repudiating with equal energy Jeffrey's 'maxims' and Coleridge's 'principles', *Blackwood's Magazine* attacked the *Edinburgh* as a 'self-elected literary tribunal' imposing outmoded and irrelevant literary standards. Jeffrey began to write, suggested John Wilson, 'when the whole inner kingdom of the European mind was undergoing . . . a revolution. . . . He set himself . . . in opposition to the change, and strove to support, by rule and precedent, the sway of the old Powers that were – antiquated, superannuated Authorities'.[26] In his retrospective essay on 'The First Edinburgh Reviewers' (1855), Bagehot amplified Wilson's charge. From his mid-century vantage point he noted 'a tinge of simplicity' in the reviewers' charmingly old-fashioned didacticism: 'Their tendency inclining to the quiet footsteps of custom, they like to trace the exact fulfilment of admitted rules, a just accordance with the familiar features of ancient merit'.[27] A decade later, Matthew Arnold, discussing 'The Function of Criticism at the Present Time', offered the following devastating formula. 'It is by communicating fresh knowledge, and letting his own judgment pass along with it, – but insensibly, and in the second place, not the first, as a sort of companion and clue, not as an abstract lawgiver, – that the critic will generally do most good to his readers'.[28]

There is a recurring irony in the history of the canon in the fact that, to modern readers, Arnold looks as much a lawgiver as Jeffrey, and Jeffrey seems closer to the nineteenth-century critics than to Warburton. Jeffrey's 'canon of general taste' is social as much as aesthetic; it governs contemporary as well as established literature; and, as a result, it suggests urgent special pleading rather than universal law. Anticipating the central problems of the modern *canon*, Romantic and Victorian critics abandon the 'rules' they associate with an older generation of critics to engage in a protracted search for more dynamic and responsive canons identified with 'the component faculties of the human mind itself, and their comparative dignity and importance', in the words of Coleridge; 'the fitness, the measure, the centrality, which is the soul of all good criticism', in the words of Arnold.[29] Far from repudiating canons, nineteenth-century critics demonstrate the recurring pattern of an aggressive anti-canonical idealism engaged in a search for 'companions' or 'touchstones', principles more widely acceptable or deeply penetrating than the inherited principles, canons in everything but name.

During the nineteenth century, Warburton's hope for a short-list of eternally fixed 'canons of criticism' gives way to an eclectic assortment of locally applied values – energy, eloquence, pathos, taste, genius, idea, imagination, fact, sanity, inwardness – drawn from rhetoric, sociology, philosophy, politics, and psychology. If the explicit 'canons' or criteria for judging literature vary immensely, it is none the less widely accepted that final judgement according to previously established rules carries no conviction. The present age, suggests John Morley, is one of 'searching criticism followed by multiplied doubts and shaken beliefs'.[30] The 'mere judgment and application of principles' will no longer do, suggests Arnold. Such a criticism 'is tautological, and cannot well give us, like fresh learning, the sense of creative activity'.[31] In the space vacated by the old 'canons of criticism', Romantic and Victorian critics substitute a dynamic, socially responsive aesthetics based not on 'the exact fulfilment of admitted rules' but on such elusive values as the 'creative imagination', 'the common language of men', and the 'criticism of life'.

There is another irony in the fact that, as the canons of criticism become more nebulous, the agencies for transmitting them assume an increasing prominence in critical debate. In *Biographia Literaria*, Coleridge, worried about the judicial functions abrogated by a new breed of reviewers, calls for the establishment of a committee 'of learned men in the various branches of science and literature' who would 'pledge themselves . . . to administer judgement according to a constitution and code of laws'.[32] Nearly fifty years later, Arnold, considering 'The Literary Influence of Academies', takes up Sainte-Beuve's proposal for 'a high court of letters' or 'central authority representing high culture and sound judgment'.[33] After canvassing the issue with considerable urgency, both critics unexpectedly drop their proposals. Coleridge evolves the less abstract idea of a 'clerisy' which will oversee education and culture at a local and personal level. Arnold replaces his 'high court of letters' with the more flexible 'touchstone': a short-list of works and authors – Homer, Virgil, Shakespeare, Dante, Milton, and, in his later criticism, the Bible – whose words can be marshalled, penetrated and juxtaposed.

In effect, Arnold does the canon in different voices. By weaving a polyphony of international voices he hopes to mime the authority of Jeffrey's 'few settled and permanent maxims'. He creates instead an almost musical canon, in which a range of counterpointed testimonies all converge on one sad theme. Arnold's 'touchstones' anticipate the proliferating functions of the modern *canon*. His frequently quoted (often unidentified) authors support an incompletely articulated set of literary, stylistic and cultural values – the 'grand style', the 'modern spirit', 'sweetness and light', 'imaginative reason'. Touchstone authors suggest the central list of works – the 'currency of criteria and valuation', as F. R. Leavis will later call it – which has transformed the critic into the model of culture and sensitivity – the human canon – he presents to his readers. And, most important of all, touchstone authors interpose what Gombrich will later call 'problem-solutions': recurring human situations – loss, grief, consolation, illumination – which their words confront and assuage. Shakespeare, for instance, becomes a touchstone because he suggests an era which heroically explored, not evaded, the most stirring and difficult currents of modern thought.

THE ASCENT OF SHAKESPEARE: *CANON* IN THE UPPER CASE

Yet the case of Shakespeare also illustrates the steadily increasing gap between the critic's perception of a 'canonical author' and the practical demands of lay audiences. To become 'canonical' Shakespeare has to function on many cultural levels; however 'universal' he appears to the writers concerned, the 'mystical' Shakespeare of the German Romantic writers and the 'energetic' Shakespeare of Arnold provide only two of several competing versions of the Bard's work. In the German theatre, Roy Pascal observes, actor-managers forced his drama to conform to 'the middle-class tragedies of the time'.[34] Even in Britain, Shakespeare became canonical only by extensive acculturation. Charles Lamb considered *King Lear* unstageable but sufficiently important to transmit to generations of young people in his *Tales from Shakespeare* (1807). From the early nineteenth century, Shakespeare's works appear in a multitude of popular editions. He is screened for family consumption by clerical editors. His wise saws guide the young through the great crises of adolescent life. His texts become the subject of study in public examinations that admit suitable candidates to the professions.

At this point it becomes a pressing concern, one that follows methods already perfected in the study of the classical authors and the Scriptures, to establish on scientific grounds a basic list of works authentically produced by Shakespeare's own hand. This list becomes

Shakespeare's 'canon'; outside it lie relegated 'apocrypha' such as *Edmund Ironside* and *Mucedorus*. As a canonical author, Shakespeare becomes a national property to be consulted in times of crisis (John Dover Wilson found *Henry V* an apposite text for the course of British history in 1914 and 1941) and quoted on ceremonial occasions (Queen Elizabeth II described her 'salad days, when I was green in judgement' when she celebrated her royal jubilee). Passing a commonly invoked test of the 'canonical' author, the epithet 'Shakespearian' comes to be applied to works written long before Shakespeare's existence. (Chaucer has frequently attracted the epithet, and E. Talbot Donaldson ended his career with a book comparing Chaucer and Shakespeare.) A canonical author will not only survive, he will actually defeat the challenge of time, so that attentive critics will catch echoes of Shakespeare in *Our Mutual Friend* as well as in *Troilus and Criseyde*.

At its most basic level, however, Shakespeare's canon represents a collection of writings, a series of plays and poems bound in a mysterious unity of the sort once thought to be possessed only by the Bible itself. Like the biblical canon, Shakespeare's canon becomes the subject of scientific tests for its authenticity, its unity, and its congruence to known paradigms of authorship. During the nineteenth century, the canonical status of *Edward III* and *Sir Thomas More* remained unsettled, as did the status of such currently accepted works as *Titus Andronicus, Timon of Athens, Love's Labours Lost, Henry VI*, and substantial portions of *Macbeth*. Early this century fourteen doubtful plays were collected in a volume called *The Shakespeare Apocrypha* (1908) by C. F. Tucker Brooke, and the category of 'apocrypha', once established, proved an all too inviting one. In the Preface to *The Shakespeare Canon* (1922), J. M. Robertson scrutinizes the stylistic evidence of Shakespeare's pen and submits that many of his plays show signs of multiple authorship. However repugnant this idea may seem to 'uncritical traditionalism', Robertson thinks that its implications for future scholarly activity must be urgently confronted:

> Cheerfully do I recognize that all attempts to disintegrate a long-received Canon, or even to carry further a disintegration already begun, are fitly to be met by severe scrutiny. I ask only that the scrutiny shall be truly critical and not prejudiced. It should be in the nature of 'Treasury control' over all new projects of public expenditure. Treasury control . . . used to proceed on the preliminary principle that in human affairs the new game is never

worth the candle. But it waived that bias when evidence to the contrary was forthcoming; and the critical attitude towards innovating theory in matters literary should be at least as accommodating to the pressure of new ideas.[35]

Unfortunately, in protecting what he ominously calls 'the Canon', the authentically Shakespearian remnant, Robertson threatens to leave Shakespeare's authorship in shreds. The result of his textual labours is a Marlowe *Richard III* and a Marlowe *Henry V. Julius Caesar* begins in the Marlowe workshop, is improved by Kyd and Chapman, and has occasional grand passages from Shakespeare's own pen. In this way, the Bard who emerges from Robertson's study becomes a more rarefied spirit than the opportunistic collaborators who surround him. Reimagined in terms of period assumptions, Greene's 'upstart crow' resembles Pater or the Georgian poets. Removed from the brutish world of the Elizabethan theatre, Shakespeare burns with a hard, gemlike flame.

In his 1907 edition of *Titus Andronicus*, E. K. Chambers had promised that his scholarship would bring 'the literary history of England . . . into contact with the scientific spirit'.[36] In 1924 Chambers fulfilled this promise by attacking Robertson's unprecedented narrowing of the canon in a thundering British Academy address called 'The Disintegration of Shakespeare'. Chambers compares the wave of assaults on Shakespeare's authorship to an eruption 'from the shades of many of Philip Henslowe's hungry troop of hack writers'. In repudiating Robertson's 'impressionistic judgements' and 'elaborate edifice of conjectural ascriptions', Chambers touches on a recurring problem in the history of the canon: the relationship between overt anti-canonical attack and veiled commitment to an alternative, inadequately scrutinized canon. He remarks:

> our heresiarch, in fact, is himself an idolater. We have all of us, in the long run, got to form our conception of the 'authentic' Shakespeare by means of an abstraction from the whole of the canon; there is no other material. Mr. Robertson abstracts through a series of rejections . . . He idealizes.

Chambers prefers to focus on the material at hand, which he characterizes as at once more diverse and more solid. As he sees it, 'the rock of Shakespeare's reputation stands four-square to the winds of Time'.[37] Chambers's formulation recalls the words of Theobald, another 'scientific' editor-critic, who compared Shakespeare's work to 'a large, a spacious, and a splendid Dome'.[38] Both editors see their subject as a monument as well as an intriguing scientific problem. Spaciousness, room for interpretative manoeuvre and leisurely enquiry, seems to both of them as important a quality in a canonical author as the power to raise and resolve a set of scientific questions. Neither critic has much in common with Robertson, who sees Shakespeare's canonicity in terms of a distilled religious essence, an aura available only at the very highest levels of creative achievement.

Canonicity seems to become a particular problem at times of turbulence, when critics try to change the cultural map by building bridges to 'world literatures' and 'forgotten' genres. During these periods an author of high status may become particularly vulnerable to hostile interpretative manoeuvres. The sceptical account of Shakespeare provided by another critic in the 1920s shows the power of 'canon' to disturb the reputation of even the most exalted author. Prosser Hall Frye's *Romance and Tragedy* (1922) offers a far-reaching account of modern literature which takes Shakespeare as its *bête noire*. Frye ponders how far Goethe's phrase 'the illusion of a higher reality' could act as a touchstone for literary production before and after Goethe. He hopes to use this phrase as 'a kind of canon or test of literature'. Not surprisingly, Frye's experiment on literary history involves him in an increasingly ambitious set of exclusions, allowing him to see 'an alarming symptom of romanticism' in modern literature and Shakespeare alike.[39] Frye apparently intends to use his 'canon' in an ecumenical spirit, as a means of negotiation across cultures, nations and time-frames. His execution, however, entails drastic exclusions and severe judgements – all the draconian instruments of canonicity wielded so severely by Augustine and Luther. It seems that, whatever the status of an author, the application of specific 'canons' encourages an almost theological rigour of exclusion.

In Shakespeare's case, the periods of exclusion rarely seem to last too long. By 1930 J. W. Mackail's popular study *The Approach to Shakespeare* had restored Shakespeare's Canon to its upper case, giving it the joint authority of spiritual vision and patriotic wisdom. Mackail even points out that *The Tempest* appeared on the British stage the same year as the King James Bible. In a code for classroom studies which has lasted until the present day, Mackail unfolds the idea of 'a progress or evolution in Shakespeare's methods and handling, in his use of language, in his management of action, in his whole dramatic treatment'. The result, in *The Tempest*, is a presentation of Shakespeare's 'implicit doctrine' about the artist and the universe. Mackail thinks that, considered as a whole, 'the Shakespearian Canon is a vision of this world'. Complementing Dante's *Divine Comedy*, Shakespeare's canon becomes 'the Human Comedy, a *Summa Anthropologiae*' or 'secular Bible of the English-speaking world'.[40]

In a manner already pioneered in the study of Virgil (to whom Mackail also devoted a book), Shakespeare finds himself accommodated to a later age and social system. His 'irrepressible English lyrical instinct' expresses the shape of English drama as a whole: 'It might be said of the English drama, as it has been said of the British Empire, that it was not made, but happened; that its structure was not planned, but grew; that it is a matter more of luck than of guidance.' Although he presents Shakespeare as 'the interpretation of and the key to life',[41] Mackail indisputably argues from a fixed, time-bound set of assumptions. As his argument unravels, he proves one point at least – that the word *canon* cannot be restricted to the authentic list of an author's works, but endlessly accommodates itself to the assumptions current at the time it is invoked. Some authorities commandeer the canonical work to host the national virtues (Hitler thought the British produced Shakespeare execrably and un-Germanically). Others see it as the source of deep spiritual wisdom (Colin Still interpreted Shakespeare's last plays as dramatizations of the Eleusinian mysteries). Others use canonical works to inspire or regulate their own productions (Schiller's *The Robbers* shows deep resemblances to Shakespeare). The result is that the secular canonical author becomes the receptacle for all kinds of interpretations asserting some deep affiliation with the subject's own essential nature. In this way *canon* becomes a kind of snowball word, accumulating meaning to the point where Shakespeare becomes a rebel *and* a conservative, a Platonist *and* a populist.

MANIFEST DESTINIES: NATIONAL CANONS AND THEIR CHALLENGERS

For many authorities, Shakespeare also becomes the quintessential 'English' author. In this way the case of Shakespeare leads us to another repeated episode in the later history of the canon, its association with national character and cultural uplift. In 1925–6, the British librarian Ernest Barker delivered a set of public lectures at the University of Glasgow as part of a series devoted to the subject of citizenship. His subject, 'National Character and the Factors in

Its Formation', made him turn to the subject of literature, and to ask his audience:

> What are the dozen books, or poems, or passages of literature most likely to be chosen, by common consent, as those which have established themselves definitely as a national possession or influence? The canon of such a list will be neither artistic excellence nor fidelity in the expression of the national genius. . . . What matters most is rather the range and vogue of acceptance, and the degree of the effect produced on social thought and imagination.[42]

Barker's choices for his canon display a bias in favour of the uplifting and the Protestant (the King James Bible, *Pilgrim's Progress, Robinson Crusoe*). But even more significant than his choices is his principle of selection, which he defines as 'range and vogue of acceptance'. Barker's criteria steer the canon towards conformity with a preconceived version of national identity. Instead of stimulating artistic creativity or independent thought, the canon must foster national solidarity.

The costs of reconstructing the canon in the national interest become apparent when American writers enlarge on Barker's outline. In 1927 Henry Canby, editor of *Saturday Review of Literature*, relayed Barker's opinions in an editorial column entitled 'An American Canon', Canby wondered whether American writing could not also yield such a canon, chosen from the works 'which have most influenced Americans and are most definitely a national possession'. The American canon becomes a slice of national real estate added to the English inheritance when the editor concludes that 'we Americans have our English heritage with an increment of our own making', the American increment representing 'an asset not always appreciated'. The pressure towards imposed conformity becomes even more obvious when Canby lists his choices for the American canon. Nonconformists like Thoreau, Melville and Whitman do not secure entry. Sinclair Lewis, whose books, 'like Bunyan's, Dickens's, Shakespeare's, have given names to the language', gains election. Harriet Beecher Stowe, whose legacy to the language in *Uncle Tom's Cabin* will subsequently prove less reassuring, Canby characterizes as a 'doubtful' case for admission.[43]

What Canby calls 'one hundred and fifty years of national history'[44] presides over his selection of canonical works. Each of these works he maps out as a chapter in the narration of a national story, which explains why he includes the Declaration of Independence in a predominantly literary list. He aims to inventory existing stock in order to harness a modest return on the nation's existing cultural capital. He has none of the visionary or charismatic goals which led Schiller and Goethe to claim Shakespeare for the German canon. The association of *canon* with the revisiting of familiar national milestones perhaps reaches its furthest limits in Daniel L. Marsh's *The American Canon* (1939). Originally delivered as the 1939 Commencement sermon at the University of Boston, Marsh's book recapitulates the multiple senses of canon as list, rule, teaching manual, and inspiration. He describes his long and solitary search for 'some documents that all Americans would accept as the undisputed creed, or "Bible", of Americanism . . . something that will set the standard of American patriotism' at a time of rising civic and international pressures. The outcome of his search becomes the seven documents introduced in his book, an 'American canon' that comprises 'certain American writings so significant, so inspired, so esteemed by Americans, so durably valuable to the American people, so pregnant with the essence of the American spirit, so revelatory of the genius of America, that, taken together, they constitute the authoritative rule of Americanism'. Marsh's is a closed canon of non-literary texts including the Mayflower Compact, the Declaration of Independence, the Constitution of the United States, George Washington's Farewell Address, Abraham Lincoln's Second Inaugural Address, and Woodrow Wilson's 'Road Away from Revolution'. Marsh's final choice – the American national anthem – represents his sole concession to the sister arts. Like Augustine and Origen, Marsh likes the secure harbour of a closed canon. Having selected his seven works, he ominously adds, 'There is no eighth'.[45]

Showing greater consistency than either Barker or Canby, Marsh realizes that a canon constructed in the national interest will not necessarily be served best by literary sources. This is why he replaces Emerson and Benjamin Franklin with Lincoln's speeches and the Star Spangled Banner. More explicitly than Canby or Barker, he deploys these materials in a storylike pattern arranged according to a governing theme. Presenting his principle of selection as 'the genesis of American democracy', Marsh arranges his texts to illuminate a spiritual vision, 'the vision of America as the messiah of nations'.[46] In this way his texts become inspired episodes in an American theodicy prefigured by the Declaration of Independence, which Marsh sees as corresponding to the Book of Genesis.

The formulations of Barker, Canby and Marsh signal an unprecedented narrowing in the scope of *canon* as a cultural instrument. For fourth-century Byzantine scholars a canon proved an indispensable way of preserving an alien culture. For late-eighteenth-century German writers, Shakespeare's canon widened contemporary creative horizons and expanded the field of European cultural history. For some early-twentieth-century critics, Shakespeare's canon seemed to conform to certain perceived national virtues. Yet even in the rousing defences of Chambers and Mackail, nationalism never becomes the sole basis of Shakespeare's canonicity. In contrast, *canon* as redefined by Barker, Canby and Marsh becomes restricted to precisely those works which support the construction of self-fulfilling models of national esteem.

Today, the ideas of Marsh and Canby have lost prestige, even if they do represent a recurrent modern campaign to annex the canon for the reactionary, the established, and the chauvinistic. Unfortunately, contemporary anti-canonists often present this annexation as the dominant norm of modern criticism, ignoring the fact that the majority of critics oscillate between canons of conformity and canons of opposition. The contemporary critic, so eager to assert radical credentials by attacking the authority of 'the canon', has a long ancestry. In fact, such a critic might be rather disturbed at the pedigree which lies waiting to be uncovered. As early as 1918, Van Wyck Brooks's influential article 'On Creating a Usable Past' noted the tendency for canonical authors to be annexed by conventional and material interests. Brooks contrasts 'the accepted canon of American literature' with the independently creative 'literatures of Europe'. He criticizes the 'American canon' for complying too readily with genteel Protestant norms that drive American artists into exile or celebrity.

Now, Brooks sounds both dangerous and outmoded when he unblinkingly invokes racial and national categories. Even so, his long campaign on behalf of an autonomous republic of letters called for literary presses independent of civic sponsorship and for careers pledged to the interests of culture rather than nationalism. Brooks sees 'culture' as a domain of the spirit working independently of regional or national politics. 'The spiritual past has no objective reality,' he asserts. 'It yields only what we are able to look for in it'.[47] In a series of influential books, including *The Ordeal of Mark Twain* (1920) and *The Pilgrimage of Henry James* (1925), Brooks exhorted his fellow authors to declare their independence of the European salon and the American small town. In all these works, he constantly emphasizes the inadequacies of American culture and the need to construct a canon according to independently formulated artistic needs. His work sets the course for an American canon interpreted as adversarial and fluctuating, a prime weapon in the long war against American conformity prosecuted in American letters from V. L. Parrington to Lionel Trilling.

The Nobel Prize for literature awarded to Sinclair Lewis in 1930 signalled that Brooks's campaign had met some success. During the same year Edwin Greenlaw's *The Province of Literary History* defined the canonical domain even more stringently. Reverting to the older meaning of 'canon' as simply a 'restricted list', Greenlaw limits the usefulness of canons to high-school education, emphasizing their inadequacy for 'our teaching, our own reading . . . our research, or in the preparation of future Shakespeares and Miltons'. Graduate-school education cannot content itself 'only with major authors and with works acknowledged as masterpieces', he asserts. There no longer seems any point in invoking 'the timeless laws of literature, whatever that term may mean'.[48] Greenlaw proposes instead a new field of study which he calls 'literary history'. As he describes it, literary history has a similar shape to the cultural studies of the 1980s and 1990s. Both disciplines take as their area the history of civilization, a subject virtually without disciplinary or pedagogic frontiers. To their apologists it is unclear, moreover, that such areas will require canons of any kind.

Two years later, Carl Van Doren's review-essay 'Toward a New Canon' continued Brooks's and Greenlaw's double task of demystifying the accepted canon and defining the grounds for a vital creative alternative. In the course of reviewing Ludwig Lewisohn's massive history of American literature *Expression in America*, Van Doren prefigures the work of such later innovators as Richard Poirier and Harold Bloom. He contrasts two ideas of *canon*, the ecclesiastical and the revelatory. He identifies the orthodox or institutional canon with 'the vested interest of publishers who had issued collected editions, or of teachers in schools and colleges who know how to "teach" Longfellow but not Emily Dickinson, Howells but not Dreiser, Irving but not Mencken'. Van Doren makes the current canon debate look rewarmed when he adds:

> Not much help can be expected from the American academy or from the universities. They will do no more than wait till the work has been done by actual workers. Then they will hold on to the revised canon with stubborn opposition to any further changes which some later age may want to insist upon.

As early as 1932, Van Doren thinks that the 'teaching' canon embodies all that is most inert in American life. Even so, he does not, like some contemporary critics, move from a hostility to the institutional canon to a call for the abandonment of all canons. Instead, he outlines a visionary canon perpetually re-created by artists from the inner light of unsanctioned revelation. In Lewisohn's narration, which he characterizes as 'a moral epic of America . . . in the process of becoming aware of itself', he sees the lineaments of this very canon. Lewisohn's history transforms an aggregate of literary works into a significant and unified narrative. Like some of his Romantic precursors, Van Doren sees this canon as 'a kind of spiritual history' of a great modern people. Following Brooks's high premium on mobility, he reaffirms that 'the canon of American literature refuses to stay fixed'.[49] The true canon is not a short-list of conformist monuments but an endlessly circulating, perpetually modified current of ideas that changes shape according to the demands of its users.

In their different ways, Brooks, Lewisohn and Van Doren all acknowledge that if the canon is to have any vigorous twentieth-century life, it must take up the creative mission bequeathed to the secular canon since the time of Novalis and Schiller. Each of these critics seems intensely aware of the vast institutional apparatus needed to elevate secular canons to publicly accredited status, or even to wrest them from those unable to grasp the germs of their imaginative potential. Significantly, the 1939 reissue of Lewisohn's book bore the title *The Story of American Literature*. Predictably, that story turns on a recurring opposition which Van Doren describes as 'a violent critical debate between decorum and candor'.[50] Not for the last time, adversarial battle lines inside a national culture become the hidden principles of canonical selection.

STANDARD BOOKS: THE CANON AND THE MASS MARKET

What the participants in the debate barely grasp is that labels such as 'decorum' and 'candour' conceal a veritable revolution in modern letters. The innovations in production and distribution, the emergence of a new, expanded public whose work afforded it unprecedented access to leisure, and the large potential audience for a new breed of artists with an exalted sense of their missionary role, all conspired to change the shape of early-twentieth-century letters. From the 1850s onwards, modern methods of industrial production had secured stretches of leisure time for groups who had never before had the opportunity to borrow books from libraries or attend lectures or visit museums. The same methods of production made reading materials for private use available at unprecedentedly low rates. But what should the successive waves of recruits to the brave new world of culture be advised to read? In a mass cultural market it becomes, paradoxically, extremely important to foster an illusion of responsiveness to individual needs. Would the established canons – the ground rules of criticism and the lists of valued texts – prove capable of penetrating this vast unknown market? Or would new lists and new critical rules have to be built up from scratch?

In these uncharted cultural waters, the distinctions between 'progressive' and 'genteel', 'canonical' and 'anti-canonical' become hard to maintain. 'Experts' in mass culture – teachers, librarians, social scientists – emerge from the shades and encourage the new public to organize its reading around short-lists of canonical works. Creative writers offer competing lists of personally valued texts. Paradoxically, the recommendations offered by the most eminent or avantgarde figures do not always suggest the greatest respect for the independence of the new readers. It is sometimes assumed that cultural entrepreneurs such as Arnold Bennett condemned tyro readers to the 'lowest common denominator' of 'middlebrow' culture, while the redemptive energies of saviours such as Ezra Pound propagated a more nuanced cultural product. We shall see that the evidence explodes this assumption. A glance at the huge wave of recommended reading lists which appeared between the 1880s and the Second World War reveals a wide range of relationships between the purveyors and the beneficiaries of canonical lists. These relationships dissolve at least two myths of the current debate: the myth of a single, imposed cultural canon; and the counter-myth of a radicalized anti-canon emanating from some higher, purified source.

The lists of recommended readings appear in periodicals, pamphlets and books. The list-makers include authors such as H. G. Wells, R. L. Stevenson, Andrew Lang and John Cowper Powys; cultural journalists such as Frederic Harrison; teachers such as Mortimer Adler; and public figures such as Theodore Roosevelt and the explorer Henry Stanley. Other sources for lists are clergymen, librarians, librarians' associations, and the catalogues for series such as Everyman's Library. Although literature (almost never by living authors) remains their stock in trade, the lists also encompass areas such as geography, history, political science and religion. W. Forbes Gray's *Books That Count* (1923 edition) lists 6,000 books in seventeen categories ranging from agriculture and engineering to sociology and philosophy.

Between 1880 and 1940 hundreds of such lists appeared. Three period assumptions explain their popularity. First, the continuing fall in the price of books produced a new market for the idea of a 'home library'. Second, the rising mountain of new books intensified the fear among the already educated of public contamination through ill-judged reading. Together, these two ideas reinforced the third assumption: that selected 'standard' books, if purchased and perused in an orderly manner, could assist in character building and, eventually, in the uplifting of a modern mass society. The reasons for the subsequent decline in the number of lists are less easy to pinpoint. Some possible explanations lie in the high rate of obsolescence produced by the acceleration of publishing, the fragmentation of the reading public, and the loss of authority through the multiplication of lists. In Britain the spread of the tax-subsidized library system from the 1850s swelled for a time the publication of lists. Books such as William Eaton Foster's *Libraries and Readers* (1883), which instructed the public in the proper use of these facilities, proliferated throughout the 1880s. But by the early years of this century the librarians, who had originally restricted their purchases of modern books (especially fiction), began to offer expert choices of the 'best' contemporary publications. The new buying policies had two consequences. First, librarians helped to make 'current' reading as respectable as the 'standard' books. Second, the library itself superseded the canonical list. Even today in Britain a widespread popular attitude exists that 'if it's in the public library, it must be worth reading'.

In the United States another important factor in the demise of the lists was the rise of book-disseminating organizations based on a completely different premise: authorized readings not of past masterpieces but of the best contemporary books. The Book-of-the-Month Club, founded in 1926, chose Sylvia Townsend Warner's *Lolly Willowes* as its first month's selection, while the Literary Guild began operations in 1927 with Heywood Brown and Margaret Leech's *Anthony Comstock*. Although the Book-of-the-Month Club employed prestigious advisers, including Arnold Bennett, H. G. Wells, André Maurois, Thomas Mann, Clifton Fadiman and Gilbert Highet, most of its early recommendations are unremembered today. Together, the public library and the book club made contemporary literature both practical and respectable; from the 1920s, 'current' literature loses its Victorian associations of worthless trivia and begins to displace the 'classic' books as essential reading for the culturally astute.

It is important to note that even at the height of their novelty in the 1880s or the height of their popularity in the 1930s, the lists were never referred to as 'the Canon'. On the contrary, several of the list-makers attack 'canons of criticism' in the same spirit as Edwards. Arnold Bennett's *Literary Taste: How to Form It* (1909) insists that 'it is harmful . . . to map out literature into divisions and branches, with different laws, rules, or canons'. 'In judging the style of an author', directs Bennett, 'you must employ the same canons as you use in judging men. In this way, you will constantly refer literature to the standards of life'.[51] In two book-lists, both published in 1923, Jesse Lee Bennett reminded readers that 'there is no inflexible criterion of taste and beauty' but rather a 'free masonry between men of real culture' that breaks down the barriers between them. Culture is the deliberate self-shaping that allows this communication to occur. Although his main emphasis is on individual development, Bennett reverts to a very old idea of *canon* when he states that the 'phases of civilization' form an orderly whole: 'An intricate building develops first in the imagination of the architect, then in the blueprints of his draughtsmen and then in the steel and stone of the builders'.[52]

In the same spirit, May Lamberton Becker, a high-school teacher, instructs her young female audience in *Adventures in Reading* (1927, 1946) not to approach contemporary fiction in the way they approach Thackeray and Scott. If they are to develop 'a discriminating, individual taste' (a recurring value during this time), her readers must view the varying conventions of all periods and genres with an 'open mind'.[53] In 1933, H. R. Huse's *The Illiteracy of the Literate: A Guide to the Art of Intelligent Reading* articulates a growing consensus among the list-makers when he states that 'the formulas, canons, and standards of the schools involve many variables'.[54] Values do not reside inside books; they have to be put there by intelligent readers, and will vary according to their skills and needs. Like most of the other list-makers, Huse believes that the educated individual sensibility, not the canonical list, must remain the ultimate criterion for judgement, even in an age of mass readership and mass education.

What principles govern the selection of books?

Frederic Harrison's article 'On the Choice of Books' in the *Fortnightly Review* of April 1879 offers a list, a commentary on Auguste Comte's list (the catalogue of his library), and an argument for lists which turns on the need for a 'rational syllabus of essential books' drawn from 'the common civilisation of Europe'.[55] James Baldwin's *The Book-Lover: A Guide to the Best Reading* (1884, revised edition 1902) details the principles of building a library of 'the highest and best achievements of the master minds of the ages'. Baldwin promises self-development through a course of reading that satisfies personal preferences within the limits of the listed 'standard' books.[56]

Sir John Lubbock's 'The Choice of Books' (1886), originally given as an address to the London Working Men's College, became the most frequently cited and reprinted of the nineteenth-century lists. Lubbock selected his 100 best books according to the number of times he had seen them recommended. He included Confucius, for instance, not because he personally admired his works but 'because they are held in the most profound veneration by the Chinese race, containing 400,000,000 of our fellow-men'.[57] Lubbock's religious selections will dismay those contemporary critics who assume that canonical lists encase students in a single hidebound culture. Besides the Bible and Confucius, they include an edition of the Koran, a book on Buddhism, the *Nibelungenlied*, the Hindu *Mahabharata* and the *Sakuntala* of Kali-Dasa, as well as works by Marcus Aurelius, Plato, Aristotle, Plutarch, Augustine, Pascal, Comte, Keble, Berkeley, Descartes, and several others. A few months later, the *Pall Mall Gazette* reprinted Lubbock's list as a special supplement, with alternative recommendations from Wilkie Collins, William Morris, Ruskin, Swinburne, and others. As Lubbock points out, very little consensus emerged; few works appeared on more than one list.

In 1909 Arnold Bennett deployed works from Everyman's Library, World's Classics, New Universal Library, and other recent series to show the reader how to amass a coherent, unified library for a small sum. From the early 1920s, the American Library series 'Reading with a Purpose' provided similar guides to more specialized areas, such as Irving Babbitt's book on *French Literature* (1928). In 1927, the Columbia College syllabus for the course *Classics of the Western World* claimed that the listed works would allow the reader to 'share in humanity's quest for ordered and significant living'.[58] By 1931 a list of lists was needed to negotiate the recommendations and reconcile the authorities. This inevitable document appeared in the shape of Asa Dickinson's publication of 1931, *One Thousand Best Books: The Household Guide to a Lifetime's Reading and Clue to the Literary Labyrinth*, which drew on nearly sixty lists published between Lubbock and the present. Dickinson reduced the confusion of lists to a numerical exercise by providing statistical tables showing which authorities recommended which books. In his 'How to Read' (1928) (expanded into *ABC of Reading* [1934]) Ezra Pound offered a half-mocking response to the whole phenomenon of the list, along with some idiosyncratic selections.

Behind the earlier lists stands Carlyle's distinction between 'good' books and 'bad' books.[59] This idea, which still thrives in popular

publishing, assumes that 'bad' books can 'poison the moral character', while 'good' books have the power to turn their readers into
marvels of human adjustment. Arnold Bennett, for instance, thinks
that 'good' literature is a unifying whole which can 'change utterly
one's relations with the world'. He objects to the association of
literary taste with the social graces on the one hand and professional
theories about literature on the other. 'A classic does not survive
because it conforms to certain canons', he thinks. 'It survives because
it is a source of pleasure.' He instructs his readers not to worry about
'literature' in the abstract, but simply to start reading any standard
author because 'in the sea of literature every part communicates with
every other part'.[60]

Like Bennett, many of the list-makers promise to build a kind of
human *canon* who can read 'standard' works with profit and in this
way gain a facility to judge the huge mass of contemporary literature.
Even the proponents of the Columbia list emphasize that the aim of
the course is not 'learning' in any mechanical sense but rather
'playing with many ideas'.[61] The classic books, agrees Mortimer
Adler, are *'the most potent civilizing forces in the world today'*.[62] Educated
readers become teachers of other readers and, in some cases, authors
themselves. All the list-makers believe that books build and impart
'character'; several of them invoke De Quincey's distinction between
'the literature of knowledge' and the 'literature of power'. Baldwin
puts it to his readers like this: 'you must eat the book – you must
crush it, and cut it with your teeth, and swallow it'.[63] However
foreign this sounds in the 1990s, the idea that a private course of
study or public curriculum in the humanities should aid the student's
self-development rather than teach a fixed set of ideas survived
through the 1960s and still remains influential today. While the 'personal development' model has lost prestige, we have not yet agreed
how to replace it, and this remains one of the hidden problems
underlying the current debate.

The idea that all readers can, with practice, become powerful and
discriminating readers means that, especially in the later lists, need
threatens to replace authority as a principle of selection. It is significant that W. Forbes Gray's 1912 *Books That Count: A Dictionary of
Standard Books* was subtitled in its expanded edition of 1923 *A Dictionary of Useful Books*. During the interwar period, a growing sense
of the differences between books and between readers threatens any
early obsolescence for that bulwark of an organized, stratified
culture, the authorized canonical list. Jesse Lee Bennett's two lists of
1923 signal an important shift in the context for these lists. *What*

Books Can Do for You: A Sketch Map of the Frontiers of Knowledge: With Lists of Selected Books sketches out a new approach to the perplexing problem of what Americans ought to read.

Bennett makes it clear that his selections are intended as aids to individual reflection, not as syllabuses to be stubbornly ploughed through. American readers should view their reading in terms of harmonious self-development, not as dead knowledge but as potential character. In his *On 'Culture' and 'A Liberal Education': With Lists of Books Which Can Aid in Acquiring Them*, Bennett questions the idea that readers should become 'cultured' by immersing themselves in the classics. As the author of *The Essential American Tradition*, he supports the attacks on American materialism made by Lewisohn, Mencken, Sinclair Lewis, and Van Wyck Brooks. However, he notes that the immediate response to these attacks has been an upsurge of cultural panaceas, fix-it recipes promising overnight self-improvement. Bennett's advice lies halfway between the old recommendation 'go read the classics' and the current wave of quack culture. Instead of starting in the past and moving forward, he recommends readers to find a middle ground. Real culture, he thinks, is a 'vigorous and robust' growth which demands a general 'mental framework'.[64] It is unlikely to be achieved by buying shelf-loads of collected classics.

Bennett's two books indicate a growing self-consciousness among list-makers of the possible shortcomings of canonical lists. From the 1920s, a recurring worry becomes the list as a short cut to knowledge. The editors of the Columbia list strongly criticize the current fad for 'how to' manuals promising self-improvement through 'fifteen-minute-a-day exercises of the intellect'.[65] In *How To Read a Book: The Art of Getting a Liberal Education* (1940), Mortimer Adler laments 'the almost total neglect of intelligent reading throughout the school system'. American teachers, who have adopted John Dewey's *How We Think* as an educators' 'Bible', have inculcated the idea that reading, unlike thought, is a passive, regimented, indoctrinating activity. On the contrary, reading demands an active 'performance' on the part of the reader, a performance conforming to, but not bounded by, numerous explicit 'rules'.[66]

The widening debate about the usefulness of lists is matched throughout this period by a recurring disagreement about their contents. Between the 1880s and the 1940s, two types of lists emerged which still remain important today: the representative and the evaluative. If Lubbock's list tried to represent diverse cultures and philosophies, the lists of Ruskin and Pound offer an overt set of preferences. In his contribution to the *Pall Mall Gazette* forum, Ruskin struck off 'the rubbish and poison' of Lubbock's religious and philosophical selections, leaving only Bacon, Jeremy Taylor, and *The Pilgrim's Progress*. Ruskin also objected, *inter alia*, to the inclusion of Sophocles, Euripides, Gibbon, Voltaire, Hume, Swift, Macaulay, Emerson, Thackeray, George Eliot, Kingsley, and Bulwer-Lytton. Surprisingly, Pound's list is more like Ruskin's than like Lubbock's. If Ruskin thinks that 'every man has his own field, and can only by his own sense discover what is good for him in it',[67] Pound invites the reader to discover the hidden principles behind *his*, the poet's, list. That principle is 'condensation', and it allows him to throw out large chunks of English literature in the guise of separating it from its accumulated canon. Pound prefers Chaucer to Shakespeare, Dante to Milton, and Homer to all Latin authors. Despite an air of iconoclasm that is new to the list-making field, Pound's recommendations are perhaps the narrowest yet mentioned. Nor do they compensate for their narrowness by demonstrating a complete liberation from the assumptions of 'the recommended list'.

In *ABC of Reading* (1934) Pound follows earlier list-makers by attacking the critics and debunking the professors. He accepts the principle that a reader needs to know 'the best of each kind', but thinks that poets, not critics, know what is best. In this way, the canonical list resurfaces as an expression of poetic power; poets – or, as Pound calls them, 'measuring-rods' – become the new list-makers. Orchestrated by a poet for other poets, Pound's anthology offers not a 'list' but a set of 'exhibits' which present 'signposts for further reading'. It seems fair to say that his minimally signposted road bears only one-way traffic and has few turn-offs for individual excursions. Canons and rules momentarily vanish, only to reappear as 'gadgets', procedures for performing artistic operations. These gadgets are invented by 'masters of the arts'; others may imitate, but rarely improve them.[68] In the age of Henry Ford, poets become their own canons, highly calibrated machines for separating the tradition-laden wheat from the custom-infected chaff. By this stage of its development, 'culture' has become a realm of almost Darwinian competition.

CANON AND THE ROOTS OF CULTURE: THE ANTI-CANONISM OF ELIOT AND HIS FOLLOWERS

Without a knowledge of the new spirit of competition that permeates modern letters, the anti-canonical vigour of its most prominent critics becomes incomprehensible. For many American critics of the early modern period, everything outside the perpetually shifting canon of spiritual self-construction can be discarded into the ashheap of Brooks's 'accepted canon'. In 1937, Malcolm Cowley dedicated to Brooks his *After the Genteel Tradition*, a collection of essays by significant modern critics on the authors – Carl Sandburg, Willa Cather, Ernest Hemingway, Sinclair Lewis, Eugene O'Neill, Theodore Dreiser, among others – who had cleared the way for American cultural independence. In this volume, an important criterion for admission to what amounts to a radical counter-canon becomes conformity to established patterns of nonconformity. Almost all Cowley's distinguished contributors praise the way their chosen authors flout the expectations of a hypothetically ordinary American audience.

John Peale Bishop praises the authenticity of Hemingway's vision and his unflinching look at 'the remorseless devaluation of nature'.[69] Newton Arvin contrasts Sandburg's bardic aspiration with his actual living conditions, noting sadly that 'his environing culture has not nourished him and his poetry as they deserved to be nourished'.[70] Hamilton Basso takes issue with Canby's 'offensive upon the so-called "confessional" school of writers'. He goes on to compare Thomas Wolfe with Dickens in *David Copperfield*, Tolstoy in *Anna Karenina*, and, in a typical canonizing gesture, 'Shakespeare in the soliloquies of *Hamlet*'.[71] Writing in the afterglow of T. S. Eliot's 'Ulysses, Order and Myth' (1923), Lionel Trilling praises the 'air of a brooding ancient wisdom' in Cather's work, but laments traces of 'the gaudy domesticity of bourgeois accumulation glorified in the *Woman's Home Companion*'. Echoing and expanding Brooks's judgement, Trilling deems American culture unable to support the vocation of art: 'In our literature there are perhaps fewer completely satisfying books and certainly fewer integrated careers than there are interesting canons of work and significant life stories.'[72] Among the most intelligent and radical American critics of this period, a suspicion lingers that a canon will represent a list of all the works an author has *not* integrated into an inwardly compelling order. The contrast with Novalis and Schiller, for whom 'canon' carries a charge of inspired unity that provides a blueprint for further creation, could hardly be more complete.

The deep current of anti-canonism in American letters perhaps explains why T. S. Eliot, so often identified as the arch-exemplar of the canonizing disposition, should take so rebarbative an approach to accepted notions of *canon*. During the last fifteen or twenty years Eliot has routinely figured as a paradigm of conservative reaction, so that in a recent article Pierre Bourdieu can casually refer to Eliot's 'canons of "pure" reading' as protocols of deprivation which take culture further and further from the social arena.[73] In fact, early-twentieth-century culture shows *canon* being pressed into the service of the same public causes – nationalism, convention, piety – from which radical critics routinely distance themselves today.

It is against this strong current of conventionality in the early-twentieth-century use of the word that we should consider the unexpectedly hostile verdict on canons which Eliot delivers in his early collection *The Sacred Wood* (1920). Anyone who opens this volume in the hope of finding Eliot embracing 'the canon' will rapidly encounter disappointment. He uses the word three times, with mounting hostility. The effect is akin to finding anti-Jesuitical sentiments in Loyola's *Autobiography*. No less than Terry Eagleton, Eliot associates 'canonical' with the stifling hand of inert orthodoxy, ritualized and only half-conscious. 'Aristotle is a person who has suffered from the adherence of persons who must be regarded less as his disciples than as his sectaries', he cautions in 'The Perfect Critic'. 'One must be firmly distrustful of accepting Aristotle in a canonical spirit; this is to lose the whole living force of him.'[74] No less than Edward Said or Jonathan Culler, Eliot associates 'canonical' with blind submission to unquestioned authority, the confusion of living guides with classical dodos. He objects to the association of *canon* with the authority of law, or even with established critical standards and usages. As René Wellek and Austin Warren point out, 'the one-time novelty of Eliot's essays was precisely their delivering themselves of no final summary or single judgement but judging all the way through an essay'.[75] In his time, Eliot's manner seemed directly contrary to the canonical disposition, for he neither followed established procedures nor drew up privileged lists of authors whose anti-canonical virtues functioned as canonical surrogates.

In *The Sacred Wood* Eliot aims to lay down critical foundations for the study of modern literature by creating the kind of political and socially independent 'usable past' required by Brooks. Although he supports Matthew Arnold's commitment to see literature not 'as consecrated by time, but . . . beyond time', he rejects Arnold's priestly approach, preferring rather the living, secular classicism of Larbaud, de Gourmont, and Gide. He particularly objects to Arnold's habit of 'seeing the masters, whom he quotes, as canonical literature, rather than as masters'.[76] In the spirit of Edward Said's attack on 'religious criticism', Eliot argues against what Said calls a 'filiative' pattern of criticism: the academic tendency to reproduce its own likeness in the objects it studies, substituting discipleship for understanding, repetition for education.

Similarly, Eliot's essay 'Tradition and the Individual Talent' is frequently characterized as the quintessence of the canonizing spirit, largely because it argues that the modern poet 'must inevitably be judged by the standards of the past'. The qualification which follows – 'I say judged, not amputated, by them; not judged to be as good as, or worse or better than, the dead; and certainly not judged by the canons of dead critics' – is seldom quoted or even remembered. This essay, so often seen as the basis for the modern academic canon, actually moves in an overtly anti-canonical direction. By 'canons' Eliot seems to mean 'accepted standards of value authorized by superseded critical practice'. Even when he argues that a modern poet's survival will depend on his acquiring 'the historical sense', Eliot scarcely functions as the typical conservative canonist. Instead he defines this 'sense' in the inward, spiritual terms familiar from Novalis and Schiller as a 'feeling that the whole of the literature of his own country has a simultaneous existence and composes a simultaneous order'.[77] Not only does Eliot's alternative to the canon prove dauntingly comprehensive rather than restrictive in its process of selection, but it also functions as a stimulus to creation rather than as a pedagogic list. Rather than seeing Eliot as a fervent canonist in these pages, it seems more useful to think of him as updating Polycletus for the age of Picasso.

Does the *canon* of *The Sacred Wood* enjoin a 'canon of "pure" reading', as Bourdieu alleges? Bourdieu's description of such a canon as 'refurbishing . . . the academic liturgy' through 'readings of isolated texts',[78] does not strictly apply to Eliot, who seems unable to consider a literary work apart from its precursors and successors. Those who blame Eliot for the closing of the modern canon forget the figure whose audacious visionary conceit of a concordance between past and present introduced a new range of exegetical and historical possibilities to early modern critics. Eliot's 'canon' originally owed its authority not to his intensive analysis of a preferred object, nor to the magnitude of his exclusions, nor to his conformity with established values, but to the weight of allusions he masses together in a framework of creative valuation. Easy to undermine and difficult to recover, such valuations are a distinctive feature of modern culture. In his essay 'My Canon and Ours' (1985), William Bowman Piper recalls how, at times of sickness and trouble, he would jumble together fragments from his own mental canon. Although the poems and popular ditties in his 'canon' make an odd assortment, they have helped him to sustain 'a systematic identity, an identifiable coherence of being'.[79] We shall see in later chapters that Ernst Gombrich testifies to the healing power of a similar 'canon of the mind', and that even Michel Foucault points to a hidden realm of valued authors when he confesses the latent presence and canonical importance of Heidegger in his work.

In the same way, Eliot speaks in the 'The Function of Criticism' of the 'unconscious community' among artists deriving from their 'common inheritance and common cause'. The early Eliot accepts only the validity of a 'canon' he has first transported to a plane of almost visionary contemplation. While acknowledging the cultural responsibilities of the modern critic, he also demands a criticism which fuses past and present, poet and critic, into a sustaining imaginative order. This order derives from the artist's

> relation to . . . dead poets and artists. You cannot value him alone; you must set him, for contrast and comparison, among the dead. . . . What happens when a new work of art is created is something that happens simultaneously to all the works of art which preceded it. The existing monuments form an ideal order among themselves, which is modified by the introduction of the new (the really new) work of art among them.[80]

Artistic works become canonical not by virtue of resemblance to the accredited monuments but by their participation in a continuously unfolding narrative pattern. Certainly, Eliot's early canon operates as an 'idea of order'. But the 'order' of 'Tradition and the Individual Talent' and 'The Function of Criticism' is an aesthetic and narrative order which inhabits a different realm from Canby's canon of national virtues or Van Doren's canon of radical energies or the canon of Christian orthodoxy from which Eliot derives the 'standards' of his later essays.

Eliot's development into that militantly orthodox critic indicates yet again that the modern canon is the product of a deeply anti-canonical spirit. Certainly, Brooks and Eliot often *sound* canonical; their styles appear authoritarian, they make rigid evaluations, they employ racial or national vocabularies. Yet they combine all this with a strong hostility towards the accepted cultural canon. By jettisoning these 'canons of dead critics' so qualmlessly, Eliot delivers criticism to modern creation. Even so, to read across his own rhetoric is to see that he has no final objections either to history or to canons. He thinks that any poet hoping to outgrow adolescence will require 'a historical sense'. And the criticism he expects his preliminary work to inspire will create new canons, re-creating the past for its own purposes in the same spirit as the makers of the New Testament or the scholars who rescued classical antiquity in the Renaissance. By aligning *canon* with the imagination as it re-creates the past and reimagines the present, the early Eliot finds himself among such unlikely company as Athanasius, Van Wyck Brooks and Novalis.

Further evidence of radical scepticism about the canon among the twentieth century's most conservative critics emerges in the work of Eliot's contemporaries and followers. For many of these critics *canon* needs to be liberated from its associations with the institutionally acceptable if it is to acquire any authority. One of the more quizzical followers is Q. D. Leavis, whose essay 'The Discipline of Letters' (1943) deplores the process by which 'Mr Eliot has become incorporated into the canon of accepted literature'.[81] Once again, the price of canonical acceptance is viewed as a conformity which replaces an artist's imaginative vision with more socially desirable qualities. Mrs Leavis sees the canonized Eliot as a sadly reduced figure who seems more appropriate company for Dorothy Sayers than for Dante.

In the same way, many of the essays collected posthumously in *Valuation in Criticism* (1986) show F. R. Leavis making an energetic attempt to distance himself from the established agencies of cultural validation. Certainly, Leavis respects what we now consider canonical virtues. He sees the nurturing of critical 'standards' as an urgent priority, and he thinks that these standards should manifest themselves as 'a practised readiness of response over a certain selective range, a habit of implicit preference and expectation'. Yet what remains surprisingly contemporary in these essays is Leavis's mistrust of cultural and educational institutions. This mistrust becomes apparent when he contrasts 'J. B. Priestley's calculating manufactures' and the 'mechanical pertinacity' of the *Times Literary Supplement* with the 'total organic culture' represented by Blake, Lawrence, T. S. Eliot, and the finest seventeenth-century authors. Like some contemporary anti-canonical critics, Leavis speaks not of a 'canon' but of 'collective wisdom and basic assumptions, a currency of criteria and valuation'.[82] Formulated as obliquely as this, the grounds of the advanced critic's separation from the parent culture can shift and dissolve as circumstances change. Whether Leavis's elasticity abandons canons or simply camouflages them becomes a doubtful point.

A similar reluctance to admit to canonical conformity marks John Crowe Ransom's *The World's Body* (1938). In 'A Poem Nearly

Anonymous', Ransom ponders the eruptions of metrical irregularity discernible beyond the apparent regularities of Milton's *Lycidas*. Behind Ransom's search lies his belief that obedience to forms and conventions constitutes the essence of civility, but that disobedience constitutes the paradigmatic modern act. 'A feature that obeys the canon of logic is only the mere instance of a universal convention,' he ruminates, 'while the one that violates the canon is an indestructibly private thing.' Yet as one canon disappears, another waits in the wings. A few pages later, in 'Forms and Citizens', Ransom replays this argument in a parable on the role of form and convention in the construction of a civilized human being. A 'canon of logic' provides the basis for the natural science which Ransom sees as governing the modern world and crowding poetry and mythology off the stage. Yet natural science produces the natural man, he decides, in a process that aspires to nothing above 'the ideal of efficient animality'. Civilization requires more: 'Art has a canon to restrain this natural man.'[83] Like Eliot, Ransom understands *canon* from the point of view of the practising artist rather than the classroom teacher. For him, the canon has an ethical as well as an aesthetic dimension; it functions as a learned refinement of natural behaviour. In this way, its very obsolescence becomes the prime guarantee of its value.

That same obsolescence intrigues Paul Claudel when he speaks of Charles Péguy. In an address to the Catholic Institute, Claudel describes Péguy as 'an upright son of our Gaul', remote from foreign influence in a way unique for a modern Frenchman. Among contemporary French writers, only Péguy retains any link to 'this established, I am tempted to say, canonical literature which stretches from Théroulde to Victor Hugo'. Claudel describes Péguy ('the soldier peasant') in terms of a vanished organic order. As he sees it, the canonical virtues run directly opposite to the spirit of the age. Claudel ponders 'the classical radiance which interlaces its roots with Latin oration and Greek grammar'. Compared with this, most contemporary authors offer no more than 'vegetation without roots, more ephemeral than the gardens of Adonis'.[84] Claudel wants to bring *'canonique'* into alliance with *'catholique'*, and in this way purge poetry of its wordly and material accretions. Like Ransom, he sees some notion of *canon* as something deeply embedded in our cultural roots, and the loss of those roots as demanding nothing short of a miraculous intervention.

W. B. Yeats combines the ideas of Ransom and Claudel when his *Autobiography* invokes *canon* as a kind of magnificently barbaric lost civility. Yeats is considering some etchings and drawings by

Augustus John. All the figures seem 'broken by labour or wasted by sedentary life'. He thinks that

> A gymnast would find in all something to amend; and the better he mended the more would those bodies, as with the voice of Dürer, declare that ancient canon discovered in the Greek gymnasium, which, whenever present in painting or sculpture, shows a compact between the artist and society.[85]

Yeats, Claudel and Ransom all want to recruit the canon for deeply conservative modernist programmes, yet none of them speaks with the voice of a man who has held office for too long. When Yeats invokes 'that ancient canon', he does so almost defiantly. All these authors imply that canonical truths will soon become forgotten truths in a world where material power lies in deeply antipathetic hands. Like Ransom, Yeats takes it for granted that canons will go the way of fairies, elaborate courtship patterns, and large country houses. Like Claudel, he associates *canon* with an ancient wisdom almost lost. All three writers view *canons* as relics of a vanishing age. For Eliot, a canon has no place in the construction of a criticism properly modern in its methods. For Yeats, a canon seals a compact between artist and society that modernity has long since shattered. For Ransom, the term *canon* evokes patterns of conformity in art and conduct that a modern life premissed on personal spontaneity and collective calculation will only discredit.

Contemporary revisionism often links early modern criticism with the orthodox in religion and the nationalist in politics. The evidence presented so far shows that the orthodoxy of an Eliot, a Yeats or a Ransom fulfils heterodox creative needs and encourages, in the case of the Leavises, distinctly heterodox disciples. A look at the work of S. L. Bethell, another Eliot follower, reminds us of the unprecedented diversity of early modern culture, a culture in which few critical canons command absolute assent. In his *Essays on Literary Criticism and the English Tradition* (1948) Bethell pays tribute to an 'English tradition', a tradition which he venerates as an avowedly Christian critic. English poets, he thinks, form a natural bond with the English Church and the English countryside. For him, these poets are as much a part of the landscape as 'the village church, the village parson'. In this traditional 'English' poetry 'common things are seen in a religious light'.

Does Bethell, in these obsolescent formulations, unwittingly tear the mask from the modern tradition, to reveal a conspiracy between nationalism and orthodoxy? Not quite. In fact, he confides that 'It has more than once been suggested to me, by reviewers and other well-wishers, that critical canons founded upon theology most necessarily be wanting in that catholicity . . . which should be the aim of every literary critic.' In practice, Bethell's criticism does not confirm this charge. Characteristically, he proceeds not from dogma to dogma but by exploring the psychological ramifications of the religious language used by his chosen authors. Although he thinks that at the beginning of *Macbeth* the hero is a 'convinced Christian', he spends much time in charting the linguistic depths of the 'internal confusion'[86] which follows Macbeth's abandonment of his beliefs. Viewed as a whole, Bethell's work suggests that 'critical canons founded on theology' may encourage habits of careful exegesis. A theory of language emphasizing its paradoxical qualities and a theory of dramatic and narrative structure which links literary works to mythic or sacred patterns remain two of the most lasting consequences of the syncretic relationship forged between theological and critical canons in the age of Eliot.

A culture that recurrently sets under fire the vestiges of older theological canons may try to usher its rules and formulae in the direction of convenience, emphasizing the usefulness of alternative, secular canons as a means of selection or as a practical way of ordering aesthetic objects. We shall see in later chapters how these ostensibly functional canons can run to grief on the theological sand their creators hoped to vacate. In the meantime, let us consider R. P. Blackmur's attempt to escape the nets of theology in his essay 'The Shorter Poems of Thomas Hardy' (1940). One of the most interesting aspects of this essay lies in Blackmur's repeated attempt to banish religious categories and their recurring tendency to return, despite his best efforts. How many of Hardy's vast number of poems, he wonders, will support close critical scrutiny? Circling around 'those remote, impressionable, germinal areas of the sensibility' that lie just beneath the 'formulaic' surface of Hardy's verse, Blackmur announces a need for 'some sort of canon – a criterion more for exclusion than for judgment'. Yet on what grounds can a critic sensitive to the disturbed conditions of modern writing perform the operation of excision? Blackmur initially decides to 'stick to those values which can be exemplified in terms of craft', a choice which pushes his idea of *canon* nearer to Polycletus than to St Paul. Yet he concedes that 'the standards engaged in the discernment of value cannot be exclusively literary standards'. Only when we press beyond the 'formulae' of the poetic craft do we discover the poet's 'personal meaning', and only if we press beyond this meaning do we reach 'the anonymous and objective level' of the greatest art. At this point the best poems dispose themselves in a wider, larger pattern, a pattern which suggests 'some sort of standard, a canon of inclusion as well as exclusion'. And the basis for this canon is not a judgement so much as an experience – an experience, in the case of Hardy, which can be characterized as a 'disturbance, a pinioning, or a liberation'.[87]

By the end of his essay, Blackmur's 'canon' has become more of a halting metaphysical stutter than a sharp-edged critical tool. His fascination with the secret world of poetic creation has moved him far away from values that can be 'exemplified in terms of craft'. As Harold Bloom pointed out in 1958, Blackmur's criticism represents a heroically misconceived effort to deliver 'a new scriptural canon out of modern poetry in English'.[88] Blackmur presents the poetic subtext, the poem's area of contact with dark personal and spiritual forces, as more canonical, more humanly valuable, than its surface rhetorical existence. By the end of his essay, the poetic surface has come to represent whatever in the poem is conventional – and therefore reproducible – and therefore less the product of an individual sensibility responding to new experiences in new, intense, liberating ways.

The reproducibility of modern art is a topic that also exercises Walter Benjamin in his influential essay 'The Work of Art in the Age of Mechanical Reproduction'. Benjamin notes that the central point of reference in the arts is no longer beauty but use. The functional canons which have invaded the arts almost unnoticed explain the renewed prestige of architecture in modern culture. Apart from the occasions when we approach recognized monuments specifically in order to look at them, we do not give 'rapt attention' to the buildings we enter but rather notice what surrounds us 'in incidental fashion'. Benjamin goes on:

> This mode of appropriation, developed with reference to architecture, in certain circumstances acquires canonical value. For the tasks which face the human apparatus of perception at the turning points of history cannot be solved by optical means, that is, by contemplation, alone. They are mastered gradually by habit, under the guidance of tactile appropriation.

In the modern world, the distraction we take to radically new experiences and art-forms becomes, paradoxically enough, the means of their survival: 'Distraction as provided by art presents a covert control of the extent to which new tasks have become soluble by apperception.' For Benjamin, film represents the supreme instance of this oblique, piecemeal mode of apprehension. What Blackmur describes as a canonical subtext, an experience more valuable than the formulaic poetic surface but too intense to be articulated in anything but formulaic terms, Benjamin presents as a 'cult value' half-concealed by the technical paraphernalia of the modern film.[89] Do our artistic values depend on a gnostic or a visionary mode of response? In his account of 'Some Motifs in Baudelaire', Benjamin tracks the peculiar effect of Baudelaire's poetry to the impression it leaves of an 'encounter with an earlier life'. In the private *'correspondances'* described in *Les fleurs du mal (The Flowers of Evil)*, he finds many traces of the long drift from established rules and precedents in modern literature. The monumental grandeur of a neoclassical canon becomes Baudelaire's private curio shop, where 'the canonical experience . . . has its place in a previous life'. Almost despite his best intentions, Benjamin, like Blackmur, links canons to subterranean, deeply worn and virtually inaccessible modes of apprehension. His discussion of Baudelaire leaves no doubt about the occult and esoteric sources which he thinks store the residues of canonicity. He notes, for instance, the modern aversion to reproducible 'historical data', the consistent substitution of 'prehistory' for the great public monuments which Baudelaire's stately Alexandrines appear to promise. He notes too that Baudelaire's *'correspondances'* rely on prolonged attention: 'There are no simultaneous correspondences, such as were cultivated by the symbolists later.'[90] In the work of Benjamin and Blackmur, we see the first traces of an important shift of meaning. For Benjamin, 'canon' becomes a kind of hidden cultural code that facilitiates both creation and audience response. For Blackmur, 'canon' suggests a point of intersection between formula and inspiration. In neither case does 'canon' evoke the conventional or regulated aspect of the art-work or even its producer's intended effects. It signifies instead the work's point of contact with deeper cultural or psychological structures.

Benjamin sees these structures as a hidden influence on every aspect of modern cultural production, bypassing traditional boundaries between producer and audience, nation and nation. In the modern world, canons dominate and control the basic processes of perception. As Benjamin represents them, the conditions of modern culture overturn the canonical hierarchies of genre and fuse the various national traditions into new, still uncharted patterns of meaning and valuation. Unfortunately, Benjamin himself became fatally pessimistic about the shape of the canons which would become visible once these complex processes were understood. For a more optimistic account of the modernist cultural formation we must turn to the work of Valery Larbaud, a French Anglophile and independently wealthy man of letters who inaugurated one of the most influential twentieth-century campaigns for a culture without frontiers. Larbaud developed his ideas, one of the strongest expressions of the need for an open, inclusive and cosmopolitan canon, from his essays on contemporary English authors, including Coventry Patmore, Hardy, Bennett, Wells, Joyce, Conrad, and others. He observes in *This Unpunished Vice* (1936) that the best critical editions 'of canonical English authors' follow the efforts of 'French and German Anglicists'. He thinks that

> We can therefore speak of a veritable collaboration between continental Anglicists and English and American specialists in the history of English literature, and one can say that these little 'chapels' that make up the work of certain great English writers are truly serviced by a cosmopolitan clergy, to whom one can apply the phrase of St Jerome, 'one religion in all languages'.

Without neglecting the enormous pressures built up by new audiences for literature, new forms of scholarship and new educational systems, Larbaud sustains the charismatic mission entrusted to the keepers of the cultural canon since the time of Novalis and Schiller. He even speaks of 'militant or missionary Anglicists' who provide for their chosen authors the detailed criticism and exegesis previously reserved for classical authors.[91] Larbaud describes culture as a collaborative enterprise carried on by scholars and artists across national boundaries in the interests of an international cultural regeneration. His work has as its backdrop the international achievement of *Ulysses* and *The Waste Land*, works themselves composed according to sacred rubrics and saturated with the structures and rhythms of ancient and European precedents.

The idea of a canon without frontiers has not lacked detractors. In *European Literature and the Latin Middle Ages* (first German edition 1948) Ernst Curtius ends his history of canon formation – a history which has taken him from Homer to Sainte-Beuve – by voicing reservations about Larbaud's views, which he acknowledges are 'subtle' and not yet fully explored by any contemporary critic. 'The concept of a world literature could not but shatter the French canon', Curtius argues. In his earlier instances of canon-making, he could always trace national, theological or political lines of affiliation. In

Larbaud's work, Curtius detects 'a program for a politics of mind which has left behind all pretensions to hegemony, and is concerned only with facilitating and accelerating the exchange of intellectual merchandise'. When canons conform to extra-literary assumptions, one group of twentieth-century critics rejects them because that conformity lessens the cause of cultural independence. When canons become recruited for the cause of an autonomous literary culture, another group regrets their lack of ultimate authority. Curtius, who combines elements of both positions, cannot square Larbaud's programme with what he sees as the traditional function of a canon: 'to safeguard a tradition' by making a short-list of classical authors or authors whose work reflects 'the cultural development and the world-wide importance' of a particular linguistic order.[92]

In their different ways, all these later instances show that the contemporary discontent with a canon sponsored by classroom practice, civic self-esteem, or politically engineered ideas of national status has a long-established precedent behind it. Peculiar as it may seem, Jonathan Culler and Edward Said both voice doubts about canons first articulated by T. S. Eliot and Van Wyck Brooks. For as long as critics seek to reimagine their whole field of operations – and the current prominence of literary theory indicates that desire is at present very strong – they can hardly avoid recourse to some version of *canon*. The contemporary view of the canon as an imposing monolith entrusted with the transmission of homogeneous cultural values is a phenomenon whose own history can be scrutinized. The canon as monolith is a fiction or myth which allows contemporary critics to get along with the business of teaching and talking about literature. By turning the canon into the first servant of ideology, contemporary critics discover a reassuring, but possibly entirely misleading, sense of their own influence over the larger cultural process. For an academic criticism which energetically and eagerly broadcasts its 'revisionary', 'subversive', even 'revolutionary' credentials, a mythical being called 'the canon' fulfils a suitably fetishized role.

Literary history destroys that fetish by showing that the canons of the past presuppose far more than a short-list of approved academic books. Those canons have supplied inspiration to artists and basic rules to students. They have provided a retrospective pattern that becomes a 'usable past' and a simultaneous order binding together literature present and past. They have supplied lines of artistic and scholarly contact across national boundaries. We have seen that canons have played a part in campaigns of cultural nationalism, and that they have also been allocated key roles in the conservative iconographies of Claudel, Ransom and Yeats. Yet we have also noticed their wider, more assimilative functions in processing the new. Even in the classroom, canons have not only conserved indigenous cultural achievement – a task easy to underestimate in an age of electronic media, but crucially important and complicated for earlier societies – but have also aided the assimilation of foreign cultures. In many of these cases canons have served the cause not of 'essentialism' but of diversity.

In one form or another canons have a long and surprisingly tenacious history. Their banishment will not be easy. In the following chapters we shall consider how some postwar critics have accommodated the idea of the canon to current needs. In the process, we shall see that the role of canons even in 'radical' criticism is at once complex, understated and misunderstood. The present chapter has shown that secular critics have viewed canons with suspicion almost from the inception of the discipline. All the critics to be discussed in later chapters register this suspicion in their work. Northrop Frye tries to cast off the long association which binds canons to political or national authority, situating them instead with our deepest apprehensions of value. Frank Kermode wants to restore the inspired and educative properties of *canon*, which he regards as our strongest lifeline between cultural present and cultural past. Edward Said's quarrel with a canon which he sees as inextricably implicated in colonial power incorporates the most important arguments of the contemporary challenge to canons, but also illustrates the difficulty of transacting cultural exchange without them. E. H. Gombrich, the critic to whom we shall turn first, wants to purge canons of their association with uniformity and blind authority and to demonstrate their practical usefulness in creative work and rational enquiry. Of all the critics whose careers we shall examine, Gombrich has worked hardest to restore the contemporary canon to its ancient prestige.

3

Sir Ernst Gombrich and the Functionalist Canon

Sir Ernst Gombrich might have been created to order by an anti-canonical critic. In recent years he has defended the canon on every conceivable occasion, his very presence at conferences and lectures reminding his audience of his eminent and orthodox career. Gombrich shares with Northrop Frye, the subject of the next chapter, not just a pre-eminent position in his discipline but an enormous prestige among the general public. If Frye has become one of the most influential figures in modern Canadian culture, Gombrich's seemingly perpetual custodianship of the humanities has reaped an equal share of European offices and honours. In 1975 the lifelong humanist accepted the Praemium Erasmianum from the city of Rotterdam. Two years later the fervent anti-Hegelian received the Hegel Prize from the city of Stuttgart. In 1985 Gombrich received the Balzan Prize for his distinguished contribution to the study of Western art. In 1972 he received a knighthood and in 1988 the Order of Merit. Gombrich's civic esteem is matched by his academic distinction. From 1959 to 1976 his period as director of the Warburg Institute ran alongside a University of London professorship in the History of the Classical Tradition. He has served as the Slade Professor of Fine Art at Oxford, delivered the prestigious A. W. Mellon lectures on the fine arts, the Romanes Lecture at Oxford, and the Wrightsman lectures at the Metropolitan Museum of Art in New York. His list of medals and awards covers twenty-one lines of *Who's Who* (1989).

As if all this were not enough, Gombrich has exceeded the ambitions of many academic anti-canonists by becoming the common reader's favourite art historian. *The Story of Art* (1950), with its sales of over a million copies, its fourteen English editions, and its translations into world languages that include Chinese, has introduced many lay readers to the grand narrative of art history, while the enormous scholarly influence of *Art and Illusion*, his important study of the psychology of pictorial representation, has earned him a comparable esteem among the learned.[1] When Gombrich defends the humanities, as he has done recently in *Tributes* (1984), against 'a

89

certain type of politician' who finds it 'fatally easy to curry favour with the philistines by speaking superciliously of useless subjects of research',[2] he speaks with the authority of a man whom governments, colleagues and public alike have furnished with the highest scholarly and civic accolades.

POLICING THE PROFESSORS:
GOMBRICH AND THE ACADEMIC CANON

It remains a constant suprise that despite his lifelong academic affiliations, Gombrich refuses to view the canon as an instrument for bolstering professional morale. To correct what he sees as a self-serving professorial myth – the canon as academic creation – Gombrich emphasizes again and again the inescapability of canons as functional elements of aesthetic creation and audience response. We cannot escape canons, he thinks, because they have a scientific basis in our most elementary perceptions. Our responses to traditionally valued works represent more complex versions of the same perceptions, which is why it will prove hopeless to try to unseat these works from their academic pre-eminence. However specialized in vocabulary and method, traditional academic valuations of Rubens and Botticelli draw their sustenance from universal human responses. Gombrich notes that 'the feeling has grown up that the canon was set up by pedantic critics', before adding, 'but this view vastly overrates the power of professors'.[3]

Gombrich's fervent defences of canons and of the Western humanist tradition have disturbed some of his earlier professorial admirers. Murray Krieger, who once considered *Art and Illusion* (1960) as responsible for 'some of the most provocative turns that art theory, literary theory, and aesthetics have taken in the last two decades', has none the less criticized Gombrich for his 'ethnocentric parochialism'.[4] Gombrich's response is sharp. He explains: 'I would have been happier to leave Professor Krieger to his agonizing, if he did not present himself as the "spokesman" for a significant body of theorists who appear to have acclaimed my book on *Art and Illusion* without ever having read it.' This kind of attack constitutes 'an alarming symptom of academic decline', for instead of asking 'What has the critic found out?', it poses the essentially trivial question 'Where does the critic stand?' The 'campus ideologies' of recent years demonstrate 'the absence of the scientific temper' Gombrich himself has repeatedly laboured to correct.[5] *His* history draws on science, not metaphysics. *His* aesthetics uses perception theory and information science to penetrate the 'social psychology of fashions and movements'. *His* area of investigation remains 'living people in concrete situations' rather than the glacial march of *Geist*.[6]

Because Gombrich sees the academy as a dangerously idealistic cultural force, his most polemical writing generally addresses itself against critical models or myths which promise special powers of cultural interpretation. Such myths, he alleges, have fostered most of the mischief of modern life, whether they come in the false pattern of a Hegelian philosophy that for years impeded the development of a rational cultural history, or in Hitler's legend of a warrior-class Germany that devastated Europe. During the Second World War, Gombrich studied Nazi propaganda broadcasts along with Ernst Kris and Hans Speier. Since then, he has espoused the cause of his long-time friend Sir Karl Popper, whose *The Open Society and Its Enemies* (1946) presents the myths of Plato, Hegel and Marx as seedbeds of modern totalitarianism. Popper, like Gombrich, views social institutions not as vehicles for mythology but as 'means to certain ends, or as convertible to the service of certain ends'.[7] These institutions reflect the rational activities of human beings who show a verifiable 'tendency to probe both the real world and its representations with a hypothesis of regularity which is not abandoned unless it is refuted'.[8] For Gombrich, art and culture are as necessary to human existence as breathing.

All too often, Gombrich thinks, we refer *culture* not to rational human activity but to some hypostatized entity. He detects this entity in histories of art organized around some external principle or metaphor, by virtue of which Baroque art becomes a product of an Age of Faith and the development of artistic forms becomes a natural cycle, in which maturity yields to decadence and decadence to renewal. Gombrich objects strongly to such analogies, emphasizing rather that we 'need to regard the organism as an active agent reaching out towards the environment, not blindly and at random, but guided by its inbuilt sense of order' (SO, 5). He shares with Popper the idea that the spider's web fashioned by Hegelian dialectic impedes the growth of rational thinking about history, freedom, culture, and art. In his own sphere, the history of art, he repeatedly betrays some impatience with a Platonic or utopian view of aesthetic theory and history, emphasizing rather the usefulness of canons in furnishing artists with the basic skills necessary for the production of art, with the conventions by which they communicate with fellow artists, and with a larger vision of the humanistic enterprise.

Gombrich's functionalism explains why it may prove seriously misleading to speak of his view of 'the canon'. The same motives that led him to begin *The Story of Art* with the famous remark 'There really is no such thing as Art. There are only artists'[9] underpin his tendency to speak of 'canons' rather than of a single all-regulating Canon. Gombrich does not want to tell a story of art that underplays the individuality of artists, since in his view canons exist in order to aid their distinct aesthetic endeavours. For a Chinese calligrapher or a medieval manuscript-maker 'art' proceeds according to centuries-old formulae. For Picasso or Gauguin 'art' exists as a tradition to be overwhelmed. In Gombrich's view, any 'story of art' that takes no account of these changes will fail to comprehend the diversity of art as an experience for its audience and as an activity for its makers.

In the same way, he refuses to elevate 'the Canon' to a point where its meaning becomes haunted by abstractions such as the 'spirit of the age' or 'humanist ideology'. He thinks that the political machinery used to characterize 'the Canon' during the current debate belongs to mythology rather than to actual human culture. As a cultural historian, he sees the word *canon* as referring to three distinct but related activities. First, canons supply a repertoire of usable skills, a set of minimum requirements that guarantee artistic proficiency. Gombrich includes in this, his most elementary and universal *canon*, rudimentary skills such as the ability to represent a plausible figure, a lifelike head, a recognizable landscape, and, at a later stage, a figure or scene in perspective, so that the canvas becomes a window on a world that resembles our own. This is the 'how to' canon which ensures that no fledgling artist starts from scratch.

Second, Gombrich presents *canon* as a set of norms and practices shared by groups of artists. Rather than setting the work of art in the context of some determining or restricting ideology, he prefers to see it as the outcome of the consistently made, empirically identifiable choices of rational actors. He suggests that 'we are unlikely to get a clear picture of any movement in art history before we try to assess the advantages it offered its adherents'.[10] These choices explain why there is a canon of Byzantine icon-makers and a canon of Dutch masters. This canon enables an artist living in a particular milieu to contribute to a certain style or school of art. Not much art history could be transmitted in universities and academies without this version of *canon*. If the first canon contains a set of 'how to' patterns, the second provides a more ambitious 'how we' paradigm, a set of culturally preferred choices and exclusions. For artists, such canons offer a groundwork of problems to be solved or conventions to be challenged. For historians, they offer a period style that makes a Dutch master as recognizable in painting as a Cavalier poet is in

literature. Without such canons, art history would lack both notations and development. If 'how to' canons offer recipes for artists,
'how we' canons supply signposts to practitioners and audience alike.
Third, Gombrich speaks of a 'canon of excellence' or 'canon of
mastery' that stretches from Raphael and Rubens to Picasso and
Cézanne. His ideas about the 'canon of excellence' derive from the
fifteenth-century humanists who first saw classical antiquity as 'the
canon of perfection'.[11] Renaissance artists adapted this idea to their
own needs, so that the perfection contemporary philosophers discovered in the art of antiquity spurred artists to assert a new relationship with organic forms. Although it is easy to see how such a canon
could translate into a narrative of decline, since the achievement of
excellence in an earlier era may oppress all later endeavour, artists
themselves have often seen the canon of masterpieces as challenges,
first to copy and then to surpass. In the canon of excellence, criticism
discovers the legislative authority for its enquiries, the basis of its
evaluations and discriminations, while artists discover some larger
unified context for their individual effort. Both artists and critics may
articulate this enlarged awareness in terms of a general aesthetic goal,
a set of indispensable values without which no great art can be produced; or, more simply, in terms of their admiration for some revolutionary work of individual mastery, the kind of 'classical'
achievement which collectors lobby to purchase and around which
tourists cluster in a museum. In all these cases, some idea of *canon* supplies the blueprint, the foundations and the capstone to the unpredictable, dynamic, continuous narrative that Gombrich simply calls
'the story of art'.

DOING THINGS WITH CANONS:
THE WORKSHOP OF CREATION

Although Gombrich has devoted many pages to each of these three
canons, the 'canon' most often cited in his own work remains the first,
the basic 'how to' canon of artistic creation. Gombrich cannot conceive of the story of art without some sustained historical discussion
of the techniques and conventions by which artists acquire the basic
skills of artistic representation. He notes, in support of the functionalism of this part of his argument, the tendency of even the most
idiosyncratic or avant-garde artists to conform to shared cultural
assumptions about the channels for their deformations, and the
tendency of most art history to reinforce these assumptions by its
close attention to the artistic environments of its canonized works.

This overwhelming emphasis on acquired techniques and conventions sets Gombrich in the teeth of influential contemporary views of art creation and art history. Even more strongly than poets and novelists, a succession of twentieth-century artists and critics has affirmed the importance of expression as the fount of aesthetic creation. According to the powerful accounts of Picasso and Van Gogh, expression validates the artist's vision by channelling to consciousness images that originate in the unconscious mind. In the same way, primitive works become for André Malraux the expression of an aboriginal unconscious, a taproot to a pristine sacredness the modern artist must re-create through long acquaintanceship with his own irrationality.

A view of art centred on expression will account for its ecstatic properties, its power to overwhelm matter with vision. But if the storehouse of expression lies in the individual visionary consciousness, what happens to the multitude of artists who are not visionaries? What of the paintings of the seventeenth-century Dutch masters, where 'the art of describing' far exceeds the art of expressing?[12] How can expression account for the fact that, from time to time, schools of art have emerged or individual artists have 'expressed' themselves in similar ways? How does an expressionist theory of art explain the similarities between a Dali and a Magritte?

Against those who champion the claims of expression lie the artists and historians who champion imitation. If the first group finds its inspiration in the individual psyche, the second searches for it in the world of nature. For this group, the field trip or modelling session replaces the dream or the psychoanalyst's couch as the stimulus to artistic activity. Yet if the idea of art as expression fails to account for the resemblances between works of art, then the idea of art as imitation elides the differences between William Morris and Sir Joshua Reynolds, who both thought they imitated nature; or between Goya and Frans Hals, whose portraits 'from the life' work from entirely different premisses.

Perhaps Gombrich's greatest contribution to art history lies in his ability to give an account of artistic production which sidesteps the extreme claims made by the champions of expression and of imitation. Presented most extensively in *Art and Illusion* (1960) and *Meditations on a Hobby Horse* (1963), Gombrich's theory derives from his close attention to the stages of artistic creation – from his forays, as it were, into the artistic workshop. To see art either as expression or as a direct, unmediated imitation of nature is, he argues, to overlook the fact that, right up to the nineteenth century, most artists 'did not follow an inner voice, but an external commission which laid down that the projected work be firmly based upon the patterns already established for works of that kind'.[13] Long before such artists created independent works, their long apprenticeship in some master's school inculcated the 'time-hallowed formulas' by which they learned to compose a recognizable face. The long-unchallenged status of these 'canonical forms' turns much of Greek art and medieval painting into the disciplined practice of an acquired skill, 'a craft demanding the mastery of traditional formulas'.[14] Such formulae supply the artist not just with a basic vocabulary for the depiction of recurrent emotions or situations but with a direct channel to audience understanding and response.

Gombrich's championship of this practical 'how to' canon, his discussions of its earlier history and of its hidden role in later, more obviously expressive art, places him in direct opposition to the two prevailing schools. On one side, artists from Reynolds to Monet advertise their concern with the representation of the visible world. On the other side, artists such as Klee and Dali plumb the unconscious in their quest for suggestive images to commit to canvas. Both these goals strike Gombrich as excessively ambitious, a bid to get too far too soon. He comments: 'Without a medium and without a schema which can be moulded and modified, no artist could imitate reality.'[15] He urges modern artists to look more favourably on what the Egyptians and Greeks called 'their schemata; they referred to them as the canon, the basic geometric relationships which the artist must know for the construction of a plausible figure' (AI, 126). Just as a language needs accidence and grammar to become comprehensible, so canons route artistic representation along familiar, recognizable grids of reference. Like Northrop Frye, Gombrich underlines the intelligible and transmissible properties of an artistic language. Both critics stand at the pole directly opposite such twentieth-century theorists as Jacques Derrida, Paul de Man, Anton Ehrenzweig and Harold Rosenberg, who emphasize the non-transmissible, uncanny or anarchic elements of perception, language, and artistic representation.

One of the most important functions of a canon, in Gombrich's view, lies in the provision of basic formulae that all artists, whether classroom doodlers or Leonardo da Vincis, need to rough out their ideas. After recalling the nursery-school method that taught him to sketch a recognizable figure in a few strokes, Gombrich describes the refinement of this process in the drawing books and design manuals which even today supply the apprentice with a repertoire of basic shapes and figures. In a more or less sophisticated form, such primers for the neophyte continue to circulate widely, schooling the young artist in the accidence and rudimentary syntax of drawing an animal or a tree. These works, observes Gombrich, 'teach a simple canon and show how to construct the required vocabulary out of basic geometric forms, easy to remember and easy to draw, like the cat I learned to draw as a child' (AI, 127).

Gombrich thinks that acceptance and use of the basic vocabulary provided by a 'how to' canon goes beyond neophytes and apprentices in the early ages of art. His investigations of the 'experiments' concluded by Renaissance artists prove that Leonardo or Ghiberti did not flout rules so much as refine them, an important rebuttal to the freewheeling anarchism of Picasso or Klee. Even in the early nineteenth century, John Constable, who reputedly described his pictorial aim as 'to forget that I have ever seen a picture' (AI, 149), consulted a drawing book by Alexander Cozens to show his pupils how to sketch a natural, lifelike cloud. Indeed, as Gombrich triumphantly points out, Constable also deployed Cozens's book in his own work to elicit 'a series of possibilities, of schemata, which should increase his awareness through visual classification' (AI, 151). In other words, what the medieval artist might have viewed as an end against which to measure his own imperfect execution, Constable used as a perceptual vehicle, a suggestive canon that served as a freely chosen aesthetic starting point rather than as a set of culturally reinforced minimum standards. As late as the eighteenth century, Gombrich remarks, 'the sway of the pattern was unchallenged' (AI, 135), as artists continued to work on more complex variants of an inherited traditional canon, learning from some pattern book 'acquired formulas' (AI, 129) for the presentation of a tree, a cloud, a madonna in mourning, or a crucifixion scene. Since 'without a medium and without a schema which can be moulded and modified, no artist could imitate reality' (AI, 126), the aid to creation supplied by a 'how to' canon will always remain, even in the art of the future, a vital artistic resource.

Gombrich details many instances of artistic use of some 'how to' canon in the later episodes of his story of art, but he finds his largest number of illustrations when he discusses the heyday of the 'how to' canon from Greek art to the Florentine trecento. Since much classical sculpture represented figures drawn from mythology (the Laocoön or the Hercules Farnese) or from recurring cultural situations (the Dying Gladiator), the 'how to' canon served an important function during the Renaissance, by enabling 'the budding artist . . . to master

the basic vocabulary of human types and gestures' (ROHA, 98).
When medieval painters and craftsmen illustrated familiar scenes
from Scripture by means of conventional figures and imagery, they
referred to a similar schema or 'canon'. In a lengthy demonstration
of the canonical basis of medieval art, Gombrich quotes approvingly
Millard Meiss's description of 'the comparatively canonical form'
(ROHA, 50) of the *sinopie* which allowed Florentine fresco painters
to divide their work into a series of preliminary programmed steps.
The status of these outlines has remained ambiguous since their
exhibition in 1958. In *Reflections on the History of Art* Gombrich tells the
story of how decay and natural hazards destroyed the surface of the
frescoes at the Campo Santo at Pisa and in this way 'revealed to the
general public the preparatory drawings known as *sinopie*' (ROHA,
46). Some historians, misled by the habit of judging all art by the standards of the latest art, have compared these *sinopie* to 'the drafts of
a great poet, recording his inspiration, his search, his rejections, and
his triumphant solutions' (ROHA, 50). For these historians –
historians whom Gombrich sees as burdened with the unhistorical
assumptions of postmedieval art, labouring to find revelations under
every stone – the *sinopie* embody the first stirrings of artistic inspiration. Gombrich himself thinks rather that they served as the
preliminary notations which the artists set down in preparation for
their final brushwork. They are, he thinks, best compared to

> the draft of a legal document which contains a large proportion of
> time-hallowed formulas. In drafting such a text the notary will not
> need to write out these formulas in full, but will simply indicate
> them with a few abbreviated scrawls which his scribe will be able
> to read and write out. These rapid strokes, then, may conceivably
> look similar to those of a poet driven along by the fury of inspira-
> tion, but their meaning bears no comparison. . . . The abbrevia-
> tions and simplifications which delight the modern observer
> because they remind him of Matisse tell the historian that once
> communication served the need of the workshop and stood in no
> need of redundancies, while today it is the public who want to feel
> part of the workshop. (ROHA, 50)

Since so much of the art of the past consisted in learning the power
of precedent, it behoves the historian of the present to pay precedent
a similar respect. Because Gombrich the aesthetician draws on
massive evidence of a human disposition to order new material in
conformity with previously acquired expectations, Gombrich the

historian emphasizes the importance of tracking down the assumptions of the artist's society and circle. 'We must try to relearn', he emphasizes, 'the difference between stimulation through self-projection . . . and that enrichment that comes from an understanding, however dim and imperfect, of what a great work of art is *intended* to convey' (MHH, 85). At all times, Gombrich powerfully states, the historian should attempt to learn the context in which communities of artists conceived of their role, the conventions by which they mediate their art to their patrons or buyers, and the intellectual milieu in which their art emerges.

And beyond all these enquiries lies the common thread of art conceived of not just as individual experience or expression but as a teachable and communicable skill. Historians of art cannot grasp the significance of the *sinopie* of the Florentine trecento unless they admit the importance of teamwork from inception to execution. For drawings such as these furnished artists with 'shorthand indications of schemata they and their apprentices almost knew by heart' (ROHA, 50). For Gombrich, the story of art begins in the workshop, as apprentice artists learn basic skills by means of a canon. 'There are few aspects of the past ', he remarks, 'that are more difficult for us to grasp and recapture than the old experience of schooling', the time customarily spent 'copying the works of the great' (AI, 134). Gombrich cannot conceive of an art that exists as a purely solitary activity, emptied of the conventions and references which allow individual makers to transcend their personal limitations and to communicate with an unknown audience.

His strong sense of artistic milieux, of social conventions and intellectual currents, encourages Gombrich to extend his account of the 'how to' canon to the art we associate with the birth of the modern world. Throughout *Art and Illusion*, a book noted for its sophisticated paradigms of artistic representation, this first canon, a canon of methods, apprenticeships, and schoolbooks, emerges with unexpected importance. In a culture fascinated by such intangibles as 'imagination' and 'inspiration', the 'will to form' of Gombrich's teacher Alois Riegl or the 'will to mastery' of his adversary André Malraux, his own practical 'how to' canon inevitably falls into oblivion. To remedy this neglect he shows how, at the height of the Renaissance, Leonardo's sketches and ideograms compiled an inventory of natural forms. This kind of work, Gombrich believes, 'has a very practical basis', since it answers the artist's need 'for a scheme with which to grasp the infinite variety of this world of change' (AI, 132-3). For artists such as Michelangelo and Leonardo, the schema recorded in an inherited 'how to' canon becomes a 'starting point for corrections, adjustments, adaptations, the means to probe reality and to wrestle with the particular' (AI, 148). Paradoxically, as Renaissance art moves towards the representation of an increasingly complex reality, it calls more and more often on such schema to provide basic laws of construction and a versatile repertoire of natural forms. In an art conceived of as the fulfilment of known expectations by familiar means, the 'how to' canon supplies basic practical skills which serve as the building blocks of a more complex achievement. Like a language, such a canon ensures that in a particular culture aspiring artists can make themselves understood. Through its means they can produce a plausible figure, a recognizable landscape, or a meaningful dramatic gesture. Ideas of plausibility, recognition and meaning will vary widely from culture to culture, but without an acceptable syntax of lifelikeness or plausibility artists would be left with the impossible daily task of reinventing their own traditions. Without such elementary conventions art could not be taught, nor could art history survive as a discipline.

BREAKING THE MOULDS: THE 'HOW TO' CANON

The 'how to' interpretation of *canon* accounts satisfactorily for the continuities in art and in art history. For artists working in stable social conditions or in a difficult aesthetic medium, such canonical formulae become an overwhelming necessity. What the 'how to' canon does less well is account for the fact that artists periodically try to change the canon, to abandon a received schema as 'implausible' and attack their fellow artists as 'unnatural'. It is at this point that Gombrich's second idea of *canon* emerges. In all his works he emphasizes again and again that no artists can learn basic skills from scratch, but he also acknowledges that few artists want to confine themselves for ever to the rehearsal of known techniques. As he conceives it, the history of art consists of a series of paradigms to be broken, where every inherited model must be rebuilt because of the individual artist's unending quest for perfection. The moment when groups of artists become self-conscious in their use of schemata, when they begin to search more widely among the available models, signals the birth of the 'how we' canon, the canon by which artists attempt to broaden the basis and heighten the significance of the conventions governing contemporary art, an art to which Gombrich gives no special status except as the art-in-the-making of each successive age.

As Gombrich emphasizes throughout his discussion of his first, 'how to' canon, even the basic sense of *canon* as an anthology of precedents for copying carries a potential metaphysical charge. For what is the status of the precedent? If artists come to see the precedent as a perfect pattern, then the story of art turns from the acquisition of skills to a quest for a past perfection. If, on the other hand, the precedent becomes a model to be transformed and refined as new knowledge appears, then art turns into a battleground between past and present, tradition and innovation. As artists raise their conception of their activities, artistic institutions share fewer and fewer similarities with masonry or carpentry. From the beginning of the fifteenth century, a significant number of painters and sculptors reject the idea of the artist transmitted to them by tradition. They no longer wish to create according to time-honoured formulae, they no longer see their patrons as controlling every detail of their commission. Instead, they view art as an enterprise conducted by practitioners who enjoy a status equal to poets, orators and philosophers, practitioners engaged in an activity whose autonomy becomes the sign and the means of its essential perfection. Artists such as Michelangelo and Bernini regard popes and princes as their equals. They conceive of their art as evoking the actual presence of the sacred rather than as a simple re-creation of clerically authorized episodes.

Gombrich illustrates this movement from the conventional to the self-conscious and innovative in his exemplary parable of Lorenzo Ghiberti's work on the 'Gates of Paradise' for the Baptistry at Florence. Ghiberti cast two doors, the first of which he rendered in a manner appropriate to the expectations of a trecento craftsman. In this work he followed the time-honoured pattern of executing a commission, matching his own door to the one constructed a century earlier by Andrea Pisano. His second door, however, marks a complete shift in reference, with its ingenious decorations and virtuoso allusions to classical art. Gombrich explains this total change in style by showing how Ghiberti's participation in the learned activities of fifteenth-century Florence transformed his artistic activity. In 'The Renaissance Conception of Artistic Progress and Its Consequences', Gombrich narrates the story of Ghiberti's attachment to a circle of orators and philosophers that included Niccolò Niccoli and Poggio Bracciolini. In this circle Ghiberti first encountered Pliny's discussion of the bronze sculptor Lysippus, who modified the canon he inherited from the Greeks in the interests of 'nature' without abandoning the pleasing regularity of art. In effect, Ghiberti made

Lysippus's achievement his own goal. Paradoxically, Ghiberti's immersion in classical precedent challenged him to match the achievement of Praxiteles and Lysippus.

By the time he joined this humanist circle, Ghiberti had already carved the first of his doors. Obviously, his reading in the classical humanists, in Pliny, Cicero, and Quintilian, spurred him to reinterpret his task as he worked on his second door. Its virtuosity, audacity and ingenuity reflect Ghiberti's philosophical sophistication and his appeal to an alternative canon derived from the standards of antiquity. As Gombrich points out, Ghiberti 'was here deliberately trying to emulate the role of Lysippus and to change the canon'.[16] Instead of fulfilling the expectations of his patrons and immediate predecessors, Ghiberti saw himself as participating in an ideal company of artists – a company united, despite their separation in time, by the goal of representing nature in art.

When he worked on his first door, Gombrich remarks, 'there is no evidence that . . . Ghiberti saw himself as anything but a craftsman who had received an important commission' (NF, 4). By the time he worked on the second door, 'the artist had not only to think of his commission but of his mission. This mission was to add to the glory of the age through the progress of art' (NF, 3). Paradoxically, it was Ghiberti's learning and the elevated conception of art fostered by his researches in art history that allowed him to revolutionize the canon. By a typical Gombrichian thrust, the impetus to Ghiberti's innovations comes from academic models and from his study of the past. As he read Pliny's discussion of ancient art, Ghiberti began to see himself 'in the stream of history, deliberately re-evoking and reliving the past and striking out towards a new future' (NF, 6). His revolution, it must be emphasized, did not involve the abandonment of the canon or even its modernization, but the revival of an older canon derived from classical art which Ghiberti deployed as part of a distinctly contemporary interpretation of his artistic mission. In Gombrich's story of art, every innovation has its precedent, every precedent has the power to attack the complacencies of the present.

Again and again, Gombrich makes it clear that the elevated view of artistic creation fostered by Renaissance humanism does not demote the inherited canons. Even in an age infected with 'this constant search, this sacred discontent' (AI, 148), those canons continued to serve as the basic unit of artistic enquiry, the base line against which the artist's search for perfection would constantly be carried out. In the Middle Ages, 'canon' suggests a schema to be observed.

In postmedieval art, 'canon' becomes a starting point for explorations and revisions, the means of charting a slippery, shifting relationship between general pattern and particular instance. The crucial distinction between medieval and modern art, in Gombrich's view, does not lie in the emergence of some new world view but in an increasing artistic willingness to modify inherited formulae in the light of contemporary experience and knowledge. As their governing paradigm shifts from precedent to experiment, artists align themselves with scientists. Their works 'exist not only for their own sake but also to demonstrate certain problem-solutions' (NF, 7). Leonardo and Raphael transform the sketch from the reproduction of a formula into an experiment, a perpetual process of theorization, observation and error. In Renaissance art, instead of serving as a 'filing system' (AI, 151), the 'new canon' (NF, 6) becomes an instrument of problem-solving. As Gombrich presents it, the 'how we' canon invoked by post-Renaissance artists serves less and less as an exemplar or ground-plan and more and more as a stimulus to natural observation and aesthetic research. In this way, the 'how we' canon fulfils the claims of 'progress' so often made by artists and art historians. This, the second of Gombrich's three canons, presents the history of art as a continuous narrative in which generations of artists rebel against their immediate predecessors by selecting alternative schemata derived from classical or primitive art, or even from nature itself.

But as Gombrich also shows, the elevation of art implicit in the 'how we' canon, added to the glorification of illustrious artists from the distant past, produces, at all periods of art, a third canon, a canon high in its claims and extremely difficult to dislodge. To speak, as Gombrich himself does quite unrepentantly, in terms of 'standards' and 'traditions' lifts the canon above the short cuts that supply a journeyman with basic skills or the visual experiments mounted in Renaissance sketchbooks. As Gombrich clearly acknowledges, a basic law of canon formation is that the canons outgrow their original premisses. If the 'how to' canon starts out as a set of provisional, *ad hoc* arrangements that instruct a tyro in some basic shorthand; if the 'how we' canon divorces individual artists from the overworked traditions of older living masters, freeing them to assert a new relationship with nature and the aesthetic past, still both canons eventually outgrow their initial requirements. At this stage emerges the third canon, the 'why we' canon or canon of perfection, a changeless model of artistic works admired by artists and audiences through the centuries.

THE PERFECT CANON

The shift from a set of initiating skills to a measuring rod of artistic and cultural perfection has far-reaching consequences for the practice and theory of art. Yet as Gombrich wryly points out, the crucial shift occurs at the very beginning of the story of art, not in its demented latter days. Greek sculpture follows the full arc of canonical possibility, beginning as a 'how to' classroom model and ending as a 'why we' model encompassing both the master-works and the values they represent. In fact, Gombrich's first instance of what he variously calls the 'canon of excellence', 'canon of mastery', and 'canon of perfection' comes as early as the fifth century BC, when Polycletus

> created what was called the perfect canon or schema of the fine body in his Doryphoros; in the fourth century, so we read in the ancient authors, Praxiteles added grace, and finally, at the time of Alexander the Great, Lysippus claimed that he followed Nature alone, in other words that a statue such as his Apoxyomenos is like a cast from nature.[17]

Gombrich's discussion shows that an institution devised to initiate inevitably transforms itself into one designed to exemplify. This is not so surprising – the average school, for example, rarely contents itself with coaching the minimum requirements from its students. Sooner or later, some ambitious teacher will raise the standards for the most promising pupils. In the same way, few writers in any period have confined their notions of excellence to the transmission of skills monitored by artists themselves. In the course of time the conditions of entry to artistic academies are raised, targets are set, and patterns of excellence become enshrined. By degrees, a loose set of arrangements designed to facilitate the production of art becomes an institution that sets ever-increasing standards of perfection.

As the 'how to' and 'how we' canons harden from an induction to an imperative, the canon changes shape from a contract to a taboo. As Gombrich is well aware, the 'why we' canon attracts with full force 'the dogmatism which so often became associated with the canon' (ROHA, 99). The academy translates the canon for its own purposes, making a set of practices originally designed to educate novices into rule books calculated to regulate their activities. The models of classical art are invested with the properties of law and instead of serving as instruments of pedagogic convenience become the arbiters of taste itself. It is at this point that sides polarize, since rejection of the canon of excellence appears 'to threaten the community of values on which civilization depends' (ROHA, 99). As *canon* shifts from a means of elementary imitation to the judge of ultimate perfection, adherence to its hardening rules becomes identified with obedience to the laws of nature itself, and an army of enforcement agencies – academies, textbooks, lectures, treatises – emerges to institutionalize the canon and to make it the basis of all future artistic achievement.

Gombrich uses the exemplary history of Greek sculpture to show the divisive consequences of this process. As he makes clear, the paradox by which an institution designed to facilitate the production of art by degrees makes art impossible will merit close investigation. In the classrooms of eighteenth-century Europe, Greek sculpture dominated the curriculum, urging on apprentices 'the implied or explicit claim of the canon to embody and to teach the "rules" of art' (ROHA, 97). Art historians and critics in the new schools of 'classical' aesthetics begin to use Greek art as a criterion of aesthetic value, invoking it as a measuring rod for the art of cultures and periods remote from Greece. Gombrich cites the example of the German philosopher Winckelmann, for whom Greek art becomes the sole arbiter of beauty: 'To him there was only one . . . perfection, the Greek canon of beauty' (ROHA, 17). Through Winckelmann's example, the preeminence of Greece stretched beyond art into ethics and philosophy, and the cult of Hellenism became the canonical creed for the devotees of what came to be known as 'high culture'. In the work of Arnold and Pater, for instance, Greece embodies a long-vanished perfection in civilized living, a perfection that stretches from art to life. For these authors, 'Hellenism' becomes a treasured value system as well as a treasure house of masterpieces, the rallying cry for a militant elite disturbed by the consequences of a new industrial order.

A backlash against this cult of the classical naturally followed, a fervently espoused nineteenth-century orthodoxy breeding in the twentieth century its corresponding dissent. As Gombrich presents it, the nineteenth and twentieth centuries become the seat of a great divide. On one side stand the supporters of the avant-garde, with their belief in artistic freedom, their cult of self-expression, and their unswayable convictions about the relativity of taste. On the other side stands the art of the academy, with its cult of precedent, its emphasis on rules learned, perfected and applied, and its impositions of the dogma of tradition on the spontaneity of youth. Gombrich describes how, during the 1950s, students at an American Midwestern college became so exasperated with drawing from classical reproductions that they hurled their plaster statues from their classroom windows. At this point he shrewdly notes that

> All would have been well if critics of the past had confined themselves to recommending the canon of ancient statues merely as a repertory of types more easily studied and less expensive to maintain than hired models. But it lies in the dynamic of this situation that soon living bodies were judged by the degree of their correspondence to the canonic figures and that few scored well on this test. (ROHA, 98)

The shift from *canon* as an instrument designed to initiate the young to *canon* as a means of regulating their activities and judging their achievements triggers off hostilities which Gombrich finds unnecessary. By confusing works of art with natural forms, the teachers at this college only widened the gap between tradition and individual creation. As Gombrich told Quentin Bell, 'What was said of astrology may also apply to the canon: "The stars incline, but they do not compel"' (II, 183).

Why does a canon of excellence offend twentieth-century assumptions so badly? In the first place, of course, it violates modern sensibilities by suggesting that creation operates by obeying rules rather than dismantling them. Modern artists reject any attempt to formulate rules for artistic creation because of a climate of opinion that views composition as a spontaneous process conforming only to the compulsions of an inner prompting. In this climate, Greece itself becomes just one more civilization, no more to be praised than any other in the light of a new relativism that owes little to Montaigne. No ideal order – no 'nature', no 'Hellenism', no 'empire' – stands behind a twentieth-century masterpiece such as Picasso's *Guernica*, although Picasso could hardly have painted his masterpiece without training and expertise in traditional forms.

In the second place, the canon of excellence offends because it confers on the past the authority to regulate the present. The student reaction Gombrich cites signals the strength of a massive twentieth-century movement away from neoclassical assumptions which presented art as the imitation of permanent models encoded by antiquity. Modern artists repeatedly speak of art as their one source of freedom in a world of perpetually increasing constraint. For this reason, the idea of a canon of excellence as a binding contract repels many practising artists. As Gombrich points out, 'No dogma of the

Classical creed is more alien to twentieth-century views of art than this acceptance of authority. . . . The acceptance of a canon of ancient statues . . . takes us a step further towards an apparently arbitrary cultural authoritarianism' (ROHA, 97–98). When 'why we' becomes a directive more than a demonstration, the prospect of a rift between artist and critic, academy and avant-garde opens up. On the one side emerge the proliferating distinctions between artists 'at the threshold', 'in reaction', 'in decline', and 'at the forefront' – the familiar terms of manifestoes from Vasari onwards; on the other side lurks a canon deplored as authoritarian or antiquarian or hostile to the unprecedented diversity of present needs.

In the third place, and perhaps worst of all, adherents of a canon of excellence insist that not all works and not all cultures rank equally. To say that some works are better or even more useful than others will win few friends in the age of Malraux's 'imaginary museum'. Although Gombrich cites universal norms and responses in order to characterize his 'canon of excellence', he confines his actual illustrations to a restricted roster of European masterpieces, the artistic productions of a tiny minority of the world's inhabitants. In addition, his opponents will note, his case for the validation of the canon of excellence rests on shifting foundations. He sometimes describes this canon as a teaching tool, sometimes as the lodestone of values underpinning civilization itself, and sometimes in terms of psychological patterning and communication with an audience. In all these ways, his suggestion that the few works admitted to the canon of excellence evoke a universal audience response seems to combine catholicity with restriction in a highly suspicious manner.

In fact, his last article in the creed of the canon of excellence points in two puzzling directions. Gombrich rests one part of his argument for such a canon on the echoes stirred in the universal bosom in the presence of Leonardo's *Mona Lisa*, Michelangelo's *David*, or Raphael's *Madonna*. He rests the second part on the way these works embody or somehow actualize the workings of a value system greater than themselves. It is not easy to reconcile either position with the functionalism of Gombrich's other two canons. His arguments for the universal emotions stirred by the works in his canon of excellence lack the scientific ballast supplied with the 'how to' and 'how we' canons. His evidence for the 'why we' canon remains largely anecdotal, as when he recalls the

old civil servant, a refugee from Austria close to his hundredth birthday, who told me that during sleepless nights, he took a walk through the Louvre, as he remembered it from the beginning of the century, and could decide in front of which painting he wanted to stop this time so that he could look at it closely. (II, 190)

Although the anecdotes remain undeniably powerful ones, they do not compare with the wealth of scientific, cultural and historical evidence Gombrich adduces in support of his other canons. When he suggests that canonical art provokes deep responses which provide the basis for the historian's culturally specific investigations, he appears to contradict his earlier influential theories about the functional basis of artistic conventions by moving from a perceptual theory of art to an emotive and perhaps even an idealist one. The attempt to anchor canonicity in a larger humanistic value system potentially undermines the theory that artistic canons conform to biological mechanisms of human response. Gombrich's idea that the works inside the canon of excellence owe their stature in some measure to their embodiment of common values, assumptions and beliefs will find few adherents in an age of pluralism.

GOMBRICH'S APPELLATE COURT: POTENT PRECEDENTS AND MIGHTY JUDGEMENTS

Can the canon of excellence be revalidated for a twentieth-century public? Final validation of any canon will prove treacherous in any age, since the pattern by which one age adduces a larger order from serial examples of excellence, an order the succeeding age strategically undermines, remains almost as old as art itself. Ever since Pliny defined 'canon' as a 'model statue' but also as 'a sort of standard',[18] a dangerous ambiguity of reference has dogged acts of canonical validation. Does *canon* refer to the work itself or to the ideas and schemata the work bodies forth? Behind this uncertainty lies a traditional pairing between *canon* as 'excellent single work, one of a line of that kind' and *canon* as 'scheme of values underlying a line of excellent single works'. A similar pairing extends to the word *classic*, which may refer to an observable set of artistic conventions but also to a nexus of values and beliefs embodied not just in art but in a whole style of living.

More often a confusion than an association, this complex background to the canon of excellence explains why proponents of this strongest and most controversial version of the canon often refer to it in two distinct ways. Employed in the first way, the canon of excellence simply refers to the individual achievements of a particular artist. Leonardo's rendering of light against shade. Dürer's depiction of the natural world, Michelangelo's biblical figures – these artists belong to the canon of excellence on the grounds of demonstrable mastery of specific tasks. But when their works are grouped together with other works and said to point to 'nature', 'culture' or 'tradition' in the abstract, a second canon emerges in which one abstraction – a set of values discerned through a group of works – serves as a defence against modernity, relativism or some other matched abstraction, or as a rigid standard by which to measure all other crea-tions. In this way, the canon of excellence does double duty as a prac-tice and as a dogma. As a practice, it appeals to discrete instances of artistic achievement; as a dogma, it becomes subsumed in some larger scheme of values or ideological blueprint.

In which of these senses does Gombrich invoke the idea of a canon of excellence? We have seen that he periodically endorses a scheme of humanist values behind art's traditionally valued works. However, despite his championship of what in 'The Tradition of General Knowledge' he calls 'the secular creed' (II, 21), he frequently stops to deplore the 'metaphysical fog' (AI, 133) which settles over many discussions of the canon of excellence, investing it with the critic's own moral or political scheme of values. Although Gombrich does not specifically cite them, T. S. Eliot and John Berger, two influential critics from varying disciplines and political camps, illustrate how this canonization of the canon occurs in similar ways in literary criticism and in art history. For Eliot, the classical combination of sensuousness and intelligence that characterizes the poetry of Andrew Marvell comes to represent the civilized values of order, maturity and faith the Anglican critic prizes in a Christian polity. For Berger, Cubist art reflects a willingness to explore possibilities of shape and space the socialist critic transfers to the utopian social order of the future. If Eliot uses Dante to read the provinces a lesson from the metropolis, then Berger looks forward to a new world which will use space as imaginatively as Picasso or Braque for the benefit of the large majority as yet untouched by art.

For Eliot the poet, Dante's fusion of 'depravity's despair and the beatific vision' becomes the grounds for what Eliot the critic calls his 'universality'. Yet, paradoxically, Dante's 'universal' properties arise in the context of an art which is 'the most *European*'. For Berger, the new art of Cubism calls for an end to the 'superstitious awe' instilled by generations of art teachers and overbearing Victorian museums. He agrees that 'great works survive their period', but not 'by virtue of a sort of resurrection'. Artists who see art as 'timeless and eternal' will produce 'still-born works'. Artists and audiences alike must 'recognize the morality of art' by ceasing 'to stand in such superstitious awe of it'. Where Eliot thinks that culture rests on a usable past, Berger links it to the usable future, daring the new public for art to 'have the courage to risk using it for our own immediate, urgent, only important purposes'.[19] Few proponents of a canon of excellence rest content with suggesting that such a canon measures only an artist's power to make satisfying images, *tout court*. Almost imperceptibly, such critics point to a scheme of values that lies behind a line of selected great works or to a desirable civilization those works somehow embody. In their different ways, Eliot and Berger participate in the longest-running story in cultural history: the story of artistic participation in some unfolding motion of the collective superstructure, some ineffable movement towards progress or faith or liberty.

Where does a self-proclaimed sceptic such as Gombrich stand in relation to this story? How can he validate the canon of excellence for twentieth-century audiences without colluding in some such idealist fiction? Gombrich acknowledges a need to defend this, the most treacherous and powerful of his canons, and sets out to meet it in two main ways. His first, perhaps less satisfactory, way involves him in a recitation of the pre-eminence of the canon of excellence in humanistic tradition. Confronted by 'the amputation of the time dimension from our culture' (II, 21) and by mounting attacks on the discredited values associated with 'civilization' and 'tradition', Gombrich has not hesitated to place his considerable authority behind every article of the canonical creed. In the time-honoured fashion of defences of culture, from Arnold's *Culture and Anarchy* to Leavis's *Two Cultures?*, he brushes off attacks on humanistic enquiry from the social sciences and the new field of cultural materialism by observing rather heatedly: 'We were born into our civilization and we owe our orientation to that tradition, which happens to be in bad odour just now' (II, 181).

During the 1970s and 1980s, as Gombrich sees it, 'tradition' merely became unfashionable. To follow or temporize with that fashion would, for a farsighted humanist historian, seem certain death. 'The historian who investigates the reliability of a chronicle cannot', he thinks, 'doubt all accounts of the past without giving up his trade' (II, 181). Of course it was in similar terms, and possibly with similar success, that Erasmus defended Christendom against Martin Luther. Gombrich overlooks the important fact that modern sceptical thinking doubts not just 'the reliability of a chronicle' but the knowledge and assumptions an investigator takes to such a chronicle – the very instruments Gombrich himself understands as fundamentally sound. Critics hostile to the universalist assumptions that provide the constant backcloth to Gombrich's thought argue that 'the common ground of universally human experience' has long been parcelled out among a privileged and cohesive social class, a class in which professors such as Gombrich play a crucial conservative role.

Because Gombrich thinks that professors perform an important custodial service, his championship of 'tradition' and 'civilization' forces him more and more deeply into disputed territory. On occasions, his defences of the canon of excellence teeter between an elucidation of particular art-works of acknowledged mastery and an argument for the social and cultural values implicit in his 'humanist's creed'. At times he seems unsure whether he defends canons of excellence as cultural products or as cultural producers; whether he sees them as the independent creations of individual artists or as pearls on a mighty string worn by 'the tradition'. In recent essays such as 'The Tradition of General Knowledge' and 'Canon and Values in the Visual Arts', Gombrich jettisons the functionalist arguments of his earlier work. These pieces, instead of discussing the canon of excellence as a historical idea or as the specific excellence of a particular artist, present it as a kind of ethical imperative, a source of spiritual illumination that transcends the imaginative organization of the works it comprehends. When Gombrich defends the canon as a humanist dedicated to pushing back the tides of relativism, perpetual innovation or simple nonconformity, his discussion turns into a testimony of faith formulated with a numinousness he would undoubtedly find insufferable in the work of, for example, André Malraux or John Ruskin.

It may be that the conventions of the genre – defences of the humanities from Shelley to Leavis continually erupt into ill-temper – ultimately work against Gombrich's gifts. His second, less controversial, defence of the canon of excellence emerges in his close attention to individual canonical works and to the ways in which artists manipulate and modify the canon in the interest of their own problem-solutions. In the course of elucidating the conventions surrounding canonical masterpieces Gombrich can present himself as a mediator, reminding apologists for the canon of its less than exalted origins as a test of simple capacity, reminding a society inclined to see 'the canon' as a vehicle for creative repression of its usefulness as a stimulus to observation and communication. Instead of characterizing artistic progress in terms of a battleground between academic reactionaries and idol-smashing dissenters, Gombrich wants to supply the materials to write a history of art which can understand change without invariably characterizing it as revolution. This is why, in a collection of essays entitled *Ideals and Idols: Essays on Values in History and in Art*, he affirms his belief that 'there is no developed culture which lacks a canon of achievements handed down in tradition as a touchstone of excellence' (II, 156).

Part of the ongoing business of art history involves the launching of new reputations and the exhumation of old movements. In the middle of all this necessary flux, Gombrich sees the canon of excellence as the stable basis for judgement and evaluation offered by a set of acknowledged masterpieces. Because it transmits authoritative judgements, the canon of excellence functions as a kind of appellate court which enables art history to persist as a unified discipline. Defenders of this discipline need never, Gombrich implies, feel apologetic. In a review of Francis Haskell's *Rediscoveries in Art*, he shows how the author gradually pares down the canon of mastery to Raphael, Titian and Rubens, and then becomes alarmed at the narrow ground on which he appears to stand. But, asks Gombrich, is Haskell's canon 'all that limited?' He adds:

> As long as we retain this canon of artistic mastery we also know what we mean by a great painting. Anyone intending to file an application for rediscovery on behalf of one of the Salon painters still has to accept the fact that the case will come before a formidable tribunal. (ROHA, 167)

As Gombrich sees it, the problems posed by artistic masterpieces will not be solved by a simple shift of critical attention to other, previously marginalized works. For this reason he has rarely entered into contemporary debates about the canon of works accredited to individual artists, the problem of whether we should expand the Poussin canon to encompass an unattractive or stylistically odd painting or the grounds of the traditional distinction between a work emanating from the Rubens studio and a Rubens masterpiece. Instead of allowing these problems to throw the whole idea of a canon of excellence into disarray, Gombrich emphasizes the need for students of art history to have a firm grounding in the shifting conventions behind artistic activity, the changing milieu of the artistic workshop. He also underlines the artists' own quest for perfection, a quest as central to art history as the discovery of perspective. Rembrandt's genius does not wane because new research proves that collaborators played a significant part in work previously regarded as purely Rembrandt's. Gombrich assumes that any historian will know in detail the materials, the working conditions, and the daily assumptions of the artists studied. He also concedes that even permanently valuable art such as Rembrandt's reflects the expectations of its original audience and the day-to-day operations of a large, complex studio. He thinks it is legitimate to ask, even for works in the canon of excellence, contingent questions such as What did it sell for? Why did she buy it? Was he mad when he painted it?

Yet paradoxically, the very ambitiousness of the canon of excellence, its tendency to pitch present and past in a battle for rivalry and pre-eminence, encourages critics and audiences to use it as a measuring rod for individual artistic achievement – beating Uccello or Botticelli with the rod of Raphael, as it were. In an attempt to right the balance, to reanchor the canon of excellence to the firm ground of artistic process, Gombrich has declared that 'the canon is our starting point, our guiding theory about that aspect of image-making we call mastery' (II, 165). Although he describes himself as a 'keeper of the canon' (II, 165), his discussions of the canon of excellence perhaps rest more securely on its first, more practical basis, the appeal to the successful individual work, than on its other, more disputed ground, the resort to some immutable court of final appeal.

When Gombrich turns from the production of art to its reception, his most convincing discussions emerge from his attempt to ground the canon of excellence in the non-doctrinal areas of artistic convention and audience response. In *Ideals and Idols*, a collection of reviews which treats such canonical instances as Greek sculpture, Leonardo, Rubens, Michelangelo and Raphael, he reaffirms his belief in the 'universality' of the canon of mastery, even as he concedes that 'cultures differ in the kind of mastery they value' (II, 156). Rather than explaining the popularity of valued works in terms of their alignment with some pervasive ideology, Gombrich measures their success by their power to communicate with an audience. 'All the arts', he observes, 'whether music, calligraphy, dancing, poetry, painting, or architecture, send their roots deep down into the common ground of universally human response' (II, 158-9). Cultural relativism has no answer to the continuing curiosity and interest stimulated by the *Mona Lisa* or the Laocoön. The invocation of specific cultural values these works are supposed to represent fails to register the surprise and awe felt in the presence of the masterpieces themselves. Time and time again, Gombrich hints at misgivings about his own effort to contain the canon of excellence in a functionalist framework, since no practical criteria he can invoke appropriately describe not just the frequency but also the intensity of certain recurring patterns of audience response.

As Gombrich does not fail to point out, contemporary repugnance towards the rhetoric of scholarly art history fails to account for the heightened sensibilities, the deepened perceptions and emotions, triggered by traditional canonical works:

> It sounds so much safer to talk of 'plastic values' or 'closed forms' than to use the language Socrates used in his talk to artists. Nobody wants to revive the gush, not even that of Winckelmann. But a fear of M. Dubuffet's strictures should not prevent us from breaking this taboo and admitting that Greek art tries to place us face to face with the illusion of beauty at its most enthralling, most human and most unreal. The relativity of this illusion can surely be overstated. Granted that the canon varies, to deny the common core in this experience would mean to deny the unity of mankind. (ROHA, 17)

This invocation of the 'most enthralling, most human and most unreal' emotions called forth by 'the illusion of beauty' aligns Gombrich's canon of excellence with Kant's criterion for the sublime, which stirs our minds with 'a reference to something *absolutely great*', while simultaneously enforcing on us an 'inner perception of the inadequacy of every standard of sense to serve for the rational estimation of magnitude'.[20] As Gombrich sees it, sublime, rather than culturally conditioned, responses to canonical works underpin their legislative authority. The canon of excellence rests, ultimately, on the inability of an audience to withhold its instinctive projection into the works this canon presents to view. The same psychological patterns that provoke the artist to creation govern the audience's initial reception and the work's lasting fame. Artist and audience share an often unconscious belief in the mystery and magic of the image; the works included in the canon of excellence simply intensify this mystery and magic to their uttermost degree. In this way, the argument for a canon of excellence becomes an argument about the human disposition towards recurring images and responses. Individual men and women do not create the canon of excellence so much as participate in it. It precedes them and lasts long after them, like nature or God.

However alien it appears to contemporary sensibilities, the 'why we' canon plays a vital role in Gombrich's programme. Beyond the practical necessity of the 'how to' and 'how we' canons, the canon of excellence reflects his continuing faith in the human organism and in its power to enforce canons of order. In *The Sense of Order* (1978), his large work on decorative art, he once again affirms his belief in a biological predisposition to order:

> We could not function if we were not attuned to certain regularities. This tuning, moreover, could never have come about by learning; on the contrary, we could never have gathered any experience of the world if we lacked that sense of order which allows us to categorize our surroundings according to degrees of regularity, and its obverse. (SO, 113)

When artists represent nature in the process of change or human beings in motion, they sophisticate their basic canon without abandoning it. Give this canon a certain prestige, complicate it by the addition of other variables, and the 'how we' canon emerges to view. But what kind of order lies behind the canon of excellence? Gombrich remains unsatisfied by the merely pedagogic order he describes when he points to the classroom authority enjoyed by certain works. If he could rest content with the suggestion that 'If you want to represent a noble warrior dying on the battlefield, study the *Dying Gladiator* and you cannot go wrong' (ROHA, 98), then his position might remain unassailable. Instead, he oscillates between a standard lodged in a particular work and a standard he imputes to universal responses shared by all audiences for art.

The pattern of these responses can be scientifically verified, but not the canonical aura which Gombrich periodically attaches to them. At times, his representations of the canon of excellence go beyond even the most complex set of rules for artistic creation and case laws for critical judgement. Although it supports his other canons in performing these functions, the canon of excellence seems to Gombrich to tap some even deeper layer of human response or projection, a layer science can confirm but not explain. Gombrich's interest in this deep area of response becomes apparent in his recollections of Churchill's funeral:

> When the barge with the coffin of Winston Churchill traveled up the river Thames the cranes on either side of the embankment lowered their long necks as if in homage to the war leader. These cranes were not images, let alone representations, but for a fleeting moment the imagination turned them into monsters of steel who joined in the universal emotion.[21]

Although he remains to this day one of the most scientific, as well as the most sceptical, of art historians, Gombrich can invoke at climactic moments some darkly appealing images and patterns. For as long as our ideas about our human origins and ends carry deep mythic resonances, a canon of excellence will manifest itself, he implies, as a kind of a ghostly, tutelary presence, a recurring feature of artistic patterns and audience responses alike.

FROM DARK PARADIGM TO DARK BELIEF: GOMBRICH'S CANONICAL CREED

Of the four critics to be analysed in detail in this book, Gombrich offers by far the most emphatic defence of the traditional canon of great masterpieces. Even so, as we have seen, Gombrich's defence of the canon remains far from untouched by the arguments of his opponents. This chapter has described the process by which he moves from the massive, unbroken and implicit declaration of faith in canons mounted in *The Story of Art* and *Art and Illusion* to the more harassed, explicit affirmations of *Ideals and Idols*. The wealth of research and documentation in Gombrich's works combines with an unusual resemblance to heroic narrative, in which giants such as Leonardo, Vermeer and Rubens, pioneers such as Giotto and Masaccio, historians such as Vasari, Wölfflin and Malraux all merge seamlessly in a massive story.

Gombrich's major contribution to the history of the canon emerges in his development of a theory and a story of art which revalidate Vasari's great narrative without necessarily subscribing to its implications for future artistic production. As Gombrich points out, Vasari's 'story of the rise of the arts to perfection' by 'the establishment of a canon of great masters' (ROHA, 173) points to an inevitable decline in artistic quality once those masters expire. Against this model of perfection and decline, Gombrich sets his more functional account of a canon that allows artists to formulate their own problems, to regulate their own activities, and to pool their shared assumptions. In all these ways, Gombrich's 'how to' and 'how we' canons allow Vasari's story to continue long after the sixteenth century. The implicit belief behind his extension of Vasari's *Lives of the Most Eminent Painters*, the belief that the story of art production and the story of art appreciation combine as double plots in one coherent and continuous narrative, strengthens his conviction that both activities originate in common powers of perception latent in any human being. Without this basic human capacity, the continuous interplay between artistic convention and innovative representation by which he propels forward his story of art would lose all its significance.

Yet Gombrich's later work obviously presses its claims for a canon latent in universal human perception with some increased sense of harassment. The publication of *Ideals and Idols* and *Tributes* displays a writer for whom the story of art has shifted from a narrative to a creed, a creed to be defended against bureaucrats from without and heretics from within. Gombrich's sense of his intellectual identity rests on a long line of family likeness that stretches from Vasari to Burckhardt, a line of succession that in recent years has been badly disturbed. For some of his successors in art history, the 'canon of excellence' remains inextricably tainted with the Eurocentric, Christian, and elitist values they see as excluding too much of the non-Christian, non-European world. How, writers such as Murray Krieger have asked, can canons of representation adopted for fifth-century Greeks remain useful for twentieth-century artists or historians? Also subject to considerable late-twentieth-century scrutiny is Gombrich's theory of artistic creation as 'piecemeal engineering', a gradual process of paradigm learning and adjustment set in the context of a common movement sharing common principles (a canon of acceptable conventions, as it were). This theory, it is suggested, reveals Gombrich's origins as a liberal of the Austro-Hungarian Empire.

Even when Gombrich traces *canon* from the accomplished artistic master-work back to the few lines jotted on paper according to some practical short cut, he plays straight into the hands of his opponents. For if a canon resembles a universal artistic language, will it not, like a language, operate according to a system of inclusion and exclusion? And will not these exclusions be determined by the priorities of larger, less neutral systems? If a canon resembles a language, does it not, like a language, operate by differences rather than by absolute distinctions? And who demarcates these differences, who elevates them into criteria of absolute value? When Gombrich makes an extended analogy between canons and languages, which alike 'have rules which must be learned and observed', and notes that 'in a total absence of such rules of the road, communication would break down' (ROHA, 97–8), he takes no account of recent shifts in the philosophy of language. For writers from Saussure to Derrida, languages operate as satellites of a more ghostly and threatening system of 'langue'. Gombrich's analogy between language and *canon* relies on the idea of a language as a natural object. Once language itself becomes an institution, a remote power to be scrutinized with vigilance and suspicion, then the grounds of its universality inevitably recede. Even the shift from 'language' to 'languages' will need to take account of the way 'languages' underpin national hegemony: the meaning of 'French' in the Algeria of the 1950s; the meaning of 'English' in South Africa today. Gombrich's triumphant analogy has implications which can explode his carefully constructed frame of reference.

For Gombrich's model for a threefold canon appears more questionable pushed beyond the overwhelming presence of art in the studio and the museum. At some point one has to ask what exactly does Gombrich think we know when he asserts that 'we know what we mean by a great painting'? Although he generally regards *canon* as a term describing an activity rather than as an essence, a verb rather than a noun, he eventually sees something beyond function at the taproot of artistic creation and audience response. In the end Gombrich detaches artistic excellence from cultural contingency, from the rallying-cries of one or another passing contemporary faction, anchoring it not just to artistic production but to a set of values its most fervent neoclassical defenders hesitated to invoke.

Although he does not advertise or belabour the fact, Gombrich's ultimate values are transcendental ones, existing prior to the works of individual artists and perhaps even prior to 'art' itself. Rejecting 'the catchwords of value' of contemporary fashion, Gombrich habitually employs such time-honoured expressions of value as 'noble' and 'healthy'. Although he concedes that such words are essentially 'metaphors', he still asserts that the responses they signify constitute 'the facets of one untranslatable experience of a plenitude of values that speaks to the whole man – as art has always done' (MHH, 29). Gombrich thinks that his ultimate canon, the canon of excellence, displays the same powers of rational order and spiritual aspiration which drive humanity and culture as a whole. This is why he argues in *Ideals and Idols* that 'the values of the canon are too deeply embedded in the totality of our civilization for them to be discussed in isolation' (II, 163). Although art 'is invariably rooted in the life and value system of its age and society, it will transcend these situations when, as we say, it "stands the test of time"' (II, 162). But do works of art pass that test by rushing into the embrace of eternity? The great works, Gombrich asserts, survive

> not as formal exercises but as an embodiment of a value system which they teach us to recognize. Michelangelo's vision of the act of creation on the Sistine ceiling is a case in point. Its continued

resonance in our culture is second only to that book of Genesis it illustrates. (II, 163)

When challenged by Quentin Bell about the militant orthodoxy these remarks appeared to promulgate, Gombrich merely observed that 'We never start from scratch, we have not invented our civilization and our values in any case, and we should not pretend we have' (II, 170–71). Behind the third and highest of Gombrich's canons lies a creed of human continuity and human order, an order which Gombrich values above all else but cannot demonstrate scientifically.

Yet in speaking of art, Gombrich generally remains awe-struck rather than dogmatic. Apart from his discoveries and analyses in the field of art history, his most important contribution to the history of canons must surely rest on his compelling narrative of the wonder of artistic representation, from its conception in the artist's head, to its construction on a canvas, to its lasting claims on the attention of generations of diverse audiences. At the start of *Art and Illusion*, Gombrich describes his fascination at 'the mysterious way in which shapes and marks can be made to signify and suggest other things beyond themselves' (AI, vii). In his celebrated essay 'Meditations on a Hobby Horse or the Roots of Artistic Form' (1951) he shows how the humble nursery hobby horse functions neither as a representation of a horse nor as an image of a horse but as a 'substitute for a horse' (MHH, 1). In the same way, it is possible to see Gombrich's 'canon of excellence' neither as a representation of an artistic order nor as a reproduction of a cultural order but as a substitute for a human order embodied in a 'secular creed' (II, 21). The strength of this creed, in Gombrich's hands, lies in the way it turns a mysterious aesthetic process into a continuous, rational activity shared by artist and audience alike. Gombrich's 'story of art', which presents Leonardo as engaged in an activity no different in kind from a draughtsman, seems more likely to increase the wonder of art than to diminish it.

The large, continuous view of art on which Gombrich's narrative rests would be inconceivable without an appeal to canons in one form or another. At every stage of that narrative canons play a central part, supplying the basic means of representation and plausibility, the principles of artistic self-identification, and the exemplary achievements of a surpassing tradition. Gombrich's canonical masterpieces come at the end of a chain of representations that link the *Mona Lisa* to a child sketching his nursery-school horse. Just as *Paradise Lost* stands at the end of a line of Renaissance schoolboys conning their alphabets and parsing their Latin, so a canonical masterpiece perfects the basic assumptions of plausibility and coherence contained in an elementary functional canon. If art remains a mystery, it remains for Gombrich a mystery universally acquired. He resists the tendency of artists from Baudelaire to Yeats to see art as the source of a secret wisdom and to rewrite its history in catastrophic terms. As Gombrich presents it, art history proceeds in an orderly, intelligible fashion. In the canon – to paraphrase Rousseau and reclaim the territory of Ricoeur – Gombrich finds the basic terms of an 'aesthetic contract', a contract which ensures, by a rationalist's miracle, that the story of art remains continuous, coherent and comprehensible. Without that contract, neither audience nor artist could make meaningful hypotheses or comprehensible innovations, since both would be reduced to projecting their own assumptions against a void.

Gombrich cannot conceive of an art which does not transmit to all who seek it the means to acquire basic skills of representation. He cannot conceive of an art existing apart from shared assumptions and inherited techniques. And he cannot conceive of any institutional authority for the story of art without reference to the surpassing masterpieces of earlier artists. His repeated invocation of art's most varied and complex idea, the idea of a canon, helps him to present the story of art as an intelligible narrative shared by artist and audience alike. In his rousing peroration to the human plenitude of which art represents one significant instance, Gombrich completes the tribute to *homo artifex* begun in Kant's *Critique of Judgement* and Schiller's *On Naive and Sentimental Poetry*.

4

Northrop Frye and the Visionary Canon

Canons play no less significant a part in the mythical literary criticism of Northrop Frye than in the art scholarship and criticism of Sir Ernst Gombrich. Although some idea of *canon* lies at the heart of the work of both Gombrich and Frye, neither writer wants to restrict 'the canon' to a critical tool, nor to reduce it to a few masterpieces preserved from oblivion by a mass of reactionary social prejudices. For both authors, canons serve the producers of art long before they fall into the hands of its receivers. If Gombrich's canons literally allow artists to see, Frye's canons nourish the artistic imagination with the myths, metaphors and lasting images that provide it with vision and structure.

Frye, like Gombrich, has devoted a distinguished academic career to the defence of a humanistic canon characterized by its inclusiveness and its popular appeal. Yet for all their similarities, it is worth noting at the outset that Gombrich and Frye part company at crucial points. Where Gombrich pledges himself to the cautious rationality of his friend Karl Popper, Frye becomes overtly utopian. Where Gombrich presents myths as the authors of all modern mischief, from Hegel's refashioned theodicy to the aggression in the name of chivalric legend mounted by Hitler's Germany, Frye presents mythology as a total scheme for interpreting the universe. Where Gombrich's rational art history always refers back to the comprehensible psychologies of individual artists, Frye's total literary canon takes on the shape of an anonymous, collective poem. When Gombrich emphasizes that artists and historians, as he has often put it, 'never start from scratch',[1] Frye's canon works towards a utopian future. Behind Gombrich's canon stands Popper's gradualist 'social engineering' and the Warburg's School's attempt to find the truth about the past through immersion in the archives. Behind Frye's canon stand the blueprints of Milton and Blake for a new Jerusalem. What seems most significantly absent from either canon-maker is the authoritarian structure of repressive values and assumptions which recent arguments assume to persist in any critic or historian who speaks approvingly of 'the canon'. The argument that canons perpetrate the values of a dominant elite by excluding all works subverting those values does not square with the careers of two of the most significant canon-makers of postwar criticism. We shall see that these influential critics share little beyond a common concern for the humanities and a desire to proselytize for them to the widest possible audience.

THE QUEST FOR A SCIENTIFIC CRITICISM: FRYE AND THE ACADEMIC CANON

As many critics have observed, Frye belongs to the great tradition of dissenting, antinomian interpretation which grew in the wake of the Reformation. Gombrich belongs rather to a line of European humanists stretching from Jacob Burckhardt to Johan Huizinga, a line of writers who view art in terms of what Gombrich has called 'the Tradition of General Knowledge'.[2] Both writers have conducted a lifelong search for intelligible patterns of human development. But where Gombrich's concerns involve research into Renaissance patronage, depth psychology, Polynesian decoration, the statue of Eros at Piccadilly Circus, and much else, Frye's work leads him to accumulate a massive stock of mythical narrative. The variousness of Gombrich's interests leads him to identify several different canons. For Frye, however, the canon remains singular, a seamless narrative held together by a universal, timeless language. Frye's canon focuses archaic perceptions through the age-old lenses of myth and folk tale. The authorship of these stories matters less than the broad patterns of fulfilment and regeneration the narratives map out. Frye views mythology as a kind of Esperanto of the soul, a universal language of the quest for a world more imaginative and more liberated than the one inhabited on earth, and, accordingly, the basis for any regenerated society of the future.

His strong sense of this humane, emancipated future explains why, among so many twentieth-century attempts to redefine the idea of *canon*, Northrop Frye's remains the most spectacular. Through a career which has spanned trends as different as new criticism and new historicism, Frye has unfalteringly campaigned on behalf of a visionary canon. In dozens of monographs and reprinted lectures, he has countered a succession of institutional attempts to substitute a canon of conformity for a perpetually fluctuating canon of myth. It is true that some of his books record on tablets of stone ideas best remembered as the brilliant, sparklike fragments glimpsed in more suggestive works. Yet at least three of Frye's books – *Fearful Symmetry* (1947), *Anatomy of Criticism* (1957) and *The Great Code* (1982) – reconstruct an entire cultural past. They do this not by offering detailed critiques of competing canons but by interposing Frye's own inclusive narrative of Western literature's recurring archetypes and themes. As we shall see, his is a canon without overt value judgements, without fixed shape or boundaries, unattached to particular works or authors – a canon, in other words, in every way opposed to the influential canons of Eliot and Leavis, canons organized on classical lines and foregrounding a limited set of historically important works by largely dead authors.

Why, one might ask, should Frye present the whole field of literature as material for his alternative, expanded canon rather than simply expunge the whole idea of a canon from the modern literary map? At times in his later works, Frye offers an engrossing vision of a literature beyond the canon, a vision he shares with Edward Said, another critic from outside the Anglo-American mainstream. For the most part, though, Frye seeks to transform our notion of a canonical text rather than to attack the canon head-on. One can see three possible reasons for Frye's need to revitalize the canon, reasons deriving from his personal circumstances and from the period in which he started to write.

Significantly, his first major critical work appeared in 1947, just after the publication of R. G. Collingwood's posthumous *The Idea of History* (1946), a book that set the course for the decade in its determination to carve out a frame of reference for the humanities dominated neither by nationalism nor by science. Collingwood hoped to return history to the realm of rational self-consciousness that Kant, Schiller, and Gombrich have all viewed as the highest expression of human power. In Collingwood's scheme, historical interpretation becomes 'an act not only of thought but of reflective thought'.[3] Collingwood wanted to cut his discipline loose from national dynasties and abstract 'isms', so that the history of the future would serve no party except the party of reflection.

In retrospect, one can see that Frye's work up to *Anatomy of Criticism* (1957) participates in a widespread postwar search for large co-ordinating principles uncontaminated by political or dogmatic commitments. As Geoffrey Barraclough observed in 1956, in words deeply relevant to a Canadian critic, 'an interpretation which surveys the background to the present almost exclusively from the point of view of western Europe has little relevance to our current problems'.[4] Not surprisingly, the prewar campaign of Henry Canby and Ernest

Barker to construct canons embodying national or civic values never appealed to Frye. Instead, from the very start of his career, he consistently objects to attempts to corral literary works for nationalist or doctrinal purposes. He actually goes even further, separating himself from a whole preceding generation of critics in his vigorous objections to what he calls the errors of 'externalized determinism', bids to ground critical authority in a non-literary frame of reference, so that the ailing text finds itself 'carried around in some kind of religious or Marxist or Freudian wheelchair'.[5]

A similar iconoclasm attaches to Frye's view of Eliot's 'tradition', the watchword that became so important for contemporaries of the 1940s and 1950s such as Allen Tate, Cleanth Brooks and L. C. Knights. In 'tradition' Frye sees only a 'magic word . . . which means that when we see the miscellaneous pile strung out along a chronological line, some coherence is given it by sheer sequence'.[6] Frye thinks that Eliot's 'tradition' merely carries over into the twentieth century a confusion between social and literary values made by Arnold eighty years before. Arnold's criterion of 'high seriousness' answered a similar need to 'create a new scriptural canon out of poetry'. Yet the need becomes bathetic, since Arnold's 'literary value-judgments are projections of social ones' (AC, 22). Frye's rejection of Arnold's criticism recalls Eliot's strictures in *The Sacred Wood*. But where Eliot accuses Arnold of making poetry a substitute for religion, Frye's target is the Arnold of Rugby and Oxford, not the Arnold of *Literature and Dogma*. Frye attacks Arnold as a critic who trades literature's revelatory possibilities for a quasi-sociological criticism secretly tied to class. In a memorable aside, he has extended this criticism to F. R. Leavis, whom he describes as 'a person . . . trying hard to be a gentleman'.[7]

Frye was among the first contemporary critics to charge Arnold and Leavis with an offence currently being levied against the institution of criticism as a whole. Contemporary critics such as Jane Tompkins have suggested that 'the literary works that now make up the canon do so because the groups that have an investment in them are culturally the most influential',[8] a criticism which matches Frye's position in *Anatomy of Criticism*: 'Every deliberately constructed hierarchy of values in literature . . . is based on a concealed social, moral, or intellectual analogy' (AC, 23). Behind every important – ordered, in print, widely available – literary text lies the conservative sponsorship of an interpretative community. This community, not necessarily great in itself, by lobbying, advertising, and proselytizing, creates greatness for the select band of authors it promotes and reflects that greatness back on its members. To undermine these powerful vested interests, Tompkins and others show how institutional sponsors ensure the longevity of canonical works by offering extraordinary critical readings, by endlessly explaining these works to students in classrooms, and by journalistic endeavours that elevate both work and critic in the minds of the community at large.

In this context, Frye's position remains a remarkable one. Although he has secured for himself virtually all the offices and privileges available to North American academics, he refrains from endorsing the authority of the platforms from which he himself customarily speaks. Unlike the anti-canonists, Frye regards the masterpieces as intrinsically valuable simply because he views *all* imaginative works as small fragments of one grand design. As he sees it, literature creates a world that

is human in shape, a world where the sun rises in the east and sets in the west over the edge of a flat earth in three dimensions, where the primary realities are not atoms or electrons but bodies, and the primary forces not energy or gravitation but love and death and passion and joy.[9]

In interview, Frye has emphasized his long suspicion of 'isms' and schools, which he describes as 'pseudo-structures', adding that 'the real, genuine advance in criticism came when every work of literature, regardless of its merit, was seen to be a document of *potential* interest, or value, or insight into the culture of the age'.[10] By implication, Frye sees every work created by the imagination as canonical – not because he wields significant powers of patronage as an influential member of the interpretative community, but because he sees each work as an episode in the imagination's coherent creative world.

As Frye conceives of it, criticism assembles the elements of a timeless story that literature has narrated from its earliest days. This project involves him in a repeated quest for origins, transformations and archetypes; by the same token, it removes him from the myths of national progress or adversarial revolution that underpin so many critical systems. In essence, Frye's critical scheme does not rely on training or expertise, nor on any exalted conception of authorship. Authors, he tells us, are rather simple people, who build what he calls a 'mythological universe . . . out of human hopes and desires and anxieties' (SM, ix). This universe does not change like the secular world, which explains why artists worldwide always remain in touch with it. In this way, the mythological world becomes a point of contact between cultures across time and space. Myth shows why art can seem as 'subtle, profound, and in touch with "reality" among Australian aborigines as among twentieth-century poets' (SM, ix). Frye sees the distinction between 'civilized' and 'primitive' as part of the great culture shift which separated myth from science. It is an institutional distinction he regards as in need of reconciliation by the boldly visionary criticism he himself has been writing since *Fearful Symmetry* (1947).

Even so, Frye, unlike many prominent contemporary critics, does not move from a scepticism about criticism as an institution to an attack on the canon as a basic element of literary response. This difference from the mainstream of contemporary criticism reflects his second impulse towards canon-making, which comes from his work as an ordained minister in the Church of Canada. Unlike the Leavisians and New Critics whom he has made the butt of his wittiest sallies, Frye sees literature as grounded on universally appealing spiritual foundations. Unlike T. S. Eliot, he refuses to tie this spirituality to dogmatic conceptions of human destiny lodged in clerical orthodoxy or in some distant cultural past. In Frye's view, a canon lays out before us a field of human knowledge and shows us how to value it. In the secular canon as in the biblical one, books gain meaning from juxtaposition and from faith. False juxtaposition and bad faith account, in both cases, for their social misuse. Instead of reinforcing authority, the visionary canon delivers us from it; instead of limiting culture to those specialized enough to receive it, it expands culture into a total intercommunicating world. As Frye understands it, the visionary canon works not to consolidate secular culture but to destabilize it from within. Repossessed as a kind of single story, the world of visionary knowledge reveals itself as 'the total body of human achievement out of which the forces come that change ordinary society so rapidly'.[11]

Frye's third impulse towards canon-making comes from his extensive institutional affiliations. Surprisingly, he has managed to reconcile his spiritual apprehensions to a distinguished professional career, not just as a minister and a Principal of the University of Toronto's Victoria College, not just as a President of the Modern Language Association of America, but also as an editor of *Canadian Forum*, as a reviewer, and as an anthologist whose services to Canadian literature gained recognition as early as 1958 when he received the Lorne Pierce Medal. Yet these many rewards and distinctions have not separated Frye from what he considers his larger public. In an uncanny revitalization of the teaching canon of Ancient Greece, he remarks in the preface to *The Great Code*: 'All my books have really been teachers' manuals'.[12] He has repeatedly emphasized that his staple audience remains the crowded undergraduate lecture hall, not the tiny graduate-school cell. One of his later books, *Northrop Frye on Shakespeare* (1986), reproduces his undergraduate lecture course at the University of Toronto. Other books suggest his wider commitment to Canadian culture. His effort to construct a working syntax of Canadian literature appears in two urbane, non-specialist collections, *The Bush Garden* (1971) and *Divisions on a Ground* (1982). One of his most difficult works, *Anatomy of Criticism*, became accessible to a surprisingly wide public in a series of talks prepared for the Canadian Broadcasting Commission and later published as *The Educated Imagination* (1964).

Frye has clearly imported his mysticism into the institution rather than institutionalized the mystic. He finds few ties between the world celebrated in literature and the world of transcontinental conferences, industrial chairs and graduate assistants. He has expressed repeated misgivings about the importance of the Ph.D, emphasizing that his own critical scheme does not address itself to the world of professional training but to the visionary design to replenish daily life we associate with Ruskin, Morris and Carlyle. Inside Frye's 'everyman's canon', professional expertise becomes irrelevant, since he sees the capacity of the canonical author to 'communicate with times and spaces and cultures . . . far removed from his own' as 'the greatest mystery of literature'.[13] And because he sees other critics as out of touch with this central human mystery, he himself, despite his long affiliation with the University of Toronto, has always worked independently, gaining many followers but never contributing to any established critical school. The independence of mind that made him write a book in 1947 whose sole indexed reference to Eliot was to George Eliot prefigured an even more single-minded scheme of critical reconstruction.

'AN EXCLUSIVE AND DEFINITIVE CANON':
FRYE'S MYTHICIZED CLASSICISM

Frye's career as an independent visionary critic falls into three main phases of ascending ambition. In each of these some version of the canon plays a significant part. In the first phase, he seeks to reclaim a poet excluded from the canons of Eliot and neo-Christian orthodoxy, namely William Blake. At this stage, Frye presents Blake's canon – his interrelated illustrated books – as an artistic object in its own right, a work creating and conforming to its own aesthetic norms. In this way Blake's *œuvre* becomes a coherent, ordered testament to posterity rather than a ragbag of odds and ends. In the second phase, Frye moves from the study of Blake to the study of literature as a whole, showing how Blake's mythical language becomes the lingua franca of poetry, the shared arteries of Virgil, Ovid, Spenser, Milton, Smart, Coleridge, Joyce, Eliot, and Stevens.

From now on in Frye's criticism, the canon expands into one enormous poem. Charged with interpreting this great poetic world, the critic must cast aside his petty preferences, abandon his desire for advocacy, and behave as a scientist investigating a planet rather than as a consumer counsellor or high court judge. The third phase of Frye's criticism marks his long-delayed confrontation with the work towards which all his theoretical premises and aesthetic interests logically direct him. In the Bible, Frye discovers the anonymous, collective, visionary testimony his previous criticism extruded from Blake, Shakespeare, Milton, and Stevens. Instead of viewing the Bible as a manual of observances and rules, Frye presents it as the source of a visionary canon which offers 'a continuous narrative beginning with the creation and ending with the Last Judgment, and surveying the whole history of mankind, under the symbolic names of Adam and Israel, in between' (EI, 111). In a single compressed work whose title, *The Great Code*, returns to the Blake of his early inspiration, Frye reinstates the authority of the Bible as the master narrative for the lost masses of humanity in search of a soul. In effect, the latest phase of Frye's visionary canon heralds the emergence of the critic as a kind of twentieth-century sage, incorporating sacred and secular poetry and the universe of knowledge into a single 'canonical myth'. This myth has as its basis the genuinely classical insight shared by Plato, Aristotle and Frye that a teacher is 'someone who attempts to re-create the subject in the student's mind' (GC, xv). Even in Frye's late-twentieth-century visionary system, that subject remains the age-old story of descent and renewal, exile and return. In Frye's work the critic is reborn as a storyteller, recording the cycle of loss and regeneration all literature endlessly retells.

Frye's earliest attempt to set the canon on visionary rather than on dogmatic foundations came in his first book, *Fearful Symmetry*, a work of radical nostalgia which attempts to restore the unity between literature and religion. *Fearful Symmetry* strenuously explores the idea that 'the conception of the Classical in art and the conception of the scriptural or canonical in religion have always tended to approximate one another'.[14] But if he urges a 'return to essential critical principles' based on a new 'catholicity of outlook' (FS, 420), Frye conspicuously refrains from calling to his aid the formidably canonical and formidably catholic figure of T. S. Eliot. Instead, he makes it clear that his idea of classicism stems from Blake's 'doctrine that all symbolism in all art and all religion is mutually intelligible among all men, and that there is such a thing as an iconography of the imagination' (FS, 420). Although Frye rarely draws attention to the fact, his uncompromising rejection of a metropolitan, hierarchical culture in *Fearful Symmetry* equals such overtly adversarial works as Raymond Williams's *The Country and the City* and Edward Said's *Orientalism*. By writing about Blake as opposed to Dante or Donne, Frye places himself on the side of the provinces rather than the metropolis, allies himself with the primitives against the moderns, and commits himself to a ministering culture instead of a dominant one.

In choosing William Blake as his subject, Frye takes up an author exiled from the canon of T. S. Eliot because of his unwillingness to get behind the big battalions of Anglo-Catholicism, monarchy and classicism. In Blake, Eliot saw only 'the crankiness, the eccentricity, which frequently affects writers outside of the Latin traditions'. What Blake lacked, he decided, was 'a framework of accepted and traditional ideas which would have prevented him from indulging in a philosophy of his own'.[15] Frye's book supplies, in the first place, a massive rejoinder to Eliot, a defence of Blake's human importance rather than an attack on his social credentials and religious preferences, a celebration of his imaginative subversions rather than an evaluation tainted, ultimately, by a hidden social agenda.

Frye's celebration of Blake starts from what he repeatedly calls Blake's 'canon'. By 'canon', at this stage, he understands those works the artist wishes to transmit to posterity, the works that display the peak of his craftsmanship and the kernel of his ideas. For Frye, this excludes both the trial balloons of the poet's apprenticeship and the unfinished works of his old age. 'The engraved poems', he notes, 'were intended to form an exclusive and definitive canon' (FS, 6). These works appear 'definitive' because a dedicated craftsman expended his imaginative energies in revisiting the same material. Because they represent the work of an artist who revised constantly as he searched for the finest embodiment of his vision and his craft, Blake's illustrated poems evince his liking for certain kinds of design and pattern, for certain metaphorical and figurative recurrences. Familiarity with the total body of an artist's work leads the critic to observe deep patterns in the designs and images chosen, so that 'once we begin to look at Blake's engraved works as a canon, we can discern certain structural principles within it' (FS, 187). Yet these structural principles do more than bind Blake's own poems together. The centrifugal impulse that leads Frye to see the engraved poems as a unified whole moves him centripetally as well, to present the poet as part of a visionary company that includes Milton, Spenser, the Bible and Shakespeare among his predecessors, and Burns, Collins and Smart among his contemporaries.

So far, Frye's reconsideration of Blake's work follows largely familiar lines. To recover from a prolific author his works of lasting value; to suggest that these works form an organic whole that conforms to verifiable structural patterns and consistent artistic principles; to move out horizontally, linking these works to a tradition of poems that share common images, metaphors and preoccupations: these activities are familiar enough for Anglo-American critics since the appearance of T. S. Eliot's *The Sacred Wood*. Yet the seeds of a more radical way of reading already appear in Frye's work. When he begins to link the idea of the canon to the idea of a hidden primitive narrative; when he speaks of Blake as participating in an 'archetypal myth' that follows the fortunes of 'man in the religious perspective, surrounded by the huge conceptions of fall, redemption, judgment and immortality' (FS, 168), then Frye stands on the brink of a criticism which would soon move far beyond Eliot.

In the first place, the structural principles that interest him, the themes he discerns at the heart of Blake's 'canon', extend beyond form and across time. 'Anything admitted to that canon, whatever its date,' he submits, 'not only belongs in a unified scheme but is in accord with a permanent structure of ideas' (FS, 14). Entry into the canon means that the works inside it assume a rich intertextual shape that enlarges the reader's imagination to encompass a whole world, a world that stretches from creation to apocalypse. In the second place, Frye refuses to follow Eliot in linking 'tradition' or 'canon' to any specific historical period. Instead, he reverses the thrust of Eliot's 'tradition' by emphasizing the universally comprehensible vision opened up by the poetic imagination rather than the pattern of historical learning a learned and 'mature' poet shares with other learned and 'mature' poets. 'A poet who looks directly at his greatest predecessors and visualizes his own work as a concretion of a literary tradition is following the Hebraic rather than the Classical tradition', Frye notes (FS, 321–2). Setting aside the Hebraic model, he presents Blake's achievement as a spiritual vision shared by authors as different as Cornelius Agrippa and Christopher Smart. When Blake recaptures this vision, the works included in 'the Blake canon' assume a spatial order, a unified structure that lays itself out as a composite statement.

In the third place, Frye utterly rejects Eliot's suggestion that Blake belongs to no identifiable 'tradition'. Had Blake been born between 1530 and 1630, Frye notes, his public would have fully understood him, seeing that he 'offered to the world, in Spenser's phrase, "a continued Allegory, or darke conceit", without being told that poets should not invent a private symbolism' (FS, 161). In Shakespearian romance, deities descend from the clouds to pronounce on mortal dilemmas. In Blake's *Songs*, youthful chimney sweeps scour a grimy London under the custodianship of benign angels. Both authors guide their audiences by presenting large, totalizing worlds that begin in jealousy but end in redemption. Both renew a world through vision they first reproduce by imitation. Frye emphasizes the enormity of scale, the sense of plenitude, both artists mysteriously convey.

All these points lead to Frye's fourth, most dramatic departure from Eliot's canon. Frye sees the canon as the poet's imaginative and prophetic instrument rather than as criticism's retrospective reinforcement of the status quo, its tacit alliance between high culture and high orthodoxy. Instead of addressing himself to an elite, Blake unfolds 'his canon as a new testament for English culture. He will teach the English how to use their imaginations, how to develop the immense reserves of power that they are leaving untapped' (FS, 407). As Frye represents it, the new canon, the canon of vision, has a spatial rather than a temporal order, an order resting on imagination rather than on convention and on present human energies rather than on inherited cultural laws. In Blake, Frye finds his paradigm for the canonical author, an author whose poetic structures sweep across time and space, who boldly takes a universally familiar text (the Bible) and interprets it by his own prophetic lights, who avails himself of the humblest forms of folk tale and proverb, who reverses conventional preferences for sanity over madness, for experience over innocence. Here, clearly, lie the seeds for Frye's own later reversals of the preferences for tragedy over comedy and for realism over romance, his iconoclastic disavowals of such critical shibboleths as 'complexity' and 'maturity'. By this point, Frye shares little with Eliot except his high regard for Elizabethan literature.

Taken together, Blake and Shakespeare give a fairly accurate sense of what Frye looks for in his canonical authors. These authors will be synoptic, visionary, and redemptive. Their redemptive wisdom will lie not in the rich distillation of orthodox ideas Eliot found in

Dante, but in their willingness to combine the demotic with the numinous, the arbitrary with the apocalyptic. Canonical authors begin by fulfilling the minimum conventions that keep an audience happy, but their work adds dimensions until it produces a vision of 'the whole progression of life itself from fall to apocalypse' (FS, 386). The canonical work 'will give to our imaginations a depth and a perspective that can take in . . . the possibility of a more intense mode of living'.[16] It begins by bursting the barriers of genre and ends by widening the horizons of perception itself. As Frye points out, 'the interpretation of Blake is only the beginning of a complete revolution in one's reading of all poetry' (FS, 11). Such a revolution abolishes every single one of the institutions of criticism – authors, genres, canons, even the accepted physical world – replacing them, albeit 'in full consciousness', with something more primitive: 'that original lost sense of identity with our surroundings, where there is nothing outside the mind of man, or something identical with the mind of man' (EI, 29). The force of Blake's canon lies in its ability to impose on society as it is a structure of ideas that will radically transform it. As he uncovers the mythic narrative of a Britain that loses its sacred destiny only to regain it through the poet's imaginative projections, Frye sketches out the visionary lines on which his own future criticism will proceed.

THE CANON OF MYTH

During the ten years between *Fearful Symmetry* and *Anatomy of Criticism* (1957), Frye expanded and consolidated his criticism in four main ways. First, his essays and reviews of this period compile an extensive collection of the narrative patterns he discovered in Blake's work. Utopian cities, lost paradises, quest romances, visionary apocalypses – all these, he begins to suggest, form part of a common stock shared by Spenser, Shakespeare and Milton on the one side and by Joyce, Stevens and Eliot on the other. And behind these master-pieces lie the great anonymous raw materials of literature – the Bible, folk tale, myth, primitive stories that outlast the ideas and assumptions in which institutions periodically entrap them. The appeal of such stories can reasonably be termed universal, their range accurately termed comprehensive. Mythical narratives describe the world's creation and imagine its destruction. They explain the esteem of some customs and tribes and describe the decline of others. They record epochal events and inventory trivial ones. As he assembles this evidence, Frye concludes that the conventions of realism mark an interruption in a continuous mythical tradition which his own criticism could fairly represent as the most lasting foundation for literary creation.

Frye takes as his second task a theoretical revaluation of myth itself. From now on, he hopes to restore it to its ancient prestige, but without linking it to Jungian or Spenglerian doctrine. Instead, he emphasizes the constructive and aggregative power of myth. The actors in literature might change, so that Homer describes men like pigs while Orwell describes pigs like men, but the basic structural patterns remain the same. In article after article from the late 1940s to the 1960s, Frye shows that work joins itself to work by these narrative patterns, not by the accidental fact of having the same content, format, or number of lines. These 'archetypes', as he begins to call them, deliver literature from time, reuniting the individual work to a family of narratives that stretches across centuries 'as fresh as ever, and as infinitely suggestive of new modes of treatment'.[17] Sometimes Frye's criticism focuses on 'archetypal' patterns of imagery, at other times on 'mythical' clusters of narrative. In either case he suggests that the work's surface devices – its genre, form, themes and diction – have less relationship with its meaning than the deeper, mythical subtext excavated by a properly synoptic, encyclopaedic criticism. Delivered from the twin burdens of falsity and naïvety, myths become for Frye shaping clusters of narrative representing climactic sequences in the cycles of human destiny and hope.

His emphasis on the inward, mythical dimension of the canon also explains Frye's third innovation during the period between *Fearful Symmetry* and *Anatomy of Criticism*. From the 1950s, he begins to jettison the notion of the period, dividing literature instead into two great eras, apocalypse and regeneration. As a literary historian, Frye resembles the medieval cartographers who measured all distances with reference to Jerusalem. He implies that literary critics make too much of periods and too much of individual authors and texts. Instead of viewing the canonical work as a form of personal testimony, an author's authentic signature for posterity, Frye presents it as a sacred narrative embodying the quest of Everyman for regeneration in a fallen world.

His research into mythical and narrative patterns also leads Frye towards his fourth innovation during this period, his tendency to view composition as a largely unconscious process. 'Great art', he argues, 'comes from harnessing a conscious intention to the creative powers beneath consciousness.'[18] His confidence in the creative power of the unconscious mind leads Frye to sever the link between poetic and ordinary language, not just at the time of composition but even at the time of reading. He thinks that 'the necessity of discarding our accustomed habits of response to words in poetry creates a peculiar psychological barrier' (NFCL, 191). As Frederick Crews subsequently argued, Frye returns art to a pre-Freudian realm where it no longer plays a leading role in managing the internal conflicts of its audience or its creators.[19] Instead of presenting the canon as a 'tradition', a 'line of wit', or a series of 'god terms' – definitions which reflect the specialized interests of a particular intellectual culture – Frye encourages his students to view it in a more receptive, Blake-like spirit. In his view, canonical art retains a connection, however 'displaced' or oblique, with a mythic original. 'Profound or "classic" works of art', he observes, 'are frequently, almost regularly, marked by a tendency to revert or allude to the archaic and explicit form of the myth in the god-story' (NFCL, 74). Frye's canon represents something more inclusive and more primitive than anything envisaged by Eliot or Leavis, something more irreparably fixed in the universal depths of the human mind of all times, societies, and cultures.

This heavy investment in myth and archetype changes the whole status of the literary canon. In Frye's terms, it no longer makes sense to speak, as critics (including Frye himself) did in the 1940s and 1950s, of the 'Auden canon' or the 'Eliot canon', since that part of Eliot or Auden which is canonical will belong not to them alone but to poetry as a whole. This makes for losses as well as gains. In the case of a poet like Blake, to raid the poems for myths and deep structures hardly needs justifying, since the surface language is so occult. But when the recovery of these structures becomes the basis for reinterpretation of Shakespeare, Dickens or George Orwell, then entry to Frye's reconstituted mythical canon carries a higher price.

A mythical reading of Blake honours the author's intentions. A mythical reading of a Shakespearian tragedy can illuminate the play for an audience, even though the reading steps back some distance from the onstage action and renders the speeches inaudible. A mythical reading of Orwell ransoms the author to Frye's system by making a social critic with a journalist's sense of context into a visionary poet in the mode of Blake. To step back from Orwell's *The Road to Wigan Pier* and discover a re-enactment of St Paul's road to Damascus is to ransom the author's declared purposes to the critic's designated system.

Certainly, Orwell scrutinizes systems of every sort – colonial, capitalist, socialist, clerical, totalitarian, and so on. Frye none the less appears to quail at his author's counterpointed concern with the suffering human subject. Orwell intended his audience first to smart at the suffering and then to ponder the larger social order, whereas Frye's system makes him see Dante's 'Inferno' at the back of *Nineteen Eighty-Four*. To argue that Orwell somehow modulates Marxist-Leninism 'from a proletarian dictatorship into a kind of parody of the Catholic Church' (NFCL, 206) is to make his anger at the human cost of political injustice secondary to the comparison between Catholic and Communist tyrannies. Whether applied to Blake, to Shakespeare, or to Orwell, in each case 'myth' will yield only one kind of experience for a reader. Always Frye seems to burn away the work's expressive surface in order to penetrate to its deep similarity with other works. In this way, a criticism that tells us how much alike works of literature become at their deep hidden core expands the canon in volume but diminishes it in variety. And in the process, the reader's equipment for dealing with difference – between work and work, work and world – falls into an alarming disuse.

Frye's determination to set Blake alongside Shakespeare in a single mental vision reflects his need to see the whole of literature as a story to which the authors of the world have contributed in serial form, but his ambitious linkage of these two authors also highlights certain properties of canonical literature which a mythicized narrative necessarily rejects. What Frye most flagrantly excludes, of course, is words. Only at considerable distance, or on certain special occasions, does Blake *sound* like Shakespeare. When poetic language works in such a centrifugal way, it becomes difficult to tell Leopold Bloom from King Lear. Frye is a studiedly unverbal critic, piercing past the rhetoric even of *Hamlet* to discover an anthology of archetypal situations and characterizations. His criticism, which displays populism at the level of structure and hermeticism at the level of language, contains no provision for identifying the distinct voice of any author. And alongside words, Frye also rejects ideas, which he views with all the suspicion of a generation that includes Cleanth Brooks and William K. Wimsatt. On more than one occasion Frye has objected to critical procedures by which 'a scholar with a special interest in geography or economics expresses that interest by the rhetorical device of putting his favourite study into a causal relationship with whatever interests him less'. He characterizes such procedures as 'determinism' because they take over critical principles 'ready-made' from fields outside literature proper (AC, 6–7).

Having excluded words and ideas, Frye has no difficulty in excluding conventions and genres. As commonly understood by literary historians, these represent the manifest means by which an author links his creation to his predecessors and his society. Frye, however, enjoins critics to look for the laws of genre inside literature itself, to cancel the contract that links tragedy to Sidney's kings and tyrants and sees comedy as the domain of Aristotle's 'worst types of men'. Frye associates genres and conventions with stock responses and neoclassical pieties, the misleading culprits that lead Thomas Rymer to misread *Othello* as a tragedy about a handkerchief or Leavis to interpret it as a parable of egoism.

What he leaves as the sole chain of connection between literary works becomes a structural similarity perceived at a certain angle and distance, so that acknowledged masterpieces share the same anonymous materials as the most primitive formulae. He refers these perceived connections to patterns derived from mythology and folk tale. Yet the structural patterns that bind together Frye's mythicized canon may prove as exclusive as Eliot's 'tradition' or Leavis's 'line of wit', for structural patterns alone reduce authors to anonymity, characters to functions, and texts to their raw material. In moving away from Blake, he forgets that Blake's canon formed an integral whole constructed by an author; the canon which evolves in the works succeeding *Fearful Symmetry* has its only begetter in the constructive and narrative powers of Northrop Frye.

TOTAL LITERARY HISTORY: *ANATOMY OF CRITICISM*

When Frye turns his attention from Blake to the cycle of literary forms unfolded in *Anatomy of Criticism*, the energies he discovered in Blake's canon shape his approaches to the whole field of Western literature. In studying Blake, he paid little attention to the juvenilia or the unfinished works. The rest he saw as a unity informed by one integrated imaginative vision. Similarly, purged of its working papers and rough drafts (he has made much sport about the expanding industry in foul papers that postwar authors have bequeathed to American universities), the Western literary heritage beckons as an integrated whole. 'You don't just read one poem or novel after another,' he told an audience for a Canadian Broadcasting Corporation broadcast, 'but enter into a complete world of which every work of literature forms part' (EI, 69).

Since the late 1950s, Frye has repeatedly tried to articulate the Eleusinian mystery this world of literature darkly reveals, the 'story of the loss and regaining of identity' which, from Terence to Shakespeare, from Ovid to Joyce, becomes 'the framework of all literature' (EI, 55). To understand that mystery fully, however, Frye's students must undergo the 'complete revolution' of their reading habits promised in his study of Blake. That revolution will have two stages, one of which would find itself realized more fully in the works that succeed *Anatomy of Criticism*. During the first stage, Frye spells out the consequences for critical theory of insights originally presented in relation to Blake. During the second stage he circulates these theories in the larger educational and social arena.

In refuting Eliot's idea of a mateless, lunatic Blake, Frye pointed to the shared stock of stories which bind this 'solitary Robinson Crusoe' to other poets. In *Anatomy of Criticism* he goes further, not just by incorporating into the canon authors even more eccentric than Blake – Hogg, Smart, Chatterton – but by showing that a canon can be wound out of literature's own entrails almost without critical help. Frye insists that literary criticism begins and ends by describing what poems share with other poems. Arguably, his methods of demonstrating this point owe more to the metaphysical conceit than to orthodox critical history or canons of evidence. Frye's metaphysical point of view means that his sweeping, visionary canon has little place for concepts of period or seriality; the fact that Dickens wrote a long time after Shakespeare will not matter if a common image or pattern can be unearthed from the comedies of both. The basis for comparison between authors now lies deep inside their work rather than beyond it in some imposed structure of critical or social ideas. Even the characters an author creates become functions rather than destinies. Shylock's Jewishness becomes accidental, because his real significance comes from his function as a blocking *senex* in a New Comedy. In every conventional area he touches – plot, character, theme, form – Frye shapes his material in order to highlight the common features apparent in the world of literature, not the common features which literature shares with the world.

One of his most audacious assertions in *Anatomy of Criticism* concerns the difference between all works inside the canon and any work outside it. Frye probably relegates to that limbo fewer works than any other canon-maker, leaving everything from detective story to cartoon as fuel for his archetypal *canon*. He even finds a place for non-fiction prose, one of the surest tests for the inclusiveness of any critical theory. Yet all these forms he now views prismatically, since he espouses a militantly non-referential view of literature that presents poems as the products of poems and the whole of literary tradition as the permutation of a few basic narratives. Instead of 'the canon' he prefers at this point to speak of 'literary history' as an autonomous field 'based on what the whole of literature actually does' (AC, 6–7).

The favourable reception accorded to the book by so many different reviewers shows how exhilarating his fellow critics found Frye's abandonment of the traditional canon for this huge uncultivated new literary field. *Anatomy of Criticism* enlarges the traditional canon by discussing Carl Sandburg alongside Virgil, James Thurber alongside James Hogg, *Macbeth* alongside *New Yorker* cartoons. As reviewers from M. H. Abrams to Frank Kermode to David Daiches attested, Frye's work encompasses a greater number of texts and genres than almost any previous theoretical work.[20] In Frye they discovered a colleague who could not only discuss Jeeves, Leporello and Matthew Merrygreek in an account of the 'tricky slave' in comedy, but could also promise a new rigour of procedure, a determination to establish modern criticism on 'scientific' grounds. Frye's remark on the difficulty of seeing literature as a large, unending story 'if we know no other canons than low mimetic ones' (AC, 138) also struck a chord. The publication of *Anatomy of Criticism* seemed to rid literary criticism of its stultifying concern with value judgement. Frye showed younger critics how they could direct their attention to the order of words that recurs in literature as a whole, rather than to the specific order of words that results in *King Lear* or *The Waste Land*.

A second look at the book perhaps lessens this sense of a vastly increased perspective. At the start of *Anatomy of Criticism* Frye suggests the need for 'a conceptual framework' or 'coordinating principle' which will 'see the phenomena it deals with as parts of a whole' (AC, 15–16). From now on, literature no longer consists of a succession of works unified by some general sense of 'the canon', but becomes instead a large ordered totality. Into this totality Frye admits, alongside the usual canon of acknowledged masterpieces, oral works and works of primitive culture. Yet these seeming additions to the canon become paradoxically the source of its reduction, for the archetypes and mythical patterns he finds in primitive works increasingly govern his valuations of more sophisticated ones. Instead of presenting the customary evaluation of the masterpiece as a more complex version of its predecessor, Frye sees myths and archetypes as more valuable than the texts they inhabit.

Moreover, Frye understands the scientific method as a basic capacity to order material, not as a set of sophisticated paradigms and provisional explanations. Invocations to 'science' notwithstanding, he lacks the scientist's cast of mind. Stripped of its scientific trappings, *Anatomy of Criticism* gains its conviction from the narrative authority inspired by a lifetime of reading, a narrative which culminates in a vision of redemption barely concealed by a universe of mutually dependent literary forms. It is unfortunate that after his vision the prophet must then descend the mountain to chart his visionary direction and order his apocalyptic syntax. Because he insists on seeing his 'total literary history' as a field of 'total coherence' (AC, 16). Frye forces himself into the position of presenting some common element in literature from *Gilgamesh* to *The Bostonians*. His common elements or 'formulae' derive he suggests, from primitive culture. Blake's canon originated in the patterns of quest, apocalypse and regeneration which *Fearful Symmetry* traced to oral and folk culture. Now, Frye argues, such formulae appear in all valuable works. He goes further, submitting that 'there seems to be a general tendency on the part of great classics to revert to them' (AC, 17).

The 'science' developed in *Anatomy of Criticism* effectively reverses the assumptions and procedures of historical criticism and scholarship. Instead of acceding to the view that *Hamlet* refines and revises the crudities of an earlier revenge tragedy, Frye suggests that Shakespeare unconsciously reverted to a primitive mythological source. If Dryden found the English language brick and left it marble, then Frye returns it to its dusty origins in the world of myth. It is, moreover, a world to which only the most learned excavators can ever gain entry, since many of the parallels Frye discovers in his quest for a pattern of 'death and revival' (AC, 138) acquire almost mathematical involutions in their presentation. Notwithstanding the importance of the Proserpine myth in English literature, Frye strains credulity when he sees it operating, at varying levels of 'displacement', in a *cento* of texts from *Cymbeline* to *Lorna Doone*. As his argument grows more complex, Frye insists on the 'universality' of the myths whose misleading outer skin he heroically sloughs off. Yet how, one wonders, can literature be universal and appear so incongruent with the empirical world? How can literary criticism become a 'science' when it organizes its material into such rudimentary mythical patterns? Like many critics interested in literature as communication, Frye invokes a normative reader who suspiciously resembles a most unusual person, the critic himself. His 'universal' language will seem as foreign to many readers as T. S. Eliot's Latin or Homer's Greek.

The 'science' or 'universal language' which Frye develops in *Anatomy of Criticism* shows more resemblance to algebra than to the empirical study of natural forms. Like a mathematician, he plots connections between his formulae in the most occult way. When, for instance, he compares the Porter scene in *Macbeth* to the satyr plays in Greek tragedy (AC, 292), we see that one critic's universality is another's learned exegetical wit. Instead of operating like an empirical scientist, by a free interplay of hypothesis, observation, corroboration, and revaluation, Frye's science proceeds from hypothesis to endless corroboration. And instead of simulating the scientist's disavowal of value judgements, he transfers those judgements from texts and authors to narratives and genres. How else can one explain his antipathy to realism, which in *Fearful Symmetry* represents 'the bondage of a dingy and nervous naturalism' (FS, 420) and in *Anatomy of Criticism* aspires no further than the 'low mimetic'?

Perhaps the fullest measure of Frye's learning emerges in the 'phases' he deploys in his chapter 'Archetypal Criticism: Theory of Myths', as he moves from a version of experience as unstructured confusion to a vision of epiphanic totality. These lines of ascent and descent take poetry further and further from participation in the ordinary world of chaos and flux and ever nearer to the most distant contemplation of the human condition. Moreover, as he ascends, Frye disturbs one hierarchy – the preference for tragedy over comedy – only to replace it by another, more latent one. *Anatomy of Criticism* sets up a round table that ostensibly includes all genres: from tragedy and irony, with their emphasis on suffering, to romance, with its emphasis on regeneration. Yet few readers can doubt where the Grail will finally come to rest. In Frye's canon, the romance which 'begins life anew in some sheltered spot' (AC, 203) exerts a sharper imaginative force and taps deeper audience responses than any of its rivals. The cyclical patterns of *Anatomy of Criticism* conceal a displaced version of a modernist artist rather than a new breed of scientifically minded postwar critic. As represented in this book, the canon becomes an occult epic, a prose *Waste Land* holding together chaos by a few fragments of mythology. As M. H. Abrams pointed out in his review, wit, not science, becomes Frye's organizing principle. If the modernist in Frye looks at myth with the eyes of Joyce, Yeats, and Thomas Mann, the metaphysical poet (the fashion of his youth, as he has frequently observed) leads him to yoke together works as apparently distinct as Ibsen's *Ghosts* and Fielding's *Tom Jones* (AC, 181), Milton's *Comus* and Hawthorne's *The Marble Faun* (AC, 150).

By the end of *Anatomy of Criticism* it has become apparent that Frye's central myth rests on a fusion of Christian and Romantic visionary patterns. Vision alone can redeem the world of waste and violence that forms the first of Frye's phases in each of the genres. It is a Romantic aspiration that sees every poet as godlike in power. It is a Romantic aesthetic that underpins Frye's definition of poetry as 'the imitation of infinite social action and infinite human thought' (AC, 125). His own chameleonic propensities, his ability to transform from scientist to sage to artist, recall a line of Romantic poet-critics from Blake to Baudelaire. And his next step, to take the insights gained from the study of literature out into the larger social world, replays in a very different postwar context the prophetic mission of the Old Testament preacher-poets and the cultural mission of Coleridge or Schiller.

MYTHS OF CONCERN: CANONS AND THE ORIGINS OF SOCIETY

After the enormously favourable reception given to *Anatomy of Criticism*, Frye increasingly occupied himself with this larger cultural mission. But unlike Coleridge and Schiller, he found a ready-made institutional base in the modern university. From this base he returns in the later part of his career to a central concern of his early work, the ties attaching *canon* to *classic*. During the 1940s and 1950s he implicitly questioned those ties by asserting that 'every poet has the right to his own canon'. At this stage, Frye saw the canon as an assertion of authorial identity rather than as an instrument of critical judgement. 'It is as an author's canon', he asserts in a 1956 review of Robert Graves's *Collected Poems*, 'that the present collection should be read' (NFCL, 230). But what lay behind all these discrete authorial canons? From the late 1950s Frye began, in effect, an unannounced campaign to reconcile the canon of creation with the canon of teaching and the patterns governing audience response. Beyond authorial identity he now glimpsed something larger than any single author, something authors and audiences shared equally. Increasingly, after *Anatomy of Criticism*, Frye presents the canon as a 'great code', a narrative pathway into a connected series of ever more primitive narratives. And since these narratives evoke 'audience response at its most fundamental level' (NFS, 154), all humanistic curricula will be revitalized by them. As Frye sees it, the deeper students dig into these reserves of canonical narratives, the wider the interconnections they perceive between them, the more radically they will articulate their society's larger future ends.

In recent years, Frye has repeatedly argued the case for a curriculum that will introduce myth at an early stage of instruction. This is the only curriculum, as he sees it, which promises to restore capacities latent in every human being, capacities stymied by a syllabus limited to a short-list of classics preselected by an elite core of metropolitan critics. Yet if Frye's orbit in his works of the 1970s and 1980s lies in the classroom, he gradually invests this classroom with the authority of an early generation of classroom visionaries, with Socrates and Plato rather than with Leavis and Knights. These visionary affiliations explain why Frye's attitude to the 'teachable' text remains an ambivalent one. During the 1960s and 1970s, his separation of a simple, clearly identifiable subtext from the dense tangle of the textual surface met demands from parents, students and university administrators for a form of literature that could be 'taught'. The resulting dilution of the inventor's intentions involved him in years of implicit and overt rebuttals.

For Frye, the value of a syllabus based on myth lies not in the student's exposure to narrative motifs but in some larger archetypal or visionary synthesis. He objects to the idea of the canonical text as a work which a teacher can process into a fifty-minute talk or a six-thousand-word article. Rather, he conceives of an education where daily pedagogic practice and advanced scholarship combine to show that 'all knowledge is personal knowledge'. For Frye, the teacher discharges a Socratic charisma by leading the student 'to recognize what he already potentially knows' (GC, xv). As an educator committed to human renovation on the broadest front, Frye sees his mission as going beyond the standard university lecture, and to this end he has devised curricula that provide access to myths and archetypes for high-school students. Most children, he argues, think in images, not concepts; they are all poets *avant la lettre*. By restoring to them the means of access to the images they grasp unconsciously in their rhymes and chants, we can ensure that their learning becomes a relearning, the restoration of a lost identity.

Frye sees a revitalized canon based on myth as the key to the integrated adult personality described in *The Educated Imagination*, where mythopoesis becomes the inevitable response to the terror and promise of an alien environment. Frye conceives of the canonical work as tapping deep, barely conscious anxieties and desires. In these mythological residues – not in Eliot's perfection of a distinct language nor in Gombrich's rational execution of practised technical skill – Frye discovers the basis of canonicity. These residues explain the permanent appeal of Dickens or Shakespeare, whose work ends as 'an exploding force in the mind that keeps destroying all the barriers of cultural prejudice that limit the response to it' (MD, Preface). For Frye, the only legitimate canon consists of a repertoire of 'genuinely popular' narratives to which any audience will respond. Although he has devised curricula for use inside and outside the university, he insists that his own type of visionary criticism transcends both formalism and reproducible content. In his patient attempts to redress what he sees as a radical misunderstanding, to explain that the mythical approach rests on an epistemology rather than on a method, Frye has given much of his time since the late 1960s to articulating what it is the mythical critic actually knows. From the framework of his revisionary poetics emerge the seeds of an epistemology and a cultural theory. Frye's 'scientific' principles in *Anatomy of Criticism* led him to forswear value judgements. As a cultural critic, he aims for a similar neutrality. Here his mythic impulses lead him to stand back from the machinery of any given culture in order to identify its deep underlying patterns. This approach becomes particularly marked in his discussions of Canadian culture in *The Modern Century* (1967), *The Bush Garden* (1971), and *Divisions on a Ground* (1982). In these works, Frye refuses to measure the achievement of Canadian art by the yardsticks of a parent or metropolitan culture, which applies 'canons of criticism' formed 'on carefully polished poetry' to work composed of 'variants of the canon of great ballads'.[21] Such a rejection follows the strict logic of Frye's own programme, which measures metropolis and colony alike against a popular and visonary canon. Frye's criticism neither reduces Canadian literature to five or six poets who sound sufficiently like T. S. Eliot or W. H. Auden nor draws up a short-list of authors who reject the parent culture most decisively. Instead, he emphasizes the wildness of Canadian poetry, a wildness that takes it back to the very roots of poetic utterance in ballad and riddle. His Canadian canon is a pioneer's canon, fostering a poetry of visionary hope and anxiety. With its harsh and thinly populated environment, Frye's Canada becomes the empty space from which all human mythologies evolve.

Because he thinks criticism should illuminate the canon of mythology shared by poets everywhere, Frye avoids the Leavisian distinction between 'major' and 'minor' literature that dogs so many accounts of regional and postcolonial literature. He returns Canadian literature to its eternal backdrop by mapping out the eschatological anxieties and archetypes it shares with other mythopoeic cultures. By 'probing into the distance . . . fixing the eyes on the skyline' (BG, 222), the Canadian poet participates in the visionary canon Frye originally identified in Blake. Surrounded by evidence of 'the world's hostility to creation', the works of E. J. Pratt, A. J. M. Smith, Archibald Lampman, and D. C. Scott build up 'glints of a vision beyond nature, a refusal to be bullied by space and time, an affirmation of the supremacy of intelligence and humanity over stupid power' (BG, 142). By standing back, Frye can reconcile Canadian or any other literature with his deep mythic structures of alienation and apocalypse, even though the resulting critique seems closer to a parable of Canadian aspiration than to a history of Canadian achievement.

Such objections have failed to dislodge Frye from his chosen critical track, his almost planetary distance from conventional letters. In his view, to realize in one's mind a 'total form of vision' that embraces art, religion, and humane criticism is to 'complete the humanist revolution' by absorbing all cultures 'into a single visionary synthesis' (FS, 420). Increasingly in his later works, that vision reaches beyond humanist culture to areas of experience unclaimed by previous champions of 'canonical myth'. In books such as *The Critical Path* and *The Educated Imagination* Frye undermines the conservatism of T. S. Eliot, John Crowe Ransom and W. B. Yeats, who all saw myth as a way of binding together societies fissured by the rise to power of natural science. Instead, Frye emphasizes the dynamic, unsettling energy of myths – the Christian myth in particular, since this has historically associated itself with 'various ascendant classes' without identifying itself with those classes to the extent of Hinduism or Confucianism. At its core, Christianity 'is in its origin a revolutionary myth' whose basis lies in 'the discovery of a whole new dimension of social time'.[22] Like the biblical scholar James A. Sanders, Frye associates canonical myths with the eschatological and the teleological, not with a vanished order to which past-haunted artists appeal as to a fabulous fairy realm.

In this way, Frye distinguishes between the dynamic narrative he calls 'the Christian myth' and the stale canon of institutional Christianity. A similar distinction underpins his approach to other cultural myths. When he uses the world honorifically – and in his later works this becomes increasingly rare – Frye understands by *canon* a collection of stories that recur again and again in the course of a society's history. When he uses the word pejoratively – and this is increasingly common – he understands it as a source of unnecessary social, cultural or ecclesiastical control. Accordingly, he describes Marxism as a coda to dogmatic Christianity when he tracks down the Marxist fable of the coming revolution, which shares with Christianity a conviction based on 'a specific historical revelation, a canon of sacred texts, an obsession with the dangers of heresy, and, above all, a dialectical habit of mind'.[23] Frye's attitude to these rival canons betrays a deep ambivalence, for it is unclear whether he attacks the debasement of certain myths into dogma or any canonization of any myths. Certainly, he often criticizes the 'canonical importance' (CP, 34) of the myths he finds everywhere in the modern world, not just in Marxist dialectic but in the images of mass art, which unknowingly or deviously reproduce the patterns and archetypes of an earlier culture. The methods of Picasso or Chagall, who present different times on one visionary plane, explain many of Frye's innovations as a cultural critic. He views the verbal and visual phenomena of modernity – commercial television, advertising, popular journalism – as a massive whispering gallery of images and patterns inherited from an earlier time. The vertiginous diversity of modern life conceals a world without depth or perspective, 'a world in which we meet the same kind of things everywhere'.[24] The electronic media use 'magic lantern techniques of projected images' which foster illusions more often than visions. Frye notices such illusions in 'movies and television, and the imitation world of sports' (MC, 28). In 'the forces of advertising and propaganda', he detects a process operating 'in much the same way that, in *Paradise Lost*, Milton depicts Satan acting on Eve' (MC, 25–6). As a cultural critic Frye operates as a kind of mythical deter-minist, reading such diverse phenomena as advertising, Shake-spearian comedy, Canadian painting and spectator sport in the light of previously established mythological patterns. In the process, these patterns become not so much socially adhesive, holding together the various strata of society, as epistemologically constitutive, condi-tioning our basic perceptions of the structure of the universe. Although it originates in a bid to counteract the narrow metropolitan basis of established cultural canons, the mythic approach easily shifts from a mode of description into an instrument of judgement. In a comment which Oscar Wilde, Karl Marx, and Edward Said would all support, Frye describes Western society as 'an anti-art, an old and worn-out creation that needs to be created anew' (MC, 86).

What does he propose instead?

His procedures as a literary historian – so quick to detect similarity, so eager to return to the primitive – strongly influence his work as a cultural critic. In general he exhibits less interest in particular religions, cultures and belief systems than in the larger patterns of alienation, apocalypse and renovation he perceives beneath ordinary social practices and institutions. In *The Critical Path* (1971) he argues strongly for the importance of myth in understanding everyday experience, pointing to a cluster of significant stories of 'canonical importance' which he collectively describes as 'a myth of concern' (CP, 36). Into this omnibus category Frye channels a host of ideas normally associated with categories such as *culture, religion, tradition* and *ideology*. He views these myths of concern as the basic building blocks of culture, the inevitable outcome of any prolonged contact between human beings and an alien universe which fails to correspond to their deepest needs. In his view, this original alienation engenders a deeply antipathetic verbal culture held together by narrative:

> Early verbal culture consists of, among other things, a group of stories. Some of these stories, as time goes on, take on a central and canonical importance: they are believed to have really happened, or else to explain or recount something that is centrally important for a society's history, religion, or social structure. These canonical stories are, or become, what Vico calls 'true fables or myths'. (CP, 34)

Such aggregations of canonical narratives outlive the simpler verbal culture of earlier eras and persist into the modern world. The force of the myths lies in their capacity to give depth to existence, to align present-day realities with humanity's momentous origins and ends.

Conventional wisdom relegates mythology to the infancy of human development. Frye's visionary wisdom reverses this valuation by suggesting that 'as a culture develops, its mythology tends to become encyclopaedic. . . . A fully developed or encyclopaedic myth comprises everything that it most concerns its society to know.' In earlier periods a canonical 'myth of concern' operated by 'binding together . . . the community in common acts and assumptions' (CP, 36). In later periods such a myth becomes an agency for revolutionary innovation by charting the path towards what Frye calls 'a third order of experience . . . of a world that may not exist but completes existence' (CP, 170). In this way, Frye's 'myths of concern' move far beyond our ordinary concept of *culture* to indicate 'man's relation to other worlds, other beings, other lives, other dimensions of time and space' (CP, 36). By this point in Frye's work, the 'canonical myth' has become internalized as narrative capacity latent in all human beings and emerging into view whenever they project visions of an integrated human identity and a non-coercive social order. Poetics, epistemology and sociology all converge in a utopian primitivism that proposes a timeless quest for a world made in the image of a radical pastoral.

Frye asserts that a 'myth of concern' is both prior to and more lastingly important than ideology, religious doctrine, or even rationality. 'I think that an ideology is always a secondary and derivative thing, and that the primary thing is a mythology', he told

Imre Salusinszky. 'People don't think up a set of assumptions or beliefs; they think up a set of stories, and derive the assumptions and beliefs from the stories.' Just as the literary critic should recognize that the myth of the king's miraculous powers precedes *Macbeth*, so the student of politics needs to understand that the myth of the social contract antedates Hobbes's theory of the state. It is as a 'collection of interconnected stories' that Frye explains the canonical force of his 'myths of concern'. As described in his later works, these canonical myths lack any regulating power but possess a compensatory capacity to tap endless reserves of loyalty, reverence and esteem through the priority in human consciousness he believes that they possess.[25]

In his quest to define the conditions of a world somehow fuller than present-day secular culture, Frye interposes these 'myths of concern' as ways of reconciling humanity's common future to its common past. Yet neither of these myths – neither Frye's myth of human origins nor his myth of a visionary future – addresses the multiple conflicts of personal and social existence in present-day Western societies. Because he sees myth as 'the basis of the world we want to live in' (SM, 89), the ultimate resting-place for our heart's desire, Frye never really addresses the conflicts between our many human myths, the fact that few of them conform to our collective histories or personal biographies, or the degree to which they conflict with science and other forms of knowledge.

Because he sees myth, as he sees literature, on the largest scale and from the most distant vantage point, magisterially independent of persons and places, Frye undermines our contemporary Western notions of *culture* only to hand us back to an even more restrictive agent, religion itself. During the 1950s, the Frye who won a bitterly fought cultural and ideological independence from Eliot often appeared a resolutely anticlerical critic, complaining wryly about the modern flood of 'ecclesiasticized poetry, full of the dilemma of modern man, Kierkegaardian *Angst*, and the facile resonance of the penitential mood' (NFCL, 232). His witty sallies against contemporary religiosity veiled for a time Frye's deep immersion in religious paradigms and structures. From the publication of *Anatomy of Criticism* he viewed literature as a quest for order parallel in structure to a religious quest which conformed to Christian precedents. As a cultural critic Frye has never discarded this model, still less suggested that the human search for order can be satisfied in purely secular ways. Yet the cluster of impulses and needs satisfied by an aesthetic ordering of experience is just as often associated with secular culture as with religion, and historically, culture has flowed through many conduits unrecognized by Frye.

At the end of Frye's programme of criticism, the canon turns from a science into a doctrine, in a transformation that cuts across the liberating role he originally assigned to the humanities. Frye tracks all cultural superstructures back to a religious and, more narrowly, to a Judaeo-Christian base. His central text, the Bible, is a series of anonymous books whose unknown authors function as vessels for the Holy Word. In the modern period, Frye suggests that both critic and artist must empty out their identities as completely as St Paul. 'A scholar, *qua* scholar,' he observes, 'cannot think for himself or think at random.' Similarly, poets and artists exist simply as 'places where something new in literature was able to take its own shape' (CP, 24). Frye presented his original, Blake-sponsored canon on the assumption that the mythic or literary way of understanding the world differs significantly from all other ways. Stealthily, and rarely explicitly, works such as *The Critical Path* and *The Myth of Deliverance* amalgamate literature with other humanistic disciplines into a narrative of composite liberation. Yet the antithesis between imagination and reality Frye initially posited cannot fuse into the narrower visionary synthesis his later criticism seeks to unfold. Frye's vision of a new cultural order gradually reveals itself as a vision already anticipated in Christian narratives of fall and redemption. In its dogmatic mutation, his recent work steers dangerously near to false prophecy.

Paradoxically, the work Frye has produced in the last ten or fifteen years suggests a writer immersed in a specific set of cultural forms rather than the disseminator of a few simple, universally recognizable stories. Does his earlier work conceal a similar immersion? Certainly, it is possible that the popularity of myth criticism from the 1950s to 1970s rested on the Anglo-Catholic tradition its creator originally set out to oppose. However simplified and universalized, Frye's vision of a redeemed future draws on imagery – Job, the Messiah, crucifixion, atonement – derived from one exclusive mythological source. However powerful, his formulations of humanity's basic concerns evade the problems of a plural culture by attaching criticism to a religious – and perhaps more narrowly, to a Christian – frame of reference. Frye gives notional assent to the existence of mythologies other than the Hebraic and Christian, but the Hebraic-Christian myth remains at the centre of his own search for a visionary synthesis.

In his quest for this synthesis Frye has recently hardened his position, jettisoning still more of the customary agencies for understanding literature. Poetic statement becomes almost a contradiction in terms, since 'the real poetic meaning' opposes itself to 'the explicit meaning'. The basis for the former rests in a family of images and archetypes that 'cannot . . . be grasped in a way that makes it possible for us to say that this is what Shakespeare really meant, or had in mind, or was trying to say' (CP, 70). Intentions and explicit meanings lie on the ash–heap of a superseded version of literary theory. What remains is the deep structure of archetype and myth on which all authors draw. But in this case, why speak of authors at all? Although he arrives at the point from special mythical premisses, the Frye of the late 1960s aligns himself with the critics who discard authors, referring instead to 'structural principles . . . conventions, genres and recurring image-groups or archetypes' (CP, 24). Having discarded authors, why speak of canons? 'An open mythology has no canon', Frye remarks in *The Modern Century* (1967, 118), contrasting the disposable imagery of a free society with the dogmatically unalterable stock of a closed one.

Frye rejects the old-style regulating and legislating canon which literary criticism borrows from institutional religion, emphasizing that the authority of any modern seer will always be tentative since no one can 'be given any authority beyond what they earn by their own merits' (MC, 118). He adds:

> Perhaps, if we think of the reality of religion as mythical rather than doctrinal, religion would turn out to be what is really open about an open mythology: the sense that there are no limits to what the human imagination may conceive or be concerned with. (MC, 120)

The fluctuating, malleable world of mythology, with its magical overlappings of mind and body, mind and matter, time and space, becomes Frye's model for a cultural canon. As he sees it, mythology produces human culture and reinforces it; mythology lies as close as we can come to the hidden force propelling history as a whole: 'A mythology rooted in a specific society transmits a heritage of shared allusion and verbal experience in time, and so mythology helps to create a cultural history' (GC, 34).

Can the Christian narrative meet the demand for a total cultural mythology? In *The Great Code* (1982) Frye strongly argues that it can, by showing how the Bible systematically flouts 'conventional aesthetic canons' (GC, xiii, xvi) of beauty, of harmony, or even of authorship. The anonymous canon of Scripture forms the natural terminus for Frye's view of literary and cultural history. The Bible finally 'evades all literary criteria' (GC, xvi), dissolving them in the interests of a deeper order. More than any other generally recognized text, the Bible exposes the roots of our mythically conditioned existence, restoring the basic truth that we live 'not directly or nakedly in nature like the animals, but within a mythological universe'. Frye characterizes this universe as 'a body of assumptions and beliefs' developed from our most basic 'existential concerns' (GC, xviii).

In *The Great Code* Frye works hard to purge the Bible of its associations with worldly notions of plausibility and historicity, which he dismisses as our 'modern canons of credibility' (GC, 41). Instead, the Bible promises nothing more binding than 'some sense of a *canon*' (GC, 33) – in other words, a series of interconnected images, themes, motifs and narrative situations which we ourselves must humanly construe. For William Empson, the Bible closes with the scandalous ascension of Christ, after his crucifixion, as God the Father, condemning humanity to the cycles of guilt and atrocity which swirl inexorably down into Hiroshima and Auschwitz. For Frye, in sharp distinction, the human history of Jesus culminates 'at the point at which master and servant become the same person, and represent the same thing' (GC, 91), a bold reversal which Shakespeare repeats at the end of *The Tempest*. At the end of the Bible there appears 'not a hierarchy but a vision of plenitude, in which everything is equal because identical with everything else' (GC, 165).

In approaching the words of the Bible, Frye's interest is 'not in doctrines of faith as such' but 'in the expanding of vision through language' (GC, 167). To this end he repeatedly selects episodes that subvert the canons of realism, plausibility, or doctrinal authority. His touchstone text, which he describes as 'the epitome of the narrative of the Bible', occupying 'the place of a poetic and prophetic Genesis' (GC, 193), almost inevitably becomes the Book of Job. Like Job himself, the Bible cannot be contained within 'the rather simpleminded Dèuteronomic framework of law and wisdom' (GC, 194). Like the humanist in a world of mass-produced images, Job endures massive alienation. In Job, the sum of all suffering, the legalistic, dogmatic canon Frye has spent his whole career in rebutting finds its decisive nemesis. The Book of Job returns Frye's visionary canon to its source in a kernel of Christian paradox.

CHARISMATIC NARRATIVE: FRYE'S GREAT CANONICAL BOOK

Priest, polemicist, revisionist, reviewer, scientist, sage – Frye has played all these roles as a critic, and his performance in each seems so self-contained that the separate identities virtually go their own way. What unites them is the effort to articulate a charismatic narrative, the story of a great canonical book in which the visionary wisdom of all ages and cultures becomes miraculously distilled. 'The canonical significance', he notes, 'which distinguishes the myth from less important fictions also causes myths to form large unified structures, or mythologies, which tend to become encyclopedic in extent, covering all aspects of a society's vision of its situation and destiny.'[26] Few twentieth-century critics have the resources to communicate such an encyclopaedic vision; in many ways, Baudelaire and Ruskin appear to be Frye's analogues rather than the professionally accredited, institutionally aligned member of the contemporary Modern Language Association.

The modern university, of course, presents neither the most likely nor the most appropriate location for the charismatic mission of a visionary critic. Part skills centre, part nesting-ground for dissent, part finishing school, it still remains, in Frye's view, the centre for 'the community of spiritual authority' (SS, 256) in the late twentieth century. In the contemporary debate about the shape and ends of the academic canon, he remains one of the few critics who refuse to validate literature by squaring it with the changing fashions of the contemporary intellectual. Against the progressive fallacy so common among those intellectuals, Frye presents his own mythical viewpoint, in which the presiding tropes are not conflict and accommodation but identity and reversal. In Frye's work, myth becomes the great leveller which enables the postcolonial culture of Canada to measure itself alongside European and American literature. Instead of a closed canon resting on metropolitan edict or institutional dogma, Frye projects an open canon emanating from desire, the universal desire to project mind into matter and the universal hope of self-transformation across space and time.

These recurring themes explain, in turn, why Frye's criticism has always based itself on a final identity between narratives and on a climactic peripeteia, a point at which canonical narratives strike out from conventional expectations. Frye uncovers such reversals in Shakespearian comedy, in Spenserian romance, in Blake's *Songs*, and in most of the works he values. And his own criticism reinforces these values through the astonishing series of reversals by which he attacks our established preferences for difference rather than identity, realism rather than romance, dogmas rather than myths. In an effort to distance himself from the darker mythologies of D. H. Lawrence and W. B. Yeats, Frye emphasizes that his is not a sexual or racial mythology, a mould into which any given society must be pressed. 'Myths are seldom if ever actual hypotheses that can be verified or refuted' (MC, 115), he observes. Frye's myths belong with the world of the possible, the 'as if' world or More and Blake, not the 'and then' world of Hitler and Mussolini. Even so, his hatred of totalitarian systems has not stopped Frye from serving as a veritable Minister of Propaganda for mythology. His role in steering Canadian poetry from a cult of irony *à la* Eliot to a poetry based on folklore and myth is documented in the many reviews he contributed to *Canadian Forum* and *University of Toronto Quarterly* during the 1940s and 1950s. In *The Modern Century* he presents culture as the sum of its mythologies, matching his vision of a world integrated by literature against the vision of his compatriot Marshall McLuhan of a global village linked by the electronic media. In this book Frye steps so far back from his material that few but his disciples will recognize his 'modern century'. Yet distance can also lend enchantment, and accordingly Frye's most audacious successes come when he subjugates time to space and the corporeal eye to the eye of vision, a process described and enacted in his recent book on Shakespeare. 'In many tales of the *Tempest* type', he concludes,

> the island sinks back into the sea when the magician leaves. But we, going out of the theatre, perhaps have it in our pockets like an apple: perhaps our children can sow the seeds in the sea and bring forth again the island that the world has been searching for since the dawn of history, the island that is both nature and human society restored to their original form, where there is no sovereignty and yet where all of us are kings. (NFS, 186)

False prophecy perhaps, but magnificent narrative. Frye has always seen Shakespeare as canonical for any vision of a better world or a finer life. Characteristically, his interpretation of Shakespearian romance focuses not on its imputed 'problem elements' but on its restorative final vision. Travelling a critical path that leads from folk tale to vision, Frye represents this quintessential canonical author not as Mackail's epitome of the English national genius but as an anarchic visionary telling a stirring, liberating story the whole of society deserves to know. In this way, the 'canonical myth' Frye borrows from Blake and replenishes for the next forty years lays the foundation for some of the most imaginative postwar criticism. Its status – as art, science, rule, or revelation – appears in the 1990s more equivocal than its creator has ever assumed. But in dislodging his visionary canon, Frye's critics will find no more compelling story of alienation and renewal, a story that rivals some of the works it interprets in its powerful narrative force.

Whether he deals with canonical Scriptures or canonical authors, Frye articulates a vision that undermines those canons from within. His ambitious rewriting of our traditional canons retains the symbolist vision of literature as a realm of latent value while insisting that value can be dispersed without dilution to the widest possible audience. His criticism rarely proceeds without the toppling of some idols, although his synoptic sweep gives him little time to dwell on the enormity of his own iconoclasm. Unlike the upholders of a closed canon from Aquinas to Eliot, Frye sees no virtue in scarcity. His conception of the 'total literary field' as a vessel of the sacred accepts Blake's axiom 'Everything that lives is holy'.

Perhaps contemporary critics reject that premise; perhaps they lack Frye's encyclopaedic learning: whatever the reason, few 'canonbusters' have tried to match his comprehensive counter-canon. Attacks on the inequality of university appointments, assaults on Leavisian assessments of canonical reputations, repudiations of ways of reading texts which enjoyed their highest authority during the 1950s – none of these rivals the wide-ranging erudition Frye takes to the construction of his all-embracing mythological canon. Among the critics who have followed him in finding the established canon politically and imaginatively harmful, only Edward Said, the subject of a later chapter, outlines a comparably inclusive alternative. Frank Kermode, the critic to whom we turn next, offers a more cautious, minimalist canon than either critic. Where Frye's canon becomes an interconnected narrative that potentially includes all authors and literary forms, Kermode weaves sophisticated webs of constantly shifting interpretation from single canonical texts. We shall see in the following chapter how Kermode juggles the competing claims of past and present into an unarrestable canonical synthesis, a fluctuating canon hospitable to all possible interpretative demands – except the demand for the final dissolution of the canonical text.

5

Frank Kermode and the Canon of Interpretation

DEEP STRUCTURES: THE CANON IN A PLURAL WORLD

At first glance, a canonical unanimity between the authors of *Forms of Attention* and *Anatomy of Criticism* might appear unlikely. It was Kermode, after all, who devoted his famous book *The Sense of an Ending* to a rebuttal of *myth*, the set of permanent forms situated at the visionary centre of Frye's work. By interposing the more provisional idea of the *fiction* in the space vacated by *myth*, Kermode signalled, as early as 1966, his readiness to lend his authority to the anti-canonists as the canon debate gradually unfurled. Kermode's fictions bear a sacred charge, but they remain instrumental rather than dogmatic, mutable rather than fixed.

Even so, one can only characterize Kermode's promise alliance with the anti-canonical critics as a troubled and perplexing one, as provisional in the end as his own fictions. For unlike other contemporary critics of the canon, Kermode comes to the debate grinding no sharp political axe. His forty-odd years as a literary critic have yielded no strong political allegiances. His many books and reviews are most stimulating when they discuss authors whose sympathies can hardly be considered radical – Allen Tate, T. S. Eliot, Wallace Stevens, W. B. Yeats. Moreover, the values which Kermode prizes in the works he examines – secrecy, paradox, learning, difficulty – leave little doubt that he has modelled his aesthetic tastes and intellectual development according to what Edward Said calls 'the canon of validation', the canon of the great moderns whose reactionary politics have long embarrassed their commentators. Even so, Kermode's very attentiveness to these moderns makes him deeply sympathetic to new ways of understanding the canon. As he has often pointed out, at the centre of twentieth-century letters lies an attempt to reimagine the past from the horizon of an anxious present. This attempt separates Kermode from some of the traditional critics he admires (and Gombrich is certainly one of these). It also moves him across the gulf that separates Edward Said from Gombrich and Frye.

In turning to Kermode and Said, the subjects of the next two chapters, we move into a world of critics who lack Frye's confidence in a universal mythical order and Gombrich's unquestioned allegiance to canonical values that rest on universal capacities of rational perception. At a time when nationality resembles a complaint from which to recover more than a virtue to affirm, when 'culture' becomes the subject of political and ideological analysis rather than a valued aspiration, canons – whether as simple rules of thumb, as mythical narratives, or as complex institutional structures – present opportunities for suspicion more than grounds for belief. Said and Kermode have both taken stock of the waves of self-doubt, interdisciplinary debate, and melancholy scepticism which have visited humanities departments in recent years. Both critics regard the territorial disputes and radical innovations of the 1970s and 1980s with considerably more sympathy than Gombrich and Frye, who exhibit an indifference verging on hostility to recent developments in poststructuralism, deconstruction, and cultural materialism.

In keeping with this new climate of sceptical assault, Kermode and Said move very tentatively indeed in their characterization of canonical activities. Not for them Gombrich's bold invocations of universal capacities for pattern-making and order, his unabashed sweep from canons of artistic excellence to the unity of humankind. Not for them Frye's *Anatomy of Criticism*, in which a cyclical classification embracing all literary forms modulates into a prophecy about the future of human society. Kermode's well-known early work, *The Sense of an Ending* (1967), takes its master pattern of human experience from a prisoner of war confined to a solitary cell, while Said's first general study, *Beginnings* (1975), resembles an extremely long Beckett play, a meditation on beginnings that permanently defers any actual beginning. Then, by a coincidence that represents rather the fruits of long methodological self-questioning and wide interdisciplinary forays than a single line of scholarship unbrokenly advanced, Kermode and Said coincidentally produced within a year of each other an important study of cultural institutions to which they themselves did not belong. During the late 1970s, each of these critics published a large synoptic study on topics one can imagine having a strong interest for Gombrich and Frye. Yet significantly, when Said writes a large narrative in his *Orientalism* (1978), he offers it as an outsider's history of a traditional scholarly discipline, while Kermode dedicates his sceptical study of the canonical Christian story, *The Genesis of Secrecy* (1979), 'to those outside'.

What remains surprising is that neither critic sees 'the canon' as the thoroughly discredited institution portrayed by the more extreme participants in the current debate, a ruined monument to the power of criticism to impose and disseminate arbitrary class, national and cultural values. Whether as legislative instrument, agency of quality control, or instruction book for the beginner, 'the canon' lies in ruins. Canons coerce, exclude and propagandize; a contemporary criticism with one eye on a more radical future can spare few good words for such an obvious relic of the past. For the 'canon-busters', the canon – always resolutely singular – functions as a cultural equivalent of the International Monetary Fund, bestowing its privilege and accumulated capital only on works that accept its parochial, but inordinately overfunded, prejudices as carrying the force of universal law. Against this backdrop of unremitting criticism, both Said and Kermode choose with considerable care their grounds of attack and defence. As I shall show, their contribution to the still-unfolding history of the late-twentieth-century canon lies in their combination of stringent criticism and sceptical reconstruction.

Needless to say, the work of reconstruction proceeds independently for each critic. Kermode's affection for the great Anglo-Saxon moderns makes his approach to the problem of the canon ultimately very different from Said's. Kermode never forgets that the Donne of T. S. Eliot and William Empson or the Marvell of *Scrutiny* seemed in their time as radically anti-canonical as Foucault and Deleuze seemed to Said in the 1980s. Where Said finds a chasm between these critics and all previous work, Kermode represents the traditional canon as the texts *worthy* of debate rather than *beyond* debate. Unlike Said, he characterizes interpretation inside the academy as motivated less by conservatism than by novelty, noting that academic advancement has traditionally required its pursuers 'to say something new about canonical texts without defacing them'.[1]

Another difference is that where Said, an intellectual willing to deploy literature in the interests of a political programme, thinks of critical debate in ultimately social terms, Kermode's allegiances remain predominantly aesthetic. Where 'debate' leads Said to the political arena – and, by degrees, to political action – Kermode moves in the opposite direction, towards the contemplation of recurring temporal and spiritual mysteries. It is no accident that much of Kermode's recent work directs itself towards exegesis of the Gospels, nor that he sandwiches between *Forms of Attention* (1985) and *An Appetite for Poetry* (1989) a study called *History and Value* which offers a powerfully non-militant critique of accepted ideas about political poetry in the 1930s and the politicization of the humanities in the 1980s. Kermode's guides are not Gramsci and Williams but (among many others) Stevens, Donne and Forster. These allegiances, in turn, explain why he conceives of the canon in terms of the sceptical contemplation of human value which is represented by a richly patterned art-work.

Like his favourite authors, Kermode remains fascinated by the way old forms and ideas – apocalypse, crisis, revelation, tradition – continue to circulate in new conditions. Unlike Said, he thinks we will never escape the shadow of the past. But does the canonical past offer a binding body of case laws, as Lawrence and Eliot sometimes suggested? Or does it rather cast an intermittent radiance on a very different contemporary environment, as Forster and Joyce prefer to think? Kermode generally takes the second approach to understanding the inherited cultural canon. Instead of viewing it as a legislative instrument, a codex from the past telling the future how to think and write, he represents the canon of excellence as an inventory of texts and images we can dispose of as we think fit, the basis of an independent modern narrative which hardly constrains us to follow narrowly in our ancestors' tracks.

Like Said, Kermode prefers to think in terms of a mobile, shape-shifting canon, always in the process of being constructed or dismantled. This mobility, in turn, explains his fascination with the range of interpretations that canonical works inspire. Where some critics see the lack of critical unanimity about important works as evidence of some deep-seated failure in the literary community, Kermode argues that rival testimonies heighten the mystery, and therefore the stature, of the interrogated texts. For Kermode, discussion, controversy, interpretation – the very virtues anti-canonical critics have recently tried to capture – underpin the whole existence and prestige of the traditional canon. In essence, Kermode's canon of interpretation seeks to liberate the traditional canon of valued texts from its associations of monolithic, immovable authority, even if this liberation weakens our sense of the stability of understanding that normally clings to canonical texts. Although Kermode has long expressed admiration for Gombrich, he does not share Gombrich's conviction that the canonical work will always remain capable of being understood. Kermode suggests, rather, that all the familiarity in the world with the original audience for *Hamlet*, the genre of its Ur-text, and the conventions of Shakespeare's contemporaries will take us no nearer to the mysteries of the play itself. Where Gombrich proceeds with absolute confidence that he can penetrate to what a work means, Kermode thinks this is impossible either for *Hamlet* or for any other masterpiece.

Kermode has also drawn Frye-like analogies between t
the secular canon and their biblical predecessors, but the ...,
narrative which for Frye constitutes the essence of the canonical
becomes for Kermode an endlessly fluctuating interpretative surplus
or potential. Frye implicitly suggests that any work virtually interprets itself. This is why much of his criticism seems to take place at
a preverbal level, at a distance where *Tom Sawyer* conforms to *The
Faerie Queene* in its patterns of ritual descent, or where *Paradise Lost*
and *Finnegans Wake* share the same pattern of quest. Because Kermode
attends to verbal texture as well as to narrative structure, his criticism
remains less concerned than Frye's with unifying motifs and systems,
so that he perpetually moves from the identification of a pattern to
the existence of a complicating countermovement. He notes approvingly that 'canonical texts . . . share with the sacred at least this
quality: that however a particular epoch or a particular community
may define a proper mode of attention or a licit area of interest, there
will always be something else and something different to say' (FA,
62). For Kermode, the canon as a whole is an open structure because
the canonical text is an open text.

Kermode thinks that the canonical text has three constant
attributes: it is hospitable to interpretation; it has sufficient depth to
support the multitude of interpretations it attracts; and, as a direct
result of these qualities, it becomes charged with mystery. One of the
qualities by which we recognize and respond to such a text becomes
what Kermode calls 'patience', a capacity for adjustment to the
changing paradigms used to explain it. Although he arrives at the
idea with more hesitancy and scepticism, Kermode, just as certainly
as Gombrich or Frye, sees the canonical text as a mysterious element
in a larger transcendent pattern. The literary *imperium* he describes as
'an imperium distorted in the transmission, subject to outrageous
claims, but in the long run still there, indeed *sine fine*'.[2] Of all contemporary critics, Kermode acknowledges most strongly the self-
conscious, constructed, primarily *narrative* properties of any canon.

It is important to realize that Kermode arrived at his idea of the
canon's patient accommodation to contemporary paradigms by an
unorthodox route. Although he spent eight stormy years, from 1974
to 1982, as holder of the pre-eminent chair of literature at an English
university, Kermode achieved this honour more in defiance of British
academic tradition than in adherence to its norms. When he suc-
ceeded to the King Edward VII Chair at the University of Cambridge, this was not a homecoming for him, as it had been for his
predecessors L. C. Knights and Basil Willey and his successors

Christopher Ricks and Marilyn Butler. Uniquely among holders of the Chair, Kermode attended the ancient English universities neither as an undergraduate student nor as a postgraduate candidate. In this way he entered Cambridge, to use his own figure, as one of 'those outside', and it is the outsider's stance that complicates his relationship with the conventions and institutions of English criticism.

As an undergraduate at the University of Liverpool, Kermode escaped not just the heavy Oxford emphasis on philology but the precisionist curriculum at Cambridge itself, with its draconian inculcation of the canonical virtues and the canonical authors. A fellow undergraduate at Liverpool was Peter Ure, who shared with Kermode the exalted view of the poetic vocation celebrated by Yeats and the Romantic poets. When Kermode moved from Newcastle to his second academic post at the University of Reading, his colleagues included D. J. Gordon and J. B. Trapp. The links between these two critics and the Warburg Institute encouraged Kermode to pursue his interest in Renaissance conventions and genre in an interdisciplinary and internationalist way.

The Warburg School, a group of eminent expatriates which has included Gertrud Bing, E. H. Gombrich, Fritz Saxl, Erwin Panofsky, Edgar Wind, Rudolf Wittkower and Frances Yates, among others, provided Kermode with a model for intellectual activity that transcended national boundaries, an important point for a young scholar from the Isle of Man who neither hailed from the metropolis nor trained at one of the major British institutions. In the works of the Warburg School, tradition becomes a latent, ever-renewable source of spiritual potential rather than a 'natural' (i.e. perpetually fixed) reflection of a cultural disposition. For the Warburgians, poetic or artistic images belong to no particular artist or society, but reflect internationally diffused aspirations and fears. This is why Warburgian cultural history frequently engages with the latent imaginative properties of images and themes circulated across national boundaries among groups of artists. It is useful to note, too, that despite their enormous respect for high culture, the Warburg critics often discuss popular art. Warburg's research took him to Native American festivals and European postage stamps. Panofsky contributed an essay on cinema to *Transition*. In her work on Renaissance culture, Frances Yates redeemed mountebanks and adventurers, placing them on a plane of vision alongside Newton and Bacon. When Dora and Erwin Panofsky studied the transformations of the image of Pandora's box, they discussed Frank Wedekind and postwar cartoons about nuclear weapons, as well as classical mythology. The seeds of Kermode's freewheeling juxtapositions of St Mark's Gospel and Thomas Pynchon perhaps lie in the wide-ranging undertakings of the Warburg critics. This background also explains why Kermode's idea of the canon differs so radically from some of his British contemporaries. Marilyn Butler, for instance, his second successor to the King Edward VII Chair, viewed the canon in her 1987 inaugural lecture 'Revising the Canon' in terms of what it is 'natural' for undergraduates in a particular community to read. Additions to the canon, she suggests, must 'emerge with time, and from consultation'. In particular, Butler wants to renegotiate our understanding of the Romantic canon, exploring it not so much through the apocalyptic, international and sacred paradigms established by Frye, Harold Bloom and M. H. Abrams, but through the gradual, social and national frames of reference that emerge if we see Wordsworth in terms of Robert Southey, Landor, and Samuel Rogers. 'It will begin to seem more natural to us in the future', she argues, 'to replace the old thin line of national heroes with a richer and more credible notion: that writers represent groups and attitudes within the community, and therefore from time to time come dynamically into contention with one another.'[3] It seems more useful to Butler for Cambridge undergraduates to trace these internal lines of affiliation than to compare Wordsworth with Aquinas and Shelley with Proust. In effect, Butler hopes to turn a visionary company into a limited or representative company, spurning mergers with foreign associates such as Novalis or de Vigny. Her view of the canon as a kind of incremental national stock is designed to address a particular institution's curricular needs; it could hardly be more opposed to the idea of *canon* Kermode discovered among the Warburg School and shares with a line of secular critics stretching from Schiller to Frye. The canon all these critics invoke is a large, atemporal sacred book stretching from Augustine to Beckett – a difficult, impersonal narrative transcending nations and authors, and therefore imbued with a charismatic aura.

CANON V. TRADITION?

Kermode's quest to define the canon in terms of imaginative potential rather than social or political property first became apparent in *Romantic Image* (1957), a study of critics and poets who 'do not always acknowledge their inheritance, and indeed are frequently associated with critical positions avowedly hostile to Romantic aesthetics'.[4] Although at this stage Kermode describes his area of investigation as a 'tradition' or 'inheritance' rather than as a canon, *Romantic Image* prefigures his subsequent thinking on canons in some important directions. First, the 'tradition' he uncovers remains a latent one; even at this early stage in his career, Kermode thinks that a historian of modernity should distinguish between stated commitments and deep but occluded concerns. Reading against the grain of Eliot's official statements, Kermode discovers a deep unity between the Romantic period and the modern world, just as the Warburgians rejected the idea of a schism between the Renaissance and antiquity. Like the Warburg School, Kermode concerns himself with recurring poetic images as vehicles for a matrix of psychological anxieties and as secular vessels for sacred energies. Like the Warburg School, he wants to suggest 'ways of looking at the past which provide valuable insights into essentially modern possibilities and predispositions' (RI, 138).

Inevitably, these suggestions also lead him to attack certain less valuable contemporary ways of looking at the past. His principal target lies in the annotations to Eliot's 'tradition' which British and American critics constructed after the appearance of *The Sacred Wood*. For Eliot could not content himself with the role of critic; he even turned intellectual and cultural historian, hinting that 'something had happened to the mind' of England that somehow made Herbert a more traditional poet than Tennyson. In his early essays, Eliot laid out a *cordon sanitaire* between the 'modern' literature practised by Pound and the 'Romantic' literature practised by Shelley and Tennyson. In effect, almost despite his own intentions, Eliot inaugurated a canon, a binding set of precedents by which to measure all subsequent achievement. From Eliot's suggestive but largely undeveloped asides, a whole set of valuations and exclusions sprang up. F. R. Leavis traced the fortunes of 'the line of wit' in *Revaluation* (1936); Cleanth Brooks distinguished between the valuable and the worthless in modern poetry in *Modern Poetry and the Tradition* (1939); L. C. Knights preserved the undissociated segments of the English tradition in successive volumes of his *Explorations* (1947, 1965, 1976); S. L. Bethell set out to discover what 'happened to the English mind' in *Shakespeare and the Popular Dramatic Tradition* (1944) and *The Cultural Revolution of the Seventeenth Century* (1951); while Patrick Cruttwell explored the Jacobean crisis outlined in Eliot's essays on Marston and Middleton in *The Shakespearean Moment* (1954). Although Cruttwell repudiated orthodox affiliations in his preface, Bethell, a Welsh clergyman, could hardly offer the same demurral, and Leavis and Knights were prominent disciples. During the 1940s and 1950s, Eliot's potent fragments were effectively becoming canon law.

Throughout *Romantic Image* Kermode chips away at the authority enjoyed by Eliot's restrictive, quasi-historical canon, showing that the 'tradition' outlined by Eliot and fleshed out by his followers represents an imaginative construction rather than a legislative instrument. Its basis, in other words, lies in story rather than in history. Eliot's compelling narrative about the fortunes of 'tradition' led to the acceptance of an essentially symbolist canon that yoked together so unlikely a group of associates as Donne, Herbert and Pound, while excluding, among many others, Milton, Wordsworth and Tennyson. 'The historical effort of Symbolism', Kermode notes,

has been to identify a period happily ignorant of the war between Image and discourse, an un-dissociated age. In the end, it is not of high importance that any age selected for this role is likely to be found wanting, except of course for the tendency to exclude particular poets and periods from the canon. (RI, 150)

Later scholarship and criticism, mistaking Eliot's fiction for the fabric of event, laboured to find the disasters and to formulate the patterns which made Eliot's story more plausible. In effect, Eliot's high-sounding abstractions glossed over a search for a more numinous age than history could offer, a search prosecuted in the work of Blake, Coleridge and Wordsworth – the very canon modern critics declared themselves against.

In *Romantic Image* Kermode shows how writers of the stature of Hulme, Yeats and Eliot bequeathed to their followers a fatal search for a non-existent canon lodged in a fabulous golden age. Each of these major early modern writers tries to 'search history for this critical moment, and because they share much the same poetic heritage, they are all looking for much the same kinds of rightness and wrongness in historical periods' (RI, 145). What is Kermode's attitude to this fatal search? The closing pages of *Romantic Image* ruthlessly demolish the historical authority of Eliot's canon. Even so, they display great sympathy with the *needs* incorporated in such a canon. Much modern literature testifies to a desire for spiritual possibilities without dogmatic constraints, a desire Kermode has no intention of gainsaying. Having returned to literary criticism after six years of war, he shows considerable sympathy with attempts to imagine a world more unified and orderly than the world of recent historical events. It is perhaps this sympathy that leads him to quote Yeats's words on the 'ancient canon discovered in the Greek gymnasium, which, whenever present in painting or sculpture, shows a compact between the artist and society' (RI, 57). Although he makes the point more tentatively than Yeats, Kermode implies that such a compact, suitably modified to meet social and individual needs, offers a paradigm for the role of every successful artist in any society which values cultural achievement.

Just as the Warburg School searched for every possible piece of imagery that might link antiquity to modernity, so the Kermode of *Romantic Image* ransacks modern literature to uncover an older romanticist canon and then, having uncovered it, traces that canon back to an ever more primitive set of literary images. As he describes the pattern of aboriginal bliss, catastrophic fall, and miraculous regeneration which turns up again and again in Romantic and modern criticism in order to justify a particular set of cultural preferences and imaginative needs, Kermode moves to some inescapable conclusions. Modern criticism has composed for itself a sacred narrative, a theodicy that justifies the ways of an obscure and difficult poetry to a fallen industrial society. Modern canons are sacred stories which aim to convert their audiences, weaning them from the modern world to a haven of images that suggests a model for unity, consensus, and homogeneity in the distant past. As fictional constructions these canons have considerable attraction for Kermode; as bodies of case law he finds them uncompelling and inadequate.

Does this recurring attraction explain his unexpected sympathy with the 'tradition' he attacks? In a sense, Kermode writes his criticism in the margins of other men's dogmatisms. However much he might later deplore what he has called 'the earnest and immodest tone of the conventicle',[5] his early intellectual choices mark him as a member of the congregation. Although he could hardly have felt the ferocity of the critical battles that resulted in the canonization of Marvell and Donne by leading Cambridge critics in the 1930s, his projected master's thesis on the poetry of Abraham Cowley would have made little sense outside assumptions sponsored by T. S. Eliot's essays on the Metaphysical poets. The self-consciousness, the scepticism, and the respect he brings in *Romantic Image* to an Eliot-sponsored 'tradition' all prefigure his own canon of interpretation – a canon open to the present, reverent of the past, yet still, at its core, difficult and paradoxical. Unlike Said, Kermode revels in the mystery the canonical work gradually accumulates. He does not credit this mystery to the operation of the political or cultural confidence trick which Said sees behind the eminence of Eliot. On the contrary, like Eliot himself, Kermode accepts that 'poets in our civilization, as it exists at present, must be *difficult*'.[6] These difficulties reflect the Luciferian ambitions of modern artists described in *Romantic Image*. But they also reflect the contradictory demands made of modern art: that it should be realistic *and* numinous, that it should draw on deep reserves of heterodox spirituality while retaining a worldly superstructure. All these contradictions Kermode sees as resting in 'the image', the vessel for sacred mysteries in an age of secular responsibilities.

Even so, Kermode's mysteries are not dogma in disguise, but reflect instead his desire to steer 'tradition' into a region of uncommitted and perpetual transience, away from its warring factions and fervent admirers. Where many other academics of the 1960s aligned them- selves either with Eliot or with the increasingly vocal counterculture, Kermode moved cautiously, conceding the institutional basis of the canon of masterpieces only to emphasize the institution's importance as the canon's first line of defence. In his essays of the early 1960s Kermode intensified his attack on the thousand ways of excluding half its major works which current English criticism presented as its unalterable, time-sanctioned mode of enquiry. In 1963, for instance, he noted that 'there is surely a *prima facie* case for thinking that a poetic tradition is impoverished by the neglect of poets formerly, and during great periods, held to be masters'.[7] For so long, he suggests, critics have set a culture's bearings by its canonical monuments, sup- posed repositories of all that is certain and unchanging. But to jet- tison these assumptions does not deliver the canon to the adversarial culture. The new academic canon envisaged by Kermode requires only that critics relinquish their claims to dogmatic certainty about an author's official intentions, along with their other irritating cer- tainty – their certainty about the resistance of interpretation to radical cultural change.

In *The Sense of an Ending* (1967), his other important work from this period, Kermode's engagement with canons is still intermittent and implicit, the tentativeness of his commitments very marked. Once again he takes an alternative, outsider's, perspective on a current Anglo-American critical idea. During the 1950s and 1960s, some North American institutions shifted the validation of a canonical text from Eliot's 'tradition' to the 'mythic' or 'archetypal' favoured by Frye and Ernst Cassirer. If *Romantic Image* undermines the canonical authority of 'tradition', *The Sense of an Ending* repeats the medicine for Frye's 'myth'. Kermode's critique of myth demands new resources of style and a wide range of reference, but at the heart of his complex argument lies a simple opposition. For Kermode, a myth is a simple story that explains everything, whereas his own preferred instrument, the 'fiction', tells complex stories that explain phenomena only provisionally.

His concern with the provisional and the fluctuating explains why Kermode compares the tentative working hypotheses of quantum physicists to the arguments of medieval jurists, suggesting that both of these reconcile precedents to new and more complex experiences rather than abandon precedents completely. The delicate reconciliations between old and new that characterize clerical debate through the centuries also apply, he argues, to a modern physicist such as Niels Bohr. In his theory of complementarity 'Bohr is really doing what the Stoic allegorists did to close the gap between their world and Homer's, or what St Augustine did when he explained, against the evidence, the concord of the canonical scriptures.'[8] Once again Kermode opposes the authority of any single scheme of value, insisting instead that clerical fictions enjoy a precarious existence as disposable instruments in a shifting, dark, sceptical enquiry. In Eliot's 'tradition' or Frye's 'myth', Kermode sees a doomed attempt to contain multiplicity in a single authoritative pattern. 'Fictions' acknowledge plurality; their reconciliations of heterogeneous phenomena always remain provisional.

In other words, the impetus behind Kermode's early reordering of cultural priorities comes from adjustment: canons, archetypes, precedents and paradigms will not survive, he argues, in a world of disturbingly rapid change. Whether in physics, in scriptural interpretation or in classical philology, a 'fiction' becomes a model of the world, a paradigm that yokes together disparate phenomena by virtue of its explanatory powers, while avoiding 'the regress into myth which has deceived poet, historian, and critic' (SE, 43). Kermode values imagination, not doctrine; he wants to make sense of experience, not to imprison it in classical notions of order. This explains why, where Eliot speaks of tradition, Kermode, like I. A. Richards, speaks of needs. As Kermode sees it, survival in the modern world calls for a delicate adjustment of precedents and accepted canons in the interest of two conflicting contemporary needs. These needs – the need for value and the need for change – justify the tactic of validation by compromise, accommodation and interpretation.

Kermode sees the point of contact between these conflicting values as the 'need to know the shape of life in relation to the perspectives of time' (SE, 3). The shadow of his later work becomes apparent in the way that, throughout *The Sense of an Ending*, he lingers longest on needs traditionally justified by religion and art. He even reports sympathetically on a recent critical attempt to see existentialism as 'an adaptation of Christian eschatology' (SE, 142). The same sympathy encourages him to set the patterned images of mortal experience provided by Aquinas and Spenser against the momentary, fictive concordances of a Sartre or a Christopher Burney. For the authoritative epic narrative of crisis and fall described in *Romantic Image*, *The Sense of an Ending* substitutes a kind of internalized canon, a pattern of complementary and antithetical needs that measure themselves against valued art-works. This shifting canon of recurring human valuations replaces the existing pattern by which canonical works are measured in relation to some non-existent cultural centre, some hypothetical Rome. Rather than applying a single measuring rod to a multiplicity of works, Kermode wants to encourage a tentative mode of assent to a method of playing off past against present which he characterizes as 'clerical sceptism' (SE, 57).

The loose, tentative, shifting canon of interpretation endorsed by the Kermodian clerkly sceptic relinquishes legislative authority for imaginative connection. For Eliot's binding, law-enforcing canon Kermode substitutes a tacit line of continuity that links Spenser, Milton, Wordsworth, Eliot, Yeats and Pound along a common thread of human need. In effect, although he never spells this out, Kermode's canon becomes an unauthorized, even an unconscious, narrative of the search for a spiritual unity unavailable from the official sources. The very idea of a canon becomes just one more instance of the search for pattern undertaken by human beings as they thrust themselves 'into the middest' (SE, 7). After reading *The Sense of an Ending*, no student of the humanities could doubt that this search recurs at all periods in history, not just at its high Anglican or high modernist peaks.

PRIVATIZING THE MONUMENTS: HOW THE CLASSICS SURVIVE

As this chapter unfolds, we shall see the three main stages mark Kermode's meditations on this ever-fluctuating canon of interpretation. During the first stage, which is represented by *Romantic Image*, he operates, by and large, as a traditional literary critic. He inspects images, compares conventions, and reports on his reading in a generally informal manner. At the second, transitional stage represented by *The Sense of an Ending* and *The Classic*, Kermode still confines his attentions to the individual canonical work rather than addressing the canon as an academic or institutional phenomenon. At this stage, however, he markedly expands his field of reference to undertake raids on areas ranging from atomic physics to structural linguistics.

At the third stage, exemplified in works such as *Forms of Attention* and *An Appetite for Poetry*, he becomes overtly concerned with the canon as a cultural institution sustained by interpretative liberty.

It is at this point that Kermode, unlike Gombrich or Frye, becomes interested in issues of interpretation and evaluation as they relate to the humanities as a whole. Moving freely between art history, psychoanalytical theory, scriptural interpretation and literary criticism, Kermode searches in his later works for the basic needs and shared tools necessary for any proficient interpretation. Such unprecedented catholicity of means and ends makes his recent criticism unusually wide-ranging, even in a period when the walls of the disciplines appear to be crumbling. At this third and latest stage of his career, he undertakes a sustained investigation of the interrelationship between sacred and secular canons and the institutions entrusted with their transmission. The result is *The Genesis of Secrecy, History and Value* and *An Appetite for Poetry*, each of which outlines the implications for literary criticism of current theological debate about the canon.

'Late periods', from Shakespeare to Blackmur, usually mark an increasing self-consciousness, and Kermode's later criticism is no exception. His recent canonical formulations do not, however, take the form of impassioned defences of traditional valuations, as they do for Gombrich in *Ideals and Idols*. Nor do they become theses nailed at the door of the academy of the sort presented by Said in *Orientalism*. In Kermode's later criticism, the criticism prefigured by *The Sense of an Ending*, his engagement with the vital contemporary questions about canons – their formation, transmission, aesthetic function; their role in the structures of university education and human need – becomes more intense but simultaneously more occult. From now on Kermode reveals himself as the Erasmus among the canonists, preferring compromise to unyielding authority and reinterpretation to outright schism. Perhaps it says something about the increasing polarization inside the humanities that his work – cautious, almost scholastic in its learning, wit and detachment – has proved remarkably controversial, attacked by conservative humanists such as Helen Gardner on the one side and by radicals such as Jane Tompkins on the other.[9]

So intent does Kermode become from the early 1970s on demythologizing the academic canon that his discussion occasionally turns it into nothing more than a rhetorical device or sketchy ground-plan. 'There tends to be a canon, variable of course', he concedes in 'The Young and the Elders' (1970), an essay written in the

United States at a time of burgeoning campus strife. But the origins and operations of this unavoidable curricular instrument reflect no great cultural plot. Instead, 'works that get into it are works particularly susceptible to the necessarily varying methods of talking and being persuasive about them'. Kermode offers no direct answer to a set of politically motivated complaints. He has no intention of disturbing the established canon; what he wants are simply 'new ways of making the monuments new, taking them out of the temporal rat race, changing them as needed'.[10] Even more strongly than Gombrich, Kermode describes the demoted, but still valuable and integral, canon of monuments in practical terms, emphasizing the central importance of a group of valued texts during a period of rapidly changing cultural values. At the same time, he wants to defuse the unpleasantness that attaches to these texts in the course of angry campus debate. In institutional terms, he asserts that the canon is nothing more than a stock of available texts about which particular instructors can talk persuasively to particular groups of students.

Yet if Kermode formulates his general arguments in terms of a canon that endures because of its powers to accommodate whatever instructor or world view happens to be current, his private interpretations of his chosen texts reflect a more introspective purchase on the mysterious or paradoxical properties of the canonical work. Kermode does not take the road followed later by Harold Bloom; he will not rest his case for canonicity on the existence of a tradition of misinterpretation. But he does concede a point unlikely to be welcomed by either Frye or Gombrich, the idea that the canonical text presents itself in many different shapes to many different minds. For Kermode, canonical survival entails the relinquishment of the work's identity to the activity of an interpreter.

In 'Survival of the Classic', a lecture published in *Shakespeare, Spenser, Donne* (1971), the problem of the canon moves for the first time to the very centre of Kermode's thought. At a time when widespread university demonstrations and unrest pointed to a climate among students that hardly made the conservation of cultural monuments a pressing international priority, Kermode emphasizes that anyone entrusted with the transmission of canonical texts might harbour 'a perfectly reasonable doubt about the fate of the classics after our day'. Now, in implied opposition to the current climate, Kermode couches his first extended discussion of the canon in terms of its preservation and defence. The classics, the time-honoured works, he sees as belonging 'to a shadowy, indefinite canon which is, for everybody concerned with survival from the lowly pastorate to the inspired theocrat – that is, from the working schoolmaster to the legislating critic – the best analogue we have to the less mutable canon of the church'.[11]

Even so, in 'Survival of the Classic' Kermode assumes that this 'urgent question', as he terms it, becomes most urgent of all inside the academy. So little of a utopian is Kermode compared with such critics of the canon as Frye, Said, or even F. R. Leavis that his hopes for canonical survival make sense only in terms of the institutional structure of an academy that can comprehend and adjust to social change without being essentially changed by it. In other words, Kermode's response to a growing climate of hostility towards classical works is to shift the plane of debate altogether. He acknowledges the political objections to canonicity but resolves them in a higher unity, soothing the ruptures of schism with the balm of mysticism. Kermode sees the academy as a church that gives all the appearance of temporal immersion while retaining a secret allegiance to its own spiritual laws. As in the church, grandly authoritative past readings encourage similar revaluations in the present.

The canonical text Kermode takes to demonstrate these points is Shakespeare's *King Lear*, whose contemporary prestige depends, he thinks, on 'a continuous tradition of valuation' (SSD, 166). Like Johnson, Kermode sees 'length of and duration of esteem' as indices to canonical value. But where Johnson saw a phalanx of witnesses offering broadly similar testimony, Kermode argues that the sheer variety of the interpretations of *King Lear* offer the key to its survival: 'That the answers will be very various is likely to have something to do with the survival of *Lear*' (SSD, 167). As his argument unravels it becomes clear that Kermode wants to dislodge the dogmatism attached to canonical works by pointing to a tradition, stretching from Johnson to Peter Brook, of what he calls ' "saving *Lear*", legiti-mating it . . . preserving, at whatever cost to the body of the play itself, its live relation to our world, as the Stoics allegorized Homer and as theologians demythologize the Bible' (SSD, 173). Kermode's search for what he calls 'the canonicity of *Lear*' leads him through a series of adjustments and interpretations that links Johnson and Tate (who flin-ched at its seemingly unalloyed pessimism) to Brook and Kott (who want to make it still more pessimistic). Pondering all these powerful attempts to grasp the play's essence, Kermode observes that it is useless to scan a canonical work in order to fix some core of determinate meaning. *Lear*, like all Shakespearian tragedies, possesses an inter-pretative surplus: there is 'too much of it for one's perception, or anybody else's, to organize' (SSD, 175). The survival of the canonical work depends on it giving up some of this surplus – breaking off, as it were, fragments from its substance while still remaining miraculously intact.

For Kermode, the work's continued survival in *our* time almost entails that it surrender itself as a dramatic event to the restless enquiries of its interpreters. This is why he can stoically accommodate himself to a *Lear* without Goneril and Regan, a *Lear* where Cordelia miraculously survives – even a Peter Brook *Lear* where Cornwall's act of charity must be elided in order to avoid 'the tint of sympathy' (SSD, 172). As Kermode envisages it in this essay, a canonical work survives in the form of sacred fragments preserved by the efforts of interpreters who can never hope to capture it whole. In effect, he describes a class of almost spiritually inspired exegetes who ensure the survival of the canonical work by their willingness to 'say, in a hundred different accents and with all the authority they can muster, "This is valuable; this endures as long as we do"' (SSD, 180). What survives is a work utterly purged of action and character yet so miraculously replete with significance that it can repay the efforts of endless, varied meditation. By the end of the essay, it has become clear that Kermode's emphasis on *Lear*'s 'obsessed, dreamlike quality' (SSD, 178) conceals his barely veiled fascination with the spiritual images and anxieties he sees as the inexhaustible raw materials of the modern classic.

In 'Survival of the Classic' Kermode's frame of reference remains the sacred story he uncovered in *Romantic Image*, refashioned to fit his own tolerant, sceptical, contemporary assumptions. None the less, it is useful to notice how much of this story he jettisons at successive stages of his career. First, his argument is couched in almost existential terms; it is about 'survival', not about vigorous cultural life. Second, he abandons the idea of a fixed canonical core, that inescapable residue of value to which Frye and Gombrich remain so tightly attached. The important point for Kermode is to keep the valued object alive, not to fix its prolonged existence according to a particular set of curricular constraints or cultural paradigms. Compared with Gombrich or Frye, Kermode's instincts seem latitudinarian, more eager to make peace with critical factions than to destroy or even to ignore them. For each faction contributes in its way to the collective story a canonical work gathers to itself. Kermode's aim is ultimately a mystical one: to illuminate one time by the light shed by another. Like the medieval and Renaissance philosophers who postulated a double nature for the monarch, Kermode thinks the canonical text lives on eternally despite its many local imperfections and its changing reputation over time.

Kermode, like Gombrich, often speaks of the 'value' that attaches to our more permanently honoured masterpieces. Even so, Gombrich's defence of those masterpieces rests chiefly on rational grounds; Kermode's, one must emphasize, does not. When Kermode speaks of 'value' it is as a matter of assumption and conviction, not of rational argument. His generalizations about canonicity repeatedly strip away what he sees as the disposable elements of the work – its author's intentions, the professed doctrine the work has been seen to embody, its manifest action, its generic envelope – to penetrate to its core of fluctuating human valuation. For Kermode, the canonical work's most valuable qualities arise from its position at the intersection of sense and absurdity, dream and reason, providence and disaster. The interpreted work remains a mystery; it resembles 'a dream in its condensations and overdeterminations' even though it appeals to our 'relatively unconsidered demands – the moralistic, the prudential' (SSD, 179).

In *Romantic Image* Kermode required canons to relinquish historical or legislative authority; after *The Sense of an Ending* he asks that they relinquish any aspirations to narrative certainty. As he presents it in 'Survival of the Classic', each canonical work becomes a little mystery, a fragment perpetually fascinating to those willing to defer the claims of determinate meaning, to allow the reconciliation of 'clarity coexistent with condensation' (SSD, 178). In effect, Kermode's *Lear* exists less as a dramatic action than as a recurring topic, a constellation of thematic concerns and figural resonances equally suited to Shakespeare's time and our own. Its centre becomes an interpretative potential rather than an actual, realized work. His growing concern with interpretation means that Kermode's later work increasingly moves from the canonical object to the institutions and tacit assumptions that render a work canonical.

When he next returns to canonical survival in *The Classic* (delivered as the T.S. Eliot Memorial Lectures in 1973) and *Lawrence* (also 1973), Kermode emphasizes that his broader topic is one 'that must be asked in some form whenever there is in process any kind of secular canon-formation, any choice of authorities in matters of doctrine and style'.[12] The perennial question 'What is a Classic?' must be asked, he thinks by any culture that wants to maintain a vital tradition of interpretation, for without such a tradition cultural transmission becomes impossible. Kermode thinks that the question of the classic becomes especially pressing when Eliot's imperial myth, which measures the canonicity of every work by its propinquity to Rome, loses its validity under pressure from new, radical ideologies that see 'universality' or 'timelessness' as bourgeois mythopoesis.

In 1966, Kermode reviewed very unfavourably Raymond Williams's *Modern Tragedy*, a book that presented the Western canon of tragedy as a case study in academic alienation from larger human sympathies and social priorities. By 1975, with the publication of *The Classic*, Kermode had shifted his ground. By this point, he had come to accept the radical challenge to present a new understanding of the canonical work's 'universality'. His theme remains the historical pattern of interpretation of traditionally valued literary texts. Even so, he begins by conceding the 'strong Latin and indeed Catholic bias' behind Eliot's answer to his question 'What is a Classic?' (C, 25). In the later chapters of *The Classic*, Kermode takes up the question discussed in *Lawrence* (1973): the problem of the modern canonical author, the author whose works shadow forth old dogmas but issue from a world where these dogmas no longer enjoy unquestioned authority.

Both books deepen the spirit of relinquishment and meditation apparent in *Romantic Image* and 'Survival of the Classic'. In *The Classic* Kermode points to the continuous history of 'accommodation' which has sustained the life and constructed the 'universality' of classical texts since the ancients. As he describes it, 'accommodation' refers to ancient methods of scriptural reading that historians of criticism have erroneously regarded as the distinctly modern invention of Eliot, Empson and Richards. By 'accommodation' Kermode means 'any method by which the old document may be induced to signify what it cannot be said to have expressly stated' (C, 40). The weakness of this formulation, of course, is that it turns the history of the canon into a history of contending despotisms, each bidding to capture the vacant canonical work for its own world view. At another point in his argument Kermode presses this idea even further, maintaining that the most appropriate canonical texts for the modern period are those which speak faintly in many voices, giving the effect of 'invitations to co-production on the part of the reader' (C, 113). To substantiate this thesis he explicates two texts which go halfway to meet it. *Wuthering Heights* and *The House of the Seven Gables* exist already as furtive, ambiguous works, strewn with dual narrators, fading voices and ambiguous signs. In effect, Kermode answers the old question 'What is a Classic?' by suggesting that there are two kinds of classic, an imperial classic that survives by cultural annexation and a modern classic on which 'the interpretative light falls differently, from the imagination and not from heaven' (C, 109).

In *Lawrence*, Kermode offers an extended demonstration of the mode of existence of a modern classic author. He wants to reduce the authority of contending despotisms by laying out a middle ground between the visionary, exhortatory Lawrence whom T. S. Eliot branded as heretical in *After Strange Gods* and the Lawrence described more cautiously in W. W. Robson's essay 'D. H. Lawrence and *Women in Love*', an author purged of his darker mythologies of sexuality, class, and the aristocracy of blood.[13] Demonstrating in his own work the accommodation he views as a central canonical virtue, Kermode tries to reconcile the messianic Lawrence to the 'Eng. Lit.' Lawrence by positing an author who habitually revised his doctrine in the course of constructing his narrative. For Lawrence the visionary Kermode substitutes Lawrence the reviser, merging the provincial overreacher who prophesied the collapse of the West with 'the great over-painter' whose 'habitual method is to confront the text again and again'. In this way, Kermode's Lawrence becomes the exemplary modern master whose belief in 'the novel as the *best* way of under- standing reality . . . encourages the fiction to take away the power of meaning from its author'.[14] The Lawrence whom Kermode des- cribes has relinquished his absolute control over his own creation, smothering his intentions in a tissue of vision and revision that makes certitude for author or critic inconceivable. When Kermode describes the modern classic as inevitably indeterminate, faltering and incom- plete, he moves from a reader who accommodates a text to a reader who virtually writes one. As he now construes it, the canonical text deprives its author of any originating voice; it demands a reader who can interpret its significance as well as construe its meaning.

The long series of relinquishments which Kermode calls for as the necessary grounds of canonical survival lead to an inevitable rise in the status of the canonical interpreter. For Kermode, the history of the canon settles into the history of interpretation, a history that respects few disciplinary or temporal boundaries. In *The Genesis of Secrecy* (1979) and *Forms of Attention* (1985), in the important essays 'The Institutional Control of Interpretation' and 'Can We Say Anything We Like?' (reprinted in *Essays on Fiction, 1971–82* [1983]), and in his two most recent works, *History and Value* (1988) and *An Appetite for Poetry* (1989), Kermode considers again and again the rela- tionship between sacred and secular interpretation.

In *The Genesis of Secrecy*, Kermode undertakes an extended investigation of the history of scriptural exegesis, emphasizing its constant oscillation between literal reading and figurative interpreta- tion. He emphasizes the 'high valuation' that 'is achieved by including the text in a canon, as for example with Mark',[15] stressing that the methods of interpretation which established the larger canon were identical to those used by the Evangelists themselves to establish their original texts. 'The Evangelists', he argues, 'used methods continuous with those by which, before the establishment of the canon, ancient texts were revised' (GS, 81). For Kermode, canon-making becomes a path to revelation, while revelation becomes a kind of charismatic editing, an operation that penetrates to the heart of a difficult, barely grasped experience or text in order to make it more widely understood.

When the individual books of the Bible became fused into a single scriptural canon, the interpretation of part and whole changed accordingly. This is why Kermode points to the epochal appearance of the New and Old Testaments as a canon, by virtue of which a compendium of narratives originally read as independent testimonies became incorporated into one all-encompassing sacred story maintained by a tradition of 'esoteric readings'. 'One would need to make much of the moment', he observes, 'when the Old Testament finally became joined to the New, when it was assured a permanent place in the Christian canon, from which there had been a determined attempt to exclude it' (GS, 18). Kermode presented a similarly continuous sacred narrative at work in *Romantic Image*. In that book his approach proved almost entirely demystifying. *The Genesis of Secrecy*, however, shows all the expertise of the later Kermode in fusing patterns and images into a sophisticated and ambiguous occult pattern. As its documentary authority fades, the Gospel of St Mark steadily aligns itself with the canon of high modernism. Like Joyce writing *Ulysses* or Pynchon at work on *Gravity's Rainbow*, the makers of the sacred canon produced a single complex, inclusive and inexhaustible text.

In 'Institutional Control of Interpretation' Kermode shows that the same pattern of increasingly complex interpretation appears inside the institutions devoted to the secular canon. Here too the whole history of institutional reading seems designed to elicit complex readings, to wean interpreters from 'the habit of literal reading', in order to conduct them 'out of the sphere of the manifest'.[16] It is because secular interpreters share the same values and motives as their sacred counterparts that we find it so hard today to 'distinguish between sacred and secular texts, those works of the worldly canon that also appear to possess inexhaustible hermeneutic potential' (GS, 40):

> Once a text is credited with high authority it is studied intensely; once it is so studied it acquires mystery or secrecy. This tradition undergoes many transformations, but is continuous. . . . The belief that a text might be an open proclamation, available to all,

coexisted comfortably with the belief that it was a repository of secrets. And this quality of sacred books is inherited by their counterparts in the secular canon. Shakespeare is an inexhaustible source of occult readings . . . yet at the same time he is believed to speak plainly, about most of human life, to any literate layman. Like the scriptures, he is open to all, but at the same time so dark that special training, organized by an institution of considerable size, is required for his interpretation. (GS, 144)

One difficulty with this position is that it conflates the text with the history of its interpretations, as if all fiction had the same oblique, fragmented form as St Mark's Gospel or Hawthorne's *The House of the Seven Gables*. In *The Genesis of Secrecy* and 'Institutional Control of Interpretation' Kermode suggests for the first time that latency and secrecy extend beyond a canonical narrative to become 'a property of all narrative, provided it is suitably attended to' (GS, 144). According to this formulation, a canon becomes a way of valuing an object rather than a collection of valued objects, and the value of the object depends on the form of critical attention it elicits. At this point, despite the depth of his own scepticism, Kermode comes close to providing a myth for the interpretative classes, a myth that explains and justifies the contemporary centrality of their activities in maintaining the canon.

Like any myth-maker, the Kermode of *The Genesis of Secrecy* tears down the walls that separate work from work and *sacred* from *secular*. In the process, 'canon' itself threatens to become a secondary, purely social formation. When he discusses Henry Green's novel *Party Going*, Kermode remarks that it is 'not yet part of the secular canon; that is, it has not been guaranteed to be of such value that every effort of exegesis is justified without argument'. The social corollary to this institutional attention is that 'a confession that one had not read *Party Going* would not be humiliating (a rule-of-thumb of canonicity)' (GS, 5). Not for Kermode the utopian and democratic virtues which Said and Frye attach to their respective canons or the age-old creative formulae which Gombrich identifies with his. The aura of freedom with which Kermode credits his canonical objects comes, it is important to note, from their relinquishment of continued identity in the course of successive interpretations.

It is difficult not to construe this freedom as a constricted one, a freedom that gathers inside an academy which is willing to discard subject disciplines while becoming increasingly restricted in its audience and methods. Gombrich's canonical affirmations rest on a latent order behind historical accident, a deep seam of value which all canonical works carry to the surface. However buried by time, this value can always be uncovered by the historical scholar, whose reformulations of it will have little to do with critical fashion or taste. Gombrich's Dürer remains Dürer, canonical in terms of a continuous commentary that tracks down his iconographic, allegorical, aesthetic and religious frames of reference. Kermode's Mark, on the other hand, exists as a constellation of mysteries deposited by a host of commentators. The kind of mystery Kermode identifies in his later descriptions of the canonical work is one without any ultimate solution – in other words, a mystery appealing to very esoteric tastes indeed. In Kermode's later criticism, *canon* no longer enjoys the status of a public code, as it does for Gombrich, nor a common end, as it does for Frye. In the end, Kermode's canonical work enjoys immortality on terms comparable to Tennyson's Tithonus.

Another difficulty with Kermode's position in *Genesis of Secrecy* and 'Institutional Control of Interpretation' is that by making interpretation the primary agent of canonical survival he delivers the canon to the custodianship of the academy, transforming one of the most catholic cultural phenomena into one of the most elite. To suggest that all important, educated interpretation engages 'in the business of conducting readers out of the sphere of the manifest' (EF, 182) liberates the text from political sponsorship and authorial intention only to deliver it to the unstable assumptions and norms of an embattled postwar humanistic academy. Some of the canonical works of English literature – *Gulliver's Travels, Wuthering Heights, King Lear* itself – have not survived by academic means alone and may not be served best by the academic interpreter's 'secret' readings.

In *Forms of Attention*, a work that originated in the Wellek Library lectures delivered at the University of California at Irvine, Kermode goes some way towards acknowledging the forces outside the academy which have helped to shape the traditional canon. Actually, he goes further, completely reversing the convention whereby an academic commentator laments the sad shoals of error attached to some canonical work. He begins by noting that an unpredictable mixture of amateur enthusiasms and professional expertise secures 'the preservation of canonical works by means of argument that may not be truly worthy of that name' (FA, 67). The modern institutionalized critic may often wish to forget it, but the inspired blunderer and independent scholar-enthusiast lie behind the high reputation of many present-day canonical works. In practice, a canonical work survives through a conjunction of interests –

amateur, professional, dogmatic and exegetical. 'Matters of fact', Kermode argues, 'will not maintain the life of a work of art from one generation to another. Only interpretation can do that, and it may be as prone to error as . . . ignorant opinion' (FA, 30).

Even when the canonical work is taken up by the academy, the basis for its assessment may not be entirely rational. The modern history of commentary and interpretation, Kermode argues, has 'developed its own inclusiveness' from specialized methods of interpretation which 'accorded to canonical books' the assumption 'that all their parts are occultly interrelated' (FA, 48). Delivering yet another bolt to his academic audience, Kermode emphasizes that canonical value is not just rediscovered but re-created. 'The need to remain modern', he concedes, 'imposes upon the chosen works transformations as great as any they may have undergone in precanonical redactions' (FA, 75). As an eminent member of the academic community, Kermode himself does not hesitate to supply such transformations. In *The Sense of an Ending* he saw canonicity in terms of a privileged relationship with time. In *Forms of Attention* he describes it as a skilful redistribution of interpretative space. In other words, interpretative sleight of hand underlies canonical survival. Although he speaks of 'impregnably canonical works' (FA, xiii), Kermode shows little interest in establishing whether the canonical text exists on the page in any pure form. The transcription of the original experience and the culturally sensitive editing of later periods both coexist in his scheme alongside modern techniques of interpretation as justifiable 'forms of attention' to some original, value-laden text. The only difference between canonical and uncanonical texts is that 'continuity of attention and interpretation . . . is reserved for the canonical' (FA, 74).

In the course of an exemplary case history – the recovery and revaluation of Botticelli over a seventy-year period from 1870 to 1940 – Kermode draws out the allegory of *fortuna* which lies behind every canonical success story. He then goes on to show that the same obscure, fathomless temporal currents account for the success of Donne: 'Donne, like Botticelli, has settled into a place in our canon; but we can now see that his admission was peculiarly the work of a past epoch, an effort controlled by historical conditions we identify as quite other than our own' (FA, 72). In a discussion of *Hamlet* Kermode cheerfully concedes that 'there can be no simple and perpetual consensus as to the proper way to join the shadow of comment to the substance of the play' (FA, 62).

A critic who has always pinned his colours to the mast of pluralism, Kermode has no intention of devising practices and assumptions that will clear the ground for a 'proper way'. The critic's aim, as he sees it, is to say 'something new about canonical texts without defacing them' (FA, 36), an end he himself duly accomplishes by interpreting *Hamlet* with psycho-rhetorical insights borrowed from Freud, Lacan, D. W. Winnicott and George T. Wright. 'This', he concludes, 'is what it means to call a book canonical.' What he hopes his own criticism will reinforce are 'canons of interpretation that are permissive rather than restrictive. . . . The canonical work, so endlessly discussed, must be assumed to have permanent value and, which is really the same thing, perpetual modernity' (FA, 62). Although he values the works included in the traditional canon, Kermode exhibits surprisingly little interest in Gombrich's 'canon of excellence' as a culturally stabilizing force. The result is the oddly mute, blank, untheatrical *Hamlet* – all potential without a stable core of action – described in *Forms of Attention*. Although Kermode believes that a dislodging of *Hamlet* from the canon would require us to live 'in a completely different world' (FA, 35), a reader will look in vain in his pages for unassailable dramatic reasons why this work has secured continuing canonical esteem.

In his last lecture he argues against current conspiracy theories of canonicity, reminding his audience that 'the canon is preserved by the multiple action of various sorts of opinion, knowledge, and mixtures of the two' (FA, 68). Laying aside the argument of *The Genesis of Secrecy* that *all* narratives contain a secret – and therefore a canonical – potential, Kermode reminds his audience that although 'the process of selecting the canon may be very long . . . once it is concluded, the inside works will normally be provided with the kinds of reading they require if they are to keep their immediacy to any moment' (FA, 75). Somewhat unnervingly, he takes the issue of canonical value for granted, acknowledging with resignation that 'opinion is the great canon-maker' (FA, 74).

Such a generalization may well hold in literary criticism. But what of the canons circulated among believers, for whom the pressure towards orthodoxy must surely prove more intense? Literary critics sometimes console themselves by imagining that their theological counterparts construct and reinforce their canons in a more draconian manner than their own secular institutions. Kermode's forays into scriptural interpretation lead him to question such assumptions. In 'The Argument about Canons', an essay reprinted in *An Appetite for Poetry*, he suggests that the makers of sacred and secular canons share similar myths, fictions and fallacies. He thinks there is magic in the web of 'canon' and 'tradition' which both groups of critics try to weave into permanent transparent truths. To enforce this point, he discusses the implications for the canon debate in literary criticism of a current theological debate about the textual authority of the biblical canon. On one side of the platform stand the arguments of Brevard S. Childs, Professor of Theology at Yale, who wants to revive the hermeneutic principle by which the Bible is read and reread through the ages as a work that makes greater sense as a whole than as a collection of parts. On the other side stand the strong counterarguments of James Barr of Oxford, who sees the separate biblical books as testimony to the words and actions of actual historical persons. As Kermode explains it, Barr argues that 'it is not the canon that gives the books their authority; it is the events and persons the books report'.[17]

In this argument between 'relevance' and 'truth', Kermode's instinct is to mediate between the two positions while tipping the discussion in favour of the first. In terms adapted from Gadamer and Rudolf Bultmann, he suggests that the very different canons of Barr and Childs hide a shared original impulse: the desire of both theologian and historian to penetrate to a 'magical', existential confrontation with the deepest layers of the biblical text – in Childs's case through a series of hermeneutic spiritual exercises; in Barr's case by stripping away the Bible's temporal accretions to reveal the complex human figures at its core. Kermode is not slow to apply these ideas to his own field of literary criticism. Whether critics call themselves historicists, new historicists, deconstructionists, or new critics, they all share 'presuppositions of which they may be largely unconscious' (AP, 206-7). Each element of literary criticism – work, period, canon – serves a common purpose in reducing a diverse field to a single hermeneutic order. The historicists have a 'mythology of period'. The new critics have a holistic conception of literary art. Twentieth-century criticism as a whole has always needed some organizational or aesthetic focus for the construction of value. However much the terms of debate may shift, Kermode argues, 'the concept of a secular canon has real force, and may even be necessary to the preservation of our disciplines' (AP, 189).

What the analogy between scriptural and secular interpretation occludes, and Kermode's essay does not address in any detail, is the canon-making role of the individual secular critic. Kermode does not disturb the assumption that 'tradition' supplies that critic with a short-list of 'standard' works, a list to which the exceptional critic may add a few favourite authors. But who validates the new list? Sometimes he speaks of legitimatization in spatial terms, as bringing the marginal into the centre. In *History and Value* (1988) he sidesteps this whole issue by discussing canon formation in more personal terms. In this book, he investigates the works he read in his youth and adolescence as a basis for a more general enquiry about why some books survive and some do not. There are, he suggests in the chapter 'Canon and Period', 'two main ways in which we try to make history manageable for literary purposes: by making canons that are in some sense transhistorical; and by inventing historical periods'. These two techniques shelter us from the sheer weight of cultural production, allowing us 'to package historical data that would otherwise be hopelessly hard to deal with'.[18] The 'period' gives us a handle on cultural production in respect of time, the 'canon' in respect of value. In other words, literary history constructs its periods and canons on foundations that conceal its architects' need for convenience. 'The canon,' Kermode reiterates, 'in predetermining value, shapes the past and makes it humanly available, accessibly modern' (HV, 117).

By arguing in this way – between the practical pole of need and the human pole of value – Kermode distances himself from a criticism which, from C. S. Lewis to Stanley Fish, has always sought to raise its own interpretative communities to a position of absolute authority. Although he admits that 'the association of canon with authority is deeply ingrained in us', he questions whether 'the literary canon is a load-bearing element of the existing power structure' (HV, 114). Better, he argues at one point, to revive the older, simpler, more functional idea of the canon as a mnemonic tool, an instrument that reverberates and expands in the mind. In a typically Olympian comment on the contemporary canon debate, he points to the existence on all sides of a

> tacit admission that there is such a thing as literature and that there ought to be such a thing as a canon. . . . The canon is what the insurgents mean to occupy as the reward of success in the struggle for power. . . . What we have here is not a plan to abolish the canon but one to capture it. (HV, 114)

Unfortunately, this formulation does not entirely settle the issue. Convenience alone does not explain the ferocity of our contemporary canon wars. Kermode asserts that a canon serves as a useful repository for cultural values, yet his own criticism emphasizes the capacity for the canonical work to surrender itself to any number of incompatible values. If this is true, why has the canon become a ground for such hectic and bitter dispute at the present time?

As a bid to recapture the canon for sceptical modernity, *History and Value* perhaps comes closest of all Kermode's books to making manifest the latent story he began to narrate in *Romantic Image*. The subject of his first section is the literature of the 1930s he read as a young man. Some of that literature now labours under the charges of moral dishonesty and armchair revolutionism levelled against it by George Orwell, while some other works, less highly valued at the time, are currently being mobilized as the expressions of an authentic working-class voice. After rejecting class as a principle of canonical survival, Kermode sets himself the challenge of presenting his own version of the period's saving residue. Predictably, he finds that residue in the authors' conformity to the great theological archetypes his own criticism has long presented as the central concern of modern letters. He finds a 'religious quality' in the political concerns of the 1930s, a belief that 'full conversion will happen only when poetry is returned to the collectivity' (HV, 38). Just as *Romantic Image* interpreted Eliot's 'tradition' as a quest for a mystic unity where art and polity became one, so *History and Value* represents the Marxism of Auden and the 1930s as an 'agent of conversion' (HV, 40). What recent Marxist critics such as Carole Snee have seen as 'the bourgeois canon' (HV, 34) of the period Kermode invests with more spiritual properties, so that the works of Auden and Isherwood embody a mystic crusade that involves a 'serious though transgressive quest, prompted in part by conscience' (HV, 28).

Once again, the operation of saving works for the canon requires that they relinquish some of their manifest existence; in this case, the Marxism of Auden and his generation foreshadows the religious ideas some of these writers later embraced overtly. When he returns to Auden's 'Spain', a poem he had characterized in *Romantic Image* as 'once greatly admired and now embarrassing' (RI, 164), Kermode emphasizes that it 'is not a marching song or a recruiting poster; it is an attempt to express what it feels like to confront a great historical crisis. At bottom such crises have elements in common' (HV, 78). Kermode's target, once again, is the imaginative residue revealed to the probing, sceptical intelligence acquainted with, but undogmatic about, the possibilities of a life that is recorded through culture but exists finally beyond history. Applied to the literature of the 1930s, Kermode's canon of interpretation testifies to a collective quest for redemption, a bid to outwit the claims of dogma, authority and sect.

To talk in this way about a literature so deeply political in its motivation and occasion, to search poetry and history for their conformity to deep figural patterns and archetypes, is to practise a religious, if undoctrinal, mode of reading. In *History and Value*, as in *Romantic Image*, Kermode unapologetically reads works against the grain of authorial intention and social occasion. In this way, his 1930s become a peculiarly dematerialized decade, a time when manifest turbulence found itself mysteriously eased by deep waves of calm contemplation. Hunger marches, strikes, and the threat of war all melt into a deep recollective tranquility, by virtue of which Kermode confides that 'a family like my own managed fairly well on £3, and people lived with enviable style on £5' (HV, 47). In this case at least, the canon of interpretation, the legislative instrument of the powerfully sceptical hermeneutic critic, elides the political and social conflicts we can confidently infer by their historical results.

It is usual to suggest that the abundance of modern critical schools and sects somehow blunts the edge of cultural masterpieces. Such is the complaint of George Steiner's *In Bluebeard's Castle* (1971) and of Geoffrey Hartman's *Criticism in the Wilderness* (1980). Kermode, on the contrary, adheres strongly to his idea of 'salvation by interpretation'. He thinks that canonical works congregate to the point where 'all the books can now be thought of as one large book' (HV, 116). 'We cannot avoid seeing them as interrelated', he thinks, 'by reason of their distinctive features and qualities' (HV, 117). What lies behind the 'quite unmistakable difference of status between canonical and uncanonical books' (HV, 115) – a status he shows little interest in disturbing – is the secret conformity of accepted canonical works to the patterns of permanence, change, crisis, renovation, decadence and apocalypse which have sustained his criticism since *Romantic Image*.

LIBERTY OF INTERPRETATION: KERMODE AND THE ACADEMIC CANON

How can we characterize Kermode's conception of a canon? On the one hand, his *canon* has virtues no greater than convenience: it will enable an informed audience to build bridges between past and present; it will allow that audience to draw up an inventory of objects which it currently values and can dispose of according to later valuations; and it will discard some of the clutter which the past accumulates. On the other hand, Kermode can speak of 'the canon' in a somewhat mystical fashion, as an order that confers perpetual modernity on objects potentially obsolescent. Canons play tricks on time, allowing T. S. Eliot to present Lancelot Andrewes or Thomas Elyot as haunting, inescapable voices beckoning down the corridors of the past. Canons harbour any number of contradictory witnesses and interpretations, and in this way they embody a world where disagreement can exist without discord. They persist even though they are perpetually broken, like the host shared among the faithful. Like the imperial cities of Virgil and Eliot, they 'are . . . famous not for the manner of their foundation but for the completeness of their destruction' (AP, 112).

In short, canons facilitate what Kermode sees as a basic human need, the need to reinterpret or reimagine the past in accordance with the claims of the present. In this way, the canon of interpretation appears to Kermode as the classics appeared to the Italian humanists and as the open canon appears to Said: a set of admired patterns that stimulate perpetual reinterpretation by educated intelligences. Kermode's canon takes on the properties of a bridge and a prism in turn: like a bridge it brings separate territories together; like a prism it presents different meanings to the mind according to the angle at which its interpreter decides to view it. Even so, the comparison with the humanists stretches only so far. For although they, like Kermode, saw themselves as writing at a time of great crisis, their response was to place their historical knowledge at the disposal of the contemporary *polis*. In sharp contrast, Kermode uses the detritus left by the sacred past to support the kaleidoscopic interpretations of a modern academic critic.

As he formulates the problem in his later criticism, the traditional canon will survive only through liberty of interpretation. Yet the price of that liberty becomes apparent even in his own restrained and civilized readings. On his canonical texts, Kermode confers the value of 'omnisignificance'. Yet in practice, 'omnisignificance' means that the works belong neither to their own time nor to our time but to an angelic eternity in which they become the source of the endless possibilities conferred by generations of commentators. Over the years Kermode's canon has become more and more spectral, more and more a chameleon canon existing by the grace of interpretative intervention. In his attempt to redeem the canon from its zealots, Kermode risks its life by relinquishing its identity, as it survives in his criticism by a process of perpetual renunciation.

The problem of the relationship between the canon and its academic trustees is a problem Kermode's criticism never completely solves. Although he never suggests that metaphysical ingenuity will become the sole criterion for canonical survival, his criticism uses exegesis as its principal agency. But will even his own free-ranging exegesis remain a lasting aspiration for academic critics? Kermode's latest book, *An Appetite for Poetry* (1989), confronts a rising generation of senior academics who voice only hostility to a canon they see as not just as 'conceptually wrong' but as 'subversive of justice' (AP, 13). Despite its popular reputation as an 'ivory tower', the modern academy has never offered itself as a quiet harbour for popularly established canonical texts. This recurring pattern of academic instability does not discourage Kermode from entrusting the transmission of the canonical objects to the authority of learned interpreters lodged in prestigious institutions, even though his own connections with any one institution have always been provisional and impermanent.

It is worth noting that Edward Said, the most direct spokesman for a canon 'in transience', has confined his professional life to the universities of Harvard and Columbia, while Frye and Gombrich forged lifelong associations with the University of Toronto and the Warburg Institute respectively. Although Kermode gives the academy a larger role than any of these critics in the canon's continuing life, he himself has survived more or less as a scholar in transit, holding full-time appointments at the Universities of Newcastle, Reading, Manchester, Bristol, London, Cambridge and Columbia, and visiting professorships at Wesleyan, Harvard, Jerusalem, and a host of other institutions. Kermode's career follows the curve he sets for the canonical object: a basic continuity set off by perpetual mutation.

Kermode's sceptical yet visionary purchase on the canon also sets him at some distance from the other critics discussed in this book. Frye and Gombrich both venerate canonical works with an almost spiritual intensity, but part of that intensity derives from their certainty about the way to apprehend those works. The urbanity of manner both critics habitually assume masks an adamantine commitment to certain ways of experiencing and understanding artistic excellence. Their criticism unrolls like a massive, continuous story. Not so Kermode's writing. With its unobtrusive switches of direction and method, its provisional commitments and occasional or even journalistic origins, it suggests in its own pages the flexible, open-ended ways in which canons persist in the modern consciousness.

What is the value of this flexibility for the modern academy? It is impossible to ignore the note of extremity that characterizes much contemporary discussion of the canon, whether the canon be Gombrich's canon of excellence, Frye's canon of utopian romance, or the diabolic canon of the current debate. In *An Appetite for Poetry* Kermode has no difficulty in demolishing the case that the modern canon has been constructed by academics in dishonourable collusion with political power. (It is worth observing that this most contemplative of contemporary critics possesses an Erasmian ferocity in argument.) Even so, one need not see Kermode's main adversary, the Jonathan Culler of *Framing the Sign* (1988), as unveiling a document of cultural emancipation in order to acknowledge Culler's threat to some of his most cherished positions.

Kermode has repeatedly characterized the academy as eager for change and eager for interpretation – what if a new eagerness for the one takes the form of an eagerness to expel the other? A generation of academics attuned to Barthes, Derrida and Foucault – to the very developments in the humanities Kermode welcomed throughout the 1970s – may well have no place for the interpretation derived from sacred precedent he himself has customarily practised. Where Kermode sees the canon and its commentators as wrapped in a mystic dialogue between permanence and change, his successors may hear only a chorus of conformity. His belief in the prismatic qualities of the canonical object and the indefatigability of canonical commentary relies on idealist premisses a self-styled cultural materialism may not even bother to undermine. For materialist critics, *Heart of Darkness* is not a dark, ever-shifting narrative but a document about ethnocentricity and the complicity between colonialism and the expatriate imagination. In contrast, Kermode's premisses would lead him to see this kind of political reading as only the latest in a succession of readings which all point to the plurality of Conrad's tale. But the latest interpretation might prove the last interpretation if its proponents no longer concede the inexhaustibility of the work in question.

In recent years canons seem to elicit little short of absolute conviction from their spokesmen, little short of unqualified opposition from their detractors. Those who find this kind of dogmatism unrewarding may well feel much in common with Kermode's self-characterization as a speaker from 'a position of moderation' (EF, 8). Even so, the potential weakness of the moderate lies in his attempt to reconcile irreconcilable positions. One of the accusations to be levelled against Kermode's canon of interpretation is that it retains the shell of the canon while discarding its substance. In *Forms of Attention*, for instance, he states that 'the canonical work is fixed in time but applicable to all time' (FA, 75), a formulation more reminiscent of theological paradox than the practical world of canon-making and revising.

Even so, as a ground-plan for a modern canon, Kermode's canon of interpretation has strengths that may well outreach its contradictions and renunciations. Gombrich remains too much of a historian to listen too long to the Siren call of the contemporary. Frye's sense of the one world and one future celebrated in myth makes him an unreliable witness to the demands of plurality or even contemporaneity. Said, the critic we shall discuss next, believes that ultimately the voices of the unheard and unenfranchised count for more than witnesses drawn almost exclusively from the privileged and powerful. Compared with all these critics, Kermode has taken most stock of the problems faced by the modern academic canon, and his twin desires to address the concerns of anti-canonical critics and to ensure the survival of traditional canonical texts make his final position on the canon the most difficult to address. Kermode comes nearer than either Gombrich or Frye to dislodging the canon. Because his canon of interpretation opens the dykes between modern and ancient, secular and sacred, unknown and familiar, it inevitably raises the question of why we need a canon at all. An enterprise that began with a desire to ensure the survival of the classic at a time of dissidence paradoxically fosters a situation where every Milton becomes mute and inglorious without an interpreter's restoring touch. A canon can survive by becoming mysterious; but it is doubtful whether it can flourish by perpetual novelty.

Kermode's criticism arguably tries to balance two irreconcilable positions: a need to conceive of an order beyond time, a tradition or myth or *aevum*, with a need for adjustment, self-consciousness, openness, provisionality. However sceptically, his canon moves inside the long shadow cast by its ecclesiastical forerunner. His sometimes abrupt, commonsensical emphasis on the opportunism of the canon-making institutions and the instability of the canons they support hides his deeper conviction about the sacred qualities of the objects inside the canon. For forty years Kermode has searched for a sanctuary inside the sanctuary, a place where canonical works can live on, protected from the larger systems that would reduce them to instruments. Throughout a long meditation which shows an unusual willingness to relinquish the claims to absolute authority made for the traditional canon, Kermode persists in his search for the mysterious residue of his canonical texts – the residue that enables them to link past to present, *there* to *here*. A canonical work, he suggests, represents 'endless chains and crossings of significance . . . as many as may be found in the created world with which the book is coextensive' (FA, 76).

6

Edward Said and the Open Canon

THE SCANDAL OF 'NORMAL SCIENCE': SAID AND THE ACADEMIC CANON

In the climate of mounting hostility to canons described in the last chapter, Edward Said has conducted one of the most probingly coherent and consistent cases against the canon. It is not just that he has actually identified a canon at work (something the 'canon-busters' have often failed to do) but he has also noted the way that a canon, in some form or other, remains part of the habits of mind and institutional behaviour of even the most radical professional academics. Like Kermode, Said acknowledges that most foes of the canon bury a canon inaugurated by Eliot only in order to rebuild a new one endowed by Derrida. Said is aware too that in the less frequent instances where new canons rest on new texts rather than on new methods, the reconditioned canon rarely does anything more novel than transcribe the social attitudes a critical faction wishes to see represented on literary syllabuses. Where the old-style canonical text operated as a Cabinet member, the new-style canonical text serves as a delegate for the cultural assumptions a particular critic or school wants to reinforce or attack.

Against this backdrop of wholesale revision, Said has not only mounted a sustained campaign against the 'Orientalist' canon by which Western culture confronts what it conceives of as its polar opposite, but he has also identified at work what we might call a canonical disposition, a tendency to construct models that conform to certain shared assumptions. As a result, he has enlarged the canon debate in three important ways. First, he argues that the academic canon propagates what he calls 'the ideology of humanism' by means of 'canons of order'.[1] Essential articles in the academic humanist's secular faith include an institutional monopoly on intellectual enquiry; a division of intellectual life into academic 'fields'; and a further separation of these fields, on the grounds of 'objectivity' or 'specialization', from society as a whole. Second, Said attacks the

political consequences of the humanist's avowedly non-political programme. He thinks that a chain of complicity links the intellectual
practices of the academy to the anti-intellectual prejudices of the
media and what, after C. Wright Mills, he calls 'the cultural
apparatus'.[2] In deliberate or unconscious collusion, these agencies
install a canon of rejection of subject cultures. Third, Said raises the
question of whether cultural canons 'are more methodologically
necessary to the order of dominance . . . than they are to the secular
study of human history'.[3] As a way of escaping this 'order of dominance', he proposes to investigate 'the notion of culture top to
bottom'. In the course of this investigation, he looks forward to a
canon of the future based on 'new narrative forms' and '*other* ways
of telling'.[4]

Said's distinct contribution to the unfolding history of the canon
lies in his repeated, authoritatively stated warnings about the latent
dogma and ritual surrounding the academic canon and the dangerous
inertia of existing paradigms. As he frequently points out, both in
analysis and with the force of personal testimony, a closeted academic
world stretching from Frankfurt to Berkeley faces the unprecedented
challenge of a postcolonial, electronic world-cultural order in which
emerging sectors struggle for definition against forces they
inevitably construe as agencies of attack. Said's often eloquent
testimony to the view from outside sets him apart from many radical
academics, especially in the United States. He does not think the
battle for cultural studies can be fought out on campus, nor does he
think that a simple change in the canonical list of works addresses
the underlying problem of the canonical habit of mind. Even worse,
he thinks that this habit is reinforced by the theories of institutional
behaviour which academic critics use to explain to themselves and
to others how their assumptions evolve, change and operate in the
classroom.

The institutional frame of reference for the canon – a frame
acknowledged in practice if not in precept by radicals and conservatives alike – derives special support from Thomas Kuhn's view of
intellectual activity as a pattern of conformity to institutional expectations. Viewed from a Kuhnian perspective, canons function as
stamps of approval in an endlessly repeated circle of institutional
validation. According to the influential theory of 'normal science'
promulgated in *The Structure of Scientific Revolutions* (1962), the
institution serves as sponsor, regulator, and ultimate guarantor of
intellectual activity and achievement. This theory, which stresses the
importance of the institution at every stage of intellectual life, has

provided a welcome injection of esteem for endangered and self-doubting liberal arts departments by convincing them that the future of the canon lies in their own hands.

It is hardly surprising that students of literature as different in orientation as Stanley Fish and Frank Kermode have adjusted Kuhn's model to the field of literary study, suggesting with greater or lesser resignation that literary interpreters screen out questions according to the assumptions and prejudices current within their institutions. For Said, however, 'normal science' represents a potential scandal. He refuses to consider the history of criticism purely in terms of its own internal laws, because he believes that such laws share suppressed lines of conformity with larger social and political systems. Arguments which follow patterns of conformity may seem innocuous enough in a discussion of *The Comedy of Errors*; the same forms of argument extended to the oil crisis of the 1970s or the Iran–Contra affair of the 1980s have catastrophic political effects.

In *The World, the Text, and the Critic* and *Beginnings*, Said argues strongly that the paradigms of conformity at work even in radical versions of intellectual enquiry, the pressure towards accepting overt or hidden institutional norms, lock university-based intellectuals in an ethnic and ethical dilemma whereby they become 'experts' for a government eager to impose its political 'canons' across the continents. Said views 'normal science' with suspicion because it honours in theory a diversity it fails to acknowledge in practice. He shares Raymond Williams's suspicion about the territorial barriers between individual disciplines, preferring to see 'literature' as just one among a broad spectrum of reports on the social production of consciousness and representation of reality. Like Williams and Gramsci, he repeatedly returns to the marginalized society and the marginalized consciousness – in his case not Wales or Sardinia but 'the Orient', an umbrella term constructed by Western intellectuals to reinforce imperialist domination.

Said shares with the 'canon-busters' the view that those who teach only the 'classics of European letters' involve the academy in the tacit suppression of monuments venerated by other cultures. Yet he also emphasizes that knowledge of these other cultures must modify in some practical, existential way our understanding of the European canon. Accordingly, his own work often pays loving attention to marginal authors such as Kipling or T. E. Lawrence, whose original celebrity has faded without any compensating rise in academic esteem. Said also admires authors like Joseph Conrad and Jonathan Swift who resist curricular categories, ideological restraint, and narrative closure. All these values explain why his own books move fluidly between disciplinary boundaries, yoking Foucault to *A Thousand and One Nights*, Swift to Dilthey, Blake to Gadamer, all in the space of one or two pages.

Said's disciplinary and rhetorical mobility, his constant questioning and relocation of own premises, make him almost as difficult to pin down as Kermode himself. Because he sees the invisible hand of empire behind the much-defended autonomy of the human sciences, he imposes on himself a perpetual self-consciousness. His criticism will accept no unity he cannot discover during the process of composition. In *Beginnings* (1975), perhaps his most self-conscious work, he describes his decision to employ the method of 'the meditative essay – first, because I believe myself to be trying to form a unity as I write; and second, because I want to let beginnings generate in my mind the type of relationships and figures most suitable to them'.[5] In *The World, the Text, and the Critic* (1984) he reaffirms his commitment to the essay as the form which lends the critic most liberty to reconstruct the texts that come to him sealed inside canonical compacts. The essay potentially disturbs the canon by showing that 'texts after all are not an ideal cosmos of ideally equal monuments' (WTC, 53). In *Orientalism* (1978) he describes his controversial decision not 'to attempt an encyclopedic narrative history of Orientalism',[6] but instead to proceed by a succession of climactic episodes and polemically reconstructed fragments. In Said's view, the imposing bulk of monuments in a canon should not spur on the anti-canonical critic to construct an equally imposing rival order. Instead, such a critic should provide significant juxtapositions, ironic comparisons, and occasional rousing denunciations.

This mobility of argument extends beyond its rhetorical occasion to become a preferred strategic position. At one point in *The World, the Text, and the Critic* Said conceives of an adversarial criticism which 'can only be practiced outside and beyond the consensus ruling the art today' (WTC, 5). Yet twenty pages later he attacks a 'contemporary criticism' which sets loose 'the unrestrained interpretation of a universe defined in advance as the endless reading of a misinterpretation' (WTC, 25). Suspicious of Barthes's '*jouissance*' as well as Eliot's 'tradition', Said none the less manages to find a place for both. As the ever-changing situation requires it, he can sound at one time like George Eliot scrutinizing sympathetically the web of social, ethical and personal relations inside the interpretative community, while at another he can sound like Foucault, piercing that web with a few glancing disintegrative thrusts. His mobility has not endeared

Said to some members of the academic community, since it is often far from clear where his work fits in a line of critical descent. In fact, it is tempting to argue that the term 'Edward Said' collapses into two discrete entities: the *Raritan* Said who composes eulogies on Foucault, leisurely meditations on R. P. Blackmur, and stately, diffuse appreciations of *Kim*; and the *Critical Inquiry* Said who discusses the politics of interpretation and the status of disciplinarity to an audience at the leading edge of theoretical discourse.

Even in so drastic a summary as this, it becomes clear that Said shares the synoptic ambitions – even the quest for some accommodating synthesis – of his less radical predecessors. His early writing shows the willingness to link old to new in a continuous narrative we have learned to expect from Northrop Frye and Frank Kermode. Like them, Said does not shrink from pursuing global lines of myth and peripeteia, continuity and discontinuity. Indeed, one surprising theme through all his books remains his respect for a criticism with 'the universality and the scope of German romance philology (with its origins in Goethe's idea of *Weltliteratur*)' (B, 334). His circuitous progress across several literatures and languages pushes Said towards an older kind of cross-cultural scholarship that opens up grand vistas of a 'new science' or field of learning. In a sense, his career starts from and returns to Ernst Curtius's repudiation of conventional literary history in *European Literature and the Latin Middle Ages* (1953). Urging critics to abandon strict canons of chronology, Curtius advocates new methods which 'will "decompose" the material . . . and make its structures visible'. Without offering specific directions, he indicates what he has in mind in an allusion to Hofmannsthal. The modern German critic, Curtius asserts, has little to work from except 'Friedrich Schlegel – and beginnings'.[7]

His affinities with this older scholarship may explain why Said has spoken so respectfully of Frye, whose interest in the primitive and in narrative repetition he compares with Lévi-Strauss and Gilles Deleuze, and whose *Anatomy of Criticism* he thinks 'has played the dominant part, and deservedly so, in giving critical discourse in English today an important share of coherence' (B, 376). Another surprise is to hear Said praise not just Ernst Curtius and Leo Spitzer but even Erich Auerbach, the philologist, historian and critic whose *Mimesis* might conceivably be retitled 'The Story of Western Literature'. And perhaps the greatest surprise of all is to watch Said repeatedly characterizing his own field of endeavour as 'the human adventure or 'the human enterprise', descriptions which recall the similarly formulated projects of Gombrich in *Ideals and Idols* and Frye in *The Stubborn Structure*.

Yet however similar the ambitions, the vocabulary, and even the procedures, Said still resists the 'canons of order' which underpin works such as *The Story of Art* and *The Great Code*. As he sees it, 'order' in an unequal society involves repression and coercion. Said joins Raymond Williams in suggesting that humanistic canons occlude 'the notion of struggle'.[8] Despite his respect for certain traditional critics, Said finally carries us across the chasm that separates Leavis and Eliot, Gombrich and Frye from Chomsky and Williams, Gramsci and Althusser. None of these writers disputes the fact that modern life follows unprecedentedly disruptive forms, but their ways of responding to these disruptions remain markedly different. Where Eliot and Leavis exempt 'tradition' and 'English' from the turbulence, presenting them as still sources of value in a world of fracture, Said and Williams implicate the canon in the crisis, presenting it as an institutional device of the intellectual classes to shrink a culture into a few valued monuments, to restrict access to those monuments, and to limit the ways in which they can be apprehended.

What are the grounds for Said's resistance to the traditional European canon and the foundations of his revisions? The basis for his resistance becomes clearer if we examine the history of his development as a critic. Born as an Episcopalian Christian in Palestine, but spending much of his adult life at an affluent private university located on the rim of Harlem, Said must be more aware than most critics of cultural diversity and dislocation. As he himself has commented, his personal history points to a chance encounter between radically distinct traditions and identities rather than to the long, Eurocentric continuities felt by Auerbach, Frye and Gombrich. Granted, Gombrich reports the massive shocks which have visited Europe in the twentieth century. He recalls the slaughters of the First World War that drove Aby Warburg into insanity. He describes the rise of Hitler that drove generations of Europeans to exile or extinction. But in the face of all these massive interruptions, 'culture' remains for Gombrich a continuously apprehended whole. To counterbalance the story of European devastation, he narrates Aby Warburg's quest to understand the classical art of the Renaissance. He even describes how one of his fellow refugees from Austria reimagined the Louvre in his head. Northrop Frye, one can concede, belongs to a society closer to the wilderness than Gombrich's Austria. Yet Frye's *The Bush Garden* still incorporates the Canadian imagination within the family of European Romantic myths, themes and images. For Frye as for Gombrich, 'culture' remains 'a structure built by human concern',[9] a common stock the humanistic critic will rework and reconsider rather than wilfully dismantle and build again.

Said argues that, as a Palestinian, few of these cultural continuities apply to him; he comes from a people whose memories can never attain the canonical status of the memories of Gombrich or Frye. Like Raymond Williams in *The Country and the City*, Said sees the convergence of different peoples and traditions in a particular geographical location in terms of the dominance one group exerts over another. Where Frye's *The Bush Garden* shows the European cultural memory as replenishing Canadian imaginations, Said and Williams present their cultural monuments at the stage of bricks, mortar and productive labour, when they appear as nothing more than bare cross-sections of sociocultural life, men, women, and raw materials disposed according to a set of unchanging blueprints designed by unseen hands. If a canon seems as natural as the leaves on the trees, then both writers make clear that this is the result of massive horticultural labour.

There remains, however, at least one important difference between Said and some of the radical European critics he admires. Where Williams and Gramsci seem solitary thinkers, Said's intelligence swarms with a multitude of influences, not all of them from the Old World and the East. If the Palestinian Said must constantly battle to extract his Eastern culture from the mists of Western misapprehension, the New York intellectual Said takes an assured place in a tradition which, since the days of Philip Rahv and William Barrett, has submitted the Anglo-Saxon Christian commonwealth of T. S. Eliot and Allen Tate to a searching political critique.

Said's longstanding residence in New York permits him easy access to the metropolitan centres of American dissent. In the 1930s, *Partisan Review* defended Soviet Marxism against American capitalism. A few years later, the journal settled into its customary mixture of cautious alliances with the progressive in politics and the avant-garde in culture. Such alliances shift the New York intellectual in opposite directions – towards Jean-Paul Sartre, Simone de Beauvoir and Alberto Moravia on one front; towards Wallace Stevens, T. S. Eliot and John Crowe Ransom on another. Whatever their inconsistencies, Dwight Macdonald, Philip Rahv and Mary McCarthy maintained open lines of communication between America and the outside world. Where many Southern writers of the 1930s acknowledged only European thinkers of the order of Dante, New York intellectuals deployed Koestler, Camus and Sartre as partners in a complex dialogue between the academy and the polity.

Shortly after the end of the Second World War, another generation of American writers, their ranks bolstered by Jewish and European exiles, renewed their intellectual ties at Princeton University, Said's undergraduate institution. The establishment of the Christian Gauss seminars in criticism at Princeton in 1949 brought together a diverse group of European and American intellectuals and rekindled earlier contacts with the European radical left, with existentialist French thinkers such as Sartre and Camus, and with social critics such as Hannah Arendt.[10] Gauss, who encouraged Edmund Wilson to write *Axel's Castle* in the early 1930s, may have inspired Said's later efforts to integrate the study of literature with the study of society. It is also worth noting that during the same period the lavish endowment of the Rockefeller Foundation allowed postwar intellectuals to mount their criticisms of American capitalism without undue fear of penury. All these factors created the climate for Said's later engagement with Gilles Deleuze, Michel Foucault and Jacques Derrida.

Another influence on Said's later work comes from his long-term professional base. Columbia University has a reputation for supporting the kind of multicultural, multidisciplinary realignment of the humanities proposed in *The World, the Text, and the Critic* and *Orientalism*. During the 1930s, Jacques Barzun and Lionel Trilling housed themselves very successfully at Columbia, where they collaborated in broad pedagogic ventures across conventional curricular boundaries.[11] If Trilling and Barzun saw culture and civilization in terms that Said would find excessively hierarchical, their wide-ranging, philosophical investigations still provided a context (some might even call it a canon) in which his own work need not start from scratch. Trilling in particular may have offered a personal example to Said, since he elaborately reconstructed his intellectual identity, displacing his Jewish, urban origins to suggest an English gentleman who had made a home at Columbia. This earlier critical displacement anticipates one of Said's favourite ideas, the modern intellectual's willingness to exchange 'filiation', an identity inherited through family and ethnicity, for 'affiliation', an identity constructed through personal election and culture.

It is also worth noting that throughout the 1960s Columbia served as one of the principal sites for American resistance to the Vietnam War, an issue centrally related to Said's twinned emphases on the role of the intellectual in society and the imposition of dominant 'canons of order' on emerging subject cultures. During this period, students

194   *The Making of the Modern Canon*

at Columbia refused to accept the canons of excellence transmitted to them by their elders. Their dissatisfaction with the official curriculum signalled a deeper dissatisfaction with the idea of a warmongering national culture. The war also made the experience of 'otherness' a pressing concern for some members of the Columbia faculty. It encouraged C. Wright Mills, for instance, to probe the responsibility of intellectuals inside an aggressive state and to examine emerging cultures in Africa and Latin America as paradigms for a global future. In all these ways, Columbia has offered Said laboratory conditions in which to conduct his examination of canons, cultures, and intellectual conformity.

THE IDEOLOGY OF HUMANISM

Said's Palestinian origins, added to this rich background of American dissident enquiry, come together in his favourite model for the modern intellectual: the nomad, the intellectual and cultural wanderer tied to no particular discipline, no particular critical method. As he remarks in *Beginnings*:

> It is less permissible today to imagine oneself as writing within a tradition when one writes literary criticism. This is not to say, however, that every critic is now a revolutionist destroying the canon in order to replace it with his own. A better image is that of a wanderer, going from place to place for his material, but remaining a man essentially *between* homes. (B, 8)

Said thinks that the model of the intellectual nomad fulfils more than his own private needs. His experience in one of the world's busiest university systems tells him that the image of the nomad suits contemporary critics better than the image of the scholar, knowing in enormous detail a closed body of texts, widening and deepening a continuous line of knowledge present and knowledge past. In *Beginnings* he describes how traditional criticism approaches its monuments in a contradictory spirit of deference and mastery. He interposes his own freewheeling cross-cultural methods as a way beyond these contradictions, a way he presents as paradigmatic for the modern critic.

Yet if *Beginnings*, a lengthy, close scrutiny of modern critical assumptions and procedures, advances a new model for scholarly activity, it also indicates very clearly the limits of its author's attack

on the canon. What Said chooses to attack at this stage is not so much
a set of texts as a set of influential early-twentieth-century critical
methods. He notes that in practice few 'practical critics' working in
the tradition of Eliot, Leavis, or the early Chicago School subscribe
to the idea of an untarnished, independent masterpiece. In his view,
academics who offer traditional 'critical readings' honour the
integrity of the canonical text in principle while breaching it in practice. Instead of viewing the text as a printed book, a finished object,
or 'as a completed edifice of some sort' (B, 193), the practical critic

> assumes, even imputes, problems to an uninterpreted text (i.e. what
> does it mean?), and after solving them offers us an object *no longer
> in need of interpretation*, partially purged . . . of its problematics. The
> text is returned to a canon, or a tradition, *more itself* than it had been
> before. (B, 194)

The most obvious analogy is to a state-sponsored psychologist or
interrogator, purging the individual before him of problems that
exist only in the minds of officials before reinserting him in a
repressive social order.

For Said, the success of the humanistic canon lies in its elision of
interpretative interference, its levelling of the rough edges of opinion
into the smooth gloss of commentary. Yet even as he dissents from
the procedures of early modern criticism and interposes other procedures derived from Foucault and Derrida, Said pays homage to the
traditional canon – even, in a sense, to practical criticism – by offering
a detailed scrutiny of a series of exemplary canonical texts. In *Beginnings* he discusses not just Freud, Vico and Renan but also *Nostromo,
The Wreck of the Deutschland*, and *The Prelude*. A newly appointed professor of English Literature, he begins his meditations on the canon
from the safety of a well-trodden field of acknowledged literary
masterpieces, his discussion of the rival Eastern tradition not stepp-
ing beyond the well-lit path of *The Seven Pillars of Wisdom* and *A Thousand and One Nights*.

Said objects to the operations which accredited academic critics
perform on accredited texts; he has no quarrel with the high valuation
of the texts themselves. On the contrary, in a series of expansive
meditations on authors from Conrad to Foucault, he signifies his
reluctance to expel from the canon the acknowledged masterpieces
already housed inside it. He wants to change, rather, the mode of
apprehension of those masterpieces, to open up the field of interpretation. It is in *Beginnings* that he quotes for the first time a section

from Nietzsche's 'On Truth and Lie in an Extra-Moral Sense' that serves as his touchstone on the canon throughout his career:

> What, then, is truth? A mobile army of metaphors, metonyms, and anthropomorphisms – in short, a sum of human relations, which have been enhanced, transposed, and embellished poetically and rhetorically, and which after long use seem firm, canonical, and obligatory to a people: truths are illusions about which one has forgotten that this is what they are. (B, 39)

Said situates himself outside the order of humanistic disciplines so that he may understand them as historical constructions built to answer needs which have been obliterated by time and institutional authority. He follows here not just Nietzsche but a distinguished body of witnesses, from Vico to Williams, who understand the uniquely unsettling, fluid characteristics of modern life as humanly constructed paradigms, not as God-inflicted wounds. Modern intellectual communities, these writers would agree, do not on the whole respond to this unsettlement with correspondingly tentative, cautious, and continually redefined institutions. Instead, these communities try to fill the gap left by the old agencies of filiation – the family, the Church, the tribe – with reconstituted ties centred on the academy and the professions. Modern intellectuals prefer Eliot's myths to Vaihinger's fictions, and the illusory solidity of the canon to the open-ended world of textual interpretation which lies outside it. In this way they end up with a more constricted, artificial version of the continuity they imagine was provided by a settled, preindustrial society.

Why, Said wonders, do so many intellectuals enlist in the service of the canon? Why do those professionally dedicated to the life of the mind choose to shelter within a stability that answers to no known conditions of modern life? How does a monument to human achievement translate into a paradigm for inertia? In his second study of Anglo-American criticism, *The World, the Text, and the Critic*, Said searches for the origins of this quest for shared certainty. He argues that the tacit precedent for the modern canon lies in the sacred canon, a canon that sets up a complex network of ties and oppositions between insider and outsider, master and disciple, source and commentary, dogma and doxa. As Said puts it, 'in the genealogy of texts there is a first text, a sacred prototype, a scripture, which readers always approach through the text before them, either as petitioning suppliants or as initiates amongst many in a sacred chorus supporting the central patriarchal text' (WTC, 46).

Because sacred interpretation determines the pattern of secular interpretation, the promoters of the modern canon repeatedly try to track their subject down to some original, unmediated intention; to peel away all the words of the canonical masterpiece leaving only a numinous core; to deny access to its meanings to all except licensed interpreters; to surrender freely their own individuality to the prior authority of the canonical text; to evolve a specialized vocabulary of worship, commentary and damnation; and, finally, to use the text which emerges at the end of their critical operations to promulgate a world view that subordinates ethnic and cultural diversity to a pattern projected into one dogmatically defended antecedent. As Said notes, 'we find the university experience more or less officially consecrating the pact between a canon of works, a band of initiate instructors, and a group of younger affiliates; in a socially validated manner all this reproduces the filiative discipline supposedly transcended by the educational process' (WTC, 21). Caught up in this endlessly duplicating educational machine, the younger affiliates must surrender their own values to understand the interpretations of their masters, whose interpretative energies derive, in turn, from some even remoter source. Then, at intervals, all this 'knowledge' is transmitted to a larger public congregation, which acknowledges the canonical texts as permanently valid in the course of its own daily living.

Said's sharp focus on the institutional and political life of canons distinguishes him from the other contemporary canon-makers we have discussed. For Frank Kermode, a canon survives by virtue of the 'patience' of the canonical work. That 'patience' allows *King Lear*, for example, to relinquish its identity to the varying perspectives of its historical audiences. For Northrop Frye, a canonical text survives because its language and its imagery correspond to the recurring eschatological hopes and anxieties of its readers. Said, however, sees the canonical work as surviving through institutional repression. He thinks that the history of literary criticism in the twentieth century follows a pattern of scriptural interpretation which he assumes to correspond to the institutional history of the Church. Just as during the medieval period Church and state came together in a Holy Roman Empire, so modern literary criticism as mediated by Arnold, Eliot, Leavis, Empson and Richards practises a similar process of adjustment, accommodation and annexation, and with an identical set of territorial objectives. Said refuses to sever 'the great tradition' validated by these critics from its national origins. Like Williams he understands 'English' as carrying a dual meaning – political and literary – that humanist critics suppress. Accordingly, he characterizes the Arnold–Eliot canon as the continuation of nationalism by pedagogic means. For these critics, Said submits, 'everything outside the Anglo-Saxon world had to bend around to Anglo-Saxon ends' (WTC, 164). In ways foreshadowed by religious criticism, critics influenced by the dominant Arnoldian paradigm of high culture reconstitute the historical referent of a text or the conditions of an author's experience in order to validate the goals and values of a particular critical community. In practice, this community wants to forge a consensus among affiliates rather than to open up a new, self-questioning intellectual field.

In *The World, the Text, and the Critic* Said pushes this argument a step further by showing how the emergence of a set of canonical texts created a need for a unified value system inside whose boundaries the new canonical authors could safely subsist. Viewed from one angle, it would seem difficult to reconcile pagan Virgil with Catholic Dante, enlightened Goethe with obscurantist Yeats. The critic bent on validating these authors for a continuous Western canon must marshal them into a suitably broad frame of reference – 'humanism', perhaps, or 'modern classicism'. As in sacred criticism, the creation of a binding canon requires a reduction of local, existential identity, so that Eliot 'saw in European poets like Dante, Virgil, and Goethe, the vindication of such Anglo-Saxon values as monarchy, an unbroken nonrevolutionary tradition, and the idea of a national religion' (WTC, 164). Against this bedrock stability in values, Said shows how the task of cultural distortion and suppression could begin. If canonical authors relinquish their existential identity in order to gain mythical permanence, then canonical texts occlude their social and historical origins as they rise to monumental status. 'For every poem or novel in the canon', Said agrees with Raymond Williams, 'there is a social fact being requisitioned for the page, a human life engaged, a class suppressed or elevated' (WTC, 23).

Some literary critics may find this description melodramatic. None the less, Said's account of the process of canonical requisitioning gains unexpected support from the work of respected scholars in other humanistic fields. Quentin Skinner, for instance, has described the process by which the keystone texts of political theory shed all contact with the political situations which produced them, leaving them free to ascend to a constellation of 'great books' which imply 'an apparently clear reference to an accepted "canon" of texts'.[12] In 'Languages and Their Implications: The Transformation of the Study of Political Thought', the introductory essay in *Politics, Language and*

Time (1973), J. G. A. Pocock shows how early political science, unsure even what to call its discipline, stumblingly organized itself into 'a canon of major works . . . isolated by academic tradition'. As this largely philosophical and historical syllabus trailed its way from Plato and Aquinas to Burke, Hegel and Marx, 'confusion set in', there was vague talk of a "collapse of the classical tradition"'. Educators became nervous as they approached the obviously political present, with the result that 'the political thought of the nineteenth and twentieth centuries has remained uncanonized by the organizers of this tradition and – where its study has not been actually discouraged – is all the better for it'.[13]

These deeply critical accounts of the history of political science support Said's view that a field organized around a canon of excellence screens out important problems and events in the interests of the most rudimentary forms of academic order. As both Pocock and Skinner repeatedly point out, a canonically organized field does not even serve particularly well the authors it elevates. Said makes a similar point in his many discussions of Conrad, a touchstone author he cites in every book. He shows that many early modern critics ignored the randomly disruptive conflux of experiences behind the novelist's works in order to set up a monument to an integral part of the modernist creed, the impersonality of art. Conrad's cross-cultural move from Poland to England; his fraught dealings with publishers; his increasing personal anguish; his 'critical place in the history of the duplicity of language' (WTC, 90): the modernist canon seals off any experiences that might disturb the monumentality of the canonized text.

Said's criticisms of the early-twentieth-century Anglo-American canon are often hard to answer. Even so, a recurrent problem in the current canon debate remains the unwillingness of the 'canon-busters' to propose an alternative set of liberating texts. Said's opponents might ask: how effectively does he himself follow the prescriptions he lays down? How far does he lead us in his quest for new ways of seeing non-traditional texts? The answer to this question would probably be ambiguous. His own chosen authors, Kipling, Hopkins, Swift and Conrad, remain solitary eminences, however disturbed by sociopolitical currents. Said's early work *Conrad and the Fiction of Autobiography* (1966) tries to lower his author from his canonical pinnacle and to immerse him in the constructive element of existential anguish, spiritual crisis and intellectual debate. Said wants his readers to see Conrad's work as a constellation of these personal and historical adversities, not as their triumphant diversion into an impersonal art. In *The World, the Text, and the Critic* he similarly argues that the canonical Swift should be returned to his daily activities as factionalist, ambitious churchman and court diarist. Accordingly, Said attacks 'the scholars who maintain the Swift canon' (WTC, 73) for dwindling their subject's pamphleteering and faction-mongering energies into the stale stereotype of a 'Tory satirist', a stereotype that drapes the very different figures of Johnson, Pope, Arbuthnot and Gay in a shared greyness. All too striking, Said implies, is the resemblance of the 'Tory humanist' to his twentieth-century counterpart.

Said emphasizes the conformity, unity and stability of the canon of validation in order to tighten his case for its wholesale rejection. Yet in drawing his vivid picture of a criticism untuned to the tension between tradition and modernity which Swift's prose mimics and echoes, he ignores the diversity of modern eighteenth-century studies, the upheavals, the debates, the friction, the turbulence at its leading edge. Studies of the kind undertaken by Claude Rawson and John Traugott pay less heed to the Tory clergyman and much more attention to the rhetorical subversions. Similarly, the Conrad of Frederick Crews or Ian Watt or even F. R. Leavis will hardly answer to the plaster saint Said discovers in what he calls 'religious criticism'. When he interposes as a model procedure his own free-floating, 'nomadic' methods, Said underestimates the mobility, the contradictions and tensions, the strong sense of cultural process already displayed in the work of his contemporaries.

In a sense, Said vies with the Auerbach of *Mimesis* by presenting the canon after Arnold as a seamless, singular line of narrative advance. Although this means that he elides the enormous differences in approach between individual critics (Winters and Eliot, Eliot and Empson), it also means that in many cases his anti-canonical narrative is elevated above the level of personal attack. His criticism thereby becomes exhortatory rather than juridical, and many readers will find themselves adding supporting examples to the larger story Said sketches out, the creation of artificial 'canons of order' by the removal of canonical masterpieces from their social and existential nests. Look, for instance, at L. C. Knights's *Further Explorations* (1965), where Ben Jonson's 'To Penshurst' is presented in exactly the terms Said identifies. Instead of discussing the social facts behind the construction of the country house, Knights venerates an 'experience' contained in the poem, an experience equated with the critic's own demonstrable mastery of verbal texture. When Knights steps away from the poem to its audience, he sees only a replica of a Cambridge tutorial. Knights's Jonson writes for an audience that consumes niceties of verbal structure without ever confronting the brutalities of the social relationships which sustain them. In the same way, F. R. Leavis's *Revaluation* (1936) proposes a set of canons of excellence according to a narrow range of incompletely articulated assumptions, and then moves from one national poetic masterpiece to the next, submitting touchstone works to extended analysis and consigning inferior ones to summary oblivion, while insinuating on every page that its younger audience must think likewise.

Said's tenacity in scrutinizing critical positions helps to illuminate the institutional role of early modern criticism. Even so, close acquaintanceship with his argument yields grounds for suspicion. Like Auerbach, he often enters into an uncanny symbiosis with his material; at times, his approach seems closer to the Victorian sage than to the modern professional critic, as he raids his material in search of some pregnant generalization or meaningful cultural pattern. Certainly, it makes for a good story to narrate the history of modern criticism in terms of 'the ideology of humanism'. Said's representation of this criticism conforms to the time-honoured ritual pattern of expelling the old and welcoming the new, but it does not conform to the canons of accurate representation.

If L. C. Knights occludes social fact in his discussion of Jonson's country house poetry, still his *Drama and Society in the Age of Jonson* (1937) bristles with social and economic references. In some ways, Knights furnishes the materials for the very kind of wide-ranging, socially anchored study Said himself presents as a desideratum. At issue here is the consistency of Knights's study of canonical monuments, not his systematic desertion of social and political evidence. Similarly, when Said characterizes early-twentieth-century criticism as 'committed to prying literature and writing loose from confining institutions', he suggests that such commitment arose from the belief that 'everyone properly instructed . . . could feel, perhaps even act, like an educated gentleman'.[14] (We have seen that Frye offers a similar criticism of Eliot and Arnold.) Yet the argument that humanist criticism trades political confrontation for decorous withdrawal smacks of the rhetorical device, the kind of enlightened demonology by which contemporary criticism defines itself in opposition to some fetishized and threatening predecessor. If the keepers of the Augustan canon suffer from a Laputan deafness, why did they assemble to hear Said's address at the Clark Library? If their standards remain so inveterately conservative, how could they pave the way for Said's own arguments? Ironically, Said's picture of the

'Tory satirist' had been drawn with equal vividness forty years before in Louis I. Bredvold's essay 'The Gloom of the Tory Satirists'.[16]

ORIENTALISM AND THE PROBLEM OF CULTURAL REPRESENTATION

In *Beginnings* and *The World, the Text, and the Critic*, Said argues that the early-twentieth-century canon of major works, the canon of validation, represents the conjunction of several overlapping interests and habits: the residue of sacred habits of interpretation; the propagandizing activities of a peculiarly modern cultural nationalism; and the nostalgia of intellectuals for a realm sealed off from the disturbances of the present. If Said's monolithic account of this canon elides much of its heterogeneity, or even its internal contradictions, his version still suits admirably the larger narrative he wishes to construct. The nature of that narrative becomes clearer in his important studies of the canon as it crosses cultures, *Orientalism* (1978) and *Covering Islam* (1981). Once they enter these two deeply anti-canonical texts, Said's readers leave behind completely the celebratory and reverential aura projected by Eliot's canon of validation. These works represent instead a massive peripeteia in Said's history of the canon, a decisive swing in canonical fortunes from reiterated validation to permanent exclusion. Both books undertake to explore the other side of the Chinese wall Eliot erected to European 'tradition' by investigating Western representations of a culture traditionally viewed as backward, irrational, devoid of logic, science and common sense.

In these books Said signals his departure from literary criticism proper into the wider field of cultural studies. His particular interest is the way in which a dominant culture represents an emerging culture in literature, in journalism, in the anthropological 'field', and in political policy statements. He suggests that although each of these areas conforms to its own separate conventions (so that the anthropologist follows vastly different criteria from the artist), shared canons govern one culture's assessment of another culture construed as inferior. These separate but mutually confirming assessments gather into what Said calls a 'canonical wisdom', which, since it has been established on so wide and apparently firm a basis, proves correspondingly difficult to dislodge.

Because Said himself is not an Arabic or Islamic specialist, he has incurred the usual reproaches from professionals in the areas he explores extraterritorially. Said's account of the Orientalist canon has been attacked on linguistic, scholarly and political grounds. Even so, it is important to remember the originality of his approach. In his cultural criticism, Said does not present himself as a linguistic specialist, nor as a colonial administrator, nor as a field worker, nor as a policy adviser, nor even as a spokesman for the oppressed. Alienated from his Palestinian background by education and profession, Said views his chosen cultures as a self-conscious outsider, stripped by education and experience of a complete identification with any party, period or school. As a self-confessed 'wanderer' or nomad, Said's angle of vision on his subject answers to no customary precedent, while his subject itself assumes a similar indeterminacy.

Very early in *Orientalism*, he states his determination to avoid 'a mindlessly chronological order' (O, 16). Instead, he hopes that his strategy of focusing on the 'highly organized and encoded system' (O, 21) of literary and critical language will show how the most apparently innocent, sympathetic representations of Oriental cultures conceal hidden assumptions of Western dominance. *Orientalism* inventories these representations from the eighteenth century to the present day, taking as its particular field 'the canonical pseudoscientific prejudices of French, British, and Italian Orientalism' (O, 296). *Covering Islam* extends this argument to contemporary images of Islam as mediated by mass-circulation magazines, press agencies and television networks. Behind all these sources, Said observes what he calls a 'canonical Orientalist opinion that the Semites never produced a great culture' (O, 289), an unshaken prejudice relayed as part of 'a canonical hymn to the beleaguered Western ethos' (CI, 35). Said views this prejudice as the last link in a chain of representations that aligns colonial past with capitalist present by cordoning off any images of an emerging East which is even now in the process of separating itself from a fadingly dominant West. As he intermittently makes clear in both books, his final concern is not just the field of East–West relations but the canons of representation in a society which has still not abandoned its vision of total cultural control.

If Said's later work constitutes neither detailed criticism of a body of Orientalist texts, nor cultural anthropology, nor radical dissent, then how can we characterize it? On one level, it constitutes a critique of representation, and in this respect it renews Said's longstanding concern with canons. For what is a canon but a culturally sanctioned representation, an image which a culture elects to preserve on the grounds of its continuing usefulness and authority? In the extended sense that Said now provides for the word, 'canon' runs along a spectrum from authoritative testimony, material to be consulted by anyone deeply interested in a discipline, to common prejudice, the unexamined ideas which happen to be current in an age or society. In a notable extension of traditional usage, he uses 'canon' to signify a body of inherited rules for representing any phenomenon, whether that phenomenon is a human body, a divine image, or a foreign culture. In *Orientalism* and *Covering Islam*, 'canon' stands for all kinds of cultural stereotypes which Said deplores. For instance, he describes Alexander William Kinglake's 'undeservedly famous and popular' ragbag of sprawling anecdotes, implausible surmise, and bone-hard prejudice in *Eothen* (1844) as 'a pathetic catalogue of pompous ethnocentricisms and tiringly nondescript accounts of the Englishman's East'. Then, almost in parenthesis, he adds that 'many of the attitudes he repeats are canonical, or course' (O, 193).

Although Kinglake is hardly canonical a century later, similar distortions enjoy a more subtle authorization today through electronic images. The dominance of these images in contemporary society ensures that the 'communal core of interpretations' (CI, 43) at the basis of any canon rests in the hands of very different kinds of experts from those entrusted with the validation of Wallace Stevens or Hart Crane. Instead, the 'canons of behavior' (CI, 29) which allow a television audience to recognize an Islamic culture come from 'television and radio networks, the daily newspapers, and the mass-circulation news magazines' (CI, 43). As Said characterizes them, these institutions have proved even less willing than the academy to explore new territory and to give credence to divergent points of view. Instead, a press half-consciously designed to protect and expand Western interests proves incapable of relaying the information necessary even to maintain them. From the Iranian revolution of the 1970s to the hostage crises of the 1980s, the American media have been forced to confront, without preparation, momentous events which they have answered, not surprisingly, with routine spasms of kneejerk prejudice.

Said tries to undermine these standardized media images in his *After the Last Sky* (1986), a pictorial exploration of a Palestine without boundaries, without recognition – a Palestine which, by a conjunction of force, prejudice, and media hostility, is 'no longer allowed to exist'. Said returns to Palestine not just in search of an authentic identity but to render 'the lived actuality' of Palestinian life.[16] Yet although he follows the implications of his argument both inside and outside the academy, Said does not want to take up the baton from F. R. Leavis or John Berger so much as to point out the implications of cross-cultural encounter for the whole notion of representation. 'The real issue', he notes in *Orientalism* (contradicting positions he implies elsewhere), 'is whether indeed there can be a true representation of anything, or whether any and all representations, because they *are* representations, are embedded first in the language and then in the culture, institutions, and political ambience of the representer' (O, 272). Such a position does not bode well for the radical intellectual, forever pledging allegiance to peoples he must inevitably misunderstand. It does not even hold out much hope for Said's own work, which rests on 'historical generalizations' about cultures he construes on the basis of information he acknowledges to be inevitably tainted at its source.

If Said clouds his discussion of these larger epistemological issues, his attack on his chosen field of cultural misrepresentation proceeds with fewer hesitancies and doubts. Having shown in his earlier books how certain works enjoyed a patriarchal authority among earlier generations of humanists, he now describes a similar line of descent inside the Orientalist canon, the traditional vehicle for Western scholarship on the societies and literatures of the East. Said shows how works such as Chateaubriand's *The Route from Paris to Jerusalem and from Jerusalem to Paris* (1811) and Sir Edward William Lane's *Manners and Customs of the Modern Egyptians* (1836) long enjoyed a status as 'pioneers, patriarchal authorities, canonical texts, doxological ideas, exemplary figures' (O, 22). When the Symbolist poet Gérard de Nerval composed a symbolic dream-poem about the Orient, a poem intimately concerned with his idiosyncratic sexual and poetic needs, he nevertheless drew on 'large swatches of Lane, incorporated without a murmur . . . as *his* descriptions of the Orient' (O, 184). Said explains this unlikely loan in terms of de Nerval's desire to take on 'the borrowed authority of a canonized Orientalist text' (O, 184), an impulse shared by the Symbolist poet as much as the colonial administrator.

The presence of fragments of a canonical text in a source so personal as Gérard de Nerval's *Tour of the Orient* (1851) emphasizes how effectively a canon can do its work, how efficiently it draws up a map later explorations will follow. Although it seems to bear the stamp of individual genius, the canonical work operates as an unseen eminence, preselecting material for later commentators, settling in advance their perspective on those materials, even governing the images they will select. And this work, in turn, will become canonical for its successors. As Said notes, 'in Lamartine, Nerval, and Flaubert, the Orient is a re-presentation of canonical material guided by an aesthetic and executive will' (O, 177). Such a canon operates in almost literally religious terms. It moves among its adherents and successors almost invisibly, imperceptibly merging its discourse with theirs. Its judgements serve as case law, so that what appears as raw experience in fact constitutes learned conditioning. Later works congregate around an Ur-text, sheltering in its authority, borrowing its aura, seeking an ever-widening field to apply its wisdom. Tragically, none of these canons for the representation of a colonized culture brings into the field of shared vision the non-threatening humanity of its members. Their silence becomes brooding malice; their volubility becomes a simmering prelude to insurrection; their complaisance signals natural inferiority; their independent organizations signify their capacity for intrigue. Times of peace become occasions for paeans to colonial administration; times of strife prove the need for its continuation. Even in scholarly and 'literary' accounts of the Orient, the canons of representation all point to the permanent inferiority of the colonized culture.

If this happens in cases where the impulse towards individual representation is very strong, what happens when it is very weak, as in journalism and political reports? As Said points out in *Covering Islam*, in these cases the authority of the canon as a principle of cultural representation becomes complete because invisible, a semi-conscious selection from previous authorities that represents itself as a direct, existential response to experiences actually witnessed. Such are the images of Islam the mass media relay to a Western audience, where the canonical decks itself out as the actual, an unfabricated slice of Oriental life:

> All in all, present coverage of Islam and of non-Western societies in effect canonizes certain notions, texts, and authorities. The idea that Islam is medieval and dangerous, for example, has acquired a place both in the culture and in the polity that is very well defined: authorities can be cited for it readily, references can be made to it, arguments about particular instances of Islam can be adduced from it – by anyone, not just by experts or by journalists. And in turn such an idea furnishes a kind of *a priori* touchstone to be taken account of by anyone wishing to discuss or say something about Islam. From being something out there, Islam – or rather, the material invariably associated with it – is turned into an orthodoxy of *this* society. It enters the cultural canon, and this makes the task of changing it very difficult indeed. (CI, 149)

In support of this argument, Said offers the instance of Iran at the time of the Tehran hostage crisis which erupted in 1979. Here, at a moment of enormous political tension, all these canonical misconceptions came together in media reports and documentaries that presented the society in question as a vortex of howling mobs. 'Canonical wisdom', observes Said, presents Islam as 'a unitary phenomenon, unlike any other religion or civilization . . . antihuman, incapable of development' (O, 296–7). In this way the possibility of seeing Iran as an emerging, politicized society, a society in the throes of complex social transition, disappears from view.

His analysis of the distortions at work in Western representations of the East aligns Said with the more radical voices in East–West relations. Yet as described up to now, his idea that political commentary matches new experiences to pre-existing patterns follows the work of predecessors not normally thought of as radical. In his description of these patterns, Said follows anthropologists such as Mary Douglas and Clifford Geertz, who think that daily life in island cultures such as Bali or mass societies like our own conforms to the process of paradigm-making Gombrich proposed for the story of art. Said, Geertz and Douglas follow Gombrich in their willingness to see everyday life as a continual process of interpretation. For all these writers, daily life becomes a pattern of paradigm-matching and paradigm-change. In their works the old theme of *Homo faber* gives way to a new image of *Homo interpretans*, and the result is the canonization of everyday life we first encounter in the work of Irenaeus and Augustine.

It is at this point that Said makes his distinct contribution. First, he points out that the Orientalist canon fits the requirements of Western imperialism, not the local conditions it purports to describe. Second, he suggests that the rules for representing Oriental societies in the days of high imperialism continue to apply in the so-called 'postcolonial' world. Third, he suggests that where the 'ideology of humanism' presents its own Western cultural monuments in a quasi-epic fashion through canons of validation, an 'ideology of difference' embalms the monuments of cultures construed as inferior or alien inside canons of rejection, canons in which irony, fantasy, or grave satire replace heroic narrative as governing tropes.

When Napoleon prepared for his expedition to the East he consulted Comte de Volney's *Travels in Syria and in Egypt* (1787), a book characterized by Said as 'an almost oppressively impersonal document' (O, 81). As in so many Orientalist texts, the appearance of neutrality masks a bedrock antipathy, 'views . . . canonically hostile to Islam as a religion and as a system of political institutions' (O, 81). If de Volney paved the way for Napoleon's territorial annexation of the Orient, Silvestre de Sacy prepares for its intellectual partitioning. De Sacy's three-volume anthology *Chrestomathie arabe* (1806), observes Said, provides 'an important link between Oriental scholarship and public policy' (O, 124). These jewels of poetry and prose reduced the diversity of Eastern cultures to a convenient unity for their Western readers. As Said points out, such works bequeath an 'Oriental presence to the West. Sacy's work canonizes the Orient; it begets a canon of textual objects passed on from one generation of students to the next' (O, 129). Instead of serving as an autonomous cultural area, 'the Orient as such' becomes 'less important than what the Orientalist made of it' (O, 127).

As the Orientalist canon hardens and sets, the East dwindles existentially, territorially and intellectually; gradually it shrinks to the point where Disraeli can say, in words Said takes as an epigraph to his book, 'The East is a career'. In a very short time, what Orientalists examine and adjudicate becomes something radically less than a cultural process. It becomes 'a *topos*, a set of references, a congeries of characteristics, that seems to have its origins in a quotation, or a fragment of a text, or a citation from someone's work on the Orient, or some bit of previous imagining, or an amalgam of all these' (O, 177). As Said represents it, the Orientalist canon becomes a grim parody of Gombrich's paradigm-making canon. Individual scholars match their own cultural stereotypes against those of their predecessors, without ever looking up from their inventory to the world outside.

If the Orientalist's procedures suggest a burlesque of Gombrich's paradigm-making and matching, then the repertoire of images the Orientalist canon compiles suggests a travestied version of Frye's myths. The result is a world that bears as much resemblance to historical reality as Disney's version of *The Jungle Book*. Because it takes the shape of a quasi-religious set of validations, the Orientalist canon offers no internal checks; because it offers no inbuilt way of monitoring its own dogmas against experience, it presents only the most limited basis for intellectual enquiry. Yet as Said points out, 'canon' in essence need mean nothing more mysterious than the process by which ideas find themselves circulated in a community, a process no less full of mistakes and misapprehensions than the process of textual transmission investigated by the bibliographical scholar.

Why, then, do we not recognize the inadequacies, the provisionalities, of our cultural canons instead of wielding them as infallible authorities? To answer this question, Said extends his attack on the canon in a pincer movement that simultaneously collapses and extends the idea: he collapses it into a congeries of rules and characteristics having little reference to the texts or groups they purport to describe; but, at the same time, he also attaches it ever more tightly to the larger political process, to the nexus of imperial and colonial interests it diligently serves to promote. The authority that underpins our standards of cultural taste, observes Said, 'is formed, irradiated, disseminated; it is instrumental, it is persuasive; it has status, it establishes canons of taste and value; it is virtually indistinguishable from certain ideas it dignifies as true' (O, 19–20).

Said returns again and again to attack two major canons: a canon of validation sustained by an ideology of humanism; and a canon of rejection supported by an ideology of difference. The first preserves national monuments; the second offers a set of rules for reinforcing national superiority by means of strategic omissions and misrepresentations of other cultures. Behind both canons stands a single vision of global Western dominance and authority. We can blame the canon, Said suggests, for the fact that the tacit acceptance of Western dominance persists long after its most militant prosecution ends. In the modern world, canons operate as highly paid servants of still-expanding postcolonial empires; they reinforce the dominance of Western economies and Western values. Canons play a major part in the tragedy which has left Western intellectuals without the will to disseminate new knowledge of cultures the popular media still consider as alien worlds.

SAID'S NOMADIC CANONS

Yet even though Said attacks the canonical disposition from several angles in four important books, the overall impression left by his work is not of the annihilation of the canon, but rather of the search for a more flexible, more provisional canon answering to a broader range of immanent cultural needs. It is worth emphasizing that this search will not necessarily spell the end of canons, since nothing in *Orientalism* or *Covering Islam* suggests that they will wither away, either in the emerging East or in the declining West. Although Said does not explore this issue very fully, he leaves no doubt that canons form an important part of the Islamic and Eastern cultures, and that in the West they have become so intertwined with our social and cultural institutions that their total eradication can barely even be conceived.

What kind of renewed cultural studies does Said propose, and what part will canons play in it? Like Curtius, who thought that 'a narrative and enumerative history never yields anything but a cataloguelike knowledge of facts',[17] Said is determined to avoid the 'mindlessly chronological' (O, 16). If Curtius saw the need for new forms of criticism in which 'European literature can . . . be seen as a whole', Said emphasizes both the danger and the potential value of the global interpenetration of critical discourse in the contemporary world. It is in keeping with his respect for at least some traditional scholarship that he periodically interrupts his argument in all four books to suggest his hopes for an easing of cultural tensions by a kind of *translatio studii* (transfer of learning), a translation of the classical or early Christian mission to a new secular, postmodern world. Although he does not explicitly employ the phrase, the hope expressed in *The World, the Text, and the Critic* for an intellectual cross-fertilization – even, eventually, a transference of cultural power – strongly resembles the access of new learning which strengthened the cultural life of imperial Rome, of medieval Europe, or of colonial America. In the late twentieth century, however, Said does not expect to renovate the cultural stock by a revival of classical learning. Instead, his *translatio studii* has two stages. First, he hopes to undermine the 'ideology of humanism' by a transference of cultural and intellectual capital from the European avant-garde to the English-speaking academy. He then (although this part of his programme is much less well developed) hopes to use this capital to enrich the interpretation of other cultures. By virtue of Gramsci, Benjamin, Derrida and Foucault, English-speaking critics will demythologize Empire and hear for the first time the voice of the colonized 'Other'.

As Said presents it, theory sets the stage for illumination; it does not exist to evolve its own internal canons and conduct its own partisan debates. The war between imagination and society that inaugurated an authoritarian, Christian, and socially homogeneous early-twentieth-century canon in a society undergoing unprecedented social and political change must not replay itself in reverse, producing what he aptly describes as 'a kind of international critical apparatus important for its activity, not by any means for the literary material it may or may not validate' (WTC, 143). As he notes, 'left to its own specialists and acolytes . . . theory tends to have walls erected around itself' (WTC, 247). To protect himself and his readers against these walls, Said devotes many pages of *Beginnings* and *The World, the Text, and the Critic* to sharp criticism of Foucault and

Derrida. Yet although he warns his fellow academics not to con-solidate the diverse testimonies of Barthes, Foucault, Gilles Deleuze, and Lévi-Strauss into 'a new canon' (WTC, 143), these authors occupy the same space in Said's work that critics of the 1950s reserved for Eliot and Richards. Said uses his touchstone authors to establish new ways of reading, tacit 'canons' for interpreting the Other. This remains the case even when he cautions his readers against elevating new methods into new monuments.

Said always suspects that the stream will prove more polluted than the source, the disciple less trustworthy than the master. He com-bines a susceptibility to charisma with extreme suspicion of its institutionalized afterlife. He admires even as thoroughgoing an academician as Lévi-Strauss for his ability to use structuralism to transform the binary opposition between 'primitive' and 'civilized' from a permanent value into a structural expediency. In contrast, when American deconstructionists cite Foucault and Derrida as authorities they restore the old hierarchical patterns of master and pupil, the old habit of deferential citation. Where Dante and Aquinas once stood, now stand Rousseau and De Man. To return to these writers, Said points out, 'as Lacan returned to Freud, is to establish them as a canon whose legitimacy is maintained with loyal devotion. . . . A new canon means . . . a new past or a new history and, less happily, a new parochialism' (WTC, 143).

Said's own books manifest a longstanding, but largely unsuc-cessful, desire to excommunicate every trace of 'loyal devotion'. The more Said wrestles with his critical angels, the more powerful they become. *Beginnings* becomes an enthusiastic meditation on the new French writers rather than a coolly evaluative intellectual report. Similarly, in his *The World, the Text, and the Critic* passages of plangently voiced cultural criticism vie for prominence with a more inward, text-haunted writer, as if the hearts of George Eliot and Walter Benjamin were to beat inside one breast. Where American intellectuals emphasize the dark, nihilistic side of modernism, con-temporary French criticism offers Said something more substantial: 'what in my opinion is an astonishing and fascinating production of thought attests to a continued belief in mind, albeit a radically altered view of scholarship' (B, 376). If Geoffrey Hartman presents criticism as an activity 'in the wilderness', Said looks beyond the wilderness towards a new intellectual territory, where new minds will find themselves fertilized by 'new cultures, new societies, and emerging visions of social, political, and aesthetic order', all of which 'now lay claim to the humanist's attention' (WTC, 21).

Ironically, it is Said's 'continued belief in mind' which lends him his place alongside the 'humanist' critics discussed in earlier chapters: critics who prefer to answer attacks on the canon by expanding or pluralizing rather than abolishing it. We have seen Gombrich, Frye and Kermode define the canon as a narrative that enlarges the dimension of critical activity by linking it to eschatological anxiety, mythic hope and fear, or simply 'the story of art'. Said ostensibly pledges himself to a narrative of a different order, but his practical energies direct him to renew the story of the modern mind envisaged by James Harvey Robinson, a predecessor at Columbia, in 1898. John Higham describes Robinson's desire to enter into an 'enthusiastic alliance with the social sciences' by encouraging students to study 'the aspects of the past that are most relevant to present needs'.[18] In Said's case, 'present needs' translate into the very special needs of the nomadic left-wing intellectual. For every page he devotes to the untold story of 'other' societies, he devotes many more pages to exemplary critical minds. Said's 'nomadic' criticism constantly returns to the exciting voices of the Left Bank – and not to the Left Bank of *mentalité* history, which has done much to bring the voices of the unheard to the attention of the academy, but to the cosmopolitan critical figures most visible to the Columbia intellectual.

Said vies with Trilling in his intoxication with the life of the critical mind. Despite his avowed intentions to force criticism to attend to the voices of the dispossessed, his pages narrate the story of an intellectual dynasty that stretches from Rudyard Kipling (an author 'appreciated but never fully canonized') to R. P. Blackmur ('the greatest of native American critics produced in the first half of the twentieth century') to Michel Foucault ('a self-born man').[19] When Said repeatedly returns to authors who exhibit the restless, nomadic qualities he values – to Foucault, to Conrad, to Nietzsche, to Vico; when he describes a 1967 dispute between Sartre and Lévi-Strauss as 'the great intellectual debate of the decade'; when he cites 'the exemplary positions' on textuality adopted by Derrida and Foucault in 1978; when he acknowledges how authors like these have helped him to understand 'a constellation of forces . . . still present in the modern era and still as unseemly in their power to engage and intoxicate',[20] he uses a language of power he attacks elsewhere as 'canonical'. With appropriate adjustments, Said's encomia recall Trilling on Freud or Arnold on Goethe. And even these critics can be inserted in a tradition of contemporary praise of the virtues of unruliness that includes Roland Barthes, Richard Poirier and, with certain qualifications, Trilling himself.

As Said no doubt appreciates, it is easier to make a declaration of independence than to achieve liberty. Even an 'open' criticism that disturbs, intoxicates, and breaches propriety communicates critical preferences and exudes intellectual enthusiasms. In Said's earlier books, many readers will remember best the many pages of excited exegesis of the new French critics, exegesis which presents them, despite Said's warning, as building blocks in a new canon, an open-ended, multidisciplinary, multinational canon that still, despite all his qualifications, remains a canon. Like Gombrich and Kermode, Said revels in difficult art, art that will transport him to a world untapped by less ambitious critics. For this reason, his search for a 'counter-narrative of liberation' cannot be prosecuted without the assistance of the great critical dynasties.

Whatever his overt intentions, Said's support for the new French critics has validated their work for a new American canon. If Paul de Man and Geoffrey Hartman introduce Poulet and Lacan to a new Yale school of criticism, Said shows students at Columbia how Foucault and Derrida fill a niche in the continuous investigation into the life of the modern mind inaugurated by Robinson and continued by Barzun, Highet and Trilling. As Said represents them to his New York audience, the new French critics operate from '*nomadic centers*, provisional structures that are never permanent, always straying from one set of information to another' (B, 376). Lévi-Strauss combines the prose of a *symboliste* with the activity of an anthropologist. Foucault moves his theatre of operations from the insane to the sick, from the sick to the criminal, from the criminal to the sexual, while constantly keeping in sight the pathology of the modern capitalist state. Instead of drawing a ring round an area they then control and defend, producing 'systems of authority and . . . canons of order whose regular effect is either to compel subservience or to gain adherents' (WTC, 290), these new critics offer novel interpretations of novel phenomena. In their willingness to present 'rethought forms of continuity, permanence, appropriation, vision, and revision' (B, 343), they demonstrate a way out of the canonical impasse: our need for canons in some shape or form; the tendency of those canons to swell from convenient instruments to large controlling powers.

Yet if it often exudes a canonical authority, Said's revitalized canon has a different shape from the early-twentieth-century 'canons of order'. The canons of Leavis or Knights operated as arguments from fixed premises that deployed a small number of preselected texts. In contrast, the open-ended 'nomadic' canon proposed by Said exploits more imaginative conventions. The warm comments Said passes on the huge field of classical scholarship or on Goethe's *Weltliteratur* reflect a similar desire to rid himself of the ache of nationalism and to strike out for the life of the mind. Similarly, his own mode of composition follows the modern artist's compulsion to tell a complex and arresting narrative rather than to settle a problem once and for all. When he attacks the Anglo-American modernist canon, Said's history of its fortunes takes the shape of a traditional tale, the story of a set of texts impounded, violated, imprisoned and rescued. When, however, he comes to narrate the sequel, the story of the canon liberated by modern French criticism, his narrative assumes the more fragmented, contradictory, gnomic thrust which Northrop Frye suggests is typical of prophetic narrative, even if the 'visions and revisions' occur not over generations but from book to book.

In *Beginnings*, for instance, Said praises the nineteenth-century religious critic Ernest Renan for his power to subdue canonical authority in the interests of fictive possibility. Like Foucault and Derrida, Renan seems less conditioned than American critics by the pressure to link his interpretations to immediate community needs. In unswerving defiance of historical convention and previous religious narrative, Renan tells the story of a revitalized, existential Jesus. 'Just as Jesus in his life and faith put himself directly next to God, so in his *Life of Jesus* Renan describes Jesus *as he could have existed* were it not for the intervening and authoritatively Christian text of the Gospels' (B, 219). Here as elsewhere, Said makes it clear that his antipathy is not to religious criticism as such, but to the institutional blanket that smothers the charismatic source. He dislikes the canonical object less than the process of canonization, which he sees as a diminution of the object's original imaginative potential. Always he affirms the value of the potential over the institutional; his approval for a Jesus 'as he could have existed' suggests a critic who hates to be tied to any binding set of assumptions.

Yet that very approval suggests why, after offering this fervent praise, Said uncanonizes his critic the next time he discusses him. In keeping with his postmodernist style of narrative, his desire to avoid at all costs traditional notions of continuity and coherence, *The World, the Text, and the Critic* paints a more hostile portrait of a less charismatic Renan, a Renan who saw in Islam only 'hatred to reason, the end of rational philosophy' (WTC, 281). While one Renan undergoes a quasi-apotheosis in his repudiation of an oppressive biblical canon, the other reveals all too human limitations in his deference to a nationalist one. In Said's work the figures and texts undergo bewildering changes of direction: no one plays hero for many pages; the reader must constantly bear in mind the shadow of the interpreter himself, provisional, tentative, constantly shifting the shape of his narrative.

As Said redefines it, the traditional *translatio studii* reorientates disciplines, monuments, even interpretations, in the direction of freedom. At every stage of the 'nomadic' critic's career, his basic approach and area of intellectual activity may – must – change shape. In *The World, the Text, and the Critic* his loosely articulated argument turns on the idea that 'for the first time in modern history, the whole imposing edifice of humanistic knowledge resting on the classics of European letters . . . represents only a fraction of the real human relationships and interactions now taking place in the world' (WTC, 21). In *Orientalism* and *Covering Islam*, which survey material from Symbolist poems to television reports, Said exposes the contradictions, the repetitions, even the plagiarism which have masqueraded as Western culture's disciplined, coherent study of the East. His less doctrinal model for the regeneration of the humanities is on display throughout his work. Moving easily from text to text and critic to critic, he describes a world resembling a kind of mental bazaar: a place of many tongues, a variety of goods, and an endless circulation of materials and people. Once installed in the bazaar, Said's critic can practise the kind of activity undertaken by Orwell's vagrant, Benjamin's storyteller, or Lévi-Strauss's *bricoleur*, middlemen who handle the fragments which come to them from a shattered canon with attention and even with respect – and then profitably relinquish them, pass them on.

For as long as canons exist as inert, blocking structures stifling the movement and trade of the bazaar, for as long as they function as a set of restrictive statutes, Said can extend to them little hospitality. Once they no longer regulate, once they no longer set up exclusive rights of representation, then he can view them with considerable warmth. Even so, there remains a large contradiction between the 'continued belief in mind' and faith in *Weltliteratur* affirmed in *Beginnings* and *The World, the Text, and the Critic* and the angry social critic glimpsed in *Orientalism* and *Covering Islam*.

From the testimony of *Beginnings* and *The World, the Text, and the Critic* one would have to describe Said as an avant-garde academician. The larger injustices described in *Orientalism* and *Covering Islam* cannot be remedied by the programmes for more open reading, more radical interpretation described in the two earlier books. *Orientalism* and *Covering Islam* do not make it clear whether Said attacks a learned canon confined to literary specialists and colonial administrators or whether he speaks as a concerned citizen addressing prejudices widely diffused through the community as a whole. It has become fashionable recently to conflate these two areas, to suggest the larger ideologies in which academic canons nest. Even so, it seems unlikely that reform of the academy, the more limited and responsive area, will transform the perceptions of an entire culture. Said's new learning can hardly hope to remove the deep cultural suspicions – the racism, the ignorance, the prejudices, the gunboat understanding of diplomacy – that characterize informal canons of cultural representation outside the academy. Indeed, he himself seems to reinforce such prejudices when he bluntly declares that the Israeli 'relationship to God' is 'impossible for me to understand'.[21] Said's enthusiasm for a new order of learning inaugurated by French critics can promise only intellectual revitalization; unless he subscribes to a more elitist view of culture than he admits, he cannot move directly from this new learning to a general social liberation.

Not surprisingly, Said's *translatio studii* has exerted most influence inside the academy. He has contributed enormously to the renewed radicalism among young academics, and in this way he has helped to reposition literary studies in the whole field of culture. Yet Said's search for 'things that otherwise lie hidden' brings him closer to what he calls 'religious criticism' (WTC, 53, 290) than he might welcome. His preference for 'historical generalizations' instead of history itself sampled scientifically and exhaustively delivers him back into the arms of Eliot and Leavis, who also swooped on their fields of study armed with some large hypothesis. Like his 'religious' predecessors, Said organizes his work around a grand crisis. For the 'religious critics' the Industrial Revolution supplied that crisis; for Said the crisis becomes colonialism. Like the 'religious critics', Said periodically sacrifices a totemic enemy ('humanism' for Eliot and Said alike, interestingly enough), halting the sacrifice only to spell forth the visionary vistas of a regenerated polity in which 'History' and 'the Other' become transcendent properties, by virtue of which the believing critic secures salvation. Paradoxically, Said's 'worldly' criticism carries an irremovable residue of the sacred and the canonical.

Yet despite (or even because of) its contradictions, Said's assault on 'religious criticism' carries more force than his revitalized 'nomadic' canon, however attractive the latter appears as a metaphor or an abstract idea. By expanding the meaning of 'canon' from a limited body of texts to a set of widely diffused cultural prejudices, Said runs the risk of diminishing the word's power either to comfort or to affront. His longstanding concern with the difficulties of textuality brings him no nearer than T. S. Eliot to 'the real human relationships now taking place in the world'. If Said explicitly describes the tragedy of the Western intellectual apparatus in one book, he implicitly plots its renewal in another by offering a rival set of readings of an only marginally adjusted order of texts, an order promulgated by a different set of Western intellectuals.

When Said recently published an essay on the question of imperialism in preparation for a long-expected sequel to *Orientalism*, he took as his text Kipling's *Kim*, a novel he praised as 'a great document of its historical moment and an esthetic milestone'.[22] This penchant for the impassioned appreciation of well-known texts remains one of the more surprising features of an intellectually very ambitious career. It is interesting too that when Said confronts a canonical text such as Conrad's *Nostromo*, his programme for a secular, radical canon withers away. In *Beginnings*, he shows how the novel outstrips its colonial contexts, noting that 'readings of *Nostromo* that overemphasize its political dimension detract from the novel's overall effect' (B, 134). Said's judgement contrasts markedly with Raymond Williams's characterization of *Nostromo* in *The English Novel from Dickens to Lawrence* as a book that measures 'the disappearance of a *social* value' by portraying 'an old and tired imperialism'.[23] Said goes far beyond Williams in acknowledging the linguistic and formal radicalism of Conrad's work; but it is his somewhat old-fashioned, sententious predecessor who confronts the book's political commitments. And when Said's closing commentary remarks that '*Nostromo* contains a highly passionate, almost religious, vision of life' (B, 136), one cannot but reflect that his place among the 'canonical' critics discussed earlier in this book is less troubled than he might like to think. In fact, as late as 1986, three years after the sustained criticisms of canons and religious criticism mounted in *The World, the Text, and the Critic*, Said told Imre Salusinszky that he valued Conrad as 'not just a great writer of stories but a great writer of parables'.[24]

In sum, Said's proposals for canonical reform run far ahead of his own textual practices. No more than Gombrich or Frye can he resist the glow of a canonical text. His intellectual *translatio studii* replenishes a canon his political shadow wants to demolish. On one front he bears down on Western intellectuals and their institutions with adamantine rigour, threatening them with the dire consequences of their cultural misrepresentations and ethnic slurs. But another side of Said remains fascinated with the life of the mind, eager to welcome the latest members of the hermeneutic circle, to lavish on them the attention extended to their distinguished predecessors – even to use the newcomers' instruments *on* their predecessors. For these reasons, Said's work amounts to an infinitely expandable canon, in which Foucault or Derrida provide an extra dimension of relevance to Swift or Conrad, where unseen dimensions of classical texts become visible to the vigilant interpreter able to tease out their hidden suggestions.

Said the writer remains entranced by the charisma of the intellectual: of Gramsci and Foucault, but also of Auerbach and Renan. For this reason, Said the citizen has done more to articulate the cause of ethnic diversity than Said the writer of cultural and literary criticism. The latter has honoured ethnic diversity in principle but has devoted himself in practice to the exegesis of the exceptional. If Said's work shapes up as the death knell for the canon, it ends as the canon's unexpected benediction, the source of much of the excitement and renewal in the life of the mind. Said undermines the authority of the canon to regulate our interpretations, but he reaffirms its imaginative resonance in his involuntary demonstrations of its power to excite them. His delight at the twilight of the idols, as when he describes how 'the Greco–Latin pedestal turns into dust',[25] only sporadically interrupts a more sustained reverie on the pleasures of canonical mastery. His campaign for 'secular criticism', with its heroic narratives, evil adversaries, ever-renewed adventures of intellectual conquering heroes, still possesses some elements of the crusade.

SAID'S VALEDICTION: THE END OF THE CANON?

I have tried to suggest that a close look at his work cannot support the conventional view of Said – or even his own self-presentation – as a militant opponent of canons. As we have seen, the drastic overhaul of our ways of seeing and valuing other cultures which he proposes in *Orientalism* and *Covering Islam* would produce a new canon. Such a canon would have little in common with the canons described by Frye or Gombrich. For Frye, a canon exists as an archive of human potential, a storehouse of origins, aspirations, epochal events and recurrent desires. Frye cannot conceive of a literary or cultural studies that sees in the images of myth, vision, and apocalypse only the imaginative reproduction of pre-existing ideologies. His canon always points finally to a liberating future rather than to a regulating past. Gombrich's very different view of the canon – progressive where Frye's is primitive, gradual where Frye's is visionary, cautious where Frye's is utopian – still shares Frye's sense of its comprehensive sweep. For Gombrich, three distinct but complementary canons guide artist and theoretician along a spectrum of artifacts that range from apprentice work to perpetual excellence.

Said's canon resembles Gombrich's in its tripartite structure and Frye's in its ultimately utopian hopes. Yet Said's canons – his canons of order, of validation, and of rejection – clash against each other rather than merge within a common picture, while his utopian hopes rest in the classroom more reluctantly than Frye's. In suggesting the conditions needed to establish a new, 'open' canon, Said moves us progressively beyond the academy, beyond existing cultural and political systems, to an order he describes as totally opposed to any bid to 'limit the human encounter between different cultures' (O, 46). Clearly, such visionary possibilities do not characterize daily behaviour in any existing canon-making institutions, where Said sees a 'canon of excellence' maintained by ritual obeisance and professional deference. Small hope here of understanding tradition along other than hierarchical, sexist and ethnocentric lines; small hope here for the construction of modified frames of reference that will enable those inside the academy to understand works departing from these authorized patterns.

If only such exclusory frames of reference were confined to the academy, where they might amount to nothing more than antiquarianism. But Said argues that these habits of conceiving all cultures, societies and races in terms of a common mould have spread to the larger culture through 'canons of rejection' circulated by electronic media and mass-circulation journalism. As more and more subject cultures become emerging cultures, and as more and more emerging cultures begin to define their identities in terms significantly different from those traditionally constructed for them, so the canons of validation and rejection will diminish in authority, to be replaced by canons of the future that will dispense images of diversity set in the interpretative frames necessary for understanding otherness.

For all these reasons, Said's work signals a valediction to the canon as a natural item in the cultural stock. After Said, the confident gesture of Horace's proverbial 'if you require a monument, look about you' becomes unavailable to contemporary critics, who must anxiously estimate the cost of the labour and raw materials which have transported and erected their chosen monuments, at the same time keeping a careful record of the precise number of groups not represented on the chosen plinth. The fate of canons in a culture more disposed to find its paradigms in politics and social science will provide the subject for the final chapter of this book. In the meantime, it is worth noting that despite his radical attack on the processes that led to the erection of the monuments of the past, Said still keeps open lines of access between adversarial and orthodox testimonies. To employ one of his own favourite metaphors, he does not aim so much at the canon's dissolution as at its 'relocation'. His unwillingness to settle for a permanently adversarial role becomes apparent in his own literary range of reference – the personal canon he invokes for practical purposes in his own work. It is significant, for instance, that he is just as likely to go to Conrad or Swift to show the workings of imperial politics as to cite Fanon or Pierre Bourdieu. Like Kermode, Said ultimately proposes not so much the abandonment of the canon as a kind of canon in transience, a flexible arrangement of valued texts that will shift its shape according to the changing contours of the larger cultural scene. It is to the less flexible arrangements of a contemporary generation of increasingly dogmatic anti-canonists to which we must finally turn.

Conclusion
Cultural Studies:
Towards a New Canon?

THE CANON CONTROVERSY:
POLEMICS WITHOUT PRECEDENT?

From time to time famous critics console themselves and their audiences by consigning the canon debate to the absurdities of contemporary cultural fashion or relegating it to a minor position in the history of intellectual life. Roger Shattuck recently told interviewers at *Harper's Magazine* that 'the canon' was a new phenomenon to him, and that his career as a distinguished cultural historian had thrown up little evidence of its importance for modern letters.

> In forty years of working in publishing and teaching, I've never heard the word *canon* except in theology. . . . The word has been introduced in the past ten years by those who consider themselves the enemies of a traditional curriculum. It is a term of opprobrium, suggesting something imposed, authoritative, reactionary.[1]

However consoling to some sensibilities, such a view will not withstand historical investigation. From 1918, when Van Wyck Brooks fired his first shots against 'the accepted canon of American literature', a sizeable body of evidence exists of a longstanding canonical debate, albeit a less bloody and less public debate than the one currently in progress. During the twentieth century canons have functioned as vehicles for national politics, as declarations of cultural independence by a critical avant-garde, as instruments to calibrate the nuances of creative excellence, and as the source of encyclopaedic, mythical or historical narratives. To step outside the twentieth century would be to add to these functions. For earlier generations, canons supplied syllabuses for basic instruction and advanced study. They stimulated creation and facilitated editorial scholarship. They furnished proof of divine inspiration, ecclesiastical authority and ecclesiastical prejudice. None of these activities occurred without controversy. A canon of ancient authorities, for example, has never

221

appeared an absolute blessing to an artist in search of spiritual self-definition. Similarly, a canon which professes to record the Word of God will always be viewed suspiciously by those who fear its manipulation by a powerful clerical hierarchy.

In the history of modern Western culture, canons have repeatedly become embroiled in controversy. In the past, the strong connection which ties *canon* to *rule* seemed to many critics – to Thomas Edwards and T. S. Eliot, to name but two – an unnecessarily rigid application of authority to a pre-eminently liberal activity. To these critics, the 'canonical disposition' implied the very opposite of the personal engagement and free enquiry that characterize the arts. As Eliot observes in a letter to Mary Hutchinson, 'Culture, if it means anything decent, means something personal', a belief that makes canonical lists and canonical rules almost impossible to follow. Shattuck, who sees the canon as a clerical institution which has somehow strayed into the field of culture, would agree with Eliot here. Yet Eliot is just as disturbed at the prospect of a completely unregulated criticism, and speculates in the same letter about the need for a 'civilisation which is impersonal, traditional', a need some have felt to be met by a canon. Not for the first time in the history of the canon, Eliot then jots down a little list of admirable authors and cultures – 'Byzantine . . . Stendhal . . . Mozart, Bach etc., Flaubert (yes), Russian ballet. . . . Russian novels.'[2] He admits that he transmits the valuations of a frivolous modern culture, for which he acknowledges an ineradicable attraction. Throughout this century, many writers exhibit a similar pattern of attraction and repulsion towards the idea of a canon.

The centrality and the ferocity of the current canon debate has a much shorter history, however. In effect, the debate dates from 1979, when Leslie Fiedler and Houston Baker Jr organized two programmes, 'English as a World Language for Literature' and 'Literature as an Institution', for the English Institute. It is a measure of the importance of this body of work that the term 'canonicity' reached the pages of the Modern Language Association Bibliography in 1980, to be followed by 'canon' in 1981. During the same year, the two programmes became a book entitled *English Literature: Opening Up the Canon* (1981). Many of Fiedler and Baker's contributors explain at length their dissatisfaction with the profession. One speaker begins his presentation by declaring: 'Where I come from, the words that are most highly valued are those which are spoken from the heart, unpremeditated and unrehearsed.'[3] These sentiments no doubt earned great applause, but would, if taken literally, overturn the protocols of an academy institutionally committed to carefully rehearsed, intensively researched discourse. Other contributors exhibit an eagerness to link the academy's presiding assumptions with conservative political systems and unjust social practices, in a way that signals the reappearance of the radical opinions voiced in the 1960s.

In general, *Opening Up the Canon* presents something of a declaration of war on a conservative profession that excludes minorities and on a nationalist discipline that squeezes English into '*The English*', repeatedly overlooking 'what men and women in the world-at-large have made of English'.[4] No longer, Baker argues, can the discipline of English confine itself to a minute section of the English-speaking world; it is time for the field to be enlarged and transformed. A profession widely perceived (especially by its victims and casualties) as dedicated to a nationalist, sexist and conservative interpretation of its activities will quickly have to change.

In 1984, another important collection appeared in the shape of Robert von Hallberg's *Canons*. Where Fiedler and Baker's contributors adopted a political and populist frame of reference, von Hallberg's collection, which originally appeared in the pages of *Critical Inquiry* between September 1983 and March 1984, proved more analytic and theoretical. *Canons* marks a resurgence of historical, rhetorical and sociological concern with canons as value-conferring institutions in the sphere of the humanities, and its contributors make use of the most up-to-date methods, deploying all the resources of the new 'theorized' academy to understand how canons work. Accordingly, the pages of *Canons* show Christine Froula using feminist and poststructuralist methods to discuss Milton, Gerald Bruns using Max Weber to understand the canon not as 'a literary category' but as 'a category of power',[5] Hugh Kenner offering an autobiographical defence of the modernist canon, and John Guillory furnishing a sociological demystification. Although *Canons* is only six years old, its catholicity and flexibility seem very distant today.

What lies behind these two important collections? Why did the canon assume so high a profile in the early 1980s and quickly became one of the most controversial, widely discussed and widely applied topics of the decade? In some ways, it is still difficult to understand how contemporary criticism has come to define the question of the canon as one of its central problems. Even W. J. T. Mitchell, the editor of *Critical Inquiry*, betrayed some bafflement about the matter. Frank Kermode recalls his saying that 'he had not planned such an issue . . . the contributions had simply arrived on his desk'.[6] The long historical unfolding of *canon* traced in this present book provides a partial explanation, by demonstrating the reappearance in the debate of longstanding critical problems. But what particular developments in postwar criticism contributed to the emergence of the canon debate at this particular moment in the 1980s and 1990s?

ORIGINS OF THE PRESENT DEBATE

We shall see in this section that three main lines of descent have shaped the current debate. First, there is the long tradition of adversarial or oppositional criticism which stands behind the Fiedler and Baker collection. Literary criticism has always attracted malcontents such as F. R. Leavis or Randolph Bourne, who hope, often with good cause, that their marginalized positions will some day come into favour. A second crucial influence is the self-conscious, metacritical concern with the nature of signifying and validating systems in the humanities which lies behind such seminal works as Roland Barthes's *The Elements of Semiology* (1964), Jacques Derrida's *Of Grammatology* (1967), Michel Foucault's *The Archaeology of Knowledge* (1969), Louis Althusser's 'Ideology and Ideological State Apparatuses' in *Lenin and Philosophy* (1971), Hayden White's *Metahistory* (1973), and Clifford Geertz's *The Interpretation of Cultures* (1973). All these works cleared the way for literary criticism to examine its own instruments for the transmission and production of value. A third influence, sociology, has also pushed contemporary criticism in a more self-conscious direction. The postwar years have seen professors of English increasingly eager to subject such terms as 'value', 'culture' and 'tradition' to sociological analysis and to build social and political bridges between valued texts and their original audiences. As early as the 1950s, F. W. Bateson told readers of his new journal *Essays in Criticism* that 'a poem . . . is not good or bad in itself but only in terms of the contexts in which it originated'.[7] Subsequent sociological criticism has travelled even further from critical absolutism by interpreting aesthetic value and reputation in terms of a continuously unfolding social process. As we shall see, the postwar criticism that paves the way for the opening of the debate transfers these three elements – the adversarial, the theoretical and the sociological – from their marginal positions at the fringes of criticism to their present place as its central constituting discourse.

One of the first critics to explore this militantly sociological criticism was Raymond Williams. In *The Long Revolution* (1961) Williams launched a sociological investigation of British authorship, highlighting such overlooked variables as the schooling and class origins of canonical authors. Two years later, in 1963, Richard Hoggart's inaugural lecture 'Schools of English and Contemporary Society', delivered at the University of Birmingham, exposed literary production to sociological analysis at every stage. What lines of communication delivered a book to a reading public? Which journals and periodicals launched important creative reputations? Hoggart called for sociological studies of the writers' audiences, of 'the opinion formers and their channels of influence . . . the organizations for the production and distribution of the written and spoken word'.[8] The postwar years, Hoggart argues elsewhere, marked ' "the entry into society" . . . of whole classes of people who were previously too poor to be able to make themselves felt'.[9] Were these people well served by an educational system which had remained unchanged since the Edwardian era? Did their emergence call for a new look at the distribution of and breadth of participation in the self-approving phenomenon called 'English culture'? In the work of Hoggart and Williams that term loses its honorific charge. The sum of both their testimonies is a massive challenge to the idea of the canon as a unifying, regulating, or even co-ordinating cultural instrument.

When 'value' and 'culture' came under scrutiny, 'tradition' could not remain long unquestioned. In 1957, at the start of *The Poetry of Experience*, Robert Langbaum wryly observes how utterly without foundation is the territory contemporary criticism sanctifies as 'tradition'. Eliot, he notes, 'talks about a tradition which the past would not have recognised'. Where some postwar critics presented 'tradition' as an inviolable alliance between custom and innovation, Langbaum sees only a set of distinctly modern anxieties about continuity, succession and authority. Eliot's canonical term, he argues, 'helps construct for us that image of ourselves which constitutes the modern pathos'.[10] Langbaum does not underrate the private imaginative significance of 'tradition' for modern poets, but he chips away at its public legitimacy, leaving an open door for his successors to reconsider the question of cultural value.

From the beginning of the 1960s more and more literary academics began to look critically at their own discipline. For instance, Graham Hough's *The Dream and the Task* (1964), originally delivered as a series of BBC radio talks, calls for drastic changes in British universities. Acknowledging that the public asks artists and commentators to fulfil an unprecedented range of spiritual and ethical functions, Hough wonders how effectively the universities are responding to these enlarged expectations. He thinks that departments of English as presently constituted separate their activities from the surrounding culture, turning literary studies 'into a kind of scripture, rigorously selecting from it a canon that makes it suitable for this purpose'. Having recently returned from a visit to Johns Hopkins, Hough sees that the study of literature at his own institution, Cambridge, proceeds by a principle of exclusion. He vigorously objects to an English syllabus arranged around a kind of nonconformist canon, a canon of intense moral uplift that makes no effort to understand the multiplicity of creative possibilities 'culture' has historically nurtured. His call for a discipline that would investigate 'the whole of man's recorded imaginative experience, not some section of it, selected to agree with some temporary social or moral prejudice' recalls the programme outlined in *The Province of Literary History* (1931) by the Johns Hopkins professor Edwin Greenlaw. In effect, Hough calls for the end of 'English' as presently constituted and its replacement by a field widened by easily available historical and anthropological knowledge'.[11]

Hough's vigorous presentation of 'the dream and the task' set the course for a long period of curricular reform and for a more thoroughgoing inspection of the inherited critical vocabulary. In 1964 C. K. Stead scrutinized this vocabulary from the unexpected perspective of a student of literature at the Universities of Auckland, Bristol and London. As a New Zealander, Stead enjoyed an oblique relationship to a 'tradition' invented by American expatriates and consolidated by cosmopolitan intellectuals. Accordingly, *The New Poetic* reflects the growing sense that nothing inherently historical or even 'national' corresponds to the early-twentieth-century traditions of Yeats, Eliot and Lawrence. Expanding the scattered polemical asides which litter F. R. Leavis's *New Bearings in English Poetry* (1932), Stead builds up a body of evidence of a road mistaken in early modern literary history. He shows that a 'literary' tradition, a collection of authors valued by other authors, does not necessarily correspond to a 'sociological' tradition, a collection of authors valued by a large, loyal readership because of their subject matter or their ability to narrate momentous public events. Modernism, Stead thinks, has its roots in 'a rejection of "public" themes designed to please a particular audience at a particular time'.[12] In societies of great diversity, 'literary history' and 'national history' will not necessarily be best served by the same practitioners. Stead's investigation of a series of important early modern terms – 'life', 'the image', 'affirmation' – reveals key items in the modern critical vocabulary as specialized constructions with little relationship to the literary preferences expressed by the public at large.

In this way, *The New Poetic* shows the beginnings of a new, uneasy relationship between the sociological and the aesthetic ways of understanding literary value. Stead's research had been supervised by L. C. Knights, whose *Drama and Society in the Age of Jonson* (1937) represented a pioneering sociocritical investigation. After that, however, the many volumes of Knights's *Explorations* accumulated into an extensive gloss on Eliot's 'tradition'. Stead's work reflects his mentor's dual allegiances to literary sociology and to modernist poetics. His sociological investigation of the works valued in early-twentieth-century England takes him down well-travelled roads, while his assessment of the 'traditions'constructed and disseminated by important modern poets takes him into distinctly different territory. Stead's critical judgement leads him to see the 'tradition' of the great moderns as the most valuable matrix for poetic achievement. A subsequent generation of critics, with a different set of critical priorities, could easily move from seeing the modern tradition as an unhistorical entity to dismissing it as a historically determined and culturally elitist testimony.

The arguments of Stead and Langbaum did not spell the demise of Eliot's 'tradition', but they certainly dislodged its monolithic structure. These critics proved that value was not a self-evident property but a sphere of interlocking interests. In this way they contributed to a growing body of calls for the detailed scrutiny of the political, cultural and aesthetic biases of those who first publicize an author's worth. Is there not something suspicious about a discipline that calls itself 'literary history' and then constructs a canon that tells us everything about the cultural preferences of the contemporary intelligentsia and nothing about the choices and biases of people in the past? Why should one generation's set of cultural monuments serve another generation's more democratic needs?

In 1970, Lionel Trilling's *Literary Criticism: An Introductory Reader* imprinted the new scepticism on college curricula by describing literature as 'an enterprise which is inherently competitive' and by informing students that 'a work of art is a commodity'.[13] During the same period, the enquiries of critics such as Stead and Hoggart also began to influence the wider public for literary culture. In 1967 James Reeves and Martin Seymour-Smith, two figures better known in the classroom and the public library than the university lecture hall, published an anthology called *A New Canon of English Poetry*. In their preface, the editors describe their innovative principle of selection and formulate their larger intentions. They go out of their way to emphasize that they have no desire to disturb the canon of literature in English built up by previous critics and teachers: 'We must insist that it is no part of our purpose to supplant the canon they laid down.' Even so, they include no poems from either the *Oxford Book of English Verse* or Palgrave's *Golden Treasury*, two standard anthologies they rename a generic *Oxgrave*. They argue that the authority enjoyed by these two volumes threatens the vitality of British cultural life. 'There is a tendency to regard them as representing "the best" in English poetry', they lament. 'Their contents are by implication stamped as canonical.' Where, in the field of finance, bad money drives out good, in the field of poetry a notion of 'the best' as the longest-lived drives out all other possibilities. As a result, 'the reader tends to enjoy a contracting canon of classic poetry'.[14]

Although Reeves and Seymour-Smith advocate a more cautious and gradualist expansion of the canon than we are accustomed to hear today, they reveal significant tacit assumptions about the unacknowledged virtues of the marginal, the value of change, and the need for variety. They hope 'to offer a substantial body of poems, mostly short, both English and American, which in our opinion deserve to rank in the canon'.[15] The editors belong to a Britain of the early 1960s whose intellectual class often believed that merit would remedy injustice, and that very moderate changes might secure extremely desirable goals. Just as premature selection in British schools produces a diminishing pool of talent for British society as a whole, so exclusive ranking lists of British poets diminish the reserves of British culture.

Later, more radical, critics would want to pay less attention to 'merit' and more attention to the values of change, marginality and variety. The 'hedges and ditches' which Reeves and Seymour-Smith thought very properly removed from sight the 'poems which Oxgrave quite rightly left out'[16] would soon gain an energetic partisan in the shape of Raymond Williams, whose *The Country and the City* (1973) implies changes to the canon much more drastic than the inclusion of Swift's 'The Lady's Dressing Room' and Dickinson's 'A Clock Stopped'. Williams impassioned defence of the virtues of the regional and the excluded locks in place a second argument of the current debate, an argument that gained strength during the same period from the voices of the marginalized themselves. Throughout the 1960s and 1970s, more and more voices from emerging cultures reached publishers' lists and sometimes even college syllabuses. For instance, from 1962 the Heinemann African Writers Series began to publish important African writers such as Chinua Achebe, Cyprian Ekwensi, Peter Abrahams, Elechi Amadi, Ayi Kwei Armah and James

Ngugi in well-printed paperback editions suitable for college use, a move which resulted in the introduction of courses in African and Commonwealth literatures in English at the universities of Leeds and Kent and elsewhere. The Penguin African Library, also inaugurated in 1962, made material available for similar courses in history and politics, as well as acquainting a wider audience with the problems and aspirations of a continent emerging from colonialism.

With this literature becoming more accessible, Williams's *The Country and the City* could sketch out some of the ironies surrounding an urban postcolonial literature written 'in the metropolitan languages which are themselves the consequences of mobility'.[17] Yet in this area at least Williams had been anticipated by Lewis Nkosi, an exiled South African writer whose essay collection *Home and Exile* appeared in 1965. Nkosi's work signals the arrival of a new cultural turbulence which rejects the accepted canon of Eliot and the high moderns as reactionary and dogmatic. He objects to 'white academicians dealing with African art and literature who find it convenient to judge African works of art entirely by European canons of criticism'. Where Reeves and Seymour-Smith see 'the canon' as a natural outcome of the critic's judicial function, Nkosi calls into question the whole idea of critical judgement. He views European critical canons as instruments of territorial authority, and suggests that they have proved useless for recognizing significant African needs. Nkosi insists that African writers understand their own traditions, and would perhaps remain sceptical about Houston Baker's suggestion that African literature should forge alliances with deconstruction and feminism in order 'to undermine the half-truths that white males have established'.[18] Nkosi especially objects to the instructional authority which Western canons enjoy in South African criticism, deploring the spectacle of 'the jejune bitter pabulum of T. S. Eliot's metaphysics buttressing an African poem'. For Nkosi, the Eliot 'canon' represents a bloodless intellectual pessimism which he sees as an affront to 'the virile masculine sensibility rooted in an essentially optimistic humanism such as is everywhere evident in Africa'.[19] Nkosi rejects the questions Western critics find so inexhaustibly important, noting that the expression 'God is dead' means nothing in a Zulu context.

Nkosi objects to the spectacle of Western criticism patrolling the world, reinforcing the metropolitan authority of 'the canon'. In his preface to the 1979 reissue of the Native American prophetic *Black Elk Speaks*, Vine Deloria challenges the Western canon on its own ground. What Nkosi argues is politically indefensible and aesthetically enervating, Deloria sees as spiritually bankrupt as well. Originally published in 1932, Black Elk's historical and prophetic testimony was presented as 'told through' John Neihardt, an independent scholar of Native American culture. Since that date the work had enjoyed a steady popularity in schools and with the general public. But is *Black Elk Speaks* just another set work or does it make greater claims on audience comprehension? Deloria argues that 'the basic works of the Black Elk theological tradition now bid fair to become the canon or at least the central core of a north American theological canon which will some day challenge the Eastern and Western traditions as a way at looking at the world'. He conceives of the canon not just as a collection of teaching texts but as the expression of a coherent world view, in this case the world view of a suppressed minority. He also considers the crucial question of Neihardt's 'literary intrusion into Black Elk's system of beliefs'.[20] If a canon constitutes the world view of a defeated people, how can their conquerors represent that canon adequately? Can the canon of a defeated subject nation renew the spiritual life of an imperial nation sickened by conquest? Does the heterogeneous collection of works taught in American classrooms constitute a similarly binding canon of Western values?

These represent the questions of a self-conscious outsider to accepted academic and professional ways of preserving the past and disseminating cultural values. What happens when aggressive voices from inside the academy start to pose similar questions? The next stage in the decline of canons arrives when the heavy theoretical artillery of European-trained theorists is aimed at its structures. From the late 1960s a systematic, even programmatic, suspicion of the canon and its monuments emanates from the European and American academy. This suspicion is very marked in two of Hans Robert Jauss's most widely read essays, 'Literary History as a Challenge to Literary Theory' (originally delivered as a speech at the University of Konstanz in 1967) and 'History of Art and Pragmatic History' (1970). Jauss sees canons as vehicles for a permanent, timeless authority which, throughout the modern period, has been made to correspond to the origins and continued existence of any known text. In his drive to raise his work above the merely pragmatic, Winckelmann, for instance, 'demands "great examples" and "decisive studies", sets up a canon. . . . The new demands of Winckelmann's *Geschichte der Kunst des Altertums* [History of Ancient Art] (1764) denigrate not only the previous "history of artists", but also the chronological presentation of previous history.' Similarly, Georg Lukács's accounts of the permanent value of his favourite artists depend on a 'time-honoured concept of the "classical" that is . . . transcendent of history'. In Lukács's 'canonization of Balzac for modern literature' and Winckelmann's 'canon' of the classical Greeks, Jauss sees a common impulse to 'bridge the gap between past and present' by an unjustified recourse to 'a timeless ideality'.[21] Yet time is the very element art cannot escape, for time determines the ensemble of structural and formal relationships available to artists and audiences alike.

A decade later, Paul de Man's essay 'Shelley Disfigured' (1979) rounds even more strongly on the canonizing disposition, which turns the textual events of the past 'into statues for the benefit of future archeologists "digging in the grounds for the new foundations" of their own monuments'. Canonization – the process of socializing textuality, of reconfiguring the fractured figures of the foreign languages inscribed in an old text – appears to de Man a disingenuous, self-serving desire to repair the ruins of time. This desire he labels 'monumentalization', a technique of reading which buries the overwhelming contingency of the literary text in 'monotonously predictable' interpretations governed by the attempt 'to define, to understand or to circumscribe' all literary phenomena 'in relation to ourselves'.[22] After de Man demystified the textual and rhetorical ploys behind canonizing authority, after Jauss described the temporal sleight of hand that masks its mode of operation, it remained only for Stanley Fish to expose the professional interests the canonizing disposition consistently served.

In 1980, Stanley Fish collected his ten-year investigation into the professional and epistemological responsibilities of the academy under the title *Is There a Text in This Class?*. His guiding theme reflects his continuing quest to subvert the canons of criticism, the basic principles he characterizes as 'the business of criticism'. In 1976, Fish had relieved his fellow professionals of the 'obligation to be right' by reinstating the norm that Friedrich Schlegel had first settled for modern criticism, the duty to 'be interesting'. Four years is a long time in the career of Stanley Fish, and by 1980 he acknowledged that these sentiments were unfortunate. He still insisted, however, that no 'standard of right exists . . . independent of community goals and assumptions'. In search of a formula that fulfils both his corporate obligations and his anarchic disposition, Fish sweeps away the time-honoured criteria of objectivity and neutrality by suggesting that an 'interesting' criticism is an interested criticism. He denies that the task of criticism is 'to decide between interpretations by subjecting them to the test of disinterested evidence'. Instead the critic should 'established by political and persuasive means (they are the same thing) the set of interpretive assumptions from the vantage point of which the evidence will hereafter be specifiable'. Fish's legal language masks a definition of literary study that pushes it in the direction of political lobbying. As he reformulates it, literary interpretation requires that texts 'will be made and remade again whenever the interests and tacitly understood goals of one interpretive community replace or dislodge the interests and goals of another'.[23] In this way the solid bulwark of canonical achievement dissolves into the fluctuating objectives of competing critical factions.

Considered as a whole, the testimony of critics from Bateson to Fish introduces nearly all the elements of the current debate. First, there is the new tendency towards sociological investigation of works previously sanctioned by tradition or taste. Second, there is the conviction that the unacknowledged merit of marginalized texts can augment the monuments valued by high culture. Third, there is a suspicion that the upholders of these monuments will never share their eminence with witnesses from other cultures, but will maintain the accepted canon by deliberately excluding them. Fourth, there is the conviction that the existing masterpieces represent a world view that social justice should overthrow, and that works already exist which can furnish culturally renewing alternatives. Fifth, there is a tendency to self-analysis in the discussion of the accepted canon, a tendency which brings to new prominence the political and persuasive mechanisms underpinning the authority of an accepted work or taught text. The sum of all this testimony is a series of major shifts in the field of literary history. From one direction, the postcolonial critique of Stead and Nkosi points to the inadequacy of homogeneous canons as a means of studying the diversity of literary and cultural history. From another direction, the sociological investigations of Williams and Hoggart indicate a need for more systematic research into the institutional history of literature. For Deloria, the canon of Western culture has lost its authority and demands countercultural replenishment. For Stanley Fish, the true motives of criticism have never been articulated, a belief that leads him to unfold new political criteria for critical argument. From all angles, literary criticism becomes a field for negotiation.

All these changes have been reinforced by concurrent work in other disciplines in the humanities, which also spent the postwar years in reconsidering their canons. We have seen that in the field of political science, J. G. A. Pocock searches with increasing complexity and nuance into the linguistic paradigms by which modern scholars reconstruct the entire political past. Educated in New Zealand, Pocock raises another significant voice from a postcolonial culture. In his *Politics, Language and Time* (1973) he confronts an academic canon that runs 'from Plato to Aristotle to Augustine to Aquinas to Marsilius to Machiavelli to Hobbes to Locke to Hume to Rousseau to Burke to Hegel to Marx', only to collapse as it faces the political problems of the modern world. The body of knowledge transmitted in departments of Political Studies has been farmed out to philosophers, historians and social scientists without ever being understood as a system of language, a conceptual world which builds the foundations of a modern discipline by constructing paradigms of legitimacy, authority and power. Studied sometimes as works of history, sometimes as philosophy, sometimes as preludes to contemporary issues, the canon of political science lacks any distinct 'universe of discourse'.[24]

Pocock considers political studies unfortunate among the historical sciences in having organized its field 'as the study of a traditional canon'.[25] Texts inside such a canon become separated from historical circumstance. The task of the demystifying, decanonizing, historically vigilant political scientist is to restore the texts to the full force of their original context. Preserved so long in the tomblike structure of the canon, the 'classic' texts of political science must circulate again as products of languages, individuals, groups, and societies in states of change. Only if it reformulates its field in this way will political science participate in the disciplinary advances made in history itself.

Their long-established freedom from canonically organized curricula has no doubt encouraged historians proper to join the front line of canonical attack in other disciplines. When Robert Darnton, for instance, reported to the *Princeton Alumni Weekly* in 1981, he delivered a severe blow to literary historians by arguing that their academic canon presents an 'arbitrary notion of literary history as a canon of classics, one which was developed by professors of literature in the 19th and 20th centuries. . . . In fact what the people of the 18th century were reading was very different. . . . It doesn't look anything like the reading lists passed out in classrooms today.'[26] The same processes which blind Western audiences to non-Western monuments also silence the witnesses of the European past. The remedy, Darnton implies, is to follow his own procedures as a historian of French culture and examine the archives of eighteenth-century printing houses, provincial registries, and previously anonymous witnesses drawn from the functionaries of the French state. At a time when metacritical enquiries exhibit a greater popularity than archival research, it must be admitted that Darnton's path remains a relatively untrodden one for literary critics.

Anthropology constitutes a third discipline which has stimulated literary critics to re-examine their field of operations. For instance, the works of Clifford Geertz enjoy a wide circulation among non-specialists, who can hardly escape the implications for their own discipline of his demystification of anthropological masterpieces by authors such as Malinowski ('a man so deeply self-engrossed as to suggest that he might have been better employed as a romantic poet'[27]) and Margaret Mead. Contemporary anthropologists have shown that works such as *The Sexual Life of Savage Societies* and *Coming of Age in Samoa* transmit identifiable Western social, political and sexual biases. Long regarded as the unvarnished reporting of pioneers in the field, these works are shot through with conventional ways of representing races construed as inferior, conventions which appear all the more dangerous when they come armed with a self-congratulating dogma of scientific objectivity and authority.[28]

English studies could hardly exempt itself from this general effort to inspect the cultural patrimony, to revaluate the monuments, and to reconstruct the discipline. The example offered by the other humanistic disciplines reinforces the internal influences discussed above – the sociological criticism widely supported inside the discipline, the testimonies of the colonial and displaced, and the theoretical self-consciousness. The result is a swelling prologue to the canon debate proper, which emerged with full fervour during the mid-1980s. From this point, the materials were in place and the course was set for one of the most dramatic changes in the field of 'English' since it became an academic discipline in the early nineteenth century: the shift from the field of 'literary studies' to a new field called 'cultural materialism' on the British side of the Atlantic and 'new historicism' on the American.

ALTERNATIVES TO THE 'ENGLISH' CANON

By what one might term the logic of dissent, the call for an end to canons has joined hands with a campaign for the departure of English. More cautious calls have been made for reform, but often they prefer such formidable charges against the existing discipline that morally and logically they amount to a call for abolition. Where so many voices are raised against it, 'English', presumably synec-dochical for any nationally conceived field of literary studies, seems unlikely to survive the present century. With the fall of English goes the fall of the canon that traditionally sustains it. Anti-canonists see the canon not as Frank Kermode's repository of inexhaustible complexity but as the vehicle for national, racial and gender superiority. The graphocentric, nationalist, phallophilic and gynophobic picture the anti-canonists paint of all known canons means that the days are numbered of English as a discipline organized around a relatively stable syllabus of traditionally valued works. Critics who object to the current canon of master-works, observes Colin MacCabe, are searching for a field with 'a very strong claim to be the democratic successor to English'. The new field, suggests MacCabe, will gain its authority from the fact it will not, unlike its predecessor, operate by 'a canon which bases itself in domination and exclusion'.[29]

What field satisfies these criteria? There is no shortage of contenders for the space currently occupied by English. Terry Eagleton's *Literary Theory* (1983) traverses the current specialisms of English and European literature before recommending a return to a semiotically inspired discipline he calls 'rhetoric' because it 'would look at the various sign-systems and signifying practices in our own society'.[30] Jonathan Dollimore and Alan Sinfield urge the case of a field called 'cultural materialism', which they characterize as 'a combination of historical and cultural context, theoretical method, political commitment and textual analysis'.[31] Yet although Eagleton has argued on behalf of semiotics and rhetoric, his own criticism focuses heavily on canonical authors such as Joyce, Richardson, Shakespeare and the Brontes. In the same way, cultural materialists often appear transfixed by the curators of the monuments venerated by a previous generation of 'essentialist humanists', so that the antipathies towards Sir Mungo William MacCallum and E. M. W. Tillyard voiced in Dollimore's *Radical Tragedy* take their place in the long history of internecine British class warfare, a warfare that repeatedly delays the construction of a new intellectual discipline.[32]

A third projected discipline comes from MacCabe, whose article 'The State of the Subject: English' sketches the concerns and pedagogic methods of an anti-canonical substitute for English he calls 'cultural studies'. As described by MacCabe, 'cultural studies' would combine freely and on a larger scale elements of semiotics, sociology, politics, history, mass communication, and the study of popular and oral cultures. In this way, says MacCabe, the new discipline would commit itself to 'an analysis of texts and their situation which would replace canonical study with a genuine cultural materialism'.[33] Of the candidates for succession to the territory once supervised by 'English', MacCabe's 'cultural studies' comes closest to a workable programme. Certainly, its broad range of constituting fields would attract to the new discipline a large number of teachers and students. Even so, to call the new area 'cultural studies' is something of a misnomer. As used by MacCabe, the term 'cultural studies' serves as a decoy for the 'genuine cultural materialism' its prosecutors are eager to make more generally acceptable. A more accurate title for the discipline envisaged by MacCabe, Dollimore and Sinfield is 'cultural politics'.

CULTURAL POLITICS

How does cultural politics work? MacCabe emphasizes that the new field seeks to replace the existing canon by a 'reading list . . . constructed in relation to a series of specific questions'. How will those questions be determined? By 'the major problems that constitute cultural studies at a particular moment'. Cultural politics operates as a problem-based discipline, its problems presumably determined by specialists in cultural politics. However, MacCabe denies that the questions raised by students of cultural politics reflect narrowly professional concerns. Instead, they are 'explicitly subject to change in relation to change within contemporary culture', a formulation which leaves unanswered whether fashion, ideology, audience reception, or civic self-improvement determines the questions asked. In the end, what MacCabe calls 'the logic of capital' seems likely to dominate the field. Is cultural politics therefore an enquiry more sociopolitical than historical? MacCabe denies that the field is restricted 'to a canonical present'. Instead, it proceeds 'in relation to genuine questions and problems . . . which will almost certainly lead back into a pre-modern past'.[34] Cultural politics jettisons the authority of the written masterpieces in order to accommodate the oral testimony of cultures not previously permitted representation in the canon of 'English'.

In a sense, cultural politics represents an effort to repopulate the literary field, which the traditional canon represents as empty of all save the mesmerizing circles of hengelike masterpieces. Proponents of cultural politics and its variants exhibit less interest in these powerful dominating monuments and more interest in combing the surrounding land for broader evidence of those who erected them. As John Barrell explains, 'Much of the poetry in the canon of English literature can also be read as writing produced by and about a particular class and gender.' This writing, he goes on, 'will produce "universal meanings" only for those who define the universal in the image of that class and gender'.[35] If Barrell's premisses are conceded, then 'English' begins to appear not so much the neutral cognomen for a legitimate intellectual discipline as a covert way of circulating the interests of a cultural elite or a political faction. Although practitioners of English have long cherished an image of their discipline as prosecuted by a saving remnant of renegade intellectuals, selflessly hostile to power and its trappings, many contemporary critics would agree with MacCabe that English studies constitutes a field 'given in advance by some mystical national identity'.[36]

Even if English does not find itself reborn as cultural politics in the form anticipated by MacCabe, the new discipline will still have to face grave questions about its canons of study. The evidence linking 'English' to the cause of England as an imperial power remains intriguing but is already a little threadbare. If canonical literary works are less 'universal' than was once thought, they may still not serve the state as self-evidently as the proponents of cultural studies assume. Indeed, the current desire to link canons with political or nationalist ideologies overlooks their less sensational alliance with instruction. The 'reading list' MacCabe describes will presumably fix, however tentatively, the shape of instruction during the lifetime of a particular course. The list may contain 'Mr MacCabe's anthology of extracts and questions' instead of *Macbeth*, *King Lear* and *Henry V*, but it will still remain a canonical list of required readings and topics for a chosen course. Moreover, because cultural politics proceeds by a set of questions constructed in conformity with academic responses to observed cultural problems, it seems likely to give considerable weight to classroom contact.

Indeed, viewed historically, cultural politics exhibits a direct, and rather surprising, line of descent from a series of twentieth-century critics who emphasized the importance of inspired teaching inside the university. As early as 1943, Q. D. Leavis's essay 'The Discipline of Letters' deplored the nepotist publicity mechanisms that canonized even authors as worthy as T. S. Eliot. Like MacCabe, Leavis sees the field of letters as a triumph of vested and orthodox interests, and recommends students of literature to construct their own non-traditional courses of study, using 'fresh contacts, cross-fertilization' in order to gain a sense 'of the complex of cultural subjects of which the study of literature forms part'.[37] Similarly, F. R. Leavis's *English Literature in Our Time and the University* (1969) argues the case for a new, collaborative field of study responsive to wider social issues.

Like MacCabe, Leavis emphasizes that 'a literature grows out of a culture'. Like MacCabe, he calls for 'a clear recognition that the world has changed, and that imperial "greatness" cannot be "great" in the old way'. Like MacCabe, he emphasizes that literature 'has its reality and life (if at all) only in the present'. Like MacCabe, he deplores the extremely narrow 'implicit canons of relevance' which more specialized scholars bring to English studies. Although he talks of 'major poetry', 'affirmation', 'intensity', 'intelligence', 'inwardness' and a whole host of other discredited values, Leavis's broader argument, the need to build up 'an English School that truly deserves the respect of those who are acquainted with intellectual standards in their own fields',[38] exhibits marked similarities to current arguments for curricular reform. And however the curriculum finally shapes up, the Leavises, like MacCabe, see the inspired, totally committed teacher as its most important element. Although she doubts that English studies can improve without 'a bloody revolution',[39] Mrs Leavis emphasizes the work of the charismatic teacher as a way of assailing the establishment on its own ground by winning over a student constituency ignored by the official discipline.

Cultural politics places a similar premium on outstanding teaching, often contrasting the innovative pedagogy offered by the polytechnics with the time-bound practices of the universities. Instead of the dead author, the live teacher. The unstated paradigm is a 'trickle up' theory, which is supposed to counteract the 'trickle down' model of Conservative Party politics. Another suggestive, if less prestigious, analogue for cultural politics lies in the civics class, a distinctly American phenomenon which suggests the strong transatlantic influence on the as yet untitled emergent discipline. Where civics teaches the virtue of adjustment to public life, cultural politics presumably proselytizes the value of subversion. Its subject matter, drawn from the great conflicts of public life – the 'crisis within the concept of nationality' described by MacCabe, the conflicts of 'class and gender' specified by Barrell, the 'struggle against the absolutist state' identified by Terry Eagleton[40] – exhibits great variety within a common field of reference, a public realm where the old categories of 'nation', 'class' and 'culture' no longer draw the support of the literary intelligentsia but where a new set of concepts and objectives still awaits wider acceptance.

As presented by MacCabe, the ideal worker in the new field resembles an uneasy amalgam between the Frankfurt School of avant-garde theory and the research and development department of a major corporation. As Jonathan Culler describes them, teachers of the new discipline operate as corporate 'producers of knowledge' in socially responsive (i.e. enrolment-sensitive) university institutions rather than as erudite individual transmitters of learning housed in protected scholarly enclaves. Situated in these new, dynamic institutions, these 'producers of knowledge' try to 'cultivate political criticism as an intentional act'.[41] But what does it mean for a literary critic to characterize his concerns as 'political'? A political scientist studies political institutions and political behaviour. A political historian discusses the varying forms of political change. A political philosopher analyses political languages and their contest for legitimacy. Which of these activities do Culler's politicized literary intellectuals practise? According to Culler, such intellectuals know 'that history will work otherwise, that the meaning of one's actions will prove other than one wished, a function of structures one does not control and which can be described only after the fact'.[42] But what can 'political' mean in such a context of almost Franciscan resignation? When students of literature describe their activities as 'political', do they merely have in mind some generalized disaffection from the structures of power in some current intellectual circle? So far, the 'political' turn in the field being vacated by English has yielded few deeply new conjunctions of new textual material. It is common nowadays for a new book to announce itself as offering an interpretation 'more radical' than the one it replaces: but what do such announcements actually mean?

New Historicism

During the 1980s a string of new movements enjoyed notoriety and acclaim: from new philology to new conservatism, from cultural materialism to new historicism. The ferment of intellectual unrest added immense weight to the mounting arguments for a 'new canon' or even for a criticism 'beyond the canon'. But how novel were these new movements? We have looked briefly at the self-formulations of the new, predominantly British field of cultural politics. Let us now examine the related, largely American area called 'new historicism'. Since its first texts began to appear in the late 1970s, new historicism has worked something of a revolution in literary studies. It has broadened the literary scholar's sphere of reference, so that canonical texts no longer seem to operate independently of their original and contemporary contexts. It has disturbed the hierarchy of the genres irreparably, blasting the teaching of literature from any lingering vestige of neoclassical norms. It has demystified the agencies of valuation, so that canonical texts no longer seem made out of inscrutable personal inspiration but according to tight, objective specifications which can be located in their authors' cultural habitat and in our own. For these reasons, new historicism stops the category of the 'literary' from enjoying the luxury of contemplative withdrawl from history, but returns it, along with its critical interpreters, to a more rigorously temporal realm. New historicists foreground culture as a socially produced activity. They acknowledge the links that tie art to power. They emphasize that art is transmitted from class to class, as well as from individual to individual. In this way both literature and criticism rejoin the secular enterprise of making sense, of understanding how other minds have understood the world.

Even so, new historicism is not so remote from an earlier movement which also called itself 'new history' and also tried to anchor the study of the past to a framework derived from present-day contexts. Indeed, some potential weaknesses in the new historicist position emerge if we compare it with a similarly named movement in American history departments of the 1920s and 1930s. 'New history' gained momentum in the classroom through the efforts of James Harvey Robinson, acquired a progressive political colouring through the formulations of Charles Beard, and was sanctioned philosophically by the Olympian scepticism of Carl Becker. Key words of the new historians include Robinson's *The New History*, Beard's *The Supreme Court and the Constitution* (both 1912), Beard's essay 'Written History as an Act of Faith' (1934), Becker's *The Declaration of Independence* (1922), his essay 'Everyman His Own Historian', and *The Heavenly City of the Eighteenth-Century Philosophers* (both 1932).

Let us briefly contrast these works with some representative new historicist texts. Appropriate examples include Stephen Greenblatt's *Renaissance Self-Fashioning: From More to Shakespeare* (1980) and *Shakespearean Negotiations* (1988), Frank Lentricchia's *Criticism and Social Change* (1983), Jerome McGann's *The Romantic Ideology* (1983) and *The Beauty of Inflections* (1985). In the first place, it is worth noting that neither movement finds it necessary to produce a comprehensive theoretical statement of its assumptions and procedures, but invokes instead a ready-made framework adapted from foreign sources (Foucault and Althusser for the new historicists; Lamprecht, Croce, and H. G. Wells for the new historians).

If cultural politics works the ideas of Leavis, Althusser and Williams into a new platform for English studies in British universities, then new historicism, like the new history of the 1930s, represents a collegiate bid by American academics to reformulate European theories for the American liberal arts curriculum. Like the new historians, the new historicists strew their texts with references to the academy. For instance, the frequent remarks on his college teaching experiences in McGann's two books recall Robinson's *The New History*, which was widely adopted as a college textbook and encouraged him to write a string of similar books. In the same way, Greenblatt's *Shakespearean Negotiations*, one of the most important documents in the new discipline, appears in a series called 'The New Historicism: Studies in Cultural Poetics'. Greenblatt himself edits the series, drawing many of his contributors from his own institution, the prestigious University of California system. A sociology of the new intellectual aristocracy and its publishing history would make fascinating reading in the hands of a twenty-first-century Robert Darnton.

What kinds of textual operations do new historicists perform on their chosen texts? It is worth noting at the outset that new historicism, like cultural politics, perfects its new techniques on the most impeccably canonical works – 'The Rime of the Ancient Mariner', the poems of Wordsworth's great decade, the tragedies of Shakespeare. In Greenblatt's hands, these tragedies become 'spectacular impostures' fulfilling our need for order, but also dramatizing its maintenance by systems of legalized torture. Shakespeare's histories nurture 'subversion, no end of subversion', but only in the margins of their manifest displays of royal power.[43] His comedies tap the disturbing world of transgressive sexuality which lies open to a single-sex stage representing a two-sex world. His romances meditate on the opportunities for performance in a world of hierarchical power.

Here is a Shakespeare, a theatrically very exciting Shakespeare, whose canon is validated through insights borrowed from Foucault, Clifford Geertz and Lawrence Stone. As he moves from probing textual analyses and potent cultural asides to magisterial historical generalizations, Greenblatt replaces the old 'Eng. Lit.' Shakespeare who transcended politics with a Shakespeare who fastidiously and opportunistically recoils from them, a Shakespeare who conforms to the disgust felt by American intellectuals during a period of burgeoning Republicanism. 'Perhaps we should imagine Shakespeare', Greenblatt speculates, on a topos beloved by Shakepearian canonizers,

writing at a moment when none of the alternatives for a resounding political commitment seemed satisfactory; when the pressure to declare himself unequivocally an adherent of one or other faction seemed narrow, ethically coarse, politically stupid; when the most attractive political solution seemed to be to keep options open and the situation fluid.[44]

This refined and elegant description of the Shakespearian malaise may fit even better the malaise of a group of American academics setting out to launch a new political discipline – all dressed up, ready for their call to arms, but with nowhere political to go except another campus and another graduate seminar. With no country left to colonize, the new disciplines may have to confine their operations to the academy, using their new discourse as the basis for a revised teaching-canon that will introduce modified versions of the old paradigms to a new, marginally more diversified, generation of students. If it intended to expose the academy to the shifting winds of contemporary history, then new historicism has not so far enjoyed much success.

It is strange that, despite their claims to introduce a new contemporary relevance to the study of canonical texts, new historicists often see history in terms of archaeology, a discipline whose very remoteness allows it to be used as a model for present-day social forces. Where the traditional historian sees the motive force behind history as the individual human agent moving through time, archaeologists often work in teams, undertaking a spatial as much as chronological analysis of their material. Archaeologists learn to read large significances from minute fragments of evidence, so that their preliminary small-scale analyses yield unexpectedly dramatic syntheses of the forces at work in the culture as a whole. It is this desire for synthesis that encourages Greenblatt to close his essay 'Invisible Bullets' with the argument:

> to understand Shakespeare's whole conception of Hal . . . we need in effect a poetics of Elizabethan power. . . . Testing, recording, and explaining are elements in this poetics, which is inseparably bound up with the figure of Queen Elizabeth, a ruler without a standing army, without a highly developed bureaucracy, without an extensive police force, a ruler whose power is constituted in theatrical celebrations of royal glory and theatrical violence.[45]

In his sweeping movement from a Shakespearian character to Shakespeare himself, from the figure of Queen Elizabeth to Elizabethan society, in his daring shifts of political, literary and historical register, Greenblatt provides a model of Elizabethan society that measures its distance from the present at a surface level while indicating its deeper affinity at the level of ideology, protest, and the struggle for power.

At this stage, during the final synthesis, comparisons between the old society and the archaeologist's own culture become especially easy to draw. As Carl Becker confessed, 'the "new history" is an old story. Since history is not an objective reality, but only an imaginative reconstruction of vanished events, the pattern that appears useful and agreeable to one generation is never entirely so to the next.'[46] For the new historians, the most pressing contemporary requirement was to alert the progressive democratic forces of the 1930s to the opportunities offered by the New Deal. For the new historicists, the past must be scrutinized with one eye on the perils and opportunities offered by the Reagan–Bush empire. If new historicism lacks the crude reductiveness of Beard's analysis of the constitution as the sum of the interests of its landowning cosignatories, still the obliquities and multiple revisions of Greenblatt's Renaissance essays rest on his need to refashion Elizabethan England in the image of Republican America, so that both appear as if controlled by a totalitarian impresario.

It is interesting to speculate whether both movements have their roots in the need for the left to make political headway in a basically conservative era, in which the classroom seems one of the most effective forums for exerting political influence. Certainly, both movements foreground the obsessions of the present over the problems and tensions of the past. Both constitute a new utilitarianism, an attempt to nudge history, through the powerful but limited agencies of the undergraduate textbook and the graduate seminar, in the directions deemed most socially responsive by a group of persuasive, upwardly mobile radical intellectuals. Over a period of years, both groups may decline in influence as the social forces that prompted their work transform their working environment, and as the personnel themselves are replaced by people who draw a different equation between present and past.

It may be objected that literary texts do not provide the best material for a discipline designed to explore ideological conflicts in the public realm. In the past, English studies cultivated the values of privacy, complexity and ambiguity, concerns which will obviously be displaced by a criticism emphasizing the linkage between literature and power. If *Macbeth* inspects the crisis in the British state, it does so obliquely and, it is possible to argue, indeterminately. I have sat on curricular reform groups where the play's ambiguities have speedily been rejected in favour of the more manifest political conflicts of *Richard III* and *Henry V*. Yet the very possibility of this choice is enough for some critics to damn Shakespearian criticism for its role in helping 'to legitimate conservative politics'.[47] Having demystified Shakespeare, new historicists have renewed our acquaintance with figures such as Sir Walter Ralegh, whom they find even more directly implicated in the construction of the Elizabethan state. Political rather than literary interest fuels materialist criticism, and the figures who emerge from it are public officials or beneficiaries rather than imaginative creators.

Such a radical rewriting of the literary past must obviously produce, in time, a spate of new textbooks. As cultural politics and new historicism gather strength, we can expect to see an increasing number of volumes centred on 'issues' and 'problems' rather than celebrating the creative contribution of an exemplary individual writer or work. In the same way, current reading lists, with their emphasis on lyric poetry and genre, will have to make way for innumerable new commentaries, new accents, and new readings. Already cultural politics is generating its own canon and its own patriarchs, who refuse to accept the ironies of the conjugation '*we* teach from a reading list, *they* proselytize through a canon, *he* mutters ineffably'. A recent visit to Dillon's Bookshop in London convinced me of the incurable canonizing of the successors to English studies. There, in the honeycombed cells of the English section, a dazed undergraduate wandered the corridors like a patient in search of a doctor, asking assistant after assistant for 'something by Terry Eagleton–*anything* by Terry Eagleton'. New disciplines inevitably canonize their founders, as the fortunes of de Man's 'rhetoric', Febvre's '*Annales*', or Freud's psychoanalysis all show. Wherever there is instruction by charismatic teachers, a canon will surely follow.

A CRITIQUE OF THE NEW DISCIPLINES

Ought one, then, to assume that cultural politics, new historicism, or one of their rivals will soon assume the space currently occupied by the study of canonical lists of English texts? Sound historical reasons support such a conjecture; sound historical evidence makes such a conjecture disturbing. English studies has always harboured what Graham Hough calls 'a fervent sense of mission whose precise direction is now not easy to discern'.[48] Some of the most influential dissident voices exhibit a displaced sense of mission rather than an abandonment of missionary goals. Fredric Jameson modestly describes his method of 'political interpretation' as 'the absolute horizon of all reading and all interpretation'. Terry Eagleton argues that 'ideology or class-struggle' is 'the very stuff of literature', while Jonathan Dollimore charts the history of Shakespearian criticism in terms of a mythic contest between 'essentialist humanism' and 'cultural materialism'.[49] Each of these critics presents himself as witness to an intellectual awakening. Awakenings usually lead to canons, and already the reiterated celebrations of a few significant reputations – Said, Gramsci, Foucault – show the lineaments of a radical counter-canon falling into place.

No writer has played a more significant part in paving the way for the new anti-canonical alliance than Michel Foucault, yet Foucault always betrayed a deeply equivocal attitude towards canons. In 1985, in the course of a last interview published in *Raritan*, he revealed a predictable hostility to any form of publicly accepted authority. He rejected utterly the idea that he might have found the Greeks he studied in preparation for the writing of *The History of Sexuality* in any way 'exemplary' or 'admirable'. Even so, in another part of the interview he discloses that 'it is important to have a small number of authors with whom one thinks, with whom one works, but about whom one does not write'. Was Martin Heidegger one of these authors? Although he never wrote about Heidegger, Foucault cheerfully admits that 'for me Heidegger has always been the essential philosopher'.[50] In Foucault's career, a canon as an authorized list of transhistorical master-works for public circulation retreats from view, but a secret canon of privileged and valued interlocutors persists. Foucault's canon no doubt awaits a next wave of demystifying materialists, who will bring the marginal and the secret to the centre of public debate. Yet there is still something curious about an intellectual avant-garde so eager to demystify all the public instruments of cultural validation while leaving its own sources of value undeclared and latent.

The powerful example of Foucault suggests that literary critics may find it difficult to abandon the search for a private realm of valuation. A canon, whether it be a canon made by fourth-century Jews or by twentieth-century cultural materialists, offers access to such a realm by narrating the history of the values held by a particular group, by detailing the stages which led to the realization of a desired goal, and by restricting entry to a limited number of religiously, sexually, politically, or intellectually qualified people. The history of canons traced in this book links them not with one permanently dominant ideology but with the ongoing and shifting construction of group goals. The group may consist of early Christian ecclesiastical authorities, fourteenth-century Florentine artists, eighteenth-century philologists, or late-twentieth-century academicians. In each case, a special intensity of conviction about the cultural importance of their work encourages them to construct a canon.

Proponents of cultural politics and the other new disciplines imply that their arguments do not work in the conventional way – that *they* articulate, and therefore uncanonize, their principles to an unprecedented degree. *Their* valuations never amount to a canonical 'totality'. *Their* 'positions' embody tentative 'figurations' which look forward to new 'configurations'. *They* valorize no 'god term' through their own 'interpretative strategies'. *Their* willingness to give free rein to academic lobbying betrays no signs whatsoever of canonicity. Yet although they have often admirably demystified the discredited values of their predecessors, practitioners of the new disciplines rarely expose to deeply critical scrutiny their own favoured terms – power, ideology, structure, and so on. Even T. S. Eliot, whose tone of unquaking authority is largely responsible for the hypostatized entity called 'the modern Anglo-American canon', proved capable of admitting that he was 'too prone to measure everything by rules derived from a dogmatic conception of literature', and that his work tended 'to become rigid and formalist'.[51] Such a confession would be unthinkable to many critics today, who rarely trace in any deeply self-conscious and explicit way their lines of affiliation with the values they seek to replace.

Throughout the twentieth century, ever since the appearance of Eliot's influential volumes of essays and poetry, a dominant value has proved to be 'difficulty'. Contemporary critics still find it hard to resist a difficult work, which becomes a kind of badge for an educated elite whose apparent disagreements on points of interpretation conceal a deeper consensus and an undemocratic commitment to the virtues of the hermetic. Even a critic such as Richard Poirier, who rejects Eliot's notion of difficulty, will succumb to the manifest difficulty of a Pynchon or the latent difficulty of a Frost.[52] Similarly, when Harold Bloom expels Eliot from the twentieth-century canon, he does so not to welcome back the simple Henry Newbolt but to usher in the equally complex Wallace Stevens, a poet first favoured by the predominantly academic audience that canonized Eliot.[53]

If we look further back into the history of criticism, to the dark days before our contemporary cultural revolution, many authorities praised literature on the grounds of its 'universality', a quality which embraces both the 'timeliness' that allows a work to gain a hearing when it first appears and the 'timelessness' that signifies its abiding worth for later generations. *Oedipus Rex, King Lear* and *Great Expectations* – these become some of the significant chapters in the universal story of great literature. What grand recurring figure will sustain cultural politics once it dislodges 'difficulty' and 'universality'? What magnet will draw discrete cultural productions into the field new historicists have made their own? How effectively will their followers comb the field for evidence of critical mystification once their opponents beat the retreat?

So far, the searchers for a 'democratic successor to English' have shelved the disciplinary objectives of English (only a front for political power to many of them, after all). The new disciplines are still a long way from following Robert Darnton into the archives, from reconstructing the lists of works that people in the past actually valued and the grounds on which they valued them. Instead, the exponents of cultural politics and its variants employ self-consciously avant-garde methods in order to destroy a canon which they conceive of as an instrument in an ideological conspiracy, a procedure which does little to remedy the deficiency in historical understanding Darnton describes.

Indeed, practitioners of cultural politics do not even acknowledge such understanding as a priority. In its zeal to colonize the cultural present, cultural politics may write off too many figures from its own disciplinary past. One figure it might confront is Aristotle, who praises the 'leaden rule' of the builders of Lesbos because of its ability to 'be bent to the shape of the stone'. As we have seen, Aristotle recommended this principle to framers of laws in all spheres of human interest, political as well as aesthetic. His 'leaden rule' has useful implications for the current debate. Practitioners of cultural politics and new historicism might start by acknowledging that political questions do not exhaust the frames of reference offered by works which have been created and enjoyed by members of a cultural community for a whole range of reasons – as moral or practical instruction, as polemical intervention; even, occasionally, as imaginative construction.

If early twentieth-century criticism overlooked the political dimensions of culture, many present-day critics overlook its anthropological dimension. For a shift from a 'culture' subsumed under nationalism or theology to a 'cultural studies' that nails its colours to the mast of the most deterministic form of politics is to exchange masters rather than to liberate intellectual enquiry. As Pocock and

Skinner have shown us, modern political analysis has become a highly nuanced activity, not one to be performed by means of a few levers labelled 'power', 'nationalism' and 'reaction'. As presently constituted, cultural politics stands at the stage of debate about the English civil war during the 1950s. That is, any number of unverified theories, unsubstantiated accusations and unlikely conjectures run a long way ahead of empirical investigation. Such debate helps to keep a discipline alive, but it does not promise an untroubled maturity for the fledgling cultural politics.

Much of the ferocity of the current canon debate stems from its protagonists' tendency to narrow the cultural and historical diversity of *canons* into one reactionary *canon*. This book will have achieved its aim if it creates an environment in which canons appear as something more than offensive weapons wielded by the disguised servants of an oppressive state. Canons have historically performed a variety of useful functions, one of which is worth bearing in mind in the current atmosphere of heated attack: the *canon* that supplies the ground rules for accuracy, evidence, and argument in the preparation of an artistic or critical work. For as long as contemporary critics usher canons of rational enquiry into the wings, supporting instead a political rhetoric of passionate persuasion, they condemn critical argument to a succession of coups; in this atmosphere, the discipline, whatever we agree to call it, will degenerate into a field without a history.

English has always sheltered so many gentlemanly affections and petty snobberies that it seems difficult to muster too many tears at its departure. Yet over the years, it has amassed a body of scholarly knowledge and professional expertise which suggests that it amounts to more than an apologia for the nation-state. Some of the 'patriarchs' of English – I. A. Richards, William Empson, René Wellek, to name but three – had complex relationships with early-twentieth-century nationalism. I do not wish to suggest that cultural politics will topple the monuments and destroy the work of centuries, allowing entry to hordes of barbarians. On the contrary, many of its proponents display predictably elite affiliations. Yet the new disciplines have still not confronted the important distinction between political conviction and professional activity. The argument that 'conservative' academics oppose the entry of feminist, Native American, or postcolonial voices to the canon on the grounds that these groups will 'lower the standards' overlooks a more powerful objection: that cultural politics may make gender or ethnic identity the sole criteria for canonicity, regardless of the teacher's or students' strong personal choice. Applied to ecclesiastical officials or Stalinist commissars, this kind of restriction looks less attractive. As Richard Wollheim has remarked, conformity can strangle cultural analysis before it even begins.[54] Moreover, although marginalized groups are welcomed in principle, cultural politics and new historicism are still some way from recovering what they actually have to say. When such authors are discovered, they are more often 'spoken for' than allowed to speak. More often than not, their patrons push the new authors into conformity with goals they may not even recognize, in the way that politicians voice the concerns of 'working people' or 'ordinary members of the public' at election time.

So far, the new disciplines are shaping up as siblings to the social sciences, catering to a readily observable student fascination with the machinery of power, the pre-eminence of status groups, and the sociology of intellectual success. A course which promises to unlock the teachable secrets of social advancement through the delightful medium of works of art will have little difficulty in filling its classrooms. Yet as developed so far, the new fields operate at a dangerously low level of conceptual sophistication. Their exponents often seem satisfied with a fervent declaration of anti-canonical convictions and a core of borrowings from appropriately radical authorities. Sometimes it appears that all the practitioners of cultural politics and its cognates aim at identical targets in identical language, so that the new field becomes a kind of 'normal ideology' or radical mutation of Kuhn's 'normal science'.

Instead of admitting new voices to the field of culture, the new disciplines are following the pattern set by their reputedly anti-democratic predecessor, in that their hostilities receive far more attention than their allegiances. Works such as Jean Howard and Marion O'Connor's *Shakespeare Reproduced: The Text in History and Ideology* (1987), Roger Sales's forthcoming *Georgette Heyer and Jane Austen: Representations of Regency England*, and Mike Wallis and Simon Shepherd's forthcoming *Gay Culture and Politics* suggest that the new fields conceive of their canons not as a pantheon of accepted monuments but as a consistent pattern of political contest. The new historicist canon focuses less on works than on reputations; it turns to questions of 'power', 'authority' and 'hegemony', where its predecessor turned to Dante, Eliot and Leavis. Its monuments will probably be tacitly rather than overtly canonical, in the way that radical critics often speak of 'the major journals' or 'the important presses' or cite a short-list of major critics by surname only. It seems arguable, however, whether a problem-centred or 'radical' canon is any less restrictive than a masterpiece-centred one.

If they are to thrive, the new disciplines need a broader subject matter and a more acute sense of their lines of descent and affiliation. As presently constituted, they have developed an enormously various way of describing social conflict and a remarkably impoverished way of describing consensus. Because they are organized on political and polemical lines, around key questions posed by the teacher, cultural politics and new historicism leave little room for conflicting evidence, and the possibility that a student would be able to recognize such evidence if it were presented seems remote. A 'canon' or set of questions designed to map out current social problems would always seem on the point of passing the threshold that separates education from indoctrination, especially given the current atmosphere of undergraduate docility and postgraduate professionalism.

Any new field offers greater career opportunities and institutional leverage than its established rivals, yet these heady opportunities do not translate into a democracy. There is no sign that the alternatives to English will constitute themselves as fields in any markedly egalitarian way. With their promises of an occult vocabulary, a radical politics, and a disciplinary centrality in the humanistic sphere, the new fields make all the claims that English made for itself in the heyday of *Scrutiny.* Yet apart from this similarity of rhetoric, no convincing links tie English studies to cultural politics or its variants in any recognizable line of succession. Every student of literature is familiar with the rough treatment literary works receive at the hands of historians and sociologists. One wonders how a trained sociologist would regard the characterizations of 'society' offered in Terry Eagleton's *Literary Theory* (1983) or Jonathan Culler's *Framing the Sign* (1988). Does the professional competence signalled by a published study of a canonical author automatically translate into a similar level of competence in analysing the ideological conflicts of modern society? It would appear not, yet MacCabe started his career with a book on Joyce, Culler with a book on Flaubert, Sinfield with a book on Tennyson, and Dollimore with an essay on Thomas Hardy's tragic view of nature which praises the author's presentation of 'an experience of common humanity' and his 'integrity of awareness'.[55] There is a correlation here with the process that earlier this century took graduates in Moderations and Greats off to India or some other colonial administration, often with distressing results for their subjects. Today, the situation remains unchanged, and few professors of English seem likely to slide any more dexterously than their Edwardian predecessors from a chair of English to a chair of cultural politics.

Certainly, if there are deficiencies in sociological or political method, they need not prove permanent. Yet one would be happier if the advanced wing of the new discipline showed any interest in characterizing 'society' as anything other than a repressive agent. As it is, every item in the apparatus of cultural politics – canons, culture, knowledge, value – becomes mobilized to the purpose of establishing the complete corruptibility of its opposition and the unassailable radical credentials of its exponents. The spectre of Caryle's disenchanted and polemical Professor of Things in General hangs over the new, as yet untitled, field. Only when the long trek towards understanding culture as a social, political and anthropological institution takes over from the guerrilla bursts that represent it as instrument of class dominance will canons once again become understood functionally, as important elements in the creation and understanding of art. Such an understanding would present culture as an ensemble of relationships inside a given community rather than as a set of eternal standards on the one side and a vehicle for systematic oppression on the other.

It is time for the field MacCabe has misleadingly labelled 'cultural studies' to declare its independence of cultural materialism, a connection that condemns students of the new discipline to protracted analysis of cultural determinants – imperialism, capital, ideology, and so on – rather than encouraging them to provide detailed investigations of the temporally and spatially restricted areas we may, for the purposes of research, call cultures: the working-class British Midlands, 1830–80; South African Cape liberal culture, 1850–1940; French artisans at the time of the Terror; and so on. Any model for a renewed cultural studies should recognize that the groups targeted for research exist outside the paradigms which contemporary intellectuals formulate on their behalf. No one overarching 'canon' answers to the various cultures which have grown up under the shadow of 'Empire'. To paraphrase E. H. Gombrich, there is no such thing as the story of culture, there is only the story of cultures. And this story really needs more plots and characters than our current story, which is danger of becoming a morality play *en travestie*. 'Early-twentieth-century British working-class culture' obviously cannot be investigated without reference to a capitalist and nationalist state. Even so, this culture has its own valuations, assumptions, idioms, productions, conflicts and practices, all of which may exist independently of the political problems some contemporary academics may wish to impute to it. In the same way, no student of Aztec culture can ignore Spanish imperialism, but not all Aztec culture can be related to this single overwhelming issue.

The full implications of the archaeological method need to be driven home to students of cultural studies. From a single potsherd discovered at a measured point in a specific dig, skilled investigators can reconstruct a whole culture. If, however, they interpret that potsherd according to some retrospective contemporary paradigm, they may as well leave it buried beneath the earth. The artifacts we uncover in the course of our research are the productions of human beings with valuations which may be distinct from our own. To bear down on every culture armed with the assumptions of our own 'interpretative community' is to compound the errors of imperialism. We ought to acknowledge, for example, that not every working–class individual who expresses an interest in 'high culture' is a political reactionary, social climber, or class traitor. By focusing so relentlessly on the diabolic institutional machinery of Christminster, students of cultural politics repeatedly overlook the need for high culture activated in Jude.

A related problem for some academics in English is how the works included in the customary 'canon of excellence' will fit into the projected field of cultural studies. The existence of the 'masterpieces' has embarrassed a theorized academy for some time now. There is no actual reason, however, why cultural studies, with its diligent archival perusal of the full range of oral and written records, the tacit validations and negations, the material and intellectual productions of any given culture, should not enhance our understanding of the institutional agencies, spiritual aspirations and psychological conflicts that underprop the privileged monuments in the cultures we elect to investigate. It is more or less taken for granted by cultural materialists that behind every great work lurks a great political machine enforcing the judgements of a repressive elite. When cultural studies starts to canvass the constituencies that respond – both favourably and with hostility – to the traditionally canonized work, then a more complex picture of the sociology and psychology of culture will emerge. At present, it is assumed that once the validating institutions behind a masterpiece have been identified, archival research can stop. Why did Orwell's *Nineteen Eighty-Four* become canonical for postwar anti-communists? How did *The Waste Land* grow famous enough to become the subject of school magazine spoofs? The answers to these questions may take us deeper into the history of publishing, education and twentieth-century politics than we have so far dared to go.

It might also prove useful, in view of the rising self-consciousness inside the humanities, if cultural studies could house a field similar to the historiography conducted in departments of History. Students of such a field would study the legitimating vocabularies, the social and intellectual contexts, the period assumptions and prejudices of the discipline of 'English' as historically constructed. It may be another unfortunate legacy of F. R. Leavis that British literary critics rarely inspect their patriarchs without hostility. This hostility would be lessened if students turned their attention to the languages of legitimacy historically circulated in British criticism. Why did 'experience' take on such significance for Raymond Williams? Why did 'maturity' loom so large for the Leavises? Was it because for them, as for no previous critics, 'teaching' became the principal forum for their critical activities? In the field of 'English', such investigations still await study, while a few reactionary totems are dragged out and impaled in public view.

WORLD POEM: THE CANON AS A WORK OF ART

The wave of self-consciousness that marks the last decades would seem to spell the death of the canon as an unquestioned part of the cultural stock. When one interest group lobbies on behalf of overlooked works, when another lobbies for new techniques which will maintain interest in works staled by obsolescent interpretation, when both stake their claims to some portion of a text or culture that answers to their own special programme, the 'Anglo-European canon', if it ever existed at all, has probably met its end. If *canon* suggests an unchanging, unquestioned body of received opinion, *canon*, in that sense at least, has permanently gone.

During the last few years, the fortunes of the canon have suffered a marked decline. On the one side, the idea of a canon has become intertwined with the idea of the classic, an idea that T. S. Eliot tried to revitalize for the 'modern experiment' and Frank Kermode has recently realigned with sceptical interpretation. On the other side, the idea of a canon has become intertwined with the idea of the curriculum, a narrower, programmatic idea about what students should be made to study rather than a wider, trickier assessment of what members of a cultural group happen to value or how artists in a culture happen to think. Recent bestselling books such as *The Closing of the American Mind* by Allan Bloom and *Cultural Literacy* by E. D. Hirsch combine both senses of 'canon', the classical and the curricular, arguing the need for a reseeding of the cultural field through an academic curriculum that would move American colleges away from the do-it-yourself majors of recent years by requiring all students to study a common core of humanistic texts. Because conservative politicians have presented knowledge of such texts as the key to national unity and advancement, 'the canon' has become an ever more deeply politicized term.

Set against the backdrop of this ongoing academic and political debate, the repudiation of the canon in some quarters on ethnic grounds, the setting out of a revised, narrower canon in other quarters on grounds of cultural solidarity, many of the critics discussed in this book represent a surprising anomaly. For an astonishing number of them draw a sharp distinction not just between *canon* and classic, but also between *canon* and curriculum. To adopt Kermode's phrase in *The Genesis of Secrecy*, few of them view with relish the 'familiar transition from the charismatic to the institutional'.[56]

However much they differ in their particular emphases and concerns, many critics would agree that the construction of canons reflects a recurring human and aesthetic need. Even Athanasius and Irenaeus describe the scriptural canon as an aesthetically pleasing group of interrelated texts and practices, as well as an instrument for expelling the heretical. The idea of a large aesthetic order in which all valued literature appears one resurfaces again and again in the history of canons, gaining its most notable expression in Goethe's idea of a *Weltliteratur* and T. S. Eliot's 'tradition'. A similar idea survives even today. In von Hallberg's *Canons*, Hugh Kenner identifies a mode of existence for the canon beyond the social or the institutional spheres when he suggests that it represents the outcome of 'a narrative of some intricacy', a narrative which offers 'a coherent sense of the world for which we and our words are unprepared'.[57] To reduce that narrative to the conjunction of market, professional or political forces inevitably tends to neglect the aesthetic dimension of the canon, a work of art itself composed of works of art. Whether created by poet-critics like T. S. Eliot or by scholar-critics like Erich Auerbach, twentieth-century canons have frequently operated as works of art, as symbolic constellations of texts constructed with the symbolist's need to link the sacred world of art to its secular analogue, to point to a latent unity in historical confusion, or, as in the case of Edward Said, to penetrate the heteroglossalian 'Other' of a culture as yet unrepresented.

Employing radically different styles of argument, writers from Ricoeur to Kermode have been intrigued by the idea that a canon can operate as a total narrative, a work of art made out of other works of art that tries to tell the 'whole story' about the origins and transmission, the interrelationships between, and the final worth of a culture's valued works of literary or visual art. In the work of critics such as Gombrich and Frye, canons become inclusive, overarching narratives, narratives that owe more to Joyce's *Ulysses* than to the *Index Librorum Prohibitorum*. In *Anatomy of Criticism*, Frye shows how the world of art provides access to a magical cyclical pattern, an imaginative structure whose apprehension can restore wholeness and connection to a humanity estranged from itself by history and by science. In *Anatomy of Criticism* and *The Great Code*, Frye presents the canon as a repository of myths and metaphors which subsumes the corpus of literary texts into the greater field of human aspiration.

The idea of the canon as a 'world poem' or total literary work supplies a recurring thread among several of the critics we have discussed. Gombrich in particular strongly supports the argument that traditional canon-making relies on imaginative inclusion rather than on draconian selection and excommunication. Gombrich began to write in Austria, where he set down nothing less than a child's *History of the World* or *Weltgeschichte*. His first influential work of art criticism, *The Story of Art*, exhibits a similar method and reach. Like Frye, Gombrich began his serious intellectual work during the Second World War, at a time when rival nationalisms revealed their full measure of brutality. Like Frye, he exhibits a strong desire to compose a comprehensive canonical narrative that will bypass national frontiers. But where Frye's quest turns on a search for imaginative structures that link human identity to the rhythms of nature, Gombrich scrutinizes the human need for visual representations. Like Frye, he sees art as serving the growth and development of the integrated self. He thinks that the universal impulse to represent the human shape signals some deeper instinct to conserve human integrity, and that a record of this collective impulse will fuel and nourish humane society. Against a background of institutional dissent and division, the strength of Gombrich's works rests in what he calls the 'universality' of canons, a quality that allows him to draw his evidence from unexpected quarters and to shower his readers with a multiplicity of sources. Again, the reach of the canon-making critic – from the Altamira cave painting to Mondrian's abstract representations of the Brooklyn Bridge – derives from the impulse to tell 'the whole story'. Like Frye, Gombrich sees such a story as illuminating much more than scholarly history. He considers representation necessary to human well-being, the basis not just of art but of civilized living as a whole.

All four of the critics whose careers I have followed in detail share an absorption in the canon as a narrative describing a complete and self-sufficient imaginative world, a world combining organized complexity and the satisfaction of ordinary human needs. However, Frye and Gombrich move far closer than Said and Kermode to presenting the canon as a blueprint for the future of humanity. Without ever reducing the canon to the interests of those who maintain it, Kermode and Said look at it sceptically as well as imaginatively. They both try to reconcile the institutional interests particular canons have historically served with their equally strong sense of the liberating power of the works those canons have brought into view.

In a situation uncannily reminiscent of the relationship between T. S. Eliot and his followers, Edward Said has become a kind of role model for the contemporary anti-canonical critic. The appearance of *Orientalism* in 1978 renewed and popularized the challenge made to existing cultural institutions by such works as Walter Benjamin's *Illuminations*, Raymond Williams's *The Country and the City*, and Michel Foucault's *Discipline and Punish*. For all these writers, culture inevitably shares in the sins of commission and omission of the national, ethnic and political institutions that support it. From this point, few critics seem able to approach the canon without some guilty pangs. After Said, the vigil at the canonical shrine, once the pursuit of all critics of good faith, has become a furtive business indeed.

Yet throughout his career, Said, a radical critic with an unusual respect for the heroic figures of traditional scholarship, intermittently takes on a visionary gleam, a longing look at an ideal canon that would present the encounter between world, text, and critic on less tainted, more open-ended, more truly imaginative lines. Said's work reflects perhaps the most challenging undertaking for the contemporary critic of canons: to develop a canon that will not run parallel with history but will actually open up a point of purchase on it. In Gombrich and Frye, we encounter the encyclopaedic and symbolist mutations of the canon. In Said we see an intriguing quest for a political canon, a canon that incorporates in its own imaginative structures antagonistic social and political forces. In my analysis of Gombrich, I suggested that his view of the canon drew on three main sources: the institutional, the aesthetic and the perceptual. We can concede that Said would have very little respect for the first, since his preferred site for critical activity remains the bazaar: the noisy marketing going on outside the temple rather than the rituals conducted inside it. Said has always urged the academy to shed its mandarin and ritualistic associations, which he perceives as the relics of a vestigial attachment to the priesthood.

Even so, he has never suggested that critics adopt instead the behaviour and assumptions of a state bureaucracy. In a world where the implied occasion for much modern criticism is the Modern Language Association Convention or Bibliography or the end-of-the-year corporate appraisal, Said sets his criticism against the backdrop of some of the most momentous present-day historical movements – the Iranian hostage crisis and the new political and cultural movements in the Middle East. At a time when many professedly 'radical' commentators have confined themselves to radicalizing the temporally distant – Elizabethan England or Swift's Anglo-Ireland – Said has elected to enter one of the late twentieth-century's most charged political arenas. As he presents it in *Orientalism* and *Covering Islam*, the Orientalist canon – a model he applies to any authoritarian canon – stands at the very crossroads of professional and public responsibility.

Perhaps because he remains unimpressed by institutional structures and concerns, Said retains more respect than most American radical critics for the distinction between *canon* and *curriculum*. He does not, in other words, move from a hostility to institutions to a total, unambiguous denial of the force of the canons they transmit. For these reasons, he remains remarkably attuned to Gombrich's two remaining senses of canon. Repeating almost point for point Gombrich's discussion of paradigms in *Art and Illusion*, Said shows in *Orientalism* and in *Covering Islam* how canon-making rests on a process of brilliant simplifications. The simplifications beget paradigms that beget unquestionable laws. Although they agree on the processes involved, Said and Gombrich remain at loggerheads over their cultural effects. When Said shows political and social life as exploiting patterns usually associated with art, he presents the superimposition of these cultural canons on political life as a process of deception and evasion. In his view, canons perpetually fall short in their adjustments to reality, screening out experience rather than accommodating to it.

As Said represents it, the principle of selection that institutes the canon by degrees becomes invisible as the canon gains in authority, and at this point the danger begins. The Orientalist's canon never submits its canonical objects to the checks and balances built into the world of Gombrich's artists. The Orientalist's canon never monitors its inventory against the movements of the world outside, whereas artists repeatedly check their constructions against the natural world. The Orientalist never presents his canon as posing problems to be solved, in the way that Gombrich's artists do. The Orientalist thinks instead of stereotypes to be reinforced – leering Arab merchants, scowling Iranian terrorists, chanting mobs. For Said, these cultural canons represent one of the tragedies of contemporary existence, a veil we draw over over all kinds of social disturbance, the bars of the 'iron cage' which Max Weber saw as the dominant image of modern life.[58]

Whether Said sees these canons as quite so dangerous in the hands of artists and critics, their primary producers, remains more doubtful. As Gombrich presents it, a rational life involves us all in a process of perceptual making and matching, of provisional orders forged in the light of pending situations. Said may not give overt assent to Gombrich's schema, to his transmitted patterns that serve as canons in the construction of images. Yet his own work uses writers such as Swift, Conrad, Hopkins, even Foucault in order to suggest the recurrence, the unfolding pattern, of the aesthetic and perceptual kaleidoscope represented in *The Story of Art*. Does Said think canons do little harm as long as they remain self-conscious and confined to artists? Despite his protestations to the contrary, his work reveals no strong desire to disturb existing creative reputations, to dislodge one author or to deprive another of pre-eminence. Instead he defines his own mission, at least in part, in terms of securing the kind of hearing for European critics and non-European cultures which was previously restricted to canonical national authors. In *Beginnings*, he provides old-style 'appreciations' of Conrad and Hopkins alongside lengthy meditations on Foucault and Derrida. The implication is that these authors too are worthy of protracted, intensive attention, that they too will take their place in a revitalized, open-ended modern order. In this way, Said has played a vital part in the modern acceptance of a canon of critics, a canon he has also helped to expand.

Said's presentation of an intellectual and interpretative canon which stretches from the earliest commentators on the Bible to the workings of an Ivy League university in the 1990s has some of the virtues displayed in works such as Williams's *The Country and the City* and Auerbach's *Minesis*. All four of the critics we have discussed exhibit a strong attraction towards narrative criticism, even if in Said and Kermode the narrative becomes fragmentary and 'postmodern'. A modernity characterized by rupture and schism will always have a place for a critic who can weave a broad, seamless pattern. This need also explains the prominence in contemporary letters of Frank Kermode, a critic who vies with Said in his quest for new forms of critical narrative that match the complexity of the works and the cultures they inhabit.

Although he is generally regarded as the more conservative of the two, Kermode arguably pushes Said's scepticism about the canon a stage further. For if Said suggests the value of an open-ended, perpetually mobile cross-cultural canon, Kermode offers us something more fragmentary still – a romantic ironist's canon, a canon that contrives to seem at once powerful and incomplete. Significantly, Kermode's first important work, *Romantic Image*, demystifies an authorized story rather than narrates the critic's own. Kermode takes issue with the idea of a 'line of tradition' by which critics like F. R. Leavis linked John Donne to T. S. Eliot. He replaces this tradition with a revisionary history that binds Eliot to a line of alien seers stretching from William Blake to Wallace Stevens. In this way, Kermode mediates between the institutional approaches to the canon articulated in the 1980s and the sense expressed by Frye and Gombrich that *canon* in its deeper sense represents the imaginative totality of an autonomous artistic world.

Kermode's sense of the modern as a period of perpetual change makes him suspicious of the inclusive and authoritative narrative favoured by Frye and Gombrich. Even so, he cannot ignore the fascinating spectacle presented by the growth, decline and inevitable rebirth of the Western literary canon. Although he views the canon as 'one of those outside' (his epigraph to *The Genesis of Secrecy*), his own work shows him drawn to confront it again and again. For so long the romantic ironist among canon-makers, Kermode has not assembled his own massive and inclusive canon but offers instead a succession of perpetually renewable canons that correspond to the plurality of needs he identifies with the fluctuating pressures of institutional life.

Instead of presenting the canon as a servant of larger ideological forces or as an assembly of texts invested with the authority of tradition, these four critics all, in their different ways, view the canon as a coherent work of art, a body of texts larger than the sum of its members, a grand cultural narrative not so different from the Hebraic canon that emerged in Ancient Israel. It is surely significant that all of them reached intellectual maturity in a world where nationalism had wrought enormous damage. Northrop Frye's canon of eschatological fears and hopes bears a close resemblance to the canon of the Old Testament, and this is why it has appropriately held up a mirror to its own workings in the Bible. Frank Kermode's canon acknowledges the pressure to open up intercourse with another world that underpins both ecclesiastical and literary canons. E. H. Gombrich sees the basis for the artistic canon in the miraculously functioning economy of a human organism. The gap between Edward Said's critical theory, which attacks 'religious criticism', and his own reading practices, which plot the desirable and creative continuities in the life of the mind made by personally valued figures and works, reinforces the connection between the contemporary radical intelligentsia and some notion of *canon*.

Although there is little unity in the way these critics describe their canons, they all exhibit a recurring interest in the canon's function as narrative. The climate for the transcendent narratives described by Frye and Kermode may well be waning, yet the impulse towards charismatic narration, the articulation of an inherited, mysteriously occluded story, has not yet ended. These four makers of the modern canon carry on the visionary mission of art and culture projected in Coleridge's *Lay Sermons* and Baudelaire's *Salon*. In *The Genesis of Secrecy* and *Orientalism*, *The Great Code* and *The Story of Art*, four very different critics undertake to create a kind of secular Scripture, an imaginative narrative which tells the whole story about the origins, transmission, history, and interrelationships of traditionally valued and customarily neglected works of literary or visual art.

Notes

INTRODUCTION: THE CANON DEBATE

1. *Aids to Reflection* (London: Taylor & Hessey, 1825), p. 6n.
2. Richard Ohmann, 'The Shaping of a Canon: U.S. Fiction, 1960–1975', in *Canons*, ed. Robert von Hallberg (Chicago and London: University of Chicago Press, 1984), p. 397. Alastair Fowler, 'Genre and the Literary Canon', *New Literary History* 11 (1979), 97–119 (97).
3. *Canons*, p. 1.
4. 'Treason Our Text: Feminist Challenges to the Literary Canon', in *Contemporary Literary Criticism*, ed. Robert Con Davis and Ronald Schleifer (New York and London: Longman, 1989), pp. 616–28 (616).
5. *Framing the Sign* (Oxford: Basil Blackwell, 1988), pp. 34, 33, 37–8.
6. Richard Ohmann, *Canons*, p. 378.
7. *Sensational Designs* (New York and Oxford: Oxford University Press, 1985), pp. 17, 23.
8. *The School of Hawthorne* (New York and Oxford: Oxford University Press, 1986), p. 5.
9. Von Hallberg, *Canons*, p. 1.
10. Gerald Graff, *Professing Literature* (Chicago and London: University of Chicago Press, 1987). Richard Bridgman, 'The American Studies of Henry Nash Smith', *American Scholar* 56 (1987), 259–68. Jonathan Arac, *Critical Genealogies* (New York: Columbia University Press, 1987).
11. *Theory of Literature*, 3rd edn. (New York: Harcourt, Brace & World, 1956), pp. 247–8.

1. MORE THAN JUST A RULE: THE EARLY HISTORY OF THE CANON

1. Herbert Oppel, *Kanōn* (Leipzig: Dieterich'sche Verlagsbuchhandlung, 1937), p. 1.
2. K. von Fritz, Review of Herbert Oppel, *Kanōn*, *American Journal of Philology* 60 (1939), 112–15.
3. Plato, *The Statesman, Philebus, Ion*, Loeb Classical Library, transl. Harold

N. Fowler and W. R. M. Lamb (London: William Heinemann, 1962), pp. 360–61.

4. Erwin Panofsky, 'The History of the Theory of Human Proportions as a Reflection of the History of Styles', in *Meaning in the Visual Arts* (Garden City, New York: Doubleday Anchor, 1955), pp. 55–107 (64).

5. C. O. Müller, *Ancient Art and Its Remains* (London: B. Quaritch, 1852), p. 115.

6. Pliny, *Natural History 9*, Loeb Classical Library, transl. H. Rackham (London: William Heinemann, 1961), pp. 168–9.

7. Galen, cited in Panofsky, *Meaning in the Visual Arts*, p. 64.

8. Cicero, *De Natura Deorum*, Loeb Classical Library, transl. H. Rackham (London: William Heinemann, 1967), pp. 44–5.

9. *Diogenes Laertius 2*, Loeb Classical Library, transl. R. D. Hicks (London: William Heinemann, 1961), pp. 556–61.

10. *Lucian 6*, Classical Library, transl. K. Kilburn (London: William, Heinemann, 1959), pp. 8–9.

11. Ibid., pp. 402–3.

12. *Demosthenes 2: De Corona and De Falsa Legatione*, Loeb Classical Library, transl. C. A. and J. H. Vince (London: William Heinemann, 1963), pp. 212–13.

13. Müller, p. 115.

14. *Euripides 1*, Loeb Classical Library, transl. Arthur S. Way (London: William Heinemann, 1966), pp. 294–5.

15. *Euripides 2*, Loeb Classical Library, transl. Arthur S. Way (London: William Heinemann, 1965), pp. 8–9.

16. *Plutarch's Moralia 2*, Loeb Classical Library, transl. Frank Cole Babbitt (London: William Heinemann, 1971), pp. 114–15.

17. *Plutarch's Lives 1*, Loeb Classical Library, transl. Bernadotte Perrin (London: William Heinemann, 1928), pp. 478–9.

18. *Plutarch's Moralia 1*, Loeb Classical Library, transl. Frank Cole Babbitt (London: William Heinemann, 1969), pp. 134–7.

19. Aristotle, *The Nicomachean Ethics*, Loeb Classical Library, transl. H. Rackham (London: William Heinemann, 1962), pp. 142–3.

20. Ibid., pp. 316–17.

21. Ibid., pp. 142–3, 316–17.

22. This section draws on these reference sources: A. R. C. Leaney, *The Jewish and Christian World 200 B. C. to A. D. 200* (Cambridge: Cambridge University Press, 1984); John H. Hayes, *An Introduction to Old Testament Study* (Nashville: Abingdon, 1979); Robert H. Pfeiffer, *Introduction to the Old Testament* (New York and Evanston: Harper & Row, 1948); Hans von Campenhausen, *The Formation of the Christian Bible*, transl. J. A. Baker (Philadelphia: Fortress Press, 1972); Gerhard Kittel, ed., *Theological Dictionary of the New Testament* (Grand Rapids, Michigan: William B. Eerdmans, 1965); Bruce M. Metzger, *The Canon of the New Testament:*

Its Origins, Development and Significance (Oxford: Clarendon Press, 1987).
23. R. Meyer, 'Supplement on the Canon and the Apocrypha', in Kittel, pp. 978–87 (982).
24. Eberhard Oberg, ed., *Amphilochii Iconiensis: Iambi ad Seleucum*, Patristische Texte und Studien 9 (Berlin: Walter de Gruyter, 1969), p. 39.
25. *Josephus 1*, Loeb Classical Library, transl. H. St J. Thackeray (London: William Heinemann, 1966), pp. 178–81.
26. James Barr, *Holy Scripture: Canon, Authority, Criticism* (Philadelphia: Westminster Press, 1983), p. 12.
27. English citations are to *The Revised English Bible* (England: Oxford University Press and Cambridge University Press, 1989). Greek citations are to *The Greek New Testament*, 2nd edn, ed. Kurt Aland *et al.* (New York and London: United Bible Societies, 1966).
28. Quoted in H. W. Beyer's article 'Kanōn', in Kittel, p. 598.
29. *Philo 6*, Loeb Classical Library, transl. F. H. Colson (London: William Heinemann, 1959), pp. 314–15.
30. Johannes Quasten, *Patrology*, vol. 3 (Westminster, Maryland and Utrecht: Newman Press and Spectrum Publishers, 1960), p. 45; J.- P. Migne, 162 vols, *Patrologiae cursus completus*, Series Graeca (Paris, 1857, reprinted Turnhout: Brepols, 1956–82), 28, 251–82. Cited hereafter as PG.
31. William Whitaker, *A Disputation on Holy Scripture*, transl. William Fitzgerald (Cambridge: Cambridge University Press, 1849), p. 48.
32. Ibid., p.28.
33. Irenaeus, *Against Heresies*, PG 7, 545–6B; Alexander Roberts and James Donaldson, *The Ante-Nicene Fathers*, 10 vols (Buffalo: Christian Literature Co., 1886), 1, 330. Cited hereafter as ANF.
34. Johannes Quasten, *Patrology*, vol. 2 (Westminster, Maryland and Utrecht: Newman Press and Spectrum Publishers, 1953), p. 7.
35. Clement, *Stromata 7*, PG 9, 525–6AB; ANF 2, 549; *Stromata 4*, PG 9, 1305–6A; ANF 2, 427.
36. Clement, *Stromata 6*, PG 9, 347–8C, 349–50A; ANF 2, 509.
37. Clement, *Stromata 6*, PG 9, 349–50A; ANF 2, 509.
38. Eusebius, *The Ecclesiastical History 2*, Loeb Classical Library, transl. and ed. J. E. L. Oulton and H. J. Lawlor (London: William Heinemann, 1964), pp. 74–5.
39. Athanasius, *Decrees*, PG 25, 455–6A.
40. Athanasius, *Festal Letter*, PG 26, 1435–6B; Philip Schaff and Henry Wace, *A Select Library of Nicene and Post-Nicene Fathers of the Christian Church*, Second Series, 14 vols (New York: Christian Literature Co. 1892), 4, 551–2. Cited hereafter as NPNF; Whitaker, p. 57..
41. Amphilochius, quoted in Oberg, p. 39; Isidore, *Epistolarum Lib. 4*, PG 78, 1185–6B; Macarius Magnes, quoted in Metzger, p. 292.
42. Athanasius, *Festal Letter*, PG 26, 1437–8BC; NPNF 4, 552.

43. *The Ecclesiastical History 1*, Loeb Classical Library, transl. Kirsopp Lake (London: William Heinemann, 1926), pp. 276-7.

44. Collected in *The Apostolic Fathers 1*, Loeb Classical Library, transl. Kirsopp Lake (London: William Heinemann, 1912), pp. 18-19, 10-11, 78-9.

45. *Eusebius 1*, pp. 506-7.

46. Clement, *Stromata 7*, PG 9, 527-8C; ANF 2, 550.

47. Basil, *Regulae Fusius Tractatae*, PG 31, 1031-2C. See also *Saint Basil: Ascetical Works*, transl. Sister M. Monica Wagner (New York: Fathers of the Church, 1950), p. 322.

48. Gregory Nazianzus, *Epistolae*, PG 37, 29-30C; NPFN 7, 448.

49. *The City of God 6*, Loeb Classical Library, transl. William Chase Greene (London: William Heinemann, 1960), pp. 18-19, 6-7.

50. *On Christian Doctrine*, transl. D. W. Robertson, Jr (New York: The Liberal Arts Press, 1958), pp. 42, 37; *Aurelii Augustini Opera: De Doctrina Christiana, De Vera Religione* (Turnholt: Brepols, 1962), pp. 41, 35.

51. *The City of God 6*, pp. 18-19.

52. *On Christian Doctrine*, p. 9; *Opera 32*, p. 8.

53. Rufinus, *A Commentary on the Apostles' Creed*, Ancient Christian Writers: The Works of the Fathers in Translation, ed. J. N. D. Kelly (London: Longmans, Green & Co., 1955), pp. 73-4.

54. Beryl Smalley, 'The Bible in the Medieval Schools', in G. W. H. Lampe, ed., *The Cambridge History of the Bible*, vol. 2 (Cambridge: Cambridge University Press, 1969), pp. 197-220 (197-9).

55. St Thomas Aquinas, *Christian Theology*, vol. 1 of *Summa Theologiae*, ed. Thomas Gilby (London: Blackfriars, 1964), pp. 31-2, 25, 33.

56. Henry Crosse, *Vertues Commonwealth or The Highway to Heaven*, ed. Alexander Grosart (Manchester: C. E. Simms, 1878), p. 81.

57. Martin Luther, *Writings*, ed. John Dillenberger (Garden City: Doubleday, 1961), pp. 37, 14; *Luther's Works*, vol. 38 *(Word and Sacrament IV)*, ed. Martin E. Lehmann (Philadelphia: Fortress, 1971), p. 33.

58. Edward Meyrick Goulburn, *The Pursuit of Holiness* (London: Rivingtons, 1870), pp. 72, 86.

59. F. Max Müller, *Introduction to the Science of Religion* (New York: Arno Press, 1978), pp. 25, 16-17.

60. Brevard S. Childs, 'The Old Testament as Scripture of the Church', *Concordia Theological Monthly*, December 1972, 709-22 (714).

61. James A. Sanders, *Torah and Canon* (Philadelphia: Fortress Press, 1972), pp. 116, 120.

62. James A. Sanders, *Canon and Community: A Guide to Canonical Criticism* (Philadelphia: Fortress Press, 1984), p. 27.

63. Paul Ricoeur, *Hermeneutic of the Idea of Revelation* (Berkeley: Center for Hermeneutical Studies in Hellenistic and Modern Culture, 1977), p. 35.

64. Ricoeur, pp. 30, 35-6.

2. A WHOLE WORLD OF READING:
THE MODERN HISTORY OF THE CANON

1. Thomas Wilson, *Arte of Rhetorique (1560)*, ed. G. H. Mair (Oxford: Clarendon Press, 1909), pp. 121–2.
2. *Miscellaneous Poems in English and Latin*, vol. 4 of *The Poetical Works of Christopher Smart*, ed. Karina Williamson (Oxford: Clarendon Press, 1987), pp. 113–26 (116, 121).
3. Samuel Johnson, *A Dictionary of the English Language* (Beirut: Librairie du Liban, 1978), p. 265; Diderot, *Encyclopédie II (Lettres B–C)*, ed. John Lough and Jacques Proust (Paris: Herman, 1976), pp. 253–64.
4. Lewis Theobald, 'Preface to Edition of Shakespeare', in *Eighteenth Century Essays on Shakespeare*, ed. D. Nichol Smith (Oxford: Clarendon Press, 1963), p. 75.
5. William Warburton, 'Preface to Edition of Shakespeare', in *Eighteenth Century Essays on Shakespeare*, pp. 94, 93.
6. *The Canons of Criticism and Glossary*, 7th edn (New York: Augustus M. Kelley Publishers, 1970), pp. 25–8.
7. *Sophocles the Dramatist* (Cambridge: Cambridge University Press, 1951), pp. 1–46.
8. *Lyrical Ballads*, ed. R. L. Brett and A. R. Jones (London: Methuen, 1965), p. 251–2.
9. Rudolf Pfeiffer, *History of Classical Scholarship: From the Beginnings to the End of the Hellenistic Age* (Oxford: Clarendon Press, 1968), p. 207.
10. See Pfeiffer, p. 207 and J. E. Sandys, *A History of Classical Scholarship*, vol. 1 (Cambridge: Cambridge University Press, 1906), pp. 129–31; and *A History of Classical Scholarship*, vol. 2 (Cambridge: Cambridge University Press, 1908), pp. 457–60 for an account of Ruhnken and the controversy surrounding his canons.
11. N. G. Wilson, *Scholars of Byzantium* (Baltimore: Johns Hopkins University Press, 1983), pp. 1–27.
12. Frank M. Turner, *The Greek Heritage in Victorian Britain* (New Haven: Yale University Press, 1981), pp. 154–70.
13. H. Taine, *Voyage en Italie*, 2 vols (Paris: Librairie Hachette, [1924]), II, 199.
14. 'Gedanke vom mündlichen Vortrag der neueren allgemeinen Geschichte' ('Thoughts for an Oral Lecture on the New Universal History') in *Kleine Schriften und Briefe* (Weimar: Hermann Böhlaus Nachfolger, 1960), pp. 17–26 (21); 'On the Imitation of the Painting and Sculpture of the Greeks', in Johann Joachim Winckelmann, *Winckelmann: Writings on Art*, ed. David Irwin (London: Phaidon Press, 1972), pp. 61–85 (61); 'Erste Prägung der ästhetischen Kategorien' (First Stamping of the Aesthetic Categories'), pp. 27–123 (30); 'Gedanke vom mündlichen Vortrag der neueren allgemeinen Geschichte', p. 23.

15. Novalis, *Schriften*, vol. 4, ed. Richard Samuel (Stuttgart: W. Kohlhammer, 1975), p. 237.

16. Novalis, *Schriften*, vol. 3, ed. Richard Samuel (Stuttgart: W. Kohlhammer, 1960), p. 449.

17. Viktor Shklovsky, *A Sentimental Journey: Memoirs, 1917–1922*, transl. Richard Sheldon (Ithaca and London: Cornell University Press, 1970), p. 233.

18. Friedrich von Schiller, *Dichter über ihre Dichtungen*, vol. 2 ed. Bodo Lecke (Munich: Heimeran, 1970), p. 129.

19. Johann Peter Eckermann, *Conversations with Goethe* (London: J. M. Dent, 1935), pp. 165–6; J. P. Eckermann, *Gesprache mit Goethe* (Leipzig: Eugin Diederichs, 1905), II, 285.

20. Friedrich Scheegel, *The Aesthetic and Miscellaneous Works of Friedrich von Scheegel* (London: Bohn, 1860), p. 270.

21. 'Poems by George Crabbe', *Edinburgh Review* 12 (1808), 131–51 (136).

22. 'The Excursion', *Edinburgh Review* 24 (1814), 1–30 (9).

23. *Lectures 1795 on Politics and Religion*, ed. Lewis Patton and Peter Mann (London and Princeton: Routledge & Kegan Paul and Princeton University Press, 1971), p. 314.

24. Letter to Robert Southey, 29 July 1802, *Collected Letters of Samuel Taylor Coleridge*, 6 vols, ed. E. L. Griggs (Oxford and New York, 1956–71), II, 449.

25. *Biographia Literaria*, 2 vols, ed. James Engell and W. Jackson Bate (London and Princeton: Routledge & Kegan Paul and Princeton University Press, 1983), II, 119, 115; I, 62.

26. John Wilson, 'On Literary Censorship', *Blackwood's Magazine* 4 (1818), 176–8 (176); 'A Preface to a Review of the Chronicles of the Canongate', *Blackwood's* 22 (1827), 531–6 (546–7)

27. 'The First Edinburgh Reviewers', in *Literary Studies* (London: J. M. Dent, 1951), I, 1–35 (11, 22–3).

28. 'The Function of Criticism at the Present Time', in *Lectures and Essays in Criticism 1*, ed. R. H. Super (Ann Arbor: University of Michigan Press, 1962), pp. 258–85 (283).

29. *Biographia Literaria*, I, 22; 'The Literary Influence of Academies', in *Lectures and Essays in Criticism 1*, pp. 232–57 (253).

30. Viscount John Morley, *Recollections* (New York: Macmillan, 1917), I, 100.

31. 'The Function of Criticism at the Present Time', p. 283.

32. *Biographia Literaria*, II, 110–11.

33. 'The Literary Influence of Academies', pp. 234, 252.

34. R. Pascal, *Shakespeare in Germany, 1740–1814* (Cambridge: Cambridge University Press, 1937), p. 15.

35. J. M. Robertson, *The Shakespeare Canon*, 5 vols (London and New York: George Routledge and E. P. Dutton, 1922–32), I, xvi.

36. E. K. Chambers, ed., *Titus Andronicus* (London: Blackie & Son, 1907), p. 6.

37. E. K. Chambers, *The Disintegration of Shakespeare* (Annual Shakespeare Lecture delivered 12 May 1924 to the British Academy) (Oxford: Milford, 1924), pp. 6, 5, 14, 8, 1.

38. *Eighteenth Century Essays on Shakespeare*, p. 59.

39. *Romance and Tragedy* (Boston: Marshall Jones Company, 1922), pp. vii, 340.

40. J. W. Mackail, *The Approach to Shakespeare*, 2nd edn (Oxford: Clarendon Press, 1933), pp. 104, 30, 48–9, 5.

41. Mackail, pp. 63, 50.

42. Ernest Barker, *National Character* (London: Methuen, 1927), p. 231.

43. Henry Canby, 'An American Canon', *Saturday Review of Literature*, 15 October 1927, pp. 191, 193.

44. Ibid., p. 193.

45. Daniel L. Marsh, *The American Canon* (New York: Abingdon Press, 1939), pp. 5–6, 9.

46. Ibid., pp. 9, 11.

47. Van Wyck Brooks, 'On Creating a Usable Past', in *Van Wyck Brooks: The Early Years*, ed. Claire Sprague (London: Harper Torchbooks, 1968), pp. 219–26 (221, 220).

48. Edwin Greenlaw, *The Province of Literary History* (London: Humphrey Milford, 1931), pp. 158, 14, 9.

49. Carl Van Doren, 'Toward a New Canon', *The Nation*, 13 April 1932, 429–30.

50. Ibid., p. 430.

51. *Literary Taste: How To Form It. With Detailed Instructions for Collecting A Complete Library of English Literature* (New York: George H. Doran [1927 ed]), pp. 32, 54, 56.

52. *On 'Culture' and 'A Liberal Education': With Lists of Books Which Can Aid in Acquiring Them* (New York: The Arnold Company, 1926), pp. 80, 86; *What Books Can Do For You: A Sketch Map of the Frontiers of Knowledge: With Lists of Selected Books* (New York: George H. Doran, 1923), p. 143.

53. *Adventures in Reading* (Philadelphia and New York: J. B. Lippincott, 1927, revised edn 1946), pp. v, 21, 204.

54. *The Illiteracy of the Literate: A Guide to the Art of Intelligent Reading* (New York and London: D. Appleton-Century, 1933), p. 247.

55. 'On the Choice of Books', *Fortnightly Review* 31, old series (April 1879), 491–512 (511).

56. *The Book Lover: A Guide to the Best Reading*, revised edn (Chicago: A. C. McClurg, 1902), p, 78. (Originally published as *The Book-Lover*, 1884).

57. *The Pleasures of Life* (London: Macmillan, 1891), p. ix. 'The Choice of Books' is reprinted pp. 60–93.

58. Everett Dean Martin, 'Sharing in the Creation of Good Books', in *Classics of the Western World*, ed. J. Bartlet Brebner and the Honors Faculty of Columbia College. With Forewords by John Erskine and

Everett Dean Martin (Chicago: American Library Association, 1927), pp. 11–16 (14).

59. Thomas Carlyle, 'Inaugural Address at Edinburgh, 2nd April, 1866: On Being Installed as Rector of the University There', in *Critical and Miscellaneous Essays*, vol. 4 (vol. 39 of Centennial Memorial Edition of Carlyle's *Works*), (Boston: Dana Estes, [1896–9]), pp. 388–420, esp. 403–4.

60. *Literary Taste*, pp. 28, 66.

61. Everett Dean Martin, in *Classics of the Western World*, p. 14.

62. *How To Read a Book* (New York: Simon & Schuster, 1940), p. 332.

63. *The Book Lover*, p. 217.

64. *On 'Culture' and 'A Liberal Education'*, pp. 9–10.

65. Everett Dean Martin, in *Classics of the Western World*, p. 11.

66. *How To Read A Book*, pp. 44, 99, 264.

67. Quoted in *The Book Lover* (1902), pp. 270, 271.

68. *ABC of Reading* (New York: New Directions, 1960), pp. 43, 87, 200.

69. John Peale Bishop, 'Homage to Hemingway', in Malcolm Cowley, *After the Genteel Tradition: American Writers Since 1910* (New York: W. W. Norton, 1937), p. 200.

70. Newton Arvin, 'Carl Sandburg', in *After the Genteel Tradition*, p. 82.

71. Hamilton Basso, 'Thomas Wolfe', in *After the Genteel Tradition*, pp. 205–6.

72. Lionel Trilling, 'Willa Cather', in *After the Genteel Tradition*, pp. 62, 53.

73. Pierre Bourdieu, 'Flaubert's Point of View', *Critical Inquiry* 14 (1988), 539–62 (542).

74. T. S. Eliot, 'The Perfect Critic', in *The Sacred Wood* (London: Methuen, 1950), pp. 1–16 (10). (Essay originally published in 3 parts in *Athenaeum*, 9 July 1920, 40–41; 23 July 1920, 102–4; 6 August 1920, 190).

75. René Wellek and Austin Warren, *Theory of Literature*, 3rd edn (New York: Harcourt, Brace & World, 1956), p. 250.

76. *The Sacred Wood*, p. xvi.

77. Ibid., pp. 47–59 (50, 49).

78. 'Flaubert's Point of View', p. 542.

79. 'My Canon and Ours', *College English* 47 (1985), 141–7 (142).

80. 'The Function of Criticism', in *Selected Essays*, new edn (New York: Harcourt, Brace & World, 1950), pp. 12–22 (13, 12); 'Tradition and the Individual Talent', in *The Sacred Wood*, pp. 49–50.

81. Q. D. Leavis, 'The Discipline of Letters: A Sociological Note', *Scrutiny* 12 (1943), 12–26 (21).

82. F. R. Leavis, 'Standards of Criticism', in *Valuation in Criticism and Other Essays*, ed. G. Singh (Cambridge: Cambridge University Press, 1986), pp. 244–52 (247, 245, 248); 'T. S. Eliot and the Life of English Literature', pp. 129–48 (131).

83. *The World's Body* (Baton Rouge: Louisiana State University Press, 1968), pp. 26, 38.

84. 'Charles Péguy: Discours Prononcé à l'Institut Catholique', in *Pages de*

Prose, ed. André Blanchet (Paris: Gallimard, 1944), pp. 174–7 (175); letter to Jacques Rivière, 19 December 1908, Jacques Rivière et Paul Claudel, *Correspondance (1907–1914)* (Paris: Librairie Plon, 1926), pp. 121–3 (122).
85. *Autobiographies* (London: Macmillan, 1955), p. 501.
86. *Essays on Literary Criticism and the English Tradition* (London: Dennis Dobson, 1948), pp. 99, 53, 29.
87. 'The Shorter Poems of Thomas Hardy', in *Form and Value in Modern Poetry* (New York: Doubleday, 1957), pp. 1–31 (1, 11, 16–17, 30).
88. 'Lawrence, Eliot, Blackmur, and the Tortoise', in *The Ringers in the Tower* (Chicago and London: University of Chicago Press, 1971), p. 197.
89. 'The Work of Art in the Age of Mechanical Reproduction', in *Illuminations* (New York: Schocken Books, 1969), pp. 217–51 (240); *Gesammelte Schriften*, ed. Rolf Tiedemann and Hermann Schweppenhauser (Frankfurt am Main: Suhrkamp Verlag, 1974), vol. 1, part II, 640.
90. 'On Some Motifs in Baudelaire', in *Illuminations*, pp. 155–94 (182); *Gesammelte Schriften*, 1, II, 505.
91. *Ce Vice impuni* (Paris: Gallimard, 1951), pp. 54–5.
92. *European Literature and the Latin Middle Ages* (New York: Harper & Row, 1963), pp. 271–2, 256, 268.

3. SIR ERNST GOMBRICH AND THE FUNCTIONALIST CANON

1. Karen Gold, 'Sceptic Who Has Never Lost His Belief in Art', *Times Higher Education Supplement*, 28 August 1987, 9.
2. *Tributes* (Oxford: Phaidon, 1984), p. 8. Cited hereafter as T.
3. 'Art History and the Social Sciences', collected in *Ideals and Idols* (Oxford: Phaidon, 1979), p. 156. Cited hereafter as II.
4. Murray Krieger, 'The Ambiguity of Representation and Illusion: An E. H. Gombrich Retrospective', *Critical Inquiry* 11 (1984), 181–94 (182, 194).
5. 'Representation and Misrepresentation', *Critical Inquiry* 11 (1984), 195–201 (195, 197, 199).
6. 'From the Revival of Letters to the Reform of the Arts: Niccolò Niccoli and Filippo Brunelleschi', in *The Heritage of Apelles* (Oxford and Ithaca: Phaidon and Cornell University Press, 1976), pp. 93–110 (93). Cited hereafter as HA.
7. Karl Popper, *The Poverty of Historicism* (London: Routledge and Kegan Paul, 1961), p. 65.
8. *The Sense of Order* (Oxford and Ithaca: Phaidon and Cornell University Press, 1979), p. 5. Cited hereafter as SO.
9. *The Story of Art*, 12th ed. (Oxford: Phaidon, 1972), p. 4. Cited hereafter as SA.
10. *The Heritage of Apelles*, p. 109. See also 'The Logic of Vanity Fair: Alternatives to Historicism in the Study of Fashions, Style and Taste', in *Ideals and Idols*, pp. 60–92.

11. 'The Renaissance – Period or Movement?' in J. B. Trapp, ed., *Background to the English Renaissance* (London: Gray-Mills, 1974), pp. 9–30 (15).

12. I take the phrase from Svetlana Alpers, *The Art of Describing: Dutch Art in the Seventeenth Century* (Chicago: University of Chicago Press, 1983).

13. 'Achievement in Mediaeval Art', in *Meditations on a Hobby Horse* (Oxford: Phaidon, 1963), p.71. Cited hereafter as MHH.

14. 'New Revelations on Fresco Painting', in *Reflections on the History of Art*, ed. Richard Woodfield (Oxford: Phaidon, 1987), p. 50. Cited hereafter as ROHA.

15. *Art and Illusion* (Oxford: Phaidon, 1960), p. 126. Cited hereafter as AI.

16. 'The Renaissance Conception of Artistic Progress and Its Consequences', in *Norm and Form* (Oxford: Phaidon, 1966), p. 6. Cited hereafter as NF.

17. 'Ideal and Type in Italian Renaissance Painting', in *New Light on Old Masters* (Oxford: Phaidon, 1986), p. 94. Cited hereafter as NLOM.

18. Pliny, *Natural History* 9, Loeb Classical Library, ed. H. Rackham (London: William Heinemann, 1961), pp. 168–69.

19. T. S. Eliot, 'What Dante Means to Me', in *To Criticize the Critic* (London: Faber & Faber, 1978), pp. 124–35 (134). John Berger, *Permanent Red* (London: Methuen, 1960), p. 152. (Published in the United States as *Toward Reality: Essays in Seeing*, with Foreword by Harold Clurman [New York: Alfred A. Knopf, 1962], p. 152.)

20. Immanuel Kant, *The Critique of Judgement*, transl. James Creed Meredith (Oxford: Clarendon Press, 1952), p. 106.

21. 'The Edge of Delusion', *New York Review of Books*, 15 February 1990, 6–9 (9).

4. NORTHROP FRYE AND THE VISIONARY CANON

1. *Ideals and Idols* (Oxford: Phaidon, 1979), p. 170.

2. Ibid., pp. 9–23.

3. R. G. Collingwood, *The Idea of History* (New York: Oxford University Press, 1956), p. 308.

4. Geoffrey Barraclough, *History in a Changing World* (Norman: University of Oklahoma Press, [1956]), p. 1.

5. *Spiritus Mundi* (Bloomington and London: Indiana University Press, 1976), p. 5. Cited hereafter as SM.

6. *Anatomy of Criticism* (Princeton: Princeton University Press, 1957), p. 16. Cited hereafter as AC.

7. Quoted in Imre Salusinszky, *Criticism in Society* (New York and London: Methuen, 1987), p.32.

8. Jane Tompkins, *Sensational Designs* (New York and Oxford: Oxford University Press, 1985), p. 5.

9. *The Educated Imagination* (Bloomington and London: Indiana University Press, 1964), p. 28. Cited hereafter as EI.

10. Salusinszky, p. 32.

11. *The Stubborn Structure* (Ithaca: Cornell University Press, 1970), p. 256. Cited hereafter as SS.

12. *The Great Code* (New York: Harcourt Brace Jovanovich, 1982), p. xiv. Cited hereafter as GC.

13. *Northrop Frye on Shakespeare* (New Haven and London: Yale University Press, 1986), p. 1. Cited hereafter as NFS.

14. *Fearful Symmetry* (Princeton: Princeton University Press, 1947), p. 420. Cited hereafter as FS.

15. T. S. Eliot, 'William Blake', *Selected Essays* (New York: Harcourt, Brace & Co., 1950), pp. 275–80 (279).

16. *The Myth of Deliverance* (Sussex: Harvester Press, 1983), pp. 89–90. Cited hereafter as MD.

17. Review of W. B. Stanford, *The Ulysses Theme* and Cleanth Brooks, ed., *Tragic Themes in Western Literature*, *Comparative Literature* 9 (1957), 180–82 (182).

18. 'The Acceptance of Innocence', in *Northrop Frye on Culture and Literature* (Chicago and London: University of Chicago Press, 1978), pp. 159–64 (160). Cited hereafter as NFCL.

19. Frederick Crews, 'Anaesthetic Criticism', collected in *Out of My System* (New York: Oxford University Press, 1975), pp. 63–87.

20. *Anatomy of Criticism* was reviewed by M. H. Abrams in *University of Toronto Quarterly* 28 (1959), 190–96, by Frank Kermode in *Review of English Studies* 10 (1959), 317–23 (reprinted in *Puzzles and Epiphanies* [London: Routledge & Kegan Paul, 1962], pp. 64–73), and by David Daiches in *Modern Philology* 56 (1958), 69–72.

21. *The Bush Garden* (Toronto: Anansi, 1971), pp. 150, 158. Cited hereafter as BG.

22. *The Critical Path* (Sussex: The Harvester Press, 1983), pp. 49, 48. Cited hereafter as CP.

23. *Divisions on a Ground* (Toronto: Anansi, 1982), p. 19. Cited hereafter as DG.

24. *The Modern Century* (London: Oxford University Press, 1967), p. 53. Cited hereafter as MC.

25. See Salusinszky, p. 31.

26. *A Study of English Romanticism* (New York: Random House, 1968), p. 4.

5. FRANK KERMODE AND THE CANON OF INTERPRETATION

1. *Forms of Attention* (Chicago and London: University of Chicago Press, 1985), p. 36. Cited hereafter as FA.

2. 'The Enduring Lear', *New York Review of Books*, 12 May 1966, 12–14 (14).

3. Marilyn Butler, 'Revising the Canon', *Times Literary Supplement*, 4 December 1987, 1349, 1359–60.

4. *Romantic Image* (London: Routledge & Kegan Paul, 1957), p. 119. Cited hereafter as RI.

5. 'Some Reservations', *New Statesman*, 25 October 1963, 569.

6. T. S. Eliot, 'The Metaphysical Poets', *Selected Essays* (New York: Harcourt, Brace & World, 1950), pp. 241–50 (248).

7. 'Survival of the Classics', *Encounter*, November 1963, pp. 82–5 (83).

8. *The Sense of an Ending* (New York: Oxford University Press, 1967), p. 62. Cited hereafter as SE.

9. Helen Gardner, *In Defence of the Imagination* (Oxford: Clarendon Press, 1982). Jane Tompkins, *Sensational Designs* (New York and Oxford: Oxford University Press, 1985). Strangely enough, many of Tompkins's arguments parallel Kermode's.

10. 'The Young and the Elders', *Partisan Review* 37 (1970), 184–98 (194, 198).

11. 'Survival of the Classic' is collected in *Shakespeare, Spenser, Donne* (London: Routledge & Kegan Paul, 1971), pp. 164–80 (165, 164). Cited hereafter as SSD.

12. *The Classic* (London and Cambridge, MA: Harvard University Press, 1983), p. 15. Cited hereafter as C.

13. W. W. Robson's essay is collected in *Critical Essays* (London: Routledge & Kegan Paul, 1966), pp. 264–84.

14. *Lawrence* (London: Fontana, 1973), pp. 18–19. Cited hereafter as L.

15. *The Genesis of Secrecy* (London and Cambridge, MA: Harvard University Press, 1979), p. 15. Cited hereafter as GS.

16. *Essays on Fiction, 1971–82* (London: Routledge & Kegan Paul, 1983), p. 182. Cited hereafter as EF.

17. *An Appetite for Poetry* (Cambridge, MA: Harvard University Press, 1989), p. 193. Cited hereafter as AP.

18. *History and Value* (Oxford: Clarendon Press, 1988), pp. 108–9. Cited hereafter as HV.

6. EDWARD SAID AND THE OPEN CANON

1. Edward W. Said, *The World, the Text, and the Critic* (London: Faber & Faber, 1984), pp. 25, 290. Cited hereafter as WTC.

2. *Covering Islam* (New York: Pantheon Books, 1981), p. 43. Cited hereafter as CI.

3. 'Opponents, Audiences, Constituencies, and Community', *Critical Inquiry* 9 (1982), 1–26 (16).

4. 'Representing the Colonized: Anthropology's Interlocutors', *Critical Inquiry* 15 (1989), 205–25 (225).

5. *Beginnings*, new ed. (New York: Columbia University Press, 1985). Cited hereafter as B.

6. *Orientalism* (New York: Vintage Books, 1979), p. 16. Cited hereafter as O.

7. Ernst Robert Curtius, *European Literature and the Latin Middle Ages* (New York and Evanston: Harper & Row, 1963), pp. 15–16.

8. Quoted in Imre Salusinszky, *Criticism in Society* (London: Methuen, 1987), p. 139.

9. Northrop Frye, *The Modern Century* (London: Oxford University Press, 1967), p. 113.

10. See Said's own essay, 'The Horizon of R. P. Blackmur', *Raritan* 6 (1986), 29–50, esp. 33–4. See also Robert Fitzgerald, *Enlarging the Change* (Boston: Northeastern University Press, 1985).

11. See Lionel Trilling, 'A Personal Memoir', in *From Parnassus: Essays in Honor of Jacques Barzun* (London: Harper & Row, 1976), pp. xv–xxii.

12. Quentin Skinner, 'Meaning and Understanding in the History of Ideas', *History and Theory* 8 (1969), 3–53 (5).

13. J. G. A. Pocock, *Politics, Language and Time* (New York: Atheneum, 1973), pp. 4–5.

14. Said, 'Opponents, Audiences, Constituencies, and Community', 4–5.

15. Louis I. Bredvold, 'The Gloom of the Tory Satirists', reprinted in James L. Clifford, *Eighteenth-Century English Literature: Modern Essays in Criticism* (New York: Oxford University Press, 1959), pp. 3–20.

16. *After the Last Sky* (New York: Pantheon Books, 1986), pp. 23, 34.

17. Curtius, p. 15.

18. John Higham, *History* (Baltimore and London: Johns Hopkins University Press, 1983), pp. 113, 111.

19. 'Kim, The Pleasures of Imperialism', *Raritan* 7 (1987), 27–64 (29); 'The Horizon of R. P. Blackmur', 36; 'Michel Foucault, 1927–84', *Raritan* 4 (1984), 1–11 (8).

20. 'The Totalitarianism of Mind', *Kenyon Review* 29 (1967), 256–68 (258); 'The Problem of Textuality: Two Exemplary Positions', *Critical Inquiry* 4 (1978), 673–714; *Beginnings*, p. 9.

21. 'An Ideology of Difference', *Critical Inquiry* 12 (1985), 38–58 (41).

22. 'Kim, The Pleasures of Imperialism', 64.

23. *The English Novel from Dickens to Lawrence* (London: Hogarth Press, 1984), pp. 150, 152.

24. Salusinszky, p. 133.

25. 'Representing the Colonized: Anthropology's Interlocutors', 224.

CONCLUSION: CULTURAL STUDIES: TOWARDS A NEW CANON

1. Shattuck contributes to the symposium 'Who Needs The Great Works?' *Harper's Magazine*, September 1989, 43–52 (49).

2. Letter of July 1919 to Mary Hutchinson, in *The Letters of T. S. Eliot: Volume 1, 1898–1922*, ed. Valerie Eliot (London: Harcourt Brace Jovanovich, 1988), p. 317.

3. Leslie Marmon Silko, 'Language and Literature from a Pueblo Indian Perspective', in Leslie A. Fiedler and Houston A. Baker, Jr, *English Literature: Opening Up the Canon* (Baltimore and London: Johns Hopkins University Press, 1981), pp. 54–72 (54).

4. Houston A. Baker, Jr, 'Introduction', in Fiedler and Baker, pp. ix–xiii (xiii).

5. Gerald Bruns, 'Canon and Power in the Hebrew Scriptures', in Robert von Hallberg, ed., *Canons* (Chicago and London: University of Chicago Press, 1984), pp. 65–83 (81).

6. See Frank Kermode, *An Appetite for Poetry* (Cambridge, MA: Harvard University Press, 1989), p. 2.

7. 'The Function of Criticism at the Present Time', *Essays in Criticism* 3 (1953), 1–27 (19).

8. *Speaking to Each Other. Volume 1: About Society* (London: Chatto & Windus, 1970), pp. 246–59 (256).

9. *Speaking to Each Other. Volume 2: About Literature* (London: Chatto & Windus, 1970), pp. 63–8 (65).

10. *The Poetry of Experience* (Harmondsworth: Penguin University Books, 1974), pp. 3, 1.

11. *The Dream and the Task* (New York: W. W. Norton, 1964), pp. 91, 98, 102.

12. *The New Poetic: Yeats to Eliot* (Harmondsworth: Penguin, 1967), p. 96.

13. *Literary Criticism: An Introductory Reader* (New York: Holt, Rinehart and Winston, 1970), pp. 1, 2. Trilling's introduction is reprinted with the title 'What Is Criticism?' in his *The Last Decade: Essays and Reviews 1965–75*, ed. Diana Trilling (New York and London: Harcourt Brace Jovanovich, 1978), pp. 57–99 (57, 59).

14. *A New Canon of English Poetry* (New York: Barnes & Noble, 1967), pp. xviii, xv.

15. Reeves and Seymour-Smith, p. xv.

16. Ibid., p. xvii.

17. *The Country and the City* (London: Chatto & Windus, 1973), p. 288.

18. 'Major Trends in Research: 22 Leading Scholars Report on Their Fields'. Houston A. Baker, Jr:. 'Literature', *Chronicle of Higher Education*, 4 September 1985, 13.

19. *Home and Exile* (London: Longmans, 1965), p. 49.

20. Vine Deloria, ed., *Black Elk Speaks* (Lincoln, Nebraska and London: University of Nebraska Press, 1979), pp. xiii, xv.

21. *Toward an Aesthetic of Reception*, transl. Timothy Bahti (Minneapolis: University of Minnesota Press, 1982), pp. 49, 13.

22. 'Shelley Disfigured', in *Deconstruction and Criticism* (New York: Continuum, 1979), pp. 39–73 (67, 68).

23. *Is There a Text in This Class?* (London and Cambridge, MA: Harvard University Press 1980), pp. 180, 174, 16.

24. *Politics, Language and Time* (New York: Atheneum, 1973), pp. 4–5, 10.

25. Pocock, p. 5.

26. 'A Journeyman's Life under the Old Regime: Work and Culture in an Eighteenth-Century Printing Shop', *Princeton Alumni Weekly*, 7 September 1981, 12. Quoted in Edward W. Said, 'Opponents, Audiences, Constituencies, and Community', *Critical Inquiry* 9 (1982), 1–26 (17).

27. *Local Knowledge* (New York: Basic Books, 1983), p. 10.

28. See also Geertz's *Works and Lives* (Stanford: Stanford University Press, 1988).

29. Colin MacCabe, 'The State of the Subject (1): English', *Critical Quarterly* 29 (1987), 5–8 (7, 5).

30. *Literary Theory: An Introduction* (Oxford: Basil Blackwell, 1983), p. 207.

31. Jonathan Dollimore and Alan Sinfield, 'Foreword: Cultural Politics', to John Barrell, *Poetry, Language and Politics* (Manchester: Manchester University Press, 1988), pp. vii–viii (vii).

32. Jonathan Dollimore, *Radical Tragedy* (Brighton: Harvester Press, 1984), pp. 189–203, 224.

33. MacCabe, p. 7.

34. Ibid., pp. 8, 6.

35. Barrell, p. ix.

36. MacCabe, p. 8.

37. 'The Discipline of Letters: A Sociological Note', *Scrutiny* 12 (1943), 12–26 (26).

38. *English Literature in Our Time and the University* (London: Chatto & Windus, 1969), pp. 41–42, 35, 7, 3.

39. Q. D. Leavis, p. 26. See also her essay 'Academic Case-History', *Scrutiny* 11 (1943), 305–10.

40. MacCabe, p. 8; Barrell, p. ix; Eagleton, *The Function of Criticism* (London: Verso, 1984), p. 9.

41. Jonathan Culler, *Framing the Sign* (Oxford: Blackwell, 1988), p. 34.

42. Ibid., p. x.

43. *Shakespearean Negotiations* (Berkeley and Los Angeles: University of California Press, 1988), pp. 65, 128.

44. Ibid., p. 175.

45. Reprinted in ibid., pp. 21–65 (64).

46. *The Heavenly City of the Eighteenth-Century Philosophers* (New Haven: Yale University Press, 1932), p. 88.

47. See Dollimore's introduction to the reissue of J. W. Lever's *The Tragedy of State* (London: Methuen, 1986), pp. vii–xiii (xv).

48. Hough's remark is quoted in Francis Mulhern, *The Moment of 'Scrutiny'* (London: New Left Books, 1979), p. 317.

49. Fredric Jameson, *The Political Unconscious* (Ithaca: Cornell University Press, 1981), p. 17; Terry Eagleton, *Literary Theory*, p. 209; Jonathan Dollimore, *Radical Tragedy*, pp. 249–71.

50. Michel Foucault, 'Final Interview', *Raritan* 5 (1985), 1–13 (2, 8–9).

51. 'Rencontre', *Nouvelle Revue Française* 24 (1925), 657–8 (658).

52. See Poirier's essay 'The Importance of Thomas Pynchon', in George Levine and David Leverenz, *Mindful Pleasures: Essays on Thomas Pynchon* (Boston: Little, Brown & Company, 1976), pp. 15–29 and *Robert Frost: The Work of Knowing* (Oxford: Oxford University Press, 1977).

53. See Harold Bloom, *Wallace Stevens: The Poems of Our Climate* (Ithaca: Cornell University Press, 1977).

54. Richard Wollheim, 'The English Dream', *Spectator*, 10 March 1961, 334–5.

55. Colin MacCabe, *James Joyce and the Revolution of the Word* (New York: Barnes & Noble, 1979); Alan Sinfield, *The Language of Tennyson's 'In Memoriam'* (New York: Barnes & Noble, 1971); Jonathan Culler, *Flaubert: The Uses of Uncertainty* (Ithaca: Cornell University Press, 1974); Jonathan Dollimore, 'The Poetry of Hardy and Edward Thomas' *Critical Quarterly* 17 (1975), 204, 214.

56. *The Genesis of Secrecy* (London and Cambridge, MA: Harvard University Press, 1979), p. 50.

57. 'The Making of the Modernist Canon', in von Hallberg, *Canons*, pp. 363–75 (373, 374).

58. *The Protestant Ethic and the Spirit of Capitalism* (New York: Charles Scribner's Sons, 1958), p. 181.

Bibliography

Sections 1 and 2 of this Bibliography list works cited in the text. Where English or parallel text editions are available, these are normally listed. Section 2 also includes a few items relevant to the modern history of the canon up to 1980. Section 3, 'The Contemporary Debate', provides a comprehensive list of books and essays on general canonical issues from 1980 to date. The number of items in this area is daunting – and growing by the day. Some essays on particular works or authors have been included in order to suggest the range of contemporary canonical enquiry. Also included for purposes of illustration are a few items beyond the sphere of this study – items on museum studies, Japanese literature, Assyriology, and so on. It must be emphasized that, in all these areas, many specialized essays have been omitted.

1. CLASSICAL AND CHRISTIAN CANONS

Ackroyd, P. R. with G. W. H. Lampe and S. L. Greenslade, eds, *The Cambridge History of the Bible*, 3 vols (Cambridge: Cambridge University Press, 1963–70)

The Apostolic Fathers 1, Loeb Classical Library, transl. Kirsopp Lake (London William Heinemann, 1912)

Aquinas, Saint Thomas, *Summa Theologiae*, 60 vols, ed. Thomas Gilby (London: Blackfriars, 1964)

Aristotle, *The Nicomachean Ethics*, Loeb Classical Library, transl. H. Rackham (London: William Heinemann, 1962)

Augustine, Saint, *On Christian Doctrine*, transl. D. W. Robertson, Jr (New York: Liberal Arts Press, 1958)

—— *The City of God 6*, Loeb Classical Library, transl. William Chase Greene (London: William Heinemann, 1960)

—— *Aurelii Augustini Opera: De Doctrina Christiana, De Vera Religione, Corpus Christianorum*, Series Latina, Vol. 32 (Turnholt: Brepols, 1962)

Barr, James, *Holy Scripture: Canon, Authority, Criticism* (Philadelphia: Westminster Press, 1983)

Basil, Saint, *Saint Basil: Ascetical Works*, transl. ister M. Monica Wagner (New York: Fathers of the Church, 1950)

Bolgar, R. R., *The Classical Heritage and Its Beneficiaries* (Cambridge: Cambridge University Press, 1954)

Campenhausen, Hans von, *The Formation of the Christian Bible*, transl. J. A. Baker (Philadelphia: Fortress Press, 1972)

Childs, Brevard S., 'The Old Testament as Scripture of the Church', *Concordia Theological Monthly*, December 1972, 709–22

—— *Introduction to the Old Testament as Scripture* (Philadelphia: Fortress Press, 1979)

—— *The New Testament as Canon: An Introduction* (Philadelphia: Fortress Press, 1985)

Cicero, *De Natura Deorum / Academica*, Loeb Classical Library, transl. H. Rackham (London: William Heinemann, 1967)

Crosse, Henry, *Vertues Commonwealth or The Highway to Heaven*, ed. Alexander Grosart (Manchester: C. E. Simms, 1878)

Demosthenes, *Demosthenes 2: De Corona and De Falsa Legatione*, Loeb Classical Library, transl. C. A. and J. H. Vince (London: William Heinemann, 1963)

Diogenes Laertius, *Diogenes Laertius 2*, Loeb Classical Library, transl. R. D. Hicks (London: William Heinemann, 1961)

Euripides, *Euripides 1*, Loeb Classical Library, transl. Arthur S. Way (London: William Heinemann, 1966)

—— *Euripides 2*, Loeb Classical Library, transl. Arthur S. Way (London: William Heinemann, 1965)

Eusebius, *The Ecclesiastical History 1*, Loeb Classical Library, transl. Kirsopp Lake (London: William Heinemann, 1926)

—— *The Ecclesiastical History 2*, Loeb Classical Library, ed. J. E. L. Oulton and H. J. Lawlor (London: William Heinemann, 1964)

Fritz, K. von, Review of Herbert Oppel, *Kanōn*, *American Journal of Philology* 60 (1939), 112–15

Goulburn, Edward Meyrick, *The Pursuit of Holiness: A Sequel to 'Thoughts on Personal Religion'* (London: Rivingtons, 1870)

The Greek New Testament, 2nd edn, ed. Kurt Aland *et al.* (New York: London and Edinburgh: United Bible Societies, 1966)

Hayes, John H., *An Introduction to Old Testament Study* (Nashville: Abingdon, 1979)

Josephus, *Josephus 1*, Loeb Classical Library, transl. H. St J. Thackeray (London: William Heinemann, 1966)

Kittel, Gerhard, ed., *Theological Dictionary of the New Testament* (Grand Rapids, Michigan: William B. Herdmans, 1965)

Leaney, A. R. C., *The Jewish and Christian World 200 B. C. to A. D. 200* Cambridge: Cambridge University Press, 1984)

Lucian, *Lucian 6*, Loeb Classical Library, transl. K. Kilburn (London: William Heinemann, 1959)

Luther, Martin, *Selections from His Writings*, ed. John Dillenberger (Garden City, N Y: Doubleday, 1961)

—— *Luther's Works*, 55 vols, ed. Jaroslav Pelikan, Helmut T. Lehmann, *et al.* (Philadelphia: Fortress Press, 1971)

Metzger, Bruce M., *The Canon of the New Testament: Its Origins, Development and Significance* (Oxford: Clarendon Press, 1987)

Migne, J.- P., *Patrologiae cursus completus*, Series Graeca, 162 vols (Paris, 1857, reprinted Turnhout: Brepols, 1956–82)

Müller, C. O., *Ancient Art and Its Remains* (London: B. Quaritch, 1852)

Müller, F. Max, *Introduction to the Science of Religion* (New York: Arno Press, 1978)

Oberg, Eberhard, ed., *Amphilochii Iconiensis: Iambi ad Seleucum*, Patristische Texte und Studien 9 (Berlin: Walter de Gruyter, 1969)

Oppel, Herbert, *Kanōn* (Leipzig: Dieterich'sche Verlagsbuchhandlung, 1937)

Panofsky, Erwin, *Meaning in the Visual Arts* (Garden City, New York: Doubleday Anchor, 1955)

Pfeiffer, Robert H., *Introduction to the Old Testament* (New York and Evanston: Harper & Row, 1948)

Plato, *The Statesman, Philebus, Ion*, Loeb Classical Library, transl. Harold N. Fowler and W. R. M. Lamb (London: William Heinemann, 1962)

Pliny, *Natural History 9*, Loeb Classical Library, transl. H. Rackham (London: William Heinemann, 1961)

Plutarch, *Plutarch's Lives 1*, Loeb Classical Library, transl. Bernadotte Perrin (London: William Heinemann, 1928)

—— *Plutarch's Moralia 1*, Loeb Classical Library, transl. Frank Cole Babbitt (London: William Heinemann, 1969)

—— *Plutarch's Moralia 2*, Loeb Classical Library, transl. Frank Cole Babbitt (London: William Heinemann, 1971)

Philo, *Philo 6*, Loeb Classical Library, transl. F. H. Colson (London: William Heinemann, 1959)

Quasten, Johannes and Angelo di Berardino, *Patrology*, 4 vols (Westminster, Maryland and Utrecht: Newman Press and Spectrum Publishers, 1951–86)

The Revised English Bible (England: Oxford University Press and Cambridge University Press, 1989)

Ricoeur, Paul, *Hermeneutic of the Idea of Revelation* (Berkeley: Center for Hermeneutical Studies in Hellenistic and Modern Culture, 1977)

Roberts, Alexander and James Donaldson, *The Ante-Nicene Fathers*, 10 vols (Buffalo: Christian Literature Co., 1886)

Rufinus, *A Commentary on the Apostles' Creed*, Ancient Christian Writers: The Works of the Fathers in Translation, ed. J. N. D. Kelly (London: Longmans, Green & Co., 1955)

Sanders, James A., *Torah and Canon* (Philadelphia: Fortress Press, 1972)

—— *Canon and Community: A Guide to Canonical Criticism* (Philadelphia: Fortress Press, 1984)

Schaff, Philip and Henry Wace, *A Select Library of Nicene and Post-Nicene Fathers of the Christian Church*, 2nd series, 14 vols (New York: and Oxford: Christian Literature Co. and Parker, 1892)

Thucydides, *History of the Peloponnesian War*, 4 vols, Loeb Classical Library, transl. Charles Forster Smith (London: William Heinemann, 1919–23)

Whitaker, William, *A Disputation on Holy Scripture: Against the Papists, Especially Bellarmine and Stapleton*, transl. William Fitzgerald (Cambridge: Cambridge University Press, 1849)

2. MAKING OF THE MODERN CANON

Abrams, M. H., Review of *Anatomy of Criticism*, *University of Toronto Quarterly* 28 (1959), 190–96

––––– *Natural Supernaturalism: Tradition and Revolution in Romantic Literature* (New York: W. W. Norton, 1971)

––––– *A Glossary of Literary Terms*, 5th ed. (New York: Holt, Rinehart & Winston, 1988)

Adler, Mortimer J., *How to Read a Book: The Art of Getting a Liberal Education* (New York: Simon & Schuster, 1940)

Alpers, Svetlana, *The Art of Describing: Dutch Art in the Seventeenth Century* (Chicago: University of Chicago Press, 1983)

Althusser, Louis, *Lenin and Philosophy and Other Essays*, transl. Ben Brewster (New York: Monthly Review Press, 1971)

Arnold, Mathew, *Lectures and Essays in Criticism 1*, ed. R. H. Super (Ann Arbor: University of Michigan Press, 1962)

Auerbach, Erich, *Mimesis: The Representation of Reality in Western Literature*, transl. Willard R. Trask (Princeton: Princeton University Press, 1953)

Bagehot, Walter, *Literary Studies*, 2 vols (London: J. M. Dent, [1951])

Baldick, Chris, *The Social Mission of English Criticism 1848–1932* (Oxford: Clarendon Press, 1983)

Baldwin, James, *The Book Lover: A Guide to the Best Reading*, revised edn (Chicago: A. C. McClurg, 1902)

Barraclough, Geoffrey, *History in a Changing World* (Norman: University of Oklahoma Press, 1956)

Barker, Ernest, *National Character and the Factors in Its Formation* (London: Methuen, 1927)

Barthes, Roland, *The Elements of Semiology*, transl. Annette Lavers and Colin Smith (New York: Hill & Wang, 1968)

Bateson, F. W., 'The Function of Criticism at the Present Time', *Essays in Criticism* 3 (1953), 1–27

––––– *Essays in Critical Dissent* (London: Longmans, 1972)

Beard, Charles A., *The Supreme Court and the Constitution* (New York: MacMillan, 1912)

—— 'Written History as an Act of Faith', *American Historical Review* 39 (1934), 219–29

Becker, Carl L., *The Declaration of Independence: A Study in the History of Political Ideas* (New York: Harcourt, Brace, 1922)

—— 'Everyman His Own Historian', *American Historical Review* 37 (1932), 221–36

—— *The Heavenly City of the Eighteenth-Century Philosophers* (New Haven: Yale University Press, 1932)

Becker, May Lamberton, *Adventures in Reading* (Philadelphia and New York: J. B. Lippincott, 1927, revised edn 1946)

Bell, Quentin, *The Art Critic and the Art Historian* (London: Cambridge University Press, 1974)

Benjamin, Walter, *Illuminations* (New York: Schocken Books, 1969)

—— *Gesammelte Schriften*, 7 vols, ed. Rolf Tiedemann and Hermann Schweppenhaüser, in co-operation with Theodor W. Adorno and Gershom Scholem (Frankfurt am Main: Suhrkamp Verlag, 1972–89)

Bennett, Arnold, *Literary Taste: How To Form It. With Detailed Instructions for Collecting A Complete Library of English Literature* (New York: George H. Doran, [1927])

Bennett, Jesse Lee, *What Books Can Do For You: A Sketch Map of the Frontiers of Knowledge: With Lists of Selected Books* (New York: George H. Doran, 1923)

—— *On 'Culture' and 'A Liberal Education': With Lists of Books Which Can Aid in Acquiring Them* (New York: The Arnold Company, 1926)

Berger, John, *Permanent Red: Essays in Seeing* (London: Methuen, 1960)

Bethell, S. L., *Shakespeare and the Popular Dramatic Tradition* (Durham, N C: Duke University Press, 1944)

—— *Essays on Literary Criticism and the English Tradition* (London: Dennis Dobson, 1948)

—— *The Cultural Revolution of the Seventeenth Century* (London: Dennis Dobson, 1951)

Blackmur, R. P., *Form and Value in Modern Poetry* (New York: Doubleday, 1957)

Bloom, Harold, *The Ringers in the Tower: Studies in Romantic Tradition* (Chicago and London: University of Chicago Press, 1971)

—— *Wallace Stevens: The Poems of Our Climate* (Ithaca: Cornell University Press, 1977)

Boltanski, Luc, 'La Constitution du champ de la Bande Dessinée', *Actes de la recherche en sciences sociales* 1 (1975), 37–59

Bourdieu, Pierre, 'Flaubert's Point of View', *Critical Inquiry* 14 (1988), 539–62

Brebner, J. Bartlet *et al.*, eds, *Classics of the Western World. With Forewords by John Erskine and Everett Dean Martin* (Chicago: American Library Association, 1927)

Bridgman, Richard, 'The American Studies of Henry Nash Smith', *American Scholar* 56 (1987), 259–68

Brooke, C. F. Tucker, *The Shakespeare Apocrypha: Being a Collection of Fourteen Plays Which Have Been Ascribed to Shakespeare* (Oxford: Clarendon Press, 1908)

Brooks, Cleanth, *Modern Poetry and the Tradition* (Chapel Hill: University of North Carolina Press, 1939

Brooks, Van Wyck, *Van Wyck Brooks: The Early Years*, ed. Claire Sprague (London: Harper Torchbooks, 1968)

Bultmann, Rudolf, *The New Testament and Mythology and Other Basic Writings*, ed. Schubert M. Ogden (Philadelphia: Fortress Press, 1984)

Canby, Henry, 'An American Canon', *Saturday Review of Literature*, 15 October 1927, 191, 193

Carlyle, Thomas, *Works*, 30 vols, ed. H. D. Traill, Centennial Memorial Edition (London: Chapman & Hall, 1896–9)

Chambers, E. K., ed., *Titus Andronicus* (London: Blackie & Son, 1907)
——— *The Disintegration of Shakespeare* (Oxford: Milford, 1924)

Coleridge, Samuel Taylor, *Aids to Reflection* (London: Taylor & Hessey, 1825)
——— *Collected Letters of Samuel Taylor Coleridge*, 6 vols, ed. E. L. Griggs (Oxford and New York: Oxford University Press, 1956–71)
——— *Lectures 1795 on Politics and Religion*, ed. Lewis Patton and Peter Mann (London and Princeton: Routledge & Kegan Paul/Princeton University Press, 1971)
——— *Biographia Literaria: Or, Biographical Sketches of My Literary Life and Opinions*, 2 vols, ed. James Engell and W. Jackson Bate (London: and Princeton: Routledge & Kegan Paul/Princeton University Press, 1983)

Claudel, Paul, *Pages de Prose*, ed. André Blanchet (Paris: Gallimard, 1944)

Clifford, James, Review of Edward Said, *Orientalism*, *History and Theory* 19 (1980), 204–23

Clifford, James L., ed. *Eighteenth-Century English Literature: Modern Essays in Criticism* (New York: Oxford University Press, 1959)

Collingwood, R. G., *The Idea of History* (New York: Oxford University Press, 1956)

Cowley, Malcolm, *After the Genteel Tradition: American Writers Since 1910* (New York: W. W. Norton, 1937)

Crews, Frederick, *Out of My System: Psychoanalysis, Ideology, and Critical Method* (New York: Oxford University Press, 1975)

Cruttwell, Patrick, *The Shakespearean Moment and Its Place in the Poetry of the Seventeenth Century*, reissue, with new introduction (New York: Random House, 1960)

Culler, Jonathan, *Flaubert: The Uses of Uncertainty* (Ithaca: Cornell University Press, 1974)

Curtius, Ernst Robert, *European Literature and the Latin Middle Ages* (New York and Evanston: Harper & Row, 1963)

Daiches, David, Review of Northrop Frye, *Anatomy of Criticism, Modern Philology* 56 (1958), 69–72

Deconstruction and Criticism, Harold Bloom, Paul de Man, Jacques Derrida, Geoffrey Hartman, J. Hillis Miller (New York: Continuum, 1979)

Deloria, Vine, ed., *Black Elk Speaks: Being the Life Story of a Holy Man of the Oglala Sioux, as told through John G. Neihardt (Flaming Rainbow)* (Lincoln, Nebraska and London: University of Nebraska Press, 1979)

De Man, Paul, *Blindness and Insight: Essays in the Rhetoric of Contemporary Criticism*, 2nd edn Theory and History of Literature, Vol. 7. (Minneapolis: University of Minnesota Press, 1983)

—— *The Resistance to Theory* Theory and History of Literature, Vol. 33. (Minneapolis: University of Minnesota Press, 1986)

Derrida, Jacques, *Of Grammatology*, transl. Gayatri Chakravorty Spivak (Baltimore and London: Johns Hopkins University Press, 1976)

Dickinson, Asa Don, *One Thousand Best Books: The Household Guide to a Lifetime's Reading and Clue to the Literary Labyrinth* (New York: H. W. Wilson Company, 1931)

Diderot, Denis, *Encyclopédie*, 4 vols, ed. John Lough and Jacques Proust (Paris: Herman, 1976)

Dollimore, Jonathan, 'The Poetry of Hardy and Edward Thomas' *Critical Quarterly* 17 (1975), 203–15

Doren, Carl Van, 'Toward a New Canon', *The Nation*, 13 April 1932, 429–30

Eagleton, Terry, *Literary Theory: An Introduction* (Oxford: Basil Blackwell, 1983)

—— *The Function of Criticism: From the Spectator to Post-Structuralism* (London: Verso, 1984)

J. P. Eckermann, *Gespräche mit Goethe* (Leipzig: Eugin Diederichs, 1902)

—— *Conversations with Goethe* (London: J. M. Dent, 1935)

Edwards, Thomas, *The Canons of Criticism and Glossary: Being a Supplement to Mr Warburton's Edition of Shakespear Collected from the Notes in that Celebrated Work, and Proper to be Bound up with It* (7th edn), Reprints of Economic Classics (New York: Augustus M. Kelley Publishers, 1970)

Eliot, T. S., 'Rencontre', *Nouvelle Revue Française* 24 (1925), 657–8

—— *After Strange Gods: A Primer of Modern Heresy* (London: Faber & Faber, 1934)

—— *The Sacred Wood: Essays on Poetry and Criticism* (London: Methuen, 1950)

—— *Selected Essays* (New York: Harcourt, Brace & Co., 1950)

—— *To Criticize the Critic and Other Writings* (London: Faber & Faber, 1978)

—— *The Letters of T. S. Eliot: Volume 1 1898–1922*, ed. Valerie Eliot (London: Harcourt Brace Jovanovich, 1988)

Fanon, Frantz, *The Wretched of the Earth*, transl. Constance Farrington (New York: Grove Press, 1968)

Febvre, Lucien, *Combats pour l'histoire* (Paris: A. Colin, 1953)

Fitzgerald, Robert, *Enlarging the Change: The Princeton Seminars in Literary Criticism, 1949-51* (Boston: Northeastern University Press, 1985)

Fish, Stanley, *Is There a Text in this Class?: The Authority of Interpretive Communities* (London and Cambridge, MA: Harvard University Press, 1980)

Foster, William Eaton, *Libraries and Readers* (New York: F. Leypoldt, 1883)

Foucault, Michel, *The Archaelogy of Knowledge*, transl. A. M. Sheridan Smith (New York: Pantheon Books, 1972)

—— *Discipline and Punish: The Birth of the Prison*, transl. Alan Sheridan (New York: Vintage Books, 1979)

Frye, Northrop, 'Canada and Its Poetry', *Canadian Forum* 43 (1943), 207–10

—— *Fearful Symmetry: A Study of William Blake* (Princeton: Princeton University Press, 1947)

—— *Anatomy of Criticism: Four Essays* (Princeton: Princeton University Press, 1957)

—— Review of W. B. Stanford, *The Ulysses Theme* and Cleanth Brooks, ed., *Tragic Themes in Western Literature*, *Comparative Literature* 9 (1957), 180–82

—— *The Educated Imagination* (Bloomington and London: Indiana University Press, 1964)

—— *The Modern Century* (London: Oxford University Press, 1967)

—— *A Study of English Romanticism* (New York: Random House, 1968)

—— *The Stubborn Structure: Essays on Criticism and Society* (Ithaca: Cornell University Press, 1970)

—— *The Bush Garden: Essays on the Canadian Imagination* (Toronto: Anansi, 1971)

—— *Spiritus Mundi: Essays on Literature, Myth, and Society* (Bloomington and London: Indiana University Press, 1976)

—— *Northrop Frye on Culture and Literature: A Collection of Review Essays*, ed. Robert Denham (Chicago and London: University of Chicago Press, 1978)

—— *Divisions on a Ground: Essays on Canadian Culture* (Toronto: Anansi, 1982)

—— *The Great Code: The Bible and Literature* (New York: Harcourt Brace Jovanovich, 1982)

—— *The Critical Path: An Essay on the Social Context of Literary Criticism* (Sussex: Harvester Press, 1983)

—— *The Myth of Deliverance: Reflections on Shakespeare's Problem Comedies* (Sussex: Harvester Press, 1983)

—— *Northrop Frye on Shakespeare*, ed. Robert Sandler (New Haven and London: Yale University Press, 1986)

Frye, Prosser Hall, *Romance and Tragedy* (Boston: Marshall Jones Company, 1922)

Fowler, Alastair, 'Genre and the Literary Canon', *New Literary History* 11 (1979), 97–119

Gadamer, Hans-Georg, *Truth and Method* (New York: Seabury Press, 1975)

Gardner, Helen, *In Defence of the Imagination* (Oxford: Clarendon Press, 1982)

Geertz, Clifford, *The Interpretation of Cultures: Selected Essays* (New York: Basic Books, 1973)

—— *Local Knowledge: Further Essays in Interpretive Anthropology* (New York: Basic Books, 1983)

—— *Works and Lives: The Anthropologist as Author* (Stanford: Stanford University Press, 1988)

Gold Karen, 'Sceptic Who Has Never Lost His Belief in Art', *Times Higher Education Supplement*, 28 August 1987, 9

Gombrich, Sir Ernst, *Art and Illusion: A Study in the Psychology of Pictorial Representation* (Oxford: Phaidon, 1960)

—— *Meditations on a Hobby Horse: And Other Essays on the Theory of Art* (Oxford: Phaidon, 1963)

—— *Norm and Form: Studies in the History of the Renaissance*, No. 1 (Oxford: Phaidon, 1966)

—— *The Story of Art*, 12th edn (Oxford: Phaidon, 1972)

—— 'The Renaissance–Period or Movement?' in J. B. Trapp, ed., *Background to the English Renaissance* (London: Gray-Mills, 1974), pp. 9–30

—— *The Heritage of Apelles: Studies in the Art of the Renaissance* No. 3 (Oxford and Ithaca: Phaidon/Cornell University Press, 1976)

—— *Symbolic Images: Studies in the Art of the Renaissance* No. 2 (Oxford: Phaidon, 1978)

—— *Ideals and Idols: Essays on Values in History and in Art* (Oxford: Phaidon, 1979)

—— *The Sense of Order: A Study in the Psychology of Decorative Art* (Oxford and Ithaca: Phaidon/Cornell University Press, 1979)

—— 'Representation and Misrepresentation', *Critical Inquiry* 11 (1984), 195–201

—— *Tributes: Interpreters of Our Cultural Tradition* (Oxford: Phaidon, 1984)

—— *Aby Warburg: An Intellectual Biography* (Oxford: Phaidon, 1986)

—— *New Light on Old Masters: Studies in the Art of the Renaissance*, No. 4 (Oxford: Phaidon, 1986)

—— *Reflections on the History of Art: Views and Reviews*, ed. Richard Woodfield (Oxford: Phaidon, 1987)

—— 'The Edge of Delusion', *New York Review of Books*, 15 February 1990, 6–9

Gray, W. Forbes, *Books that Count: A Dictionary of Useful Books*, 2nd ed. (London: A. & C. Black, 1923)

Greenlaw, Edwin, *The Province of Literary History* (London: Humphrey Milford, 1931)

Harrison, Frederic, 'On the Choice of Books', *Fortnightly Review* 31, old series (April 1879), 491–512

Hartman, Geoffrey H., *Criticism in the Wilderness: THe Study of Literature Today* (New Haven and London: Yale University Press, 1980)

Haskell, Francis, *Rediscoveries in Art: Some Aspects of Taste, Fashion and Collecting in England and France* (Oxford: Phaidon, 1980)

—— and Nicholas Penny, *Taste and the Antique: The Lure of Classical Sculpture, 1500–1900* (New Haven and London: Yale University Press, 1981)

Higham, John, *History: Professional Scholarship in America* (Baltimore and London: Johns Hopkins University Press, 1983)

Hoggart, Richard, *Speaking to Each Other: Volume 1. About Society* (London: Chatto & Windus, 1970)

—— *Speaking to Each Other: Volume 2. About Literature* (London: Chatto & Windus, 1970)

Hough, Graham, *The Dream and the Task: Literature and Morals in the Culture of Today* (New York: W. W. Norton, 1964)

Hubbell, Jay B., *Who Are the Major American Writers? A Study of the Changing Literary Canon* (Durham, N C: Duke University Press, 1972)

Huse, H. R. *The Illiteracy of the Literate: A Guide to the Art of Intelligent Reading* (New York and London: D. Appleton-Century, 1933)

Jameson, Fredric, *The Political Unconscious: Narrative as a Socially Symbolic Act* (Ithaca: Cornell University Press, 1981)

Jauss, Hans Robert, *Toward an Aesthetic of Reception*, Theory and History of Literature, vol. 2, transl. Timothy Bahti, introduction by Paul de Man (Minneapolis: University of Minnesota Press, 1982)

Jeffrey, Francis, 'Poems by George Crabbe', *Edinburgh Review* 12 (1808), 131–51

—— 'The Excursion', *Edinburgh Review* 24 (1814), 1–30

Johnson, Samuel, *A Dictionary of the English Language* (Beirut: Librairie du Liban, 1978)

Kant, Immanuel, *The Critique of Judgement*, transl. James Creed Meredith (Oxford: Clarendon Press, 1952)

Kermode, Frank, *Romantic Image* (London: Routledge & Kegan Paul, 1957)

—— 'Some Reservations', *New Statesman*, 25 October 1963, 569

—— 'Survival of the Classics', *Encounter*, November 1963, 82–5

—— 'The Enduring Lear', *New York Review of Books*, 12 May 1966, 12–14

—— 'Tragedy and Revolution', *Encounter*, August 1966, 83–5

—— *The Sense of an Ending: Studies in the Theory of Fiction* (New York: Oxford University Press, 1967)

—— 'The Young and the Elders', *Partisan Review* 37 (1970), 184–98

—— *Shakespeare, Spenser, Donne* (London: Routledge & Kegan Paul, 1971)

—— *Lawrence* (London: Fontana, 1973)

—— *The Genesis of Secrecy: On the Interpretation of Narrative* (London and Cambridge, MA: Harvard University Press, 1979)

—— *The Classic: Literary Images of Permanence and Change* (London and Cambridge, MA: Harvard University Press, 1983)

—— *Essays on Fiction, 1971–82* (London: Routledge & Kegan Paul, 1983)
—— *Forms of Attention* (Chicago and London: University of Chicago Press, 1985)
—— 'Canons', *Dutch Quarterly Review* 18 (1988), 258–70
—— *History and Value* (Oxford: Clarendon Press, 1988)
—— *An Appetite for Poetry* (Cambridge, MA: Harvard University Press, 1989)
—— and Robert Alter, *The Literary Guide to the Bible* (Cambridge, MA: Harvard University Press, 1987)
Knights, L. C., *Drama and Society in the Age of Johnson* (London: Chatto & Windus, 1937)
—— *Further Explorations* (Stanford: Stanford University Press, 1965)
Krieger, Murray, 'The Ambiguity of Representation and Illusion: An E. H. Gombrich Retrospective', *Critical Inquiry* 11 (1984), 181–94
Kuhn, Thomas S., *The Structure of Scientific Revolutions*, 2nd edn (Chicago: University of Chicago Press, 1970)
Langbaum, Robert, *The Poetry of Experience: The Dramatic Monologue in Modern Literary Tradition* (Harmondsworth: Penguin, 1974)
Larbaud, Valery, *Ce Vice impuni, la lecture: Domaine anglais*, vol. 3 of *Oeuvres Complètes*, ed. G. Jean Aubry, Robert Mallet and Vincent Milligan (Paris: Gallimard, 1951)
Leavis, F. R., *New Bearings in English Poetry: A Study of the Contemporary Situation* (Harmondsworth: Penguin, 1963)
—— *English Literature in Our Time and the University* (London: Chatto & Windus, 1969)
—— *Revaluation: Tradition and Development in English Poetry* (Harmondsworth: Penguin, 1972)
—— *Valuation in Criticism and Other Essays*, ed. G. Singh (Cambridge: Cambridge University Press, 1986)
Leavis, Q. D., 'Academic Case-History', *Scrutiny* 11 (1943), 305–10
—— 'The Discipline of Letters: A Sociological Note', *Scrutiny* 12 (1943), 12–26
Lever, J. W., *The Tragedy of State*, new edn (London: Methuen, 1986)
Lewisohn, Ludwig, *Expression in America* (New York and London: Harper, 1932)
Lubbock, Sir John, *The Pleasures of Life* (London: MacMillan, 1891)
MacCabe, Colin, *James Joyce and the Revolution of the Word* (New York: Barnes & Noble, 1979)
Mackail, J. W., *The Approach to Shakespeare*, 2nd edn (Oxford: Clarendon Press, 1933)
McKeon, Richard, 'Canonic Books and Prohibited Books: Orthodoxy and Heresy in Religion and Culture', *Critical Inquiry* 2 (1976), 781–806
Malraux, André, *The Voices of Silence* (London: Secker & Warburg, 1954)
Marsh, Daniel L., *The American Canon* (New York: Abingdon Press, 1939)

Mills, C. Wright, *Power, Politics, and People: THe Collected Essays of C. Wright Mills*, ed. Irving Louis Horowitz (New York: Ballantine Books, 1963)

Morley, Viscount John, *Recollections*, 2 vols (New York: Macmillan, 1917)

Mulhern, Francis, *The Moment of 'Scrutiny'* (London: New Left Books, 1979)

Nkosi, Lewis, *Home and Exile* (London: Longmans, 1965)

Novalis, *Schriften*, 5 vols, ed. Richard Samuel *et al.* (Stuttgart: W. Kohlhammer, 1960–88)

Panofsky, Dora and Erwin, *Pandora's Box: The Changing Aspects of a Mythical Symbol* (New York: Pantheon Books, 1962)

Pascal, R., *Shakespeare in Germany, 1740–1814* (Cambridge: Cambridge University Press, 1937)

Pfeiffer, Rudolf, *History of Classical Scholarship: From the Beginnings to the End of the Hellenistic Age* (Oxford: Clarendon Press, 1968)

Pocock, J. G. A., *Politics, Language and Time: Essays on Political Thought and History* (New York: Atheneum, 1973)

Poirier, Richard, 'The Importance of Thomas Pynchon', in George Levine and David Leverenz, *Mindful Pleasures: Essays on Thomas Pynchon* (Boston: Little, Brown & Company, 1976), pp. 15–29

―――― Robert Frost: The Work of Knowing (Oxford: Oxford University Press, 1977)

Popper, Karl, *The Poverty of Historicism* (London: Routledge & Kegan Paul, 1961)

Pound, Ezra, *ABC of Reading* (New York: New Directions, 1960)

Preminger, Alex, ed., *Princeton Encyclopedia of Poetry and Poetics*, enlarged edn (Princeton: Princeton University Press, 1974)

Ransom, John Crowe, *The World's Body* (Baton Rouge: Louisiana State University Press, 1968)

Reeves, James and Martin Seymour-Smith, *A New Canon of English Poetry* (New York: Barnes & Noble, 1967)

Richter, Melvin, 'Reconstructing the History of Political Languages: Pocock, Skinner, and the Geschichliche Grundebegriffe', *History and Theory* 29 (1990), 38–70

Rivière, Jacques and Paul Claudel, *Correspondance (1907–1914)* (Paris: Librairie Plon, 1926)

Robertson, J. M. *The Shakespeare Canon*, 5 vols (London and New York: George Routledge/E. P. Dutton, 1922–32)

Robinson, Herbert Spencer, ed., *English Shakesperian Criticism in the Eighteenth Century* (New York: H. W. Wilson, 1932)

Robinson, James Harvey, *The New History: Essays Illustrating the Modern Historical Outlook* (New York: Macmillan, 1912)

Robson, W. W., *Critical Essays* (London: Routledge & Kegan Paul, 1966)

Said, Edward W., *Conrad and the Fiction of Autobiography* (Cambridge, MA: Harvard University Press, 1966)

—— 'The Totalitarianism of Mind', *Kenyon Review* 29 (1967), 256–68

—— 'The Problem of Textuality: Two Exemplary Positions', *Critical Inquiry* 4 (1978), 673–714

—— *Orientalism* (New York: Vintage Books, 1979)

—— *Covering Islam: How the Media and the Experts Determine How We See the Rest of the World* (New York: Pantheon Books, 1981)

—— 'Opponents, Audiences, Constituencies, and Community', *Critical Inquiry* 9 (1982), 1–26

—— 'Michel Foucault, 1927–84', *Raritan* 4 (1984), 1–11

—— *The World, the Text, and the Critic* (London: Faber & Faber, 1984)

—— *Beginnings: Intention and Method*, new edn (New York: Columbia University Press, 1985)

—— 'An Ideology of Difference', *Critical Inquiry* 12 (1985), 38–58

—— *After the Last Sky: Palestinian Lives*, with photographs by Jean Mohr (New York: Pantheon Books, 1986)

—— 'The Horizon of R. P. Blackmur', *Raritan* 6 (1986), 29–50

—— '*Kim*, The Pleasures of Imperialism', *Raritan* 7 (1987), 27–64

—— 'Representing the Colonized: Anthropology's Interlocutors', *Critical Inquiry* 15 (1989), 205–25

—— 'Third World Intellectuals and Metropolitan Culture', *Raritan* 9 (1990), 27–50

Salusinszky, Imre, *Criticism in Society: Interviews with Jacques Derrida, Northrop Frye, Harold Bloom, Geoffrey Hartman, Frank Kermode, Edward Said, Barbara Johnson, Frank Lentricchia, and J. Hillis Miller* (New York and London: Methuen, 1987)

Sandys, J. E., *A History of Classical Scholarship*, 3 vols (Cambridge: Cambridge University Press, 1958)

Schiller, Friedrich von, *Naive and Sentimental Poetry, and On the Sublime: Two Essays*, transl. Julius A. Elias (New York: Frederick Ungar, 1966)

—— *Dichter über ihre Dichtungen*, 2 vols, ed. Bodo Lecke (Munich: Heimeran, 1970)

Schlegel, Friedrich, *The Aesthetic and Miscellaneous Works of Friedrich von Schlegel*, transl. E. J. Millington (London: Bohn, 1860)

Shklovsky, Viktor, *A Sentimental Journey: Memoirs, 1917–1922*, transl. Richard Sheldon (Ithaca and London: Cornell University Press, 1970)

Sinfield, Alan, *The Language of Tennyson's 'In Memoriam'* (New York: Barnes & Noble, 1971)

Skinner, Quentin, 'Meaning and Understanding in the History of Ideas', *History and Theory* 8 (1969), 3–53

Smart, Christopher, *The Poetical Works of Christopher Smart*, 4 vols, ed. Karina Williamson and Marcus Walsh (Oxford: Clarendon Press, 1980–87)

Smith, D. Nichol, ed., *Eighteenth Century Essays on Shakespeare* (Oxford: Clarendon Press, 1963)

Snee, C., 'Working-Class Literature or Proletarian Writing?', in Jon Clark et al., eds, *Culture and Crisis in Britain in the Thirties* (London: Lawrence & Wishart, 1979), pp. 165–91

Steiner, George, *In Bluebeard's Castle: Some Notes towards the Redefinition of Culture* (New Haven: Yale University Press, 1971)

Stead, C. K., *The New Poetic: Yeats to Eliot* (Harmondsworth: Penguin, 1967)

Stone, Lawrence, *The Past and the Present* (London: Routledge & Kegan Paul, 1981)

Taine, H., *Voyage en Italie*, 2 vols (Paris: Librairie Hachette, [1924])

Trilling, Lionel, *Literary Criticism: An Introductory Reader* (New York: Holt, Rinehart & Winston, 1970)

——— 'A Personal Memoir', in *From Parnassus: Essays in Honor of Jacques Barzun* (New York and London: Harper & Row, 1976), ed. Dora B. Weiner and William R. Keylor), pp. xv–xxii

——— *The Last Decade: Essays and Reviews, 1965–75*, ed. Diana Trilling (New York and London: Harcourt Brace Jovanovich, 1978)

Turner, Frank M., *The Greek Heritage in Victorian Britain* (New Haven: Yale University Press, 1981)

Waldock, A. J. A., *Sophocles the Dramatist* (Cambridge: Cambridge University Press, 1951)

Weber, Max, *The Protestant Ethic and the Spirit of Capitalism* (New York: Charles Scribner's Sons, 1958)

Wellek, René and Austin Warren, *Theory of Literature*, 3rd edn (New York: Harcourt, Brace & World, 1956)

White, Hayden, *Metahistory: The Historical Imagination in Nineteenth-Century Europe* (Baltimore: Johns Hopkins University Press, 1973)

Williams, Raymond, *The Long Revolution* (London: Chatto & Windus, 1961)

——— *Modern Tragedy* (London: Chatto & Windus, 1966)

——— *The Country and the City* (London: Chatto & Windus, 1973)

——— *The English Novel from Dickens to Lawrence* (London: Hogarth Press, 1984 [reissue of 1970 edn])

Wilson, John, 'On Literary Censorship', *Blackwood's Magazine* 4 (1818), 176–8

——— 'A Preface to a Review of the Chronicles of the Canongate', *Blackwood's Magazine* 22 (1827) 531–6

Wilson, N. G., *Scholars of Byzantium* (Baltimore: Johns Hopkins University Press, 1983)

Wilson, Thomas, *Arte of Rhetorique (1560)*, ed. G. H. Mair (Oxford: Clarendon Press, 1909)

Winckelmann, Johann Joachim, *Kleine Schriften und Briefe* (Weimar: Hermann Böhlaus Nachfolger, 1960)

——— *Winckelmann: Writings on Art*, ed. David Irwin (London: Phaidon, 1972)

Wollheim, Richard, 'The English Dream', *Spectator*, 10 March 1961, 334-5

Wordsworth, William, *Lyrical Ballads*, ed. R. L. Brett and A. R. Jones (London: Methuen, 1965)

Yeats, W. B., *Autobiographies* (London: Macmillan, 1955)

3. THE CONTEMPORARY DEBATE

[*Note:* Many discussions of the canon appear in the American professional journals *ADE Bulletin* (Association of Departments of English), *Curriculum Review* (Curriculum Advisory Service), *English Journal* (National Council of Teachers of English), and *Profession* (Modern Language Association of America)]

Adams, Hazard, 'Canons: Literary Criteria/Power Criteria', *Critical Inquiry* 14 (1988), 748-64

Allan, George, 'The Process and Reality of an Educational Canon', *Contemporary Philosophy*, 12, No. 9 (May 1989), 3-8

Alter, Robert, 'The Difference of Literature', *Poetics Today* 9 (1988), 573-91

—— *The Pleasures of Reading in an Ideological Age* (New York: Simon & Schuster, 1989)

Arac, Jonathan, *Critical Genealogies: Historical Situations for Postmodern Literary Studies* (New York: Columbia University Press, 1987)

Armstrong, Paul B., 'The Conflict of Interpretations and the Limits of Pluralism', *PMLA* 98 (1983), 341-52

Baker, Houston A., Jr, 'Literature', in Symposium 'Major Trends in Research: 22 Leading Scholars Report on Their Fields', *Chronicle of Higher Education*, 4 September 1985, p. 13

—— 'The Promised Body, Reflections on Canon in an Afro-American Context', *Poetics Today* 9 (1988), 339-55

Barker, Stephen, 'Canon-Fodder: Nietzsche, Jarry, Derrida (The Play of Discourse and the Discourse of Play)', *Journal of Dramatic Theory and Criticism* 4 (1989), 69-83

Barrell, John, *Poetry, Language and Politics* (Manchester: Manchester University Press, 1988)

Batsleer, Janet, Tony Davies, Rebecca O'Rourke, and Chris Weedon, eds, *Rewriting English: Cultural Politics of Gender and Class* (London: Methuen, 1985)

Bercovitch, Sacvan, 'America as Canon and Context: Literary History in a Time of Dissensus', *American Literature* 58 (1986), 99-108

—— ed., *Reconstructing American Literary History* (Cambridge, MA: Harvard University Press, 1986)

—— and Myra Jehlen, eds, *Ideology and Classic American Literature* (Cambridge: Cambridge University Press, 1986)

Bishop, Rand, *African Literature, African Critics: The Forming of Critical Standards, 1947–1966*, Contributions in Afro-American and African Studies, No. 115 (New York: Greenwood Press, 1988)

Bloom, Allan, *The Closing of the American Mind: How Higher Education Has Failed Democracy and Impoverished the Souls of Today's Students* (New York: Simon & Schuster, 1987)

Bredahl, A. Carl, Jr, *New Ground: Western American Narrative and the Literary Canon* (Chapel Hill: University of North Carolina Press, 1989)

Brodhead, Richard, *The School of Hawthorne* (New York and Oxford: Oxford University Press, 1986)

Brownstein, Michael C., 'From Kokugaku to Kokubungaku: Canon-Formation in the Meiji Period', *Harvard Journal of Asiastic Studies* 47 (1987), 435–60

Bruce-Nuova, Juan, 'Canonical and Noncanonical Texts', *Americas Review* 14 (1986), 119–35

Buell, Lawrence, 'Literary History without Sexism? Feminist Studies and Canonical Reconception', *American Literature* 59 (1987), 102–14

Butler, Marilyn, 'Revising the Canon', *Times Literary Supplement*, 4 December 1987, 1349, 1359–60

Cafarelli, Annette Wheeler, 'Johnson's *Lives of the Poets* and the Romantic Canon', *The Age of Johnson: A Scholarly Annual*, 1 (1987), 403–35

Cain, William E., *The Crisis in Criticism: Theory, Literature, and Reform in English Studies* (Baltimore: Johns Hopkins University Press, 1984)

——— 'Criticism and the Complexities of the Canon', *Centennial Review* 34 (1990), 6–16

Carafiol, Peter, 'The New Orthodoxy: Ideology and Institution of American Literary History', *American Literature* 59 (1987), 626–38

Castro-Klarén, Sara, 'By (T)reason of State: The Canon and Marginality in Latin American Literature', *Revista de estudios hispánicos* 23 (1989), 1–19

Charney, Maurice, ed., *'Bad' Shakespeare: Revaluations of the Shakespeare Canon* (Rutherford, NJ: Fairleigh Dickinson University Press, 1988)

Conforti, Michael, 'Expanding the Canon of Art Collecting', *Museum News* 68, No. 5 (September/October 1989), 36–40

Corral, Wilfrido H., 'La recepción canónica de Palacio como problema de la modernidad y la historiografía literaria Hispanoamericana', *Nueva Revista de Filología Hispánica* 35 (1987), 773–88

Culler, Jonathan, *Framing the Sign: Criticism and Its Institutions* (Oxford: Basil Blackwell, 1988)

Curriculum Integration: Revising the Literary Canon, Southwest Institute for Research on Women, Working Paper No. 20 (Tucson: University of Arizona Press, 1985)

Davis, Robert Con, and Ronald Schleifer, eds, *Contemporary Literary Criticism* (New York and London: Longmans, 1989)

Dejean, Joan and Nancy K. Miller, eds, *Yale French Studies*, No. 75 (1988), special number on 'The Politics of Tradition: Placing Women in French Literature'

DeKoven, Marianne, 'Gertrude Stein and the Modernist Canon', in Shirley Neuman and Ira B. Nadel, eds, *Gertrude Stein and the Making of Literature* (Boston: Northeastern University Press, 1988), pp. 8–20

Diffley, Kathleen, 'Reconstructing the American Canon: E Pluribus Unum?', *Journal of the Midwest Modern Language Association* 21 (1988), 1–15

Dollimore, Jonathan, *Radical Tragedy: Religion, Ideology, and Power in the Drama of Shakespeare and His Contemporaries* (Brighton: Harvester Press, 1984)

Elliott, Emery, 'The Extra: The Politics of Literary History', *American Literature* 59 (1987), 268–76

Farrell, John P., 'Introduction: Mathew Arnold: The Writer as Touchstone', *Victorian Poetry* 26 (1988), 1–10

Fehn, Ann Clark, 'Relativism, Feminism, and the "German Connection" in Allan Bloom's *The Closing of the American Mind*', *German Quarterly* 62 (1989), 384–94

Felperin, Howard, 'Canonical Texts and Non-Canonical Interpretations: The Neohistoricist Reading of Donne', *Southern Review* 18 (1985), 235–50

Fiedler, Leslie A. and Houston A. Baker, Jr, eds, *English Literature: Opening Up the Canon. Selected Papers from the English Institute, 1979* (Baltimore and London: Johns Hopkins University Press, 1981)

Fleischmann, Fritz, 'On Shifting Grounds: Feminist Criticism and the Changing Canon of American Literature', *Works and Days* 4, No. 1 (1986), 43–56

Flynn, Elizabeth A., ed., *Reader*, No. 15 (Spring 1986), special number on 'Teaching Noncanonical Literature'

Fokkema, Douwe W., 'The Canon as an Instrument for Problem Solving', in *Sensus Communis: Contemporary Trends in Comparative Literature*, Festschrift for Henry Remak, ed. János Riesz, Peter Boerner and Bernard Scholz (Tübingen: Gunter Narr, 1986), pp. 245–54

Friedman, Ellen G., '"Utterly Other Discourse": The Anticanon of Experimental Women Writers from Dorothy Richardson to Christine Brooke-Rose', *Modern Fiction Studies* 34 (1988), 353–70

Foucault, Michel, 'Final Interview', *Raritan* 5 (1985), 1–13

Furbank, P. N. and W. R. Owens, *The Canonization of Daniel Defoe* (New Haven: Yale University Press, 1988)

Gates, Henry Louis, Jr, 'Talkin' That Talk', *Critical Inquiry* 13 (1986), 203–10
—— 'Whose Canon is It, Anyway?', *New York Times Book Review*, 26 February 1989, p. 1

Glazer, Nathan, 'Canon Fodder: The Joke's on Stanford', *New Republic*, 22 August 1988, 19–21

Gless, Darryl J. and Barbara Herrnstein Smith, eds, special number on 'The Politics of Liberal Education', *South Atlantic Quarterly* 89, No. 1 (Winter 1990)

Golding, Alan, 'English Departments and the Literary Canon', *Publications of the Mississippi Philological Association*, 1987, 47–61

Graff, Gerald, *Professing Literature: An Institutional History* (Chicago and London: University of Chicago Press, 1987)

Graff, Harvey J., 'Critical Literacy versus Cultural Literacy – Reading Signs of the Times?', *Interchange* 20 (1989), 46–52

Greenblatt, Stephen, *Renaissance Self-Fashioning: From More to Shakespeare* (Chicago: University of Chicago Press, 1980)

────── *Shakespearean Negotiations: The Circulation of Social Energy in Renaissance England* (Berkeley: University of California Press, 1988)

────── ed., *Representing the English Renaissance* (Berkeley: University of California Press, 1988)

Guillory, John, 'Canonical and Non-Canonical: A Critique of the Current Debate', *English Literary History* 54 (1987), 483–527

────── 'Canon', in *Critical Terms for Literary Study*, eds, Frank Lentricchia and Thomas McLaughlin (Chicago and London: University of Chicago Press, 1990), pp. 233–49

Gumbrecht, Hans Ulrich, '"Phoenix from the Ashes" or: From Canon to Classic', *New Literary History* 20 (1988), 141–63

Hallberg, Robert von, ed., *Canons* (Chicago and London: University of Chicago Press, 1984)

Hallo, William W., 'Assyriology and the Canon', *American Scholar* 59 (1990), 105–8

Hamp, Steven K. and Michael J. Ettema, 'To Collect or To Educate? Some History Museums Discover They Can't Do One without the Other', *Museum News* 68, No. 5 (September/October 1989), 41–4

Hay, John, 'Canonical and Colonial Texts: English Appropriations and Misappropriations', in Bruce Bennett, *A Sense of Exile: Essays in the Literature of the Asia-Pacific Region* (Nedlands, Western Australia: University of Western Australia, 1988), pp. 15–21

Heinzelman, Susan Sage, 'Hard Cases, Easy Cases and Weird Cases: Canon Formation in Law and Literature', *Mosaic* 21 (1988), 59–72

Helprin, Mark, 'The Canon under Siege', *New Criterion* 7, September 1988, 33–40

Hirsch, E. D., Jr, *Cultural Literacy: What Every American Needs To Know* (Boston: Houghton Mifflin, 1987)

Hitchens, Christopher, 'The Toy Canon: Don't Take Stanford's Core List Seriously', *Harper's Magazine*, June 1988, 54–5

Hitt, Jack, moderator, 'Forum: Who Needs the Great Works', *Harper's Magazine*, September 1989, 43–52 (with E. D. Hirsch, Jr, John Kaliski, Jon Pareles, Roger Shattuck, Gayatri Chakravorty Spivak)

Howard, Jean E. and Marion F. O'Connor, eds, *Shakespeare Reproduced: The Text in History and Ideology* (New York: Methuen, 1987)

Hyland, Peter, *Discharging the Canon: Cross-Cultural Readings in Literature* (Singapore: Singapore University Press, 1986)

Joyce, Joyce A., 'The Black Canon: Reconstructing Black American Literary Criticism', *New Literary History* 18 (1987), 335–44. With 'Commentary' by Henry Louis Gates, Jr ('What's Love Got To Do With It?: Critical Theory, Integrity, and the Black Idiom', 345–62) and Houston A. Baker, Jr ('In Dubious Battle', 363–9) and 'Reply' by Joyce (' "Who the Cap Fit": Unconsciousness and Unconscionableness in the Criticism of Houston A. Baker, Jr and Henry Louis Gates, Jr', 371–84)

Keefer, Michael H., 'History and the Canon: The Case of Doctor Faustus', *University of Toronto Quarterly* 56 (1987), 498–522

Kibel, Alvin C., 'The Canonical Text', *Daedalus* 112, No. 1 (Winter 1983), 239–54

Kimball, Roger, 'The Academy Debates the Canon', *New Criterion* 6, September 1987, 31–43

Krieger, Murray, 'Literary Invention and the Impulse to Theoretical Change: Or, "Whether Revolution Be the Same"', *New Literary History* 18 (1986), 191–208

Krupat, Arnold, *The Voice in the Margin: Native American Literature and the Canon* (Berkeley: University of California Press, 1989)

Lauter, Paul, *Reconstructing American Literature: Courses, Syllabi, Issues* (Old Westbury, NY: Feminist Press, 1983)

—— 'Race and Gender in the Shaping of the American Literary Canon: A Case Study from the Twenties', in Judith Newton and Deborah Rosenfelt, eds, *Feminist Criticism and Social Change: Sex, Class, and Race in Literature and Culture* (New York: Methuen, 1985), pp. 19–44

—— 'Caste, Class, and Canon', in Marie Harris and Kathleen Aguero, eds, *A Gift of Tongues: Critical Challenges in Contemporary American Poetry* (Athens, Georgia: University of Georgia Press, 1987), pp. 57–82

Lecker, Robert, 'The Canonization of Canadian Literature: An Inquiry into Value', *Critical Inquiry* 16 (1990), 656–71; Frank Davey, Critical Response I: Canadian Canons, 672–81; Robert Lecker, Critical Response II: Response to Frank Davey, 682–89

Lentricchia, Frank, *After the New Criticism* (London: Athlone Press, 1980)

—— *Criticism and Social Change* (Chicago: University of Chicago Press, 1983)

—— *Ariel and the Police: Michel Foucault, William James, Wallace Stevens* (Madison, Wisconsin: University of Wisconsin Press, 1988)

Lefevere, André, 'Power and the Canon; Or, How To Rewrite an Author into a Classic', *Tydskrif vir Literatuurwetenskap* 2 (1986), 1–14

Leventhal, Robert S., 'The Parable as Performance: Interpretation, Cultural Transmission and Political Strategy in Lessing's *Nathan der Weise*', *German Quarterly* 61 (1988), 502–27

Loomba, Ania, *Gender, Race, and Renaissance Drama* (Manchester: Manchester University Press, 1989)

Lüsebrink, Hans-Jürgen, ed., 'Literarische Kanonbildung', special number of *Komparatistische Hefte* 13 (1986)

MacCabe, Colin, 'The State of the Subject (1): English', *Critical Quarterly* 29 (1987), 5–8

McCrea, Brian, *Addison and Steele Are Dead: The English Department, Its Canon, and the Professionalization of Literary Criticism* (Newark: University of Delaware Press, 1990)

McGann, Jerome, *The Romantic Ideology: A Critical Investigation* (Chicago: University of Chicago Press, 1983)

—— *The Beauty of Inflections: Literary Investigations in Historical Method and Theory* (Oxford: Clarendon Press, 1985)

—— *Social Values and Poetic Facts: The Historical Judgement of Literary Work* (Cambridge, MA: Harvard University Press, 1988)

—— *Towards a Literature of Knowledge* (Chicago: University of Chicago Press, 1989)

Maguire, James H., 'The Canon and the "Distinguished Thing"', *American Literature* 60 (1988), 643–52

McKay, Nellie, 'Reflections on Black Women Writers: Revising the Literary Canon', in Christie Farnham, ed., *The Impact of Feminist Research in the Academy* (Bloomington: Indiana University Press, 1987), 174–89

Marty, Martin E., 'The American Religious History Canon', *Social Research* 53 (1986), 513–28

Merrill, Robert, 'Demoting Hemingway: Feminist Criticism and the Canon', *American Literature* 60 (1988), 255–68

Meese, Elizabeth with Leonore Hoffmann and Deborah Rosenfelt, 'The Whole Truth: Frameworks for the Study of Women's Noncanonical Literature', in *Teaching Women's Literature from a Regional Perspective* (New York: Modern Language Association of America, 1982), 15–22

Modern Language Studies 18, Number 1 (Winter 1988), special number on 'Making and Rethinking the Canon: The Eighteenth Century'

Michaels, Walter Benn and Donald E. Pease, eds, *The American Renaissance Reconsidered* (Baltimore: Johns Hopkins University Press, 1985)

Müller-Michaels, Herro, 'Aktualität oder Historizität? Zur Kontroverse über leitende Prinzipien der Kanonbildung', in Alberecht Schöne, Klaus Grubmüller, and Günter Hess, *Bildungsexklusivät und volkssprachliche Literatur: Literatur vor Lessing – nur für Experten?*, vol. 7 of *Kontroversen, alte und neue* (Tübingen: Niemeyer, 1986), pp. 216–25

Mullen, Edward, 'The Emergence of Afro-Hispanic Poetry: Some Notes on Canon Formation', *Hispanic Review* 56 (1988), 435–53

Myers, D. G., 'The Bogey of the Canon', *Sewanee Review* 97 (1989), 611–21

Nadel, Alan, *Invisible Criticism: Ralph Ellison and the American Canon* (Iowa City: University of Iowa Press, 1988)

Newcomb, John Timberman, 'Canonical Ahistoricism vs. Histories of Canons: Towards Methodological Dissensus', *South Atlantic Review* 54 (1989), 3–20

Nussbaum, Felicity and Laura Brown, *The New Eighteenth Century: Theory, Politics, English Literature* (New York: Methuen, 1987)

O'Brien, Sharon, 'Becoming Noncanonical: The Case against Willa Cather', *American Quarterly* 40 (1988), 110–26

Ohmann, Richard, *Politics of Letters* (Middleton, CT: Wesleyan University Press, 1987)

Perloff, Marjorie, 'Can(n)on to the Right of Us, Can(n)on to the Left of Us: A Plea for Difference', *New Literary History* 18 (1987), 633–56

―――― 'Canon and Loaded Gun: Feminist Poetics and the Avant-Garde', *Stanford Literature Review* 4 (1987), 23–46

Piper, William Bowman, 'My Canon and Ours', *College English* 47 (1985), 141–7

Proceedings of the Ninth Congress of the International Comparative Literature Association, No. 1, special number on 'Classical Models in Literature' (Innsbruck: Institut für Sprachwissenschaft der Universitäts Innsbruck, 1979)

Renza, Louis A., 'Exploding Canons', *Contemporary Literature* 28 (1987), 257–70

Ricks, Christopher, 'What is at Stake in the "Battle of the Books"?', *New Criterion* 8, September 1989, 40–44

Rodden, John, *The Politics of Literary Reputation: The Making and Claiming of 'St. George' Orwell* (New York: Oxford University Press, 1989)

Rosenfelt, Deborah S., 'The Politics of Bibliography: Women's Studies and the Literary Canon', in Joan E. Hartman and Ellen Messer-Davidow, eds, *Opportunities for Women's Studies Research in Language and Literature*, vol. 1 of *Women in Print* (New York: Modern Language Association of America, 1982), pp. 11–35

Salmagundi, No. 72 (Fall 1986), special number 'On Cultural Literacy: Canon, Class, Curriculum' (with Robert Scholes, E. D. Hirsch, J. Mitchell Morse, Marjorie Perloff, Elizabeth Fox-Genovese, John P. Sisk)

Schwartz, Lawrence H., *Creating Faulkner's Reputation: The Politics of Modern Literary Criticism* (Knoxville: University of Tennessee Press, 1988)

Seeba, Hinrich C., 'Critique of Identity Formation: Toward an Intercultural Model of German Studies', *German Quarterly* 62 (1989), 144–54. See also Michael T. Jones, 'Identity, Critique, Affirmation: A Response to Hinrich C. Seeba's Paper', 155–7

Scott, Patrick, 'From Bon Gaultier to *Fly Leaves*: Context and Canon in Victorian Parody', *Victorian Poetry* 26 (1988), 249–66

Sherry, Vincent, 'Canon Fodder', *Times Literary Supplement*, 19 August 1988, 914

Schoeck, R. J., 'Intertextuality and the Rhetoric Canon', *Bucknell Review* 31 (1988), 98–112

Siemon, Stephen, ' "Carnival" and the Canon', *Ariel*, 19, No. 3 (July 1988), 59–75

Smith, Allan Lloyd, 'Salvos against Hawthorne and the Canon' (Review Essay), *Journal of American Studies* 23 (1989), 95–9

Smith, Barbara Herrnstein, 'Value/Evaluation', *South Atlantic Quarterly* 86 (1987), 447–55

―――― *Contingencies of Value: Alternative Perspectives for Critical Theory* (Cambridge, MA: Harvard University Press, 1988)

Stange, G. Robert, '1887 and the Making of the Victorian Canon', *Victorian Poetry* 25 (1987), 151–68

Stone, Albert, 'Canon and Method' (Review Essay), *American Studies* 29, No. 2 (Fall 1988), 91–3

Stow, Glenys and Patricia Dooley, 'Canon Formation: The Problem of Choice', in Perry Nodelman and Jill P. May, eds, *Festschrift: A Ten Year Retrospective* (West Lafayette, Indiana: Children's Literature Association Publications, 1983), pp. 48–51

Tate, Claudia, 'Laying the Floor; Or, The History of the Formation of the Afro-American Canon', *Book Research Quarterly* 3 (1987), 60–78

Tiger, Virginia, 'Canonical Evasions and William Golding', *Contemporary Literature* 29 (1988), 300–304

Tompkins, Jane, *Sensational Designs: The Cultural Work of American Fiction 1790–1860* (New York and Oxford: Oxford University Press, 1985)

Vanderbilt, Kermit, *American Literature and the Academy: The Roots, Growth, and Maturity of a Profession* (Philadelphia: University of Pennsylvania Press, 1986)

Verthuy, Maire E. and Jennifer Waelti-Walters, 'Critical Practice and the Transmission of Culture', *Neohelicon* 14 (1987), 405–14

Wald, Alan, 'Hegemony and Tradition in America', *Humanities in Society* 4 (1981), 419–30

Walker, Pierre A., 'Arnold's Legacy: Religious Rhetoric of Critics on the Literary Canon', *Stanford Literary Review* 5 (1988), 161–77

Weimann, Robert, 'Shakespeare (De)Canonized: Conflicting Uses of "Authority" and "Representation" ', *New Literary History* 20 (1988), 65–81

West, Cornel, 'Minority Discourse and the Pitfalls of Canon Formation', *Yale Journal of Criticism* 1 (1987), 193–201

Wexman, Virginia Wright, 'Evaluating the Text: Canon Formation and Screen Scholarship', *Cinema Journal* 24 (1985), 62–5

Whelchel, Marianne, 'Transforming the Canon with Nontraditional Literature by Women', *College English* 46 (1984), 587–97

Williams, Mark, 'Looking Sideways: English Studies, Tradition, and Cross-Cultural Comparisons', *Span* 28 (1989), 22–39

Index

Matthiessen, Francis Otto, 3
Maurois, André, 70
Mead, Margaret, 234
Meiss, Millard, 97
Melville, Herman, 64
Mencken, H. L., 67, 74
Metzger, Bruce M., 263
Meyer, R., 263
Michelangelo Buonarotti, 53, 98,
    100, 106, 108, 112, 117
Middleton, Thomas, 160
Mills, C. Wright, 187, 194
Milton, John, 41, 58, 67, 75, 81,
    118, 120, 127, 129, 131, 139,
    144, 157, 161, 165, 185, 223
Mitchell, W. J. T., 233
Mondrian, Piet, 255
Monet, Claude, 95
Montaigne, Michel de, 105
Montanus, 27
Moravia, Alberto, 192
More, Thomas, 151
Morley, John, 58
Morris, William, 72, 94, 126
Moses, 32
Mozart, Wolfgang Amadeus, 222
Mucedorus, 60
Mulhern, Francis, 275
Müller, C. O., 11, 15
Müller, F. Max, 38, 39, 42
Mussolini, Benito, 151

Neihardt, John, 230
Nekrasov, Nikolai Alekseyevich,
    54
Nero, 29
Nerval, Gérard de, 205
New Historicism, 55, 239-53
New Universal Library, 72
New Yorker, 137
Newbolt, Sir Henry, 246
Newton, Sir Isaac, 53, 158
Ngugi, James (Ngugi Thiong'o),
    228-9
Nibelungenlied, the, 72
Niccoli, Niccolò, 100

Nicea, Synod of, 27
Nietzsche, Friedrich, 51, 196, 212
Nkosi, Lewis, 229, 232
Novalis, 54, 55, 68, 76, 78, 80, 86,
    159

O'Connor, Marion, 249
O'Neill, Eugene, 76
Ohmann, Richard, 1, 3
Oppel, Herbert, 9, 10
Origen, 27, 33, 65
Orwell, George, 132, 133, 134,
    180, 215, 252
Ovid, 127, 135
Oxford Book of English Verse, the,
    228

Palgrave, Francis, 228
Palladio, Andrea, 53
Pallas, Athene, 56
Panofsky, Dora, 158
Panofsky, Erwin, 10, 11, 12, 158
Parrington, V. L., 67
Pascal, Blaise, 72
Pascal, Roy, 59
Pater, Walter, 61, 104
Patmore, Coventry, 86
Paul, St, 22, 23, 24, 31, 44, 45, 46,
    50, 56, 83, 147
Péguy, Charles, 81
Penguin African Library, 229
Pentateuch, the, 20
Pfeiffer, Robert H., 262
Pfeiffer, Rudolf, 51
Phidion, 15
Philo (of Alexandria), 23
Piazzetta, Giovanni Battista, 53
Picasso, Pablo, 78, 92, 93, 94, 96,
    105, 108, 144
Pierce, Benjamin Franklin, 3
Piper, W. B., 78
Pisano, Andrea, 100
Plato, 4, 9, 10, 11, 12, 13, 72, 91,
    127, 141, 199, 233
Pliny the Elder, 11, 100, 101, 107
Plutarch, 9, 16-17, 72